D1556269

SECOND BEST

THE RISE OF THE AMERICAN VICE PRESIDENCY

FIRST EDITION

By James E. Hite

CLACKAMAS COMMUNITY COLLEGE LIBRARY PROPERTY
WITHDRAWN

cognella
San Diego, CA

Bassim Hamadeh, CEO and Publisher
Christopher Foster, General Vice President
Michael Simpson, Vice President of Acquisitions
Jessica Knott, Managing Editor
Kevin Fahey, Cognella Marketing Manager
Jess Busch, Senior Graphic Designer
Becky Smith, Acquisitions Editor
Sarah Wheeler, Project Editor
Stephanie Sandler, Licensing Associate

Copyright © 2013 by James E. Hite. All rights reserved. No part of this publication may be reprinted, reproduced, transmitted, or utilized in any form or by any electronic, mechanical, or other means, now known or hereafter invented, including photocopying, microfilming, and recording, or in any information retrieval system without the written permission of the author.

First published in the United States of America in 2013 by Cognella, Inc.

Trademark Notice: Product or corporate names may be trademarks or registered trademarks, and are used only for identification and explanation without intent to infringe.

Printed in the United States of America

ISBN: 978-1-62131-269-7 (pbk)

CLACKAMAS COMMUNITY COLLEGE LIBRARY PROPERTY

www.cognella.com 800.200.3908

This book is dedicated to Dylan, Max, Calvin, and Lisa:
You all are my love, you all are my life.

CONTENTS

ACKNOWLEDGMENTS

Upon the completion of this manuscript I would like to acknowledge the encouragement and support of several people. To start, I wish to thank Dan Rubin for taking on the chore of copyediting an early draft of the manuscript. His suggestions were invaluable, and throughout the process he consistently displayed his great skill as an editor; more importantly, by taking on this project he demonstrated his friendship, and it is that for which I am most grateful to Dan. In addition, I wish to offer my sincere thanks and gratitude to Professor Melody Rose and likewise acknowledge the significant role she has played in the development of my academic and professional career. Professor Rose has been a helpful academic advisor to me and an excellent teacher whom I have learned much from. As such, I am grateful for all she has done for me, and though it is surely not enough: thank you, Dr. Rose.

I also want to take this opportunity to acknowledge my family, beginning with my parents, Max and Marty Hite. Their love and encouragement in every endeavor I pursued never wavered. Although they are no longer here, every day they are present in my mind and in my heart.

My children, Dylan, Max, and Calvin, bring me so much joy. They have been patient and supportive as my research and writing on the vice presidency has taken a great deal of time. In this time they have played "categories" on long car rides, agreeing to vice presidents as the topic, all the while knowing I was sure to win. They have gamely listened to stories of the vice presidents that I uncovered in my research. And they have asked questions about my work that often times have led to new ways for me to approach particular facets of the vice presidency. In the process, I can state with confidence that they have become the three most informed young people on the American vice presidency in the nation. They are a never-ending source of inspiration, laughter, and love; they are truly my life.

Finally, I gratefully acknowledge the support of my wife, Lisa. With all my work on the vice presidency, Lisa has been there for me every step of the way, as she is in every facet of our life. She is a constant source of encouragement and praise and never fails to assure me that every word I write is the best she has ever read.

PREFACE

In the course of over four years research—conducted for this manuscript, as well as for a trilogy of articles and an academic treatise—original source documents, personal interviews and communications, oral histories, diaries, published notes, autobiographies, biographies, records of Congress, journal articles, and periodicals have all been utilized in an effort to comprehensively examine and thus better understand the American vice presidency. The resources cover a lengthy span of time and include material written in the eighteenth, nineteenth, twentieth and twenty-first centuries; for this reason, it is necessary to address the etymology, as it were, of the words vice president, vice presidency, and vice-presidential, and how the forms these words have taken have varied over time.

For example, this has included capitalizing both words (Vice President); and hyphenating and capitalizing each (Vice-President); and has similarly been applied to commensurate variations for all forms of the words. In addition, hyphenation has been applied to all forms, even when presented in lower case script (vice-presidency). In order to remain true to original source documents, all quotations are reproduced as is, hence reflecting the accepted capitalization and hyphenation for the time period the material was written. This rule has been adhered to with more recent material, as well; the only exceptions are transcripts of the debates between the vice-presidential candidates, which are originally transcribed only for the exactness of the words spoken in the debate, and without concern to the preciseness of the written word.

In light of the foregoing considerations, it is impossible to maintain consistency throughout the manuscript and remain true to original source documents. Oftentimes, such inconsistencies apply to the various forms used when writing about the president, as well as other words that, in retrospect, appear to be capitalized at random. For this manuscript, however, the appropriate capitalization and hyphenation for vice president and president have been used, and in all forms, as delineated by the Chicago Manual of Style, 15th edition; therefore, these are acknowledged as the correct forms for the words at this time.

Another note on the use of various reference materials: although the temptation is great for modern researchers to simply gather information from websites whenever possible, on those occasions when material was initially located via the Internet, hard copies were obtained directly at a university library location, or by way of the inter-library loan system. Not only does this practice ensure the accuracy of page citations, it is, quite simply, an antiquated preference of this author to have the actual material in hand. Whether it was bound copies of long-forgotten journal articles retrieved from the basement of a library or a well-worn copy of a manuscript which traveled across the country, courtesy of a generous lending-library, original hard copies of reference materials have consistently been accessed, including material from the author's extensive personal collection. And for any material initially retrieved online: thank you, fittingly, to Vice President Al Gore for inventing the Internet.

1

INTRODUCTION

The American Vice Presidency Reconsidered

I am forced to look up to it, and bound by duty to do so, because there is only one breath of one mortal between me and it.

– Vice President John Adams

The American vice presidency today is an infinitely different political institution than the one conceived by the Framers. In essence, an office proposed at the Federal Convention at practically the last moment has developed into something profound and perhaps even dangerous, becoming almost a fourth branch of the United States government. It is a gross distortion of the story of the vice presidency, however, to suggest that it is an institution which has simply evolved over time. Indeed, the vice presidency is an institution that has been manipulated by specific presidents, who have granted, as well as retracted, great responsibilities and authority to their vice presidents. Of equal importance, stealthily ambitious vice presidents, such as Aaron Burr and Dick Cheney, have helped shape the vice presidency by seizing power for themselves, at the expense of both strong and weak presidents.

So for what reasons would this matter?

Despite the outward growth of the vice presidency, many of those who aspire to the presidency today continue to give scant consideration—beyond dubious electoral benefits—to the individual they choose for their running mate. Along these lines, Robert Kennedy once observed that his brother, when deciding on a vice-presidential running mate in 1960, found the entire experience disquieting, remarking that "the President thought how terrible it was that he only had twenty-four hours to select a Vice President. He really hadn't thought about it at all. He said what a mistake it was, when it was such an important position, that you only had twenty-four hours to think about it."[1]

And when it comes to the American electorate, even with the widely recognized influence of two recent vice presidents—Al Gore and Dick Cheney—much of the voting public continues to treat the vice presidency as scarcely more than a political punch line. Yet the conflux of institution, individual, ambition, and power which now rests in the modern vice presidency has the potential to undermine the democratically elected president and set the stage for a shadow government—a scenario, it could be argued, that was realized in the presidency of George W. Bush.

Another salient reason the vice presidency matters is one of simple arithmetic. Of the forty-three individuals to serve as president—Grover Cleveland was elected as both the twenty-second and the twenty-fourth president—fourteen were first vice president, with nine arriving in the Oval Office upon the death or resignation of the president, and five other presidents served in the vice presidency prior to earning their own term in the White House.[2] Furthermore, in recent decades the vice presidency has proven to be one of the better indicators of future presidential nominees. Richard Nixon, Hubert Humphrey, Walter Mondale, George H.W. Bush, and Al Gore all served as vice president prior to winning the presidential nomination of their party.

But the likelihood of any vice president ascending to the presidency via succession should not be casually dismissed. In the twentieth century alone, two sitting presidents were assassinated (William McKinley and John Kennedy), two died of natural causes (Warren Harding and Franklin Roosevelt), and one resigned from office (Richard Nixon). Furthermore, there was a concerted attempt to assassinate President Harry Truman by two Puerto Rican nationalists, two attempts were made on the life of President Gerald Ford during his brief tenure, and President Ronald Reagan nearly lost his life when he was hit by a would-be assassin's bullet.

Finally, when it comes to the vice president as potential substitute for the president, presidential inability and determinations of when a president is unable to fulfill their duties must be taken into account. Although the Twenty-fifth Amendment to the Constitution established provisions for managing cases of presidential inability, prior to the ratification of the Twenty-fifth in 1967, there was no constitutional means in place to respond, should circumstances call for it.[3] Again, in the twentieth century, President Woodrow Wilson was incapacitated by a stroke during his second term in office, which by any measure would have called for the temporary, or perhaps permanent, relinquishment of his presidential powers.

Irrespective of the number of times vice presidents have moved up to the presidency, and regardless of the specific circumstances dictating the ascension of the fourteen presidents who were first vice president, the vice presidency, as an institution, has consistently been derided and discounted. Emblematic of the broad disregard for the vice presidency was the 180 years which elapsed before any mechanism was established for replacing the vice president should the vice president succeed to the presidency, resign from office, or die. Because of this oversight, and again, before the ratification of the Twenty-fifth Amendment, which finally established a constitutional means for filling vacancies in the vice presidency, the office remained unoccupied on a number of occasions for well over three years. And in three instances—after John Tyler and Andrew Johnson succeeded to the presidency, and when Vice President William King died within weeks of being sworn into office—the nation went without a sitting vice president for nearly four years.

Table 1.1   Vacancies in the Vice Presidency

Vice President	Term	Cause of Vacancy	Date of Vacancy	Duration of Vacancy		
				Year	Months	Days
George Clinton	1809–1813	Death	4/20/1812	0	10	12
Elbridge Gerry	1813–1817	Death	11/23/1814	2	3	9
John Calhoun	1829–1833	Resigned	12/28/1832	0	2	4
John Tyler	1841–1845	Succession	4/4/1841	3	11	0
Millard Fillmore	1849–1853	Succession	7/9/1850	2	7	23
William King	1853–1857	Death	4/18/1853	3	10	14
Andrew Johnson	1865–1869	Succession	4/15/1865	3	10	17
Henry Wilson	1873–1877	Death	11/22/1875	1	3	10
Chester Arthur	1881–1885	Succession	9/19/1881	3	5	13
Thomas Hendricks	1885–1889	Death	11/25/1885	3	3	11
Garrett Hobart	1897–1901	Death	11/21/1899	1	3	11
Theodore Roosevelt	1901–1905	Succession	9/14/1901	3	5	18
James Sherman	1909–1913	Death	10/30/1912	0	4	5
Calvin Coolidge	1921–1925	Succession	8/2/1923	1	7	2
Harry Truman	1945–1949	Succession	4/12/1945	3	9	8
Lyndon Johnson	1961–1965	Succession	11/22/1963	1	1	28
Spiro Agnew	1973–1977	Resigned	10/10/1973	0	1	26
Gerald Ford	1973–1977	Succession	8/9/1974	0	4	8

What the preceding adds up to is this: the vice presidency has been left vacant eighteen times, for a combined total of almost thirty-eight years. The sheer number of days, months, and years the office was unoccupied, as represented by the data in Table 1.1, is sobering. And while the Congress periodically addressed succession and the need to manage a possible double-vacancy in the two nationally elected executive offices, the impression of an expendable vice-presidential institution is plain.

The notion that one of every three presidents first served as vice president presumably would have engendered numerous assessments of the American vice presidency—past, present and future. Yet, the paucity of research and literature devoted exclusively to the vice presidency is startling. Through the years there have been occasional attempts at addressing aspects of the vice presidency, but typically such inquiries have been peripheral, at best. For example, in 1915 the *American Historical Review* published an article devoted to those times when vice presidents had cast tie-breaking votes in the United States Senate.[4] The article devoted barely six pages of text for measuring 126 years of vice-presidential votes in the Senate.

There have likewise been cursory considerations of the vice presidency; however, not just scholars have weighed in, as rising politicians have presented their views as well. For instance, four years prior to gaining the Republican Party nomination for vice president, Theodore Roosevelt wrote an essay conjoining history with a topical review of the candidates standing for vice president in the election of 1896.[5] Although the aim of Roosevelt's essay was to highlight the candidates for vice president, at the outset he pointed to the paradox of the vice presidency in relation to the presidency; it was a paradox, at the time he was writing, informed by over 100 years of derision directed at the institution, and an unwillingness on the part of many to settle for a position which clearly stood second to the president. Roosevelt observed that "the presidency being all important, and the vice-presidency of comparatively little note, the entire strength of the contending factions is spent in the conflict over the first, and very often a man who is most anxious to take the first place will not take the second, preferring some other political position."[6]

Twenty-four years later, when Theodore Roosevelt's cousin Franklin sought the vice presidency on the Democratic ticket of 1920, he too wrote about the office.[7] But Franklin Roosevelt was not satisfied writing a simple retrospective overview, nor did he lament the historical neglect of the vice presidency. Instead, in his essay, the younger Roosevelt argued that the vice president should be put to better use. He was acknowledging the underutilization of this particular officer of the government, while underscoring another contradiction intrinsic to the vice presidency.

Roosevelt's point was that the vice president is one of only two officers of the government elected by the entire nation and voted for with the chief executive, and yet the vice president is given no ongoing executive duties and only marginal duties in the legislative branch. Of the vice president's role in the legislative branch: even there, the vice president is limited to one chamber of a bicameral legislature. So where does the vice president belong in the government? Or, restated, what is the vice president to do? By Roosevelt's estimation:

> The duties of the Vice President in relation to the Senate are, in short, largely perfunctory. He has no duties in relation to either the executive or judicial branch of the Government. There is no little truth, then, in the witticism that the Vice President constitutes a kind of fourth branch of the Government—a branch condemned by tradition to sit in lonely grandeur with remote responsibilities but very little to do. If, in fact, there ever was a waste of man power it would seem to be here ... One would think that the grotesqueness of the predicament of the Vice President would have been apparent to everyone long ago.[8]

But the predicament of the vice president must not have been as apparent as Roosevelt assumed, for serious studies of the institution were sporadic from the time Roosevelt's article appeared, continuing to the present. Apart from the anemic body of literature devoted to the vice presidency and vice presidents, at one point there was a concerted effort at improving the efficacy of the vice presidency in relation to the presidency. This came about with the work of the Hoover Commission, chaired by former president Herbert Hoover in the 1950s. Because the ideas of the Hoover Commission are referenced later in the text, and at more than one juncture when telling the story of the vice presidency, it merits a brief introduction here.

The Hoover Commission was founded expressly to study and recommend a broad reorganization of the executive branch of the federal government. Ironically, the Hoover report did not recommend revamping what was then understood to be an ineffectual vice-presidential institution. Instead, Hoover and the other members of the commission proposed adding a second vice president to the executive government who was to be employed only in administrative duties.[9] The objective being, the second vice president would relieve some of the burdens of the modern American presidency. Obviously the proposal has yet to be implemented; nevertheless, a remedy that included creation of a second office of the vice president indicated much about the potential inherent to the institution, and was similarly a sign of how far the American presidency had come by the middle of the twentieth century.

Returning to published studies of the vice presidency: of the articles to appear in academic journals over the years, many have suggested making the most of the existent office; conversely, some scholars have devoted time to electoral calculations and the value, or not, of vice-presidential candidates; and then there has been the occasional scholar who suggests that the answer to the riddle of the vice presidency might just be to abolish the office.[10] In the 1950s, an interpretation of the vice presidency up to that point in time was issued. The main title was innocuous enough, *Second Consul*; however, the subtitle spoke volumes: *The Vice Presidency: Our Greatest Political Problem.*[11]

By the 1980s, serious and less dramatically titled texts were on occasion presented; still, a substantial oeuvre on the American vice presidency never gelled.[12] Typically, of the few academic texts available, nuances of the institution and its occupants were overlooked. For example, despite the dearth of substantial individuals to hold the office in the nineteenth century, there were specific vice presidents who, due to the relationship they sustained with the president they served, warranted at least perfunctory appraisals. Alas, reports on such unions were not produced.

In the twenty-first century there has been some renewed academic interest in the vice presidency, but on the whole, wide-ranging evaluations of the institution are absent and tend instead to focus on exclusive spheres or individuals. For instance, one text that came out in 2009 was devoted entirely to the vice president's role in foreign policy; it failed, however, to include the contributions of several vice presidents prior to the forty-second vice president, Walter Mondale.[13] Although the involvement of various vice presidents in foreign policy is featured when appropriate to the narrative of this text, at this juncture another mischaracterization perpetuated by the aforementioned text should be pointed out. Even if many of the author's conclusions on the five vice presidents under review might be sound, the description of the vice presidency as "semi-institutionalized" is a flawed categorization.[14] Frankly, at this point in the history of the institution, it is inaccurate to argue the American vice presidency is in some way incomplete.

Then again, attaining a precise understanding of the structure and the status of the vice presidency never has been simple. In 1908, Woodrow Wilson posited a classification for institutions wherein an institution may be accepted as an established entity, yet not necessarily be sanctioned by the Constitution, let alone by scholars. Wilson put it this way:

> We sometimes attach a very artificial significance to the word 'institution.' Speaking in the terms of history, and particularly of political history, an institution is merely an established practice, an habitual method of dealing with the circumstances of life or the business of government. There may be firmly established institutions of which the law knows nothing.[15]

Wilson's elastic characterization is apropos to the proposition that the American vice presidency is undeniably a political and government institution. For that matter, the vice presidency has been an institution since its inception—a hollow institution, perhaps, but an institution, nonetheless.

It is important to emphasize that any text issued prior to 1993 is unavoidably missing assessments of two remarkable vice-presidential tenures—those of Al Gore and Dick Cheney. As for Cheney, since the end of his second term in office, a spate of books have come out that delve into the machinations of his unwavering rise to power when he served at the side of President George W. Bush. But such texts fail to place Cheney's ambition and success in the appropriate context and by doing so ignore the many presidents and vice presidents who unwittingly abetted him in his assumption of power and prerogative.

If, however, the modern American vice presidency is portrayed as solely the work of Dick Cheney, then the vice presidency remains an enigma. It is the complete story of the institution, and of the individuals who have served as vice president, that must be examined in order to gain a meaningful understanding of where the vice presidency is today, and what that portends for politics and governance in the United States. Ultimately, it is the necessary breadth of analysis of the American vice presidency that is wanting in the scant academic and popular literature that bothers to venture into appraisals of the institution.

This then leads to the 2008 presidential election and the vice-presidential nominees chosen by the two major political parties. Undoubtedly, increased time and emphasis should be given to the selection of vice-presidential nominees by the presidential nominees, as well as by the delegates to the nominating conventions. In recent years, last minute decisions made at the conventions have given way to a deliberative process that is commonly systematic and extensive. Using such vetting processes to examine potential vice-presidential nominees has become the norm for many of the presidential nominees and their campaign organizations. The 2008 presidential election, however, offers a notable case study of the dichotomy in approach taken by the presidential nominees of the two major American political parties when both were set to select vice-presidential running mates.

For one presidential nominee, this meant implementation of a selection process equally dynamic and methodical, and for the other, the selection of the vice-presidential nominee was made absent of process, founded almost entirely in reaction to the opposition presidential nominee's measured choice. With the former, the extent of the process was an acknowledgement of the significance of the modern vice presidency, whereas the latter was an exercise in retrogress, emblematic of the historic tendency to discount the vice presidency and all who seek and serve in the office. The transparent disparities in approach taken by the two presidential nominees when picking their running mates underscore not only why the American vice presidency matters, but also the paradoxical view of the vice presidency that endures. Regrettably, the preceding points hamper a precise and inclusive understanding of, and appreciation for, the modern institution and the individuals who occupy it.

In the lead-up to the 2008 Democratic Party nominating convention, the manner and method for winnowing, and then vetting, the field of contenders for the party's vice-presidential nomination was organized and extensive. Senator Barack Obama had assembled a trio of talented individuals to undertake a wide-ranging vetting process of potential vice-presidential nominees.[16] He had begun this process well before the reluctant admission by his remaining primary campaign opponent, Senator Hillary Clinton, of his likely being the party's standard-bearer.[17] Obama's approach typified what inarguably should be the standard for all presidential nominees once their own nomination is secure and the time has arrived to focus on the choice of a running mate. Hence, this seriousness of purpose reflected Obama's respect for the orderly process utilized by several previous presidential nominees; it was presumably also in recognition of the power and resources that now reside within the vice-presidential institution.

Prior to the Democratic convention, Obama spoke candidly about the process he established for selecting a vice-presidential running mate and of the value he placed on choosing the right individual for the job; more importantly, he was unequivocal about the type of association he envisioned he would have with his vice president. Obama said,

> the vice presidency is the most important decision that I'll make before I'm president. And it's something that I take very seriously ... So we've got a committee ... They are going to go through the procedure and vet and talk with people and get recommendations. I will meet with a range of people... And I will be deliberate and systematic about it, because this will be my final counselor when I'm making decisions in the White House. And I want to make sure that I get it right.[18]

Still, Obama's task was not as straightforward as it might otherwise have been. Complicating his search for a suitable running mate was the length and ferocity of his battle with Clinton for the nomination, and the subsequent pressure to put her on the ticket.[19] Yet having a vice-presidential nominee who was married to a former president—one who brought assets as well as distractions to the scene—coupled with the palpable ill will existent at that time between Obama and both Clintons, was surely too much for any campaign to bear.

Obviously Obama might have made a cynical decision, casting aside many of the potential negatives in selecting Clinton and focusing on the presumed electoral advantage she held among women and the working class. Instead, Obama chose to implement an exact and rigid methodology when choosing a running mate. Evidently he placed a premium on finding a vice-presidential nominee competent and capable of succeeding to the presidency—which Clinton certainly was—but, of more significance to Obama's long-term purposes, he wanted a running mate who was ultimately compatible to govern by his side.

Conversely, the Republican presidential nominee, Senator John McCain, opted for a visceral and less orderly process when making his choice for a running mate. In the weeks prior to the Republican convention, McCain had signaled privately that his favorite for the number two spot on the ticket was, oddly enough, the Democratic nominee for vice president in 2000, Senator Joseph Lieberman.[20] Aside from Lieberman's registration with the Democratic Party, his liberal positions on many issues precluded his ever being selected; regardless, considerable attention was devoted to the possibility of an offer of the vice-presidential nomination to Lieberman. Cognizant of the resistance he was certain to encounter from ardent conservative Republicans if Lieberman was picked, McCain chose instead to rely on his instincts—instincts apparently informed most by the timing of the opposition party convention. Since the convention for the Republican Party began in the immediate aftermath of the Democratic National Convention, McCain held a distinct advantage in knowing Senator Joe Biden was the Democratic vice-presidential nominee. Undoubtedly, having confirmation of the opposition vice-presidential nominee, McCain could not help but be influenced when making his choice.

If Barack Obama had picked Hillary Clinton for the vice-presidential nomination, in all likelihood John McCain would not have chosen Alaska's governor, Sarah Palin. It was a selection initially viewed auspiciously for the sheer dynamism Palin presumably brought to the ticket, in tandem with the residual electoral benefits her presence might add. Ultimately, McCain's choice of Palin seemed ill conceived, perhaps risky, and eventually proved a drag on the ticket.[21] At its core, McCain's approach to the process was imprudent and reflected a curious ignorance of what the modern vice presidency has become. What is more, by his dismissal of a serious vetting process prior to offering the nomination to Palin, McCain indicated a fundamental absence of concern for the presidency, and the prospect of the vice president succeeding to the higher office. Equally disconcerting, McCain's actions suggested a level of political calculation emblematic of earlier selection processes, when too often the result was the nomination and election of insubstantial and unprepared vice presidents.

When presidential nominations are certain relatively early in the primary season, as it was for McCain by the spring of 2008, presidential nominees feasibly may take more time to review possible running mates. This has been the scenario for a number of modern presidential nominees, with some taking advantage of the additional time to make a measured, prudent selection. Likewise, the benefit of a concerted evaluation of a potential vice president is borne out by the two occasions when the selection process was removed from electoral politics. This came about when the Twenty-fifth Amendment was invoked and President Richard Nixon nominated Gerald Ford to replace Spiro Agnew as vice president, and it occurred when President Ford nominated Nelson Rockefeller for his own replacement in the second office. In both instances, the efficacy of thoroughly reviewing the qualities and qualifications of possible vice presidents was well supported.

Certainly Ford and Rockefeller had their weaknesses, yet the linked congressional investigations and confirmation hearings their respective nominations prompted gave Congress and the public reasonable depictions of what both nominees brought to the vice presidency. Of greater consequence, and regardless of where Ford and Rockefeller landed on the political spectrum, the detailed examination of their experience and qualifications for the second highest office in the land indicated that they had been confirmed because they were prepared to serve as vice president, and quite possibly president. For in the long run, it is the presidency that continues to make the American vice presidency matter.

Continuing the consideration of electoral politics and vice-presidential nominations, the benchmark for all presidential nominees when picking a running mate should be parity with the opposition party's vice-presidential nominee. Obviously the burden for choosing an equivalent or even superior running mate falls on the presidential nominee with the nominating convention that follows the opposition party's convention. To Obama's credit, it seemed that his first priority was a running mate equipped to succeed to the presidency. This is not to infer Biden's foreign policy credentials or his attractiveness to working class constituencies were not reasons for his selection; however, the preceding factors, in conjunction with his acknowledged political stature, added a level of gravitas to the ticket, and likewise reassured voters that he could competently assume the presidency should the need arise.[22]

In contrast, the confidence of the electorate in Governor Palin as a potential vice president or president was much lower than that for Senator Biden. Palin failed to achieve a measure of parity with Biden, whether it was in regard to preparedness, seriousness of purpose, or the capacity to govern a large and diverse nation. According to one poll, 66 percent of voters suggested Biden possessed the requisite experience to serve as president, whereas 50 percent said the same about Palin.[23] Most telling, in the same poll, while 21 percent of the respondents claimed Biden did not have the experience to assume the presidency if there was cause for his elevation, twice as many respondents, 42 percent, doubted Palin possessed the necessary experience to take on the presidency.[24]

Senator McCain's decision to pick Palin was likely aimed at capitalizing on the gender of his running mate and then, in theory, gaining the support of disaffected women supporters of Senator Clinton. What is striking about the entire episode, however, is that McCain opted for an individual who was so ideologically disparate from Clinton and, in terms of preparedness and experience, so inferior to the opposition vice-presidential nominee. But his choice of Palin might also have been informed by the consistent data indicating that Senator Obama had more support with women voters. Specifically, a Gallup tracking poll showed when voters, in the aggregate, were asked their preference of presidential candidates, Obama was favored by 49 percent of women voters, to McCain's 39 percent.[25]

Apart from the political drama underscoring the selections made by the 2008 presidential nominees, any meaningful consideration of potential vice-presidential nominees should be guided by a simple truth: modern vice presidents step into a vastly changed institution, with access to power a given and tangible institutional resources readily available. Whereas the strengths and weaknesses of each president's relationship with their vice president goes far in determining the influence any vice president has within an administration—a theme considered throughout this book—modern vice presidents have benefited from the incremental establishment of precedents, as well as the accrual of numerous institutional resources. Quite simply, it is unlikely that what the vice presidency has become will ever be cast aside.

Even if John McCain, when making his choice for the vice-presidential nomination, demonstrated a critical misunderstanding of how far the American vice presidency has come since 1789; it also reinforced a collective supposition about those who run for vice president. More specifically, it is taken for granted that vice-presidential nominees will make a difference in elections and, at the very least, will carry their home state. It is reasonable to suggest that McCain adhered to the premise that his running mate could deliver a decided electoral advantage, and with a particular demographic, irrespective of her perceived or actual preparedness for the vice presidency or presidency. What McCain discovered was that the vote of the electorate is determined by their view of the presidential candidates, and typically without an overriding concern for the attributes of the vice-presidential candidates.

Sarah Palin also seemed to underestimate the increased importance of the modern vice presidency and even went so far as to overstate the role the Constitution fixed for the vice president to play in the legislative branch. This occurred nearly seven weeks after Palin won the Republican nomination for vice president, with her assertion that, as vice president, she would be "in charge of the Senate [and therefore could] really get in there with the senators and make a lot of good policy change."[26] As the vice-presidential nominee of a major American political party, Palin's lack of clarity on what the vice president actually does was a poignant reminder of the broad misunderstanding that persists about the office.

What is fascinating about the nominations of Biden and Palin, and by the same token beguiling, is that their nominations occurred in the aftermath of the substantial vice-presidential tenure of Al Gore, and while Dick Cheney was serving in the office. Both Gore and Cheney exercised considerable influence and authority and used the institutional resources of the modern vice presidency completely. Moreover, Gore and Cheney were partners to the presidents they served; as such, their time in office highlighted the role that any individual elected to the vice presidency will likely play in the future. And, in the choices Obama and McCain made, they offered two conflicting views about what the vice presidency has become in recent years.

For Barack Obama, Joe Biden appears to have been a choice made in recognition that the vice president is more than the presiding officer of the United States

Senate and instead may be, at a minimum, a governing partner with the president, akin to Gore and Cheney. Biden certainly held such a view of the office, and he had agreed to run for vice president only after being assured that he was to play a substantial role in an Obama administration.[27] Of his likely role, Biden offered at the vice-presidential debate that "Barack Obama indicated to me he wanted me with him to help him govern. So every major decision he'll be making, I'll be sitting in the room to give him my best advice."[28]

In contrast, John McCain's selection of Sarah Palin looked as if he had simply dismissed the necessity of a governing partnership like that which characterized the Clinton-Gore pairing as well as the reign of Bush and Cheney. Having met with Palin for no more than three hours before making his choice known, it is improbable that McCain was well enough acquainted with his running mate to then anticipate a future relationship on par with more recent presidents and vice presidents.[29]

As for Palin, she indicated in the vice-presidential debate that the part she anticipated playing in a McCain administration was less as an equal partner to the president, and instead was more in the vein of a loyal supporter and advocate for the president's agenda. In her inimitable manner, Palin delineated her role in a future McCain administration in this way: "I'm thankful that the Constitution would allow a bit more authority given to the vice president if that vice president so chose to exert it in working with the Senate and making sure that we are supportive of the president's policies and making sure too that our president understands what our strengths are."[30]

The American vice presidency must not be gauged exclusively by the candidates who have recently sought the office, nor should it be valued only by the performance of its most recent occupants. Likewise, the "grotesqueness of the predicament of the Vice President," of which Franklin Roosevelt wrote so long ago, should not continue to define the office. Instead, the vice presidency today is the sum of its rich and colorful history. And if there have been good, and even brilliant, vice presidents who have served their nation with dignity, the office has equally been occupied by a murderer, traitors, and a fair number of individuals who spent the better part of their tenure yearning for the power and prestige that rests with the other nationally elected officer of the United States—the president.

As it stands, those who have served in the vice presidency represent the best and the worst the American political system has to offer; and yet, at the end of the day, it is the indissoluble connection of the vice presidency to the presidency that makes the second office count. Still, the vice presidency, and all that it was and all it has become, is long overdue for a comprehensive analysis. For the vice presidency today stands firmly alongside the presidency as a singular political institution, worthy of consideration.

2

IN THE BEGINNING

VICE-PRESIDENTIAL SELECTION, AARON BURR, AND THE TWELFTH AMENDMENT

Every body is aware of that defect in the constitution which renders it possible that the man intended for Vice President may in fact turn up President.
– Alexander Hamilton

HOW THE AMERICAN VICE PRESIDENCY CAME TO BE

The position of vice president was of almost no concern to delegates of the Federal Convention of 1787. James Madison would make note of the office, though not by name, two months into the Convention proceedings, and then only when discussing how to sort out the selection of the chief executive.[1] To this point, Madison recorded that one delegate, Hugh Williamson of North Carolina, had "observed that such an officer as vice-President was not wanted. He was introduced only for the sake of a valuable mode of election which required two to be chosen at the same time."[2] Williamson was referring to the proviso that electors of the Electoral College should be required to cast at least one of their two electoral votes for a candidate from a state other than their own. Hence the office arose, at least in part, from the desire to elect a president who was representative of the entire nation, and not just of a single state.[3]

In what would prove critical to the earliest contests for president, the result of casting two electoral votes for the same office was to make the vice presidency a consolation prize; it was a practice that even after it was altered continued to inform the view taken by most toward the office, and still does to this day. Simply put, the outcome of casting two votes for the same office was that ultimately someone had to lose. Thus, when the recipient of a majority of the vote had been determined, and had therefore won the office of president, the vanquished candidate, coming in second, was entitled to the vice presidency. As will become apparent later in this chapter, the "valuable mode of election which required two to be chosen at the same time" would unravel in the aftermath of the fourth presidential election.

In addition to being one part in the mechanics of electing a president, the principal use of the vice president emerged when making the second officer in the land the president of the Senate; it was a position which was the outgrowth of the debate and compromise on competing designs for the new government at the Federal Convention.[4] Eventually, as a product of that debate, the vice presidency was embedded in the Constitution, albeit with considerable resistance. Still, even what opposition there was to the office did not escape vigorous challenge, as there were advocates for including a vice president, and Alexander Hamilton, for one, could be counted among those who argued for a vice president, and he merits credit for initially suggesting establishment of the office.

In the course of the Federal Convention's proceedings, Hamilton responded to the alternative schemes for organizing the government by outlining his own "Plan of Government."[5] In it, Hamilton recognized the need for a secondary executive officer who would assume the duties of the president—or "governor," the original title Hamilton proposed for the individual commanding "Supreme Executive authority"—were that officer to die, resign or be removed from office.[6]

What Hamilton was proposing was not the paradigm for a novel government officer; instead, he was modeling a new national officer on that of the lieutenant governor—an office that could be found in ten of the states, and with fairly commensurate duties attached to it.[7] Though Hamilton did not recommend in his plan that such a secondary officer would be designated the "vice president," he did proffer the already suggested "President of the Senate" for the post. Later, when he was promoting the ratification of the Constitution—in unison with James Madison and John Jay, via a series of editorial letters known collectively as *The Federalist*—Hamilton was unequivocally calling for the establishment of a vice-presidential officer in the new government. To Hamilton, the vice president would resemble "a Lieutenant-Governor, chosen by the people at large, who presides in the Senate, and is the constitutional substitute for the Governor, in casualties similar to those which would authorize the Vice-President to exercise the authorities and discharge the duties of the President."[8]

Hamilton was never one to retreat from his critics, particularly when the form of the Constitution was at stake, hence he vigorously advocated for the inclusion of the vice presidency within the document. In order to better elucidate the reasons for instituting the vice presidency, Hamilton advanced, via *Federalist No. 68*, the following arguments:

> The appointment of an extraordinary person, as Vice-President, has been objected to as superfluous, if not mischievous. It has been alleged, that it would have been preferable to have authorized the Senate to elect out of their own body an officer answering that description. But two considerations seem to justify the ideas of the convention in this respect. One is, that to secure at all times the possibility of a definite resolution of the body, it is necessary that the President should have only a casting vote. And to take the senator of any State from his seat as senator, to place him in that of President

of the Senate, would be to exchange, in regard to the State from which he came, a constant for a contingent vote. The other consideration is, that as the Vice-President may occasionally become a substitute for the President, in the supreme executive magistracy, all the reasons which recommend the mode of election prescribed for the one, apply with great if not with equal force to the manner of appointing the other.[9]

With Hamilton's assertion that "the Vice-President may occasionally become a substitute for the President," he had made a passing allusion to the prospect of the vice president, under certain conditions, taking on the responsibilities delegated to the president. But designating the vice president as the president-in-waiting appears never to have been the intent of delegates to the Federal Convention. Filling a vacancy in the presidency, be it temporary or permanent, was consistently viewed as the ideal fit for the president of the Senate—an officer initially meant to be drawn from among the members of the upper chamber—and to serve only until a new president was selected.[10]

Having the vice president the designated successor to the president led one delegate, Gouverneur Morris, to draw attention to the futility of the idea, and of the office. To this point Morris suggested, with a bit of humor, that "the vice president then will be the first heir apparent that ever loved his father. If there should be no vice president, the President of the Senate would be temporary successor, which would amount to the same thing."[11] Therefore, and with no readily apparent use for a vice president, it came to pass that the presiding officer of the Senate was to be the vice president of the United States.

Hamilton suggested another proviso with regard to the assumption of the duties of the president by the vice president. Although it never made it into the Constitution, Hamilton maintained that the vice president should take over for the president if the president had occasion to travel abroad and was therefore physically absent from the United States—an absence that first had to be approved by both houses of Congress.[12]

Clearly then, besides being the designated stand-in for the president, should circumstances dictate, the vice president was expected to serve a legislative role by presiding over the Senate. With this, the vice president was to be given a vote in the Senate, contingent on the chamber being equally divided. This meant the vice president could vote in the Senate, but only when a tie occurred. All the same, having even a limited vote was not intended to empower. Many of the Framers were determined to establish a strong national legislature, yet it was meant to be an institution unable to usurp the powers of the states and their respective senators.

Therefore, as Hamilton had put forward in the earlier selection from *Federalist No. 68*, a permanent presiding officer drawn from outside the legislative branch would mean no state would ever lose one of its two constitutionally provided votes in the chamber, as neither senator from any state would have to routinely take the chair to preside over the Senate. To this point, Roger Sherman, a delegate to the Federal Convention from Connecticut, emphasized that placing a senator in the presiding officer's chair would merely guarantee that the senator was "deprived of his vote."[13] Sherman also wryly hinted at the paradox that shadowed those serving as vice president for years afterwards, remarking, "If the vice-President were not to be President of the Senate, he would be without employment."[14]

Evidently, having the vice president preside over one chamber of the legislature caused unease for some at the Federal Convention.[15] In part, this may be traced to the odd duality of the institution, with the vice president ostensibly belonging to two of the three branches of the United States government—a distinction afforded no other official in the federal government. Accordingly, the ratification of the Constitution cemented the vice president's connection with the executive branch in the following ways: the vice president was to be chosen at the same time and in the same manner as the president; the vice president, under specific, detailed conditions was the constitutionally designated substitute for the president; and the vice presidency was instituted in Article II of the Constitution—literally in the company of the other national executive, the president. Presumably, the vice presidency was to be counted as part of the executive branch.

But giving the vice president a job in the Senate, noted previously and expressed without equivocation in Article I of the Constitution, landed the vice president squarely in the legislative branch, too. For that matter, by including the vice president with the Congress in Article I, a place for the office was reserved prior to any mention of the president in the document.

It was this outward show of executive intrusion into the legislature that most concerned delegates, such as Elbridge Gerry of Massachusetts and George Mason of Virginia. James Madison reported that Gerry, who was against the addition of a vice president to the new government, had announced that Convention delegates "might as well put the President himself at head of the Legislature. The close intimacy that must subsist between the President & vice-president makes it absolutely improper."[16] Along these same lines, Madison documented the sentiments of Mason, who "thought the office of vice-President an encroachment on the rights of the Senate; and that it mixed too much the Legislative & Executive, which as well as the Judiciary departments, ought to be kept as separate as possible."[17]

Ironically, Elbridge Gerry and George Mason, joined by Edmund Randolph of Virginia, were the only three delegates active in the Convention not to sign the finished document. Even more ironic, Gerry later went on to serve as James Madison's second vice president. It is equally telling that when objecting to the vice president's presence in the Senate, Gerry had insisted that the nature of the president's association with the vice president necessitated "close intimacy." As such, Gerry's words would prove to be a prescient description of the relationship that typically characterizes modern presidents and their vice presidents.

Even if the Constitution is ambiguous in places, it is a rigid document and confers no flexibility in its placement of the vice president in the government. Put another way: other than some initial uncertainty that arose the first time presidential succession was tested, the Constitution, without fail, has assigned the vice president solely to the presiding officer's chair.

Second Place Finisher

Whereas the office of vice president was an outwardly impotent, though firmly established position in the Constitution, determining who was to occupy the office was dependent entirely on the election of the president. Therefore, the method for selecting the vice president was set forth in the Constitution as follows:

> The Electors shall meet in their respective States, and vote by Ballot for two Persons, of whom one at least shall not be an Inhabitant of the same State with themselves ... The Person having the greatest Number of Votes shall be the President ... In every Case, after the Choice of the President, the Person having the greatest Number of Votes of the Electors shall be the Vice President.[18]

The implications of the foregoing excerpt from the Constitution on the American vice presidency were two-fold. First, it initiated the precedent of selecting a president and a vice president from dissimilar regions of the country. This was a standard subsequently adopted by the political parties, and later followed by individual presidential candidates, during the nomination process.[19] And since presidential electors were compelled to cast at least one ballot for a candidate of another state, it was impossible for electors from a single state to dominate the two highest offices in the land, subsequently ensuring the national character of the presidency and the vice presidency. As Alexander Hamilton asserted in a segment of *The Federalist*: casting two votes for president would "establish him in the esteem and confidence of the whole Union, or of so considerable a portion of it as would be necessary to make him a successful candidate for the distinguished office of the President of the United States."[20]

And second, the preceding passage from the Constitution ostensibly guaranteed that the occupant of the vice presidency possessed relatively equal qualities and abilities to the president's. In other words, with the electors being able to choose from a number of presidential aspirants, all of whom were estimated to be of presidential caliber, the second place finisher was presumably equal to the winning candidate.[21]

If, when choosing the president and vice president, the preceding two outcomes were indeed the Framer's intent, then the first three presidential elections were a success on both accounts. President George Washington heralded from Virginia, and the first vice president, John Adams, was a native of Massachusetts; consequently, the rural and commercial divisions of the new nation were uniformly represented in the executive branch.[22] Similarly, with the ascension of John Adams to the presidency in 1797 and the election of Virginian Thomas Jefferson as the replacement vice president, the provincial cast of the executive was preserved. Fortunately for the new nation, Washington, Adams, and Jefferson were made of exceptional minds and talents, setting a standard that proved, unfortunately, elusive for many of their successors.

Alas, the selection of presidents and vice presidents possessing outstanding qualities was not to remain a characteristic of American elections for long. And so, by the fourth inauguration of a vice president, the standing of the institution was significantly diminished. For after John Adams and Thomas Jefferson had served as the first and second vice president, respectively, it became something of a challenge to locate individuals of their intellect and ability willing to settle for the vice presidency. Even though the third vice president, Aaron Burr, was a clever and gifted political strategist, it was widely agreed that Burr was in equal measure a person of dubious character.[23]

POLITICAL PARTIES AND THE ELECTORAL COLLEGE

Political parties were not instrumental in the creation of the American vice presidency. For that matter, political parties as they are known today did not exist when the vice presidency was established. As a result, political parties played no part in determining the outcome of the first two contests for president, and the ensuing determination of the vice president. Those elections, held in 1789 and 1792, have since proved unprecedented in the annals of American politics; never again were political parties absent from the machinations of electing presidents and vice presidents. Nonetheless, by the time President Washington chose not to run for a third term, thus setting the two term precedent that held for nearly 140 years, political parties—in theory and in practice—began to emerge as the driving force of the nascent American political scene.

This is not to suggest that political parties, or at least something resembling such associations, were entirely unknown to the architects of the Constitution. James Madison had famously cautioned against the mischief of factions, pejoratively describing a faction as "a number of citizens, whether amounting to a majority or a minority of the whole, who are united and actuated by some common impulse of passion, or of interest, adverse to the rights of other citizens, or to the permanent and aggregate interests of the community."[24] But Madison, despite the direness with which he described factions and the potential such groups held for disruption of the political process, was resigned to the inevitability of factions, further noting "that the causes of faction cannot be removed, and that relief is only to be sought in the means of controlling its effects."[25]

George Washington, too, warned against the rise of permanent factions, but Washington was not averse to calling factions what they actually were: political parties. In Washington's Farewell Address to Congress, itself a body of brewing factious elements, the president cautioned that those who are "of a party ... may now and then answer popular ends, [but] they are likely, in the course of time and things, to become potent engines, by which cunning, ambitious, and unprincipled men will be enabled to subvert the Power of the People, and to usurp for themselves the reins of Government; destroying afterwards the very engines which have lifted them to unjust dominion."[26]

It was the election of 1796 that set the stage for the first transparent manifestation of political parties, and the gamesmanship that has since colored presidential politics. As is the case in the United States today, two distinct political associations dominated politics in 1796: one group was commonly denoted as the Federalists; the other was alternately described as the Democratic-Republicans or Jeffersonian Republicans.[27] Initially the Federalists arose as a loosely connected group advocating for the adoption of the Constitution, yet by 1796 the incumbent vice president, John Adams, was the acknowledged head of a more formal, recognizable party of Federalists.[28] As it turned out, the Federalists were not long on the political scene, with their perceptible demise beginning with the election of 1800, and their run was almost complete at the finish of the election of 1804.[29]

As the Federalists weakened, and then eventually ceased to operate, a number of other minor political factions appeared and disappeared; all, however, failed to coalesce into more permanent associations. One political party, the Whigs, did succeed in intermittently electing presidents and vice presidents; specifically, the teams of William Henry Harrison and John Tyler; and Zachary Taylor and Millard Fillmore. Curiously, both elected Whig vice presidents succeeded to the presidency upon the death of the elected Whig presidents, thus making four Whig presidents in all. It was, perchance, foreshadowing of the demise of an organized Whig element in American politics.

Conversely, the Democratic-Republican coalition came from a fellowship of politicos who adhered primarily to the words and deeds of Thomas Jefferson; it was an association that, after 1796, achieved greater success than the Federalists. Eventually most Democratic-Republicans drifted toward Andrew Jackson as their leader, condensed their name to simply the Democratic Party, and effectively dominated the national government for all but eight of the next thirty-two years.[30]

In effect, Jackson's Democrats were only intermittently challenged for control of the national government, and not seriously until the election of 1860. In that year, victory came to the Republican Party—a coalition of party regulars, most of whom had identified with the National Republican Whig Party just four years prior. By 1860, many of the same National Republican Whigs were instead known as Republicans, and from their nominating convention they delivered Abraham Lincoln and Hannibal Hamlin to run for president and vice president, respectively.

In 1796, however, there were not yet nominating conventions; instead, the political parties chose their candidates for president for the first time by means of the congressional caucus.[31] Still, in that year the two party caucuses were merely perfunctory exercises, for it was widely assumed the Democratic-Republicans would nominate President Washington's former secretary of state, Thomas Jefferson, for president, and the Federalists were sure to nominate Vice President Adams for his opponent.[32] Both parties also indicated a preference for vice president—at that time, the runner-up in the presidential contest—with Aaron Burr the acknowledged second to Jefferson and Thomas Pinckney, as Burr's equivalent, to stand with Adams.

Of the four principal candidates, Aaron Burr would prove most like a modern candidate in a presidential campaign. Burr's behavior was suggestive of future vice-presidential candidates, as he vigorously campaigned for the Democratic-Republican team for several weeks, whereas Jefferson, Adams, and Pinckney were essentially absent from any campaign activities.[33] Yet Burr's aggressive electioneering raised suspicions among some in his own party that his real target was the presidency, and not the vice presidency—a charge against him that was echoed in the election of 1800.[34]

In addition to the part played by Aaron Burr, on many levels the election of 1796 could be viewed as the model for future political party campaign activities, with both

Democratic-Republican and Federalist partisans introducing a variety of campaign tactics in their competing efforts to gain the presidency.[35] This is not to suggest that such activities equally matched those of modern campaigns, but the rudimentary elements of campaigning were definitely taking form. Some of these tactics were entirely new to the political landscape, some were familiar but vastly extended by Burr during the campaign, and all would swiftly become staples of American political campaigns from that time forward. Ultimately, Democratic-Republican activists were the more discerning of the two competing groups, as they deliberately cultivated support for their candidates from the people. Apparently Democratic-Republicans recognized that the future of presidential elections might actually lie outside the domain of traditional political elites.[36]

Beyond their increasing appreciation for innovative campaign techniques, political leaders of the era also understood that the president and vice president of the United States were not elected exclusively by direct popular vote. Instead, the president and vice president were chosen by the electors of the Electoral College, the mechanics of which are dictated by the Constitution.[37] In brief, the Constitution instructs the legislatures of each state to determine how to select their own state's electors, with each state having no more electors than the number of senators and representatives granted to the state. Next, the electors are to list all the candidates voted for, and then send the tally of the vote to Congress. At that point, prior to the adoption of the Twelfth Amendment, the person with the most votes was elected president, and the second place finisher was elected vice president. Finally, in the event that a candidate fails to gain a majority of the appointed electors, then and now, the House of Representatives determines, with one vote per state, the winner of the presidency; the Senate is empowered to proceed in the same fashion with respect to settling on the vice president.

In 1796 sixteen states sent electors to the Electoral College. Of those sixteen states, six chose their electors by popular vote, and the remaining ten states formed their slate of electors by way of their state legislature. As such, in those states choosing electors via the legislature, the political party that dominated the legislature plainly had the edge in elector selection. Adding to the potential for political intrigue was, and still is, this quirk in the design of the Electoral College: electors are in no way required to vote for specific candidates. And it was this procedural loophole that President Washington's secretary of the treasury, Alexander Hamilton, hoped to exploit to his own political satisfaction.

At some point in 1796, Alexander Hamilton decided to try and propel the accepted Federalist candidate for vice president, Thomas Pinckney, into the presidency.[38] It apparently did not matter to Hamilton that John Adams was his party's presidential candidate, as Hamilton, a long-time adherent of George Washington, could never entirely accept Adams as the heir apparent to the first president. Furthermore, Hamilton's intimacy with President Washington had kept him conveniently near the apex of power and influence for many years, leaving Adams more of an irritant than a threat. But with Washington approaching the threshold of retirement, Adams seemed a most unlikely conduit to power for Hamilton. Hamilton understood his best chance to preserve influence in the capital lay in his depriving Vice President Adams of ever becoming President Adams.[39]

Setting what was to become the foundation for practically every future vice-presidential selection, Aaron Burr and Thomas Pinckney were chosen for the electoral advantage each presumably brought to their respective political parties. The attachment of Burr was expected to make the difference for Jefferson in winning New York's highly coveted electors, and in Pinckney, the Federalists hoped to gain the requisite electors from the South.[40] Conversely, Alexander Hamilton was focused, unlike his Federalist brethren or the opposition Democratic-Republicans, on a less transparent aim than regional ticket-balancing. Hamilton anticipated using the Federalist vice-presidential hopeful in a manner that would, in the long-term, be of considerable value to him. Put simply, Hamilton's objective was to divert just enough Federalist electors away from Adams to elevate the Federalist vice-presidential candidate to the presidency.[41] When Hamilton's plotting was eventually uncovered, concerned members of his own party made sure it did not come to fruition, leaving Hamilton's ambitions unfulfilled and Pinckney no closer to the presidency, nor, as it would turn out, any closer to the vice presidency.[42]

In the end, John Adams prevailed in the Electoral College by earning seventy-one votes to Thomas Jefferson's sixty-eight votes; next was Thomas Pinckney with fifty-nine votes, followed by Aaron Burr's thirty votes, with the remainder of electoral votes scattered among nine other individuals. In the short term, Adams's victory afforded the vice presidency greater cachet, for it temporarily set an expectation for the sitting vice president to be the logical successor to the president.

The election of Thomas Jefferson to the vice presidency had a further, discernable effect on both the institution and the American political psyche. First, Jefferson's ascension to the second highest office in the land, and even his acceptance of the job, added further prestige to a position that Adams initially made credible. And second, Jefferson's success as the leader and candidate of the Democratic-Republicans signaled the transparent arrival of a new and competitive political party—a party poised to contest the Federalists' control of an adolescent American government.

Although the election of 1796 marked the most tangible manifestation of political parties up to that stage in American history, it likewise served as the starting point for deliberately indicating a preference for vice-presidential candidates. But apart from the preceding watershed events, the campaign and election of 1796 would also prove noteworthy for the following reasons: a candidate meant for the vice presidency campaigned in lieu of the active participation of the presidential candidate; specific individuals were chosen as vice-presidential candidates because of a presumed electoral advantage that might come to the political party from making that choice; and lastly, in 1796 the designated vice-presidential candidates were the objects of considerable interest, and even intrigue, but when the votes were tallied, it was the presidency that mattered most.

AARON BURR AND THE PRESIDENTIAL ELECTION OF 1800

Midway through the presidential election year of 1800, America's first two genuine political parties utilized a caucus of their congressional members as the method for formally nominating candidates for the national executive. Even if the political parties were different in form than they are today, the rudimentary outline of political party machinery was existent in nearly every state, beginning with the election of 1796, and confirmed during the electoral season of 1800. The sitting vice president, Thomas Jefferson, was the preferred presidential nominee of Democratic-Republican partisans, and the sitting president, John Adams, was the choice of most Federalists. It was a contest that pitted, again, two of the foremost political figures of the era against one another. Moreover, it was a clash informed by ideological differences that separated the principals, differences underscored by fundamental disagreements about how the practices of the government, the presidency, and the vice presidency should transpire. From a historical vantage, the real significance of the election of 1800 lies in its anomalous nature, for never since has the incumbent president run for reelection against the incumbent vice president, as they did that year.

Not surprisingly, a lesser match-up colored the vice-presidential contest. Aaron Burr was once more the acknowledged Democratic-Republican choice for vice president, and this time John Adams would have Thomas Pinckney's brother, the Federalist enthusiast Charles Cotesworth Pinckney, as his intended vice president. Although the party nominations were not formalized until after several preliminary state contests, all four men had been the probable contenders for some time; still, there were certain obstacles to overcome before the Democratic-Republican caucus settled on Burr.[43] And yet, of more significance than any of the nominees to surface were the compacts the parties made within their respective caucuses. While the compacts were rudimentary—a pledge to cast both electoral votes exclusively for the two, respective nominees of their party—the minimalism of this strategy belied the decided impact it was to have on the outcome of the election.[44]

The election of 1800 brought Aaron Burr to the vice presidency. To better understand the circumstances by which Burr arrived there, it is necessary to briefly revisit the political world of New York at the onset of the nineteenth century. At that time, leadership of New York Democratic-Republicans was under three primary spheres of influence: future vice president George Clinton and his family, the extensive Livingston tribe, and Aaron Burr and his numerous steadfast followers.[45] Of the three groups just cited, only one vigorously entered into the fray. Hence, in the prelude to New York's selection of its twelve electors to the Electoral College, the Clintons and the Livingstons acquiesced to Aaron Burr's domination of the process.[46] The decision by the two clans to restrain themselves in the conduct of the campaign and election had consequences none could have foreseen.

Burr's efforts began with the construction of a slate of capable and attractive Democratic-Republican candidates for the state legislature. Success in this effort was crucial, as New York's legislature was responsible for selecting the state's twelve presidential electors. As a consequence, the legislature had the power to deliver or to deny the partisan composition of electors who then contributed New York's vote to the Electoral College's tally for president and vice president.[47]

More than one biographer has chronicled Burr's innovative tactics in 1800, wherein he organized the drive in New York much like a modern political campaign, exceeding what he had done for the 1796 election.[48] For instance, on top of targeting specific supporters for financial contributions and setting up ward-level committees, Burr compiled an inclusive list of New York City's eligible voters, delineating such details as "the voter's political preferences, the degree of his zeal in their pursuit, his temperament, his willingness to serve the cause as a volunteer, his financial standing, etc."[49] It is the twentieth century politician and Speaker of the House of Representatives Thomas "Tip" O'Neil who is widely credited with saying that "all politics is local." But it is an axiom especially applicable to Burr more than a century prior, when Burr's labors at the local level proved so vital to the outcome of a national election.

Of course none of the preceding is meant to imply that Burr had New York to himself, for Alexander Hamilton, one of the leading Federalists of that state, functioned as Burr's natural counterpart. To be sure, Hamilton was proactive for the Federalist cause, piecing together the legislative slate for his party and coordinating the electoral ground game in New York City.[50] Still, when all the campaigning was over and the votes were tallied, Hamilton's efforts had been for naught. As a tactician, Hamilton proved no match for Burr; he had not sufficiently organized for, nor had he delivered in, New York's preliminary election competition. Therefore, and as a result of Burr's cunning and strategic prowess, Hamilton was prevented from retaining sufficient Federalist control of the state legislature.

In the main, three of the four principal candidates in 1800—John Adams, Thomas Jefferson, and Charles Pinckney—avoided much in the way of overtly campaigning for the national executive positions. For Adams and Jefferson, this meant maintaining dignified and to some extent removed presidential candidacies. Yet, neither Adams nor Jefferson was entirely idle in the lead-up to the election. For Adams this meant arranging some well-timed travel, no doubt effectively arousing broader awareness of his candidacy in the upcoming election.[51] And for Jefferson, a restrained candidacy was defined by profusely writing letters brimming with politics, as well as actively overseeing the written work of others—all of which transparently indicated Jefferson was in the race for the presidency.[52] As to Aaron Burr: in stark contrast with his presumed rival for the vice presidency, Pinckney, Burr kept a comparatively high profile throughout the year, focusing on different regions and states when they came into play.[53]

One of the more effective efforts made towards influencing the outcome of the 1800 election came, not from the words or deeds of any of the principal candidates that year, but instead from the pen of Alexander Hamilton. Hamilton had chosen to write and publish, in the form of an open letter, a vicious attack on John Adams that cast a dark pall on his character; it no doubt undermined the Federalist cause broadly, all the while contributing to a further decline in support for Adams specifically.[54] As in 1796, Hamilton knew well that his influence in the next administration was sure to be stymied if Adams or Jefferson won the presidency, but the ascension of either Pinckney brother might have given him the access to power he craved.[55]

When the outline of the electoral vote was pieced together, state-by-state, it appeared that the incumbent vice president would likely defeat the incumbent president. The real question, then, was this: who was to be vice president for the next four years? And when, in late December, the Electoral College tally was at last complete, every Democratic-Republican elector had kept their caucus pledge, casting both electoral votes exclusively for their party ticket, whereas Federalist electors fell short in fully honoring their own comparable vow. As a consequence, the Electoral College voting went as follows: Thomas Jefferson and Aaron Burr each received seventy-three votes for president, John Adams received sixty-five votes, Charles C. Pinckney received sixty-four, and John Jay gained one electoral vote—a single vote from the state of Rhode Island that, had it been cast for Jefferson or Burr, could have averted what came next.[56]

SETTLING THE ELECTION FOR PRESIDENT AND VICE PRESIDENT IN 1800

The tie between Jefferson and Burr presented an extraordinary opportunity to settle a presidential election for the first time in Congress. To begin with, the Constitution is explicit on the method for resolving those instances when the Electoral College balloting for president results in a tie: members of the House of Representatives are left to decide the outcome, with each state delegation having a single vote to cast. Under most circumstances the mechanics for settling the election would proceed in a fairly seamless manner; however, in place to decide the outcome of the election was a House membership composed of a polarized but decidedly Federalist majority.

Clearly then, the tie vote for president was owned entirely by the opposition political party, with the defeated party poised to select the victors for the offices of president and vice president from among the opposition candidates. As it stood, the vote of the House of Representatives would determine the winner of the presidency, with the second-place finisher left with the vice presidency. This constitutional edict was complicated even further when the top two candidates for president were members of the same political party and had run for office, presumably, as a team. What is more, the tie between Jefferson and Burr meant the vice-presidential nominee was unexpectedly a contender for the presidency, thus flipping the intended hierarchy of the ticket.

When the House of Representatives met in early 1801 to decide the fate of the presidency and vice presidency, sixteen state delegations participated. A modest majority of nine states was necessary to win, and yet there was nothing simple about this particular election, and so the intrigue, accusations, and political maneuvers grew with each vote taken by the House. What ensued were deadlocks, reports of assassination plots, and threats of secession.[57] Over the course of six days, the House voted for president thirty-five times; each time Thomas Jefferson won eight states and Aaron Burr six, with two abstentions.

At some point in the process of choosing the next president, Federalist James Bayard of Delaware, among others, began to seek a compromise for ending the stalemate. Unlike his Federalist brethren, Bayard had an unusual advantage in the proceedings:

being the only House member from Delaware, he was in control of a delegation of one.[58] Bayard knew, as did every other Federalist in Congress, that a president had to be chosen sooner or later, and the two alternatives for president were members of the opposition party. What made Bayard finally decide to abstain, which along with other shifts in the voting gave the election to Jefferson, is unclear. But what is certain is that the anxiety most Federalist members of Congress maintained about a Jefferson presidency was, in the end, assuaged with the deliverance of Aaron Burr to the vice presidency instead.

There has long been speculation that Thomas Jefferson agreed to certain Federalist demands in an effort to obtain the necessary support in the House that would allow him to move from the vice presidency to the presidency.[59] It is possible that Federalist members of Congress, when faced with a choice between Jefferson and Aaron Burr, could not reconcile themselves to a president with as questionable a character as Burr allegedly possessed. Or perhaps Jefferson was willing to barter with his Federalist foes, so long as he would not have to serve another term as vice president—this time under Burr. Either way, it is quite likely that some covert dealings transpired to tip the election.

To this end, one historian posited that if "Jefferson abandoned any of his original plans, and in that sense bargained away any of his principles to win the office, [it] is extremely unlikely; but when he entered the White House it was after satisfying the Federalists that he and they had come to some kind of understanding."[60] At any rate, Thomas Jefferson's selection as president and Aaron Burr's as vice president was eventually determined by the House of Representatives, and on the thirty-sixth ballot. The final tally stood at ten states for Jefferson, four states for Burr, and two states opting for abstention from the historic electoral contest.

Surely the presidential election of 1800 will be recalled for the anomalous tie between Thomas Jefferson and his running mate Aaron Burr, yet the election will be remembered equally for the political intrigue that marked the entire contest. Much of the scheming that year can be traced to disgruntled Federalists, particularly Alexander Hamilton. As it turns out, it was the scheming of Hamilton and others which laid the groundwork for the demise of the Federalists as an organized political party. Nonetheless, political discord in the Federalist camp did not arise solely from within. When the opportunity presented itself, Burr, for one, did what he could to stoke the internal quarrels of the Federalists.[61] Early on, Burr discerned that if events fell into place he might become the president, instead of the vice president, as was planned.

The complexities to arise in resolving the election of 1800, in stark contrast to the three prior presidential elections, signaled that something was seriously amiss in the method used to select the president and vice president of the United States. As Hamilton presciently observed in 1789: "Every body is aware of that defect in the constitution which renders it possible that the man intended for Vice President may in fact turn up President."[62] At the time, Hamilton was expressing his own baseless suspicions that John Adams was planning to propel himself to the top spot over the expected president—George Washington—but in making his concern for the Washington-Adams contest known, he had laid out a scenario that nearly unfolded in the presidential election of 1800.

THE TWELFTH AMENDMENT AND THE ELECTION OF THE VICE PRESIDENT

In the immediate aftermath of the election of 1800, Aaron Burr's willingness to usurp Thomas Jefferson's claim to the presidency gave cause for altering how the president and vice president were to be selected. What is more, being a leading political figure of the era, Burr's complacency in tying the presidential nominee of his own party in the vote of the Electoral College was troubling. The predicament the tie vote created—in tandem with Burr's apparent satisfaction if the election went in his favor—heightened concerns that the system in place was ill equipped for the emergence of political parties, and especially when such an outcome might have come about so early in the nation's history.

With an individual of Aaron Burr's suspect character so dangerously close to winning the presidency, coupled with the increasingly competitive and partisan nature of American politics, Congress chose to act. The move Congress made was toward constructing a new method for formally electing the president and vice president. In order to affect such a change, however, the Constitution had to be amended. On this account, there are just two ways the document may be amended, though, as of this writing, only one has ever been used. That method is as follows: the vote of two-thirds of both houses of Congress is necessary to propose an amendment to the document, and then approval of three-fourths of the state legislatures is required to ratify the amendment the Congress originally agreed upon.[63]

Despite competing proposals and incidences of acrimonious debate, the amendment that developed in Congress was uncomplicated in purpose; the principal aim was the separate election of the president and vice president by the vote of the electors to the Electoral College. Henceforth, the electors were instructed to cast one of their two electoral votes explicitly for president and their second vote specifically for vice president. After only four presidential elections, the vice presidency would no longer be a consolation prize for losing presidential candidates; it was to be, at least within the balloting of the Electoral College, finally a stand-alone elective office.

But reaching consensus on what became the Twelfth Amendment to the Constitution was not easily achieved, and the proposal was met with considerable resistance. In large part this may be explained by there never having been a great reserve of affection for the vice presidency. Over the course of the congressional debate on the Twelfth Amendment, the principal complaints against the office, initially articulated sixteen years earlier at the Federal Convention, were revisited. This included discomfort in even establishing the vice president as an officer of the federal government.

Along these lines, a member of the House of Representatives from Connecticut, Samuel Dana, reminded his listeners of the historical haphazardness with which the vice presidency was instituted. Dana professed "that there is no necessity for this office ... The idea of a Vice President did not suggest itself until the idea of a double ballot was introduced ... Unless some great good result from the office of Vice President, no argument for its continuance can be deduced from the necessity of having an eventual successor."[64]

Like others in the Congress, Representative Dana did not approach the proposed amendment to the Constitution solely as a means to improve the manner in which the president and vice president were chosen. Instead, Dana was seizing on the amendment as a convenient way to excise the vice presidency from the document and from the government. As such, a large share of the debate within the Congress focused on the few places where the vice president fit. From there the debate, based almost entirely on the irrelevance of the institution, was a systematic argument for the abolishment of the office.[65]

One tack taken by those attempting to purge the Constitution of the vice presidency was to address the core principle of the amendment—that being to redirect the electors of the Electoral College to cast separate votes for president and vice president—and then juxtapose that with the original intent of the Framers, which gave the vice presidency to the second place finisher for president. On the original arrangement, James Madison had proffered to the Federal Convention that the outcome of casting two votes for president might very well be that "the second best man in this case would probably be the first, in fact."[66]

Altering the feature of presidential selection that filled the second spot in government with individuals of presumably presidential caliber might result in the vice presidency having even less appeal than was already the case. What is more, the amendment put the presidency itself at stake. Since the electors to the Electoral College would be casting separate votes for president and vice president, but the vice president was still presumed to be the designated successor to the president, a candidate never proposed for the presidency might easily end up there.

It was a plausible outcome that caused concern for many in Congress and led one, Vermont's James Elliot, to assert that "the amendment will make the Constitution worse than it now is, believing as I do that it may bring a man into the Presidency, not contemplated by the people for that office."[67] Then again, as one representative pointed out, should "the office of Vice President ... be abolished, every Elector will give one vote, and that vote will be for President."[68]

And what of the responsibilities that came with the vice president's other title, president of the Senate? Roger Griswold, another member of Connecticut's House delegation, posed and then answered the most forthright of questions with regard to the necessity of the vice president presiding in the Senate. Speaking of the vice president, Griswold asked: "Will he be wanted to preside in the Senate? That will not be necessary, for the Senate sit half their time without the Vice President, and I have not understood that the business is not as well done without as with him."[69]

When it came to the president and the vice president, succession, and altering the procedures of the Electoral College, Representative Griswold was no less forgiving. Arguing against passage of the amendment, Griswold claimed that the value of the vice presidency, assuming there was some value there, would be diminished by casting ballots specifically for president and vice president. According to Griswold, such a method would cultivate an arrangement whereby the "Vice President will be carried to market to purchase the votes of particular States ... If it be your desire to consider the Vice

President as heir apparent to the Presidency, elect him not in this manner, for he must be the mere child of corruption!"[70]

When the amendment was finally approved by both houses of the Congress, the ratification process began, and the projected Twelfth Amendment then went from state to state for ratification. In New York, Alexander Hamilton was the chief advocate for the amendment and the sole author of the "Proposal for the New York Legislature for Amending the Constitution."[71] Hamilton argued that ratification of the Twelfth Amendment was imperative "as a necessary safeguard in the choice of a President and Vice President against pernicious dissensions [and] as the most eligible mode of obtaining a full and fair expression of the public will in such election."[72] For Hamilton, and others of his ilk, the best way to steer clear of any disagreeable electoral incidents, akin to what transpired in the 1800 election, was to ensure that "the persons voted for shall be particularly designated by declaring which is voted for as President and which as Vice President."[73]

Less than a year after Congress initiated the ratification process, and following ample deliberation on the merits of the amendment in the state legislatures, thirteen of the seventeen states then in the Union had agreed to the changes delineated by Congress. In part, the Twelfth Amendment reads:

> The Electors shall meet in their respective states, and vote by ballot for President and Vice-President, one of whom, at least, shall not be an inhabitant of the same State with themselves; they shall name in their ballots the person voted for as President, and in distinct ballots the person voted for as Vice-President, and they shall make distinct lists of all persons voted for as President, and of all persons voted for as Vice-President, and of the number of votes for each, which lists they shall sign and certify, and transmit sealed to the seat of the government of the United States, directed to the President of the Senate ... The person having the greatest number of votes for President, shall be the President ... The person having the greatest number of votes as Vice-President, shall be the Vice-President.[74]

Apart from the antiquated language of the Twelfth Amendment, the mechanics of the amendment were straightforward: directing the electors of the Electoral College to isolate their vote for president, and to then do the same with their vote for vice president. Yet the simplicity of this revision to the rules for electing the president and vice president did not portend the subsequent, long-term impact the amendment was to have on the vice presidency.

To begin with, a major consequence of the Twelfth Amendment was that defeated presidential candidates were unlikely to occupy the office of vice president, for having lost a bid for the presidency, few were willing to run expressly for the vice presidency in a future election. In addition, with the second place finisher for president no longer relegated to the vice presidency, the initiation of the Twelfth Amendment effectively tempered genuine interest in the vice presidency for many capable individuals who might have viewed it as a stepping stone to the highest office in the land—as it had been for John Adams and Thomas Jefferson. This then became a contradiction unique to the Twelfth Amendment: while it provided for the transparent election of a specific individual for vice president, it also dramatically reduced the pool of high quality individuals willing to settle for the office.

The Twelfth Amendment also cemented the pattern of political parties presenting a team of candidates for the two highest offices, a practice that actually began with the first contest between Adams and Jefferson.[75] As was already indicated, the appearance of political parties was to have a major impact on the system that had worked so well for the first two presidential elections. In essence, the intent and integrity of the original system had been corrupted by the machinations of political parties. And even if those responsible for constructing the Constitution had prepared for many contingencies, the document was lacking any reference to political parties. To this end, the Framers were remiss in not better preparing for the appearance of political parties—or at least something resembling such groups. Because, as one scholar has pointed out, by 1800 the political parties had successfully "upset the applecart on the two-votes-for-President system."[76] It was reasonable to assume political parties would not stop there.

For a number of years then, the caliber of individuals to assume the vice presidency fluctuated greatly. This is partly attributable to the absence of any genuinely attractive powers and responsibilities coming with the office. Still, and irrespective of the want in functions for the vice president, if many of the individuals to land in the vice presidency were unremarkable, some of the earlier occupants of the office—such as Elbridge Gerry and John Calhoun—were gifted political leaders in their own right. While acknowledging that some of the earliest vice presidents possessed commendable intellect and political aptitude does further the narrative of the institution, there was another unanticipated consequence from the implementation of the Twelfth Amendment that deserves attention. For after the Twelfth Amendment, there was an undeniable and striking change in the age of some of the individuals elected to the office.[77]

For instance, whereas Aaron Burr was inaugurated as Thomas Jefferson's first vice president when he was just forty-five, Jefferson took George Clinton, at the age of sixty-five, for his second vice president. Clinton went on to serve nearly all of a second term in the vice presidency in the service of President James Madison, though he eventually died while in office when he was seventy-three. Similarly, Clinton's immediate successor, Elbridge Gerry, came to the vice presidency at the advanced age of sixty-nine. Like Clinton, Gerry too died in office, less than two years into his term.

Even if electing elderly vice presidents failed to be a long-term trend, it was indicative of the value placed at that time on those who were candidates for vice president. Further contributing to the perception that the vice president was dispensable was that, up to April of 1841, no president had died while in office. For this reason, it was not until the death of the ninth president, William Henry Harrison, and the elevation of John Tyler from the vice presidency to the presidency, that there was any concern for who served as vice president—and even that concern soon receded.

Then again, as late as the 1904 presidential election, the Democratic Party selected a transparently bigoted octogenarian, Henry Davis, for the vice-presidential nomination. What was curious about the choice of Davis was that leading the opposition Republican

Party ticket was the incumbent president, Theodore Roosevelt, a man who, upon the assassination of President William McKinley, had ascended from the vice presidency to the presidency just four years earlier. As such, Roosevelt was the embodiment of what every vice president might become in an instant.

Adding to the rather puzzling choice of the ripened Henry Davis was the point at which presidential history in the United States had reached. By 1904, undoubtedly all of the electorate was aware of the assassination of McKinley. Furthermore, of those same voters, presumably most were alive at the time of the assassination of James Garfield, and even many of those same voters would have been living when Abraham Lincoln was killed. As it turned out, Lincoln and Garfield were succeeded by two of the more inadequate vice presidents in American history: Andrew Johnson and Chester Arthur, respectively. Consequently, with so much death and succession filling the collective memory of the electorate—as three presidents were assassinated over the course of thirty-nine years—it would seem that the public and the partisans alike should have noted the ease with which the second executive of the nation may become the first.

THE AMERICAN VICE PRESIDENCY

THE PRE-MODERN ERA

I have become Vice President willy-nilly, and anticipate the necessity of enduring heavy and painful and protracted sacrifices, as the consequence.

– Vice President George Mifflin Dallas

The historical record of the American vice presidency is considerably more vibrant than the popular perception of the institution that persists. By no means is this meant to suggest that the depiction of an institution wanting for power and prestige and ripe for derision is wholly unwarranted. But as evidenced in this chapter, there have been notable vice presidents among the many banal individuals who have inhabited the office, and moving forward it becomes apparent that a more significant role has been played by certain vice presidents than is widely known, if and when their presidents permitted. As a consequence, there are specific vice presidents who have contributed over time, and most often subtly, to the complexity of the most misunderstood institution of the United States government.

THE COMMENCEMENT OF THE AMERICAN VICE PRESIDENCY (1789–1801)

Elected the first vice president of the United States, John Adams could not help but set the mold for those who were to follow him in the office, for he was taking on a newly conceived position, in an untried government. And even if the position of lieutenant-governor, at that time found in nearly every state, did share certain features with the vice president, establishing the office of vice president in the national government was an innovative feat.

Whereas Adams faced uncertainty about how to proceed, the Constitution was precise in defining what was expected of the vice president: preside over the Senate, cast a vote in the Senate in cases of a tie, and assume the responsibilities of the president under specific circumstances. That was it. Therefore, being the first presented a quandary for Adams, particularly in how he was to bring meaning to a position that was so inherently insubstantial, yet might become much more. In an often-quoted speech before the Senate, Adams captured the essence of the new office best when he proclaimed: "I am Vice-President. In this I am nothing, but I may be everything."[1]

From the outset, Adams was preoccupied with formal, procedural titles for the president and vice president.[2] More specifically, the first vice president wanted to know how to address the first president when the latter appeared before Congress. At one point in the debate over titles, Adams lamented: "I am Vice-President ... But I am president also of the Senate. When the President comes into the Senate, what shall I be? I can not be [president] then. No, gentleman, I can not, I can not. I wish gentleman to think what I shall be."[3] Critics maintained that the vice president's concern with titles stemmed from his predilection for all things aristocratic, but Adams insisted that titles, which might strike some as haughty, would facilitate the perception of preeminence that he felt the national government needed in its relations with the states, as well as for its broader standing in the world.[4] The deliberations on titles lasted not quite three weeks, with at one point "His Highness the President of the United States of America and Protector of the Rights of the Same" a contender.[5] Eventually, the consensus of separate reports from Senate and House committees was to settle on an easy, unadorned designation for George Washington: President of the United States.

Adams did, however, have concerns beyond titles; he was also curious as to his salary. The reason for the first vice president's keen interest in this area was because he knew that he was responsible for financing his own housing when Congress was in session. Since his presence in the Senate was expected, and because he had never been a wealthy man, Adams was therefore worried about how he was going to pay for a home in the capital as well as one in Massachusetts. Indeed, housing for the vice president was a concern not just for Adams, but likewise for thirty-nine of the vice presidents who came to office after him. It was not until July of 1974—the last full month of Gerald Ford's abbreviated tenure as vice president—that the federal government finally acquired a permanent residence for the vice president.[6] But due to Ford's timely elevation to the presidency, it was the forty-first vice president, Nelson Rockefeller, who had sufficient time to move into the vice president's home on Observatory Hill. Ironically, Rockefeller possessed ample financial resources, and so he could afford to decline public housing. He subsequently opted not to stay in the vice president's residence and instead used the house solely for social events.

As to the vice president's salary, the first Congress was divided on how much to pay the second officer of the national government. There were those who argued that the vice president may well be absent from the Senate, scarcely be missed, and yet continue to draw a salary; for those critics the answer was simple: the vice president "should be paid only on a per diem basis."[7] The counter argument to paying the vice president by the day was that within an instant the vice president might assume the responsibilities of the chief executive; it was therefore imprudent for the vice president to have to work at a side vocation out of financial necessity.[8] There were others who contended that the proposed annual salary of $6,000 was far too much; conversely, $8,000 was also suggested as the more appropriate compensation.[9] In the end, and after extensive discussion and compromise, Congress approved a $5,000 annual salary for the vice president, with no allowance for housing, while the president was appropriated an annual salary of $25,000, and in time, a permanent residence.[10] Without question, the difference in pay grade was reflective of the relative value Congress placed on the first and second executives of the nation.

Throughout his vice presidency, John Adams took the role of presiding officer of the Senate seriously. Adams sought to maintain order and decorum in the upper chamber of Congress, while seeking any means for wringing substance from his position. To this end, he recognized that he could command the attention of the Senate from the presiding chair. Besides, the vice president's tie-breaking vote gave him a tool for interjecting the viewpoint of President Washington, as well as his own, into the legislative process. No doubt Adams appreciated having a public forum to convey his political thoughts, regardless of the constitutional limits imposed on the position he held. All told, Adams cast twenty-nine tie-breaking votes in his eight years as vice president—a record for any vice president, which holds to this day.[11]

If some of his votes were of more significance than others, it did not matter; what mattered were those occasions when the vice president's deciding vote accentuated the long-term goal Adams held for a strong national executive.[12] More times than not, the stalemate compelling his vote arose from a fairly contentious issue; in these instances, Adams, by virtue of the Constitution, was required to abandon the supposed impartiality of the presiding officer's position and publicly take a stand.[13] This forced Adams to become engaged in the debate, likewise committing him on issues vital to the fledging nation; an ancillary outcome was that he was then publicly at odds with the views of certain segments of his fellow citizens.

Adams did use his tie-breaking vote on one occasion that, though it did not enhance the vice presidency per se, did facilitate the expansion of presidential prerogative and thus establish an executive precedent. Cast in the summer of 1789, the vote affirmed the authority of the president to remove any member of the executive branch who had been appointed by the president and confirmed by the Senate. The vote was significant because it dampened the check the Senate had over presidential appointments. As it was, the president was still required to submit certain appointments to the Senate for approval, yet because of Adams, the president was not obligated to gain approval for the removal of those he appointed.[14]

If John Adams was never celebrated for his modesty, he always seemed cognizant that his place, as vice president to George Washington, forever relegated him to the shadow of an undisputedly historic figure.[15] But irrespective of where either man eventually landed in recorded history, the relationship between Washington and Adams was at all times one of mutual respect.[16] Washington knew Adams was a smart and seasoned diplomat, and he was satisfied seeking, and regularly taking, his vice president's advice on foreign affairs; conversely, he was less prone to ask Adams for counsel on the domestic front.[17] And from the beginning Washington encouraged Adams to attend cabinet meetings in his absence, although on those occasions when Adams did take part, he professed a reluctance to be involved and on the whole felt unwelcome amongst the group.[18]

Adams no doubt viewed presiding in the Senate as the more appropriate venue for his presence and participation; besides, the vice president was never designated a member of the cabinet. For that matter, nowhere in the Constitution is mention made of a cabinet, as such, though the Framers did give the president the power to "require the Opinion, in writing, of the principal Officer in each of the executive Departments, upon any Subject relating to the Duties of their respective Offices."[19] It was the practice of the executive department chiefs meeting with the president that led to the concept of a presidential cabinet. But distancing the vice president further from the principal officers of the executive departments, or cabinet, was that all such officers are appointed by the president, and then confirmed by the Senate; hence, the entire membership of the cabinet, unlike the vice president, is made up of unelected officers of the government.[20]

Perhaps the assumed separation of the vice presidency from the executive branch worked for Adams because constitutional boundaries ostensibly kept the personal relationship between the president and vice president free from rivalries that might otherwise arise.[21] Nevertheless, it must have been difficult for a man like Adams to accept that he was an elected national executive, with no tangible executive powers, and relegated to presiding over one chamber of the Congress. And yet, he seemed resigned to the place of the vice presidency, asserting in a letter to a friend that "the office I hold is totally detached from the executive authority and confined to the legislative."[22]

If Adams humbly, though unhappily, accepted the limits of the vice presidency, he was profoundly aware that his station in the government marked him as the perpetual president-in-waiting. But Adams, being deferential in his relations with President Washington, was sensitive to any accusations that he overtly coveted the presidency. At one point he addressed such charges directly; in doing so, he expressed what being vice president meant in relation to the president stating: "I am forced to look up to it, and bound by duty to do so, because there is only one breath of one mortal between me and it."[23]

At the conclusion of his eight years of service, John Adams had every reason to take pride in being the first vice president of the United States. Adams had done the best that could be expected in occupying a position in the government devoid of significant responsibilities, widely seen as insubstantial, and wholly unwanted in many quarters. Of course, none of the preceding had escaped his notice, and he had even contemplated resigning for these reasons.[24] But Adams erred in trivializing the vice presidency. Being the first individual elected to an untried office in an incomparable system of government, Adams had contributed immensely to the great American democratic experiment.

Like John Adams before him, the nation's second vice president, Thomas Jefferson, brought stature to the vice presidency, leaving a distinct imprint on the office. This is not meant to infer that Jefferson relished the opportunity to serve in the office, but rather that he had previously established himself in government and politics, and therefore his résumé was not wanting for embellishment. And when Jefferson raised his impending situation in the government, in a message sent to James Madison, his ambivalence towards taking on the vice presidency was evident, confessing that "it is the only office in the world about which I am unable to decide in my own mind whether I had rather have it or not have it."[25]

History has shown Jefferson to be an exceptional individual, and his vice-presidential tenure was likewise incomparable. However, when it came to the vice presidency, Jefferson stood apart because he did not share the same political party with the president he served. For this reason, his presence in the Senate chamber was equivalent to the loyal opposition typically found in parliamentary systems. But in his comportment, Jefferson never conveyed even a modicum of the passion and frenzy that on occasion arises when a parliamentary body assembles.[26] No doubt this was by design. Jefferson chose to keep his musings on the opposition to himself, all the while never reconciling his political differences with the president and remaining aloof from Adams and the administration of which he too was a member.[27]

Regardless of the disparities in their political opinions, Jefferson did not subscribe to the notion that Adams was undeserving of the presidency, nor was he of a mind that the position should necessarily have been his. For a time, Jefferson was disposed to the idea that Adams's hold on the presidency was the natural order for the careers of both men. To this, Jefferson acknowledged: "I can particularly have no feelings which would revolt at a secondary position to Mr. Adams. I am his junior in life, was his junior in Congress, his junior in the diplomatic line, his junior lately in the civil government."[28]

For the most part, Jefferson was reticent when in the Senate chamber; he seemed to find irregular attendance more to his liking.[29] But for Jefferson, this did not mean that he was determined to intrude into the executive sphere of the government, instead. To some degree this was impractical by virtue of the uniqueness of the vice president and the president identifying with opposing political parties; it was an arrangement guaranteeing that Jefferson was forever an unwelcome intruder in the Adams administration. But even if they had been of the same political party, Jefferson was adamant about where the vice president belonged, at one point declaring: "I consider my office as constitutionally confined to legislative functions, and that I could not take any part whatever in executive consultations, even if it were proposed."[30]

Throughout his public life, Thomas Jefferson routinely left his mark with the written word, and the vice presidency proved no exception. This did not come about because he wrote expressly of the vice presidency; instead, it was the result of his authorship of the *Manual of Parliamentary Practice*. With the *Manual*, Jefferson elegantly delineated a set of rules to guide the proceedings of the Senate—in effect, institutionalizing numerous legislative procedures.[31]

That Jefferson took the time to write the *Manual* underscores two remarkable facets of the vice presidency, as the eighteenth century was coming to a close. First, having only to attend to the limited constitutional duties assigned to the vice president, Jefferson apparently had ample time to compose what became an indispensable manuscript. And second, Jefferson's presumption that it fell within his purview to systemize the procedures of the Senate affirms of which branch of government the second vice president considered he was most a part.

Although Jefferson's *Manual* was considered necessary at the time of its publication, the vice president delimiting the practices of the Senate and its members was not precedent setting. Overall, and apart from the *Manual*, Jefferson served out his term as scarcely more than an observer of events. Most of his time was spent idly, waiting for the next election, and watching as the Adams administration incrementally imploded.

The Vice Presidency Served: By Ambition and the Aged (1801–1812)

In 1797, Thomas Jefferson sent a note to future vice president Elbridge Gerry, telling him "the second office of the government is honorable and easy, the first is but a splendid misery."[32] At the time, Jefferson was the newly inaugurated vice president and had yet to experience much of the honor or the ease of the vice presidency, and not a moment of the splendid misery of the presidency. No doubt when Jefferson eventually made it to the White House, Vice President Aaron Burr brought ample misery to Jefferson's first term as president.

As previously recounted, the circumstances of the election of 1800 and Aaron Burr's actions therein, actual and alleged, were sufficient cause for Thomas Jefferson to distance himself from Burr the moment the election was finally settled. Jefferson's transparent mistrust of Burr precluded any consultation with the latter on the new president's cabinet selections—a practice that took place with future, more closely allied presidents and vice presidents.[33] And so, denied a role as counsel to the president, and ostracized from the administration generally, Burr had to content himself with the minimal rigors of his job in the Senate. Yet even there, as the presiding officer, Burr achieved lasting renown, as he did, for better or for worse, in all facets of his personal and political life.

Presiding in the Senate, Burr personified the poise and dignity of the upper chamber; likewise, he was an acknowledged master of parliamentary procedure. By one account: "Burr was one of the most skilled parliamentarians to serve as president of the Senate, a striking contrast to Adams and a worthy successor to Jefferson."[34] These were talents Burr no doubt used to benefit himself more than his president. With a suspicious and overtly derisive Thomas Jefferson restricting his future as a Democratic-Republican, Vice President Burr sided increasingly with Federalist senators, in opposition to his party and to his president.

Always the clever politician, Burr was never so brazen as to openly reveal his sentiments or his plans. Instead, Burr would cast his tie-breaking vote with his own party only when necessary—covertly indicating to opposition senators his tacit sympathies with their views—and then, by means of his vote, and the manipulation of Senate practices, Burr would extend support to those senators opposed to Jefferson and the administration.

A case in point arose when President Jefferson sought repeal of the Judiciary Act of 1801, legislation President John Adams had pushed through in the closing hours of his administration with the intent of securing a Federalist presence on the federal bench. On that occasion, Vice President Burr voted first with the administration, then cast a tie-breaking vote in favor of the Federalist scheme for a select committee to attach amendments to the bill, and finally, he stacked the select committee with members sympathetic to the interests of Federalists and moderate Democratic-Republicans.[35]

Despite Burr's undisputed intelligence and political acuity, he is best remembered for a single deed; it was a deed that secured his infamy for the ages. This came about as Burr struggled to resuscitate his political career, aware that because of his behavior in 1800, he had no chance for a second term as vice president. To this end, Burr set his sights on the governorship of New York, mounting a spirited campaign and plying all of the political tactics that had served him so well in the past. But it was to no avail, since there were no longer any political factions in New York closely aligned with the vice president, and he suffered a convincing defeat. Among those opposed to Burr, yet again, was Alexander Hamilton. Hamilton, unlike Burr, was highly regarded in New York, and he used his political capital in the state to the disadvantage of Burr. When Burr learned of scornful remarks Hamilton had directed at him, Burr challenged the latter to a duel.

Aaron Burr shot and killed Alexander Hamilton in their duel. For Hamilton, Burr's challenge obviously brought a premature death; it also brought martyrdom—an outcome that a man with Hamilton's ego surely would have appreciated, if only he could have. Yet for Burr the match brought a decidedly different outcome; he lived, but victory in the duel earned him notoriety and wide-ranging contempt. Even more devastating for Burr, murdering Hamilton put a swift end to his own ambitious political life.

The fateful Burr-Hamilton duel is an exhaustively documented historical event. What is less well-known, however, is that not long after the duel Burr returned to an uneasy Senate, where he retook the presiding officer's chair, notwithstanding indictments in both New Jersey and New York for the murder of Hamilton.[36] Eventually Burr was acquitted of the charges against him in New Jersey, and the charges were reduced in New York. As luck would have it, over two hundred years passed before a sitting vice president, this time Dick Cheney, achieved notoriety for shooting another human— clearly it was not wise to antagonize Aaron Burr or to go hunting with Dick Cheney.[37]

With the end of Aaron Burr's first term nearing, and his political future permanently clouded, Thomas Jefferson was in need of a replacement vice president. For this, Jefferson turned to George Clinton. But before Burr's term ended, he was granted a parting address before the Senate. Poignantly, Burr opted to tell his audience they would do well to remember that the Senate chamber "is a sanctuary; a citadel of law, of order, and of liberty;" and therefore, "resistance [should] be made to the storms of political phrensy [sic] and the silent acts of corruption; and if the Constitution be destined ever to perish by the sacrilegious hands of the demagogue or the usurper, which God avert, its expiring agonies will be witnessed on this floor."[38] With that Burr was done—in politics, in the Senate, and with the vice presidency.

Thomas Jefferson's second vice president was picked for three reasons. First, George Clinton was in his mid-sixties and plainly in the twilight of his political career; therefore, he offered Jefferson a welcome reprieve from the manifestly ambitious, and much younger, Aaron Burr. Second, Clinton was a New Yorker, and for that reason, his addition afforded the regional equilibrium expected of a ticket headed by the incumbent president from Virginia. And third, mindful of Clinton's advanced age, Jefferson was convinced that his personal choice for the next presidential contest, James Madison, would prevail over any challenge from Clinton.[39]

Being a political boss in New York for many years, as well having been elected governor of the state on six occasions, Clinton was unaccustomed to powerlessness in politics and government. Consequently, experience and personal nature made the vice presidency a frustrating position for him to hold; it also extinguished any hope of his ever developing a working relationship with Jefferson, or later with Madison, when Madison was president. Nor did Clinton ever display any mastery of the tasks of a presiding officer, in essence shirking the most transparent responsibility of the vice president. This dereliction of duty was aptly captured when one historian described how Vice President Clinton "would frequently forget points of order and even miscounted votes. Under such conditions it is not surprising that the Senate had scant respect for the man and that the office began to be thought of in terms of the incumbent's characteristics."[40]

In terms of the history of the American vice presidency, George Clinton did leave a mark by his association with the office. In one instance this came about because of his efforts to manipulate the mechanics for nominating presidential and vice-presidential candidates. The second distinction of his vice presidency was reflected in the outcome of the election of 1808. And the third event to mark Clinton's tenure was one entirely beyond his control.

As just noted, Clinton was Thomas Jefferson's second vice president, elected to serve during Jefferson's second term as president. In keeping with the example set by George Washington, Jefferson decided not to seek a third term, in 1808, and instead openly backed the nomination of James Madison, the man he had long preferred for his successor. But even when facing the daunting power and influence of Thomas Jefferson, Clinton would not be dissuaded from his pursuit of the presidency. This involved a twofold strategy, with Clinton seeking the Democratic-Republican nomination for president at the same time that he pursued the nomination for vice president.[41]

Clinton achieved this by a series of deft maneuvers and well-timed publications, whereby he indicated to supporters his availability for the presidential nomination, while encouraging others to return him to the vice presidency if Madison should prevail.[42] Even as Clinton was putting this matchless strategy in motion, the man who had been Jefferson's minister to Britain, James Monroe, also was seeking the presidential nomination. Yet when some of Monroe's supporters began to doubt he could acquire the nomination, they plotted to advance Monroe as Clinton's vice-presidential running mate, instead. It was a morbid ploy based on the premise that Clinton's age and health precluded an extended occupancy of the White House.[43]

Eventually, when the party overwhelmingly went for Jefferson's favorite, James Madison, Clinton was rewarded once more with the vice-presidential nomination, and subsequently reelected to the office. The outcome of the 1808 election did secure Clinton's place in history, distinguishing him as the first of only two vice presidents—the other being John Calhoun—to serve with two presidents. For Clinton's supporters, it might have seemed as if this double-bill signified that an indispensable political figure had again found employment in the vice presidency. In reality, Clinton's reelection in 1808 merely accentuated the impression of a dispensable government position, filled by any individual willing to consent to taking the job.

The final significant event of George Clinton's vice presidency was one of mortality. Clinton's death while serving in office denoted the departure of a long-time fixture on the political scene; it also created the first vacancy in the American vice presidency. Presumably such an occurrence should have been anticipated when the Constitution was constructed, and yet the document was missing any prescribed means for replacing the vice president. In other words, for 180 years the Constitution was—from the time of its establishment at the Federal Convention of 1787 to the ratification of the Twenty-fifth Amendment in 1967—absent a constitutional mechanism for replacing the vice president should the vice president die, be incapacitated, resign from office, or succeed to the presidency. For this reason, on those occasions when any of the preceding occurred, the vice presidency remained vacant for a combined total of nearly thirty-eight years. It was a phenomenon emblematic of an institution plainly unwanted and undervalued from the beginning.

THE SUCCESSION ACTS

The death of Vice President George Clinton introduced a fundamental predicament for the scheme of the American government, and it was one the Framers never spent a great deal of time preparing for. The impasse arose from succession and determining how it should be implemented. More to the point: who should succeed to the presidency if both the president and the vice president resigned, were removed from office, or died? Hence, with Clinton's death being the first for an incumbent vice president or president, succession was naturally of concern. Yet in this regard, Clinton's contemporaries were at a loss, for the Framers had failed to indicate a preference for succession, leaving such matters for the Congress to decide.[44]

Congress did try to rectify the lack of direction on presidential succession—although not on vice-presidential succession—crafting and eventually approving the Presidential Succession Act of 1792. In the prelude to passage of the act, much of the debate centered on whether the secretary of state should be next in line to the presidency or if the president pro tempore of the Senate and the Speaker of the House should be the designated successors. Aversion to making the secretary of state the successor to the president came primarily from outside of the Congress, and in the form of Alexander Hamilton. Hamilton was consumed by inflated fears that his long-time adversary, Thomas Jefferson, who was then serving as the nation's first secretary of state, might stealthily enter the presidency by way of succession.[45] Although some members of Congress were reluctant to designate one of their own as the successor to the president, simply because it could disrupt the separation of powers built into the Constitution, it was not enough of a concern to dissuade either house of Congress from passing the act.[46]

Congress waited a mere ninety-four years before it again crafted and passed legislation to deal with presidential succession. In the interim, five vice presidents had died while in office, one had resigned, and four had ascended to the presidency upon the death of the president. But the move by Congress in 1885 to address presidential succession was not founded on disquietude with the inadequacies of the original succession provision of the Constitution. It was driven instead by partisan politics and a perfectly reasonable unease that control of the executive branch could shift to the opposition party on those occasions when the president and vice president were not of the majority political party in Congress.

The solution Congress devised was straightforward and effective: moving the line of succession away from itself and over to the cabinet. Not only did this ensure that potential presidential successors were of the same political persuasion as the president, it also retained the spirit of the Constitution in calling for an officer of the United States to act as president. This principle had been violated with passage of the Presidential Succession Act of 1792 and the introduction of members of Congress into the line of succession. Subsequently, President Grover Cleveland signed the Presidential Succession Act of 1886, making officers of the cabinet presidential successors upon the death, resignation, or inability of both the elected president and vice president.[47] Naturally, the Succession Act of 1886 failed to even consider, let alone devise, a method for filling vacancies in the vice presidency; it would take another eighty-one years and a constitutional amendment before that deficiency in the Constitution was rectified.

Congress next revisited presidential succession in 1945, following the death of President Franklin Roosevelt. Roosevelt's death made his third vice president, Harry Truman, president, less than three months from the day of their inauguration. Given that Truman did not have a vice president for almost four years, it made sense when he called for revisions to the law on presidential succession.[48] Truman's principal objection to the Presidential Succession Act of 1886 rested with the unelected status of cabinet members. Because the cabinet was composed of individuals nominated by the president and approved by the Senate, Truman noted it was at his discretion to nominate a potential successor, and this, he argued, was undemocratic.[49]

Ultimately, Truman's preferred line of succession prevailed and he signed the Presidential Succession Act of 1947.[50] The 1947 act established a line of succession that began, after the vice president of course, with the Speaker of the House, followed by the president pro tempore of the Senate, and finally the cabinet. The order of succession from within the cabinet started with the secretary of state, followed by each cabinet secretary, with their place determined by when the executive departments had been established.

There was poignancy to President Truman signing the Presidential Succession Act of 1947. Being a former vice president who had ascended to the presidency upon the death of the president, Truman intimately understood the significance of the succession provision of the Constitution. Moreover, by 1947 Truman was serving his third year as president—the entire time without a vice president. But just as it was with each of the previous attempts to organize presidential succession, the Presidential Succession Act of 1947 failed to address how vacancies in the vice presidency should be filled. Evidently the president and the Congress did not consider the vice president an indispensable officer of the government.

Mediocrity Reigns (1813–1825)

With the death of Vice President George Clinton in 1812, the vice presidency began a pronounced drift into mediocrity. Undoubtedly what precipitated the decline of the institution was the ratification of the Twelfth Amendment. In providing for the separate election of the president and the vice president, the Twelfth Amendment guaranteed that an office with no power or perks remained so. Besides, from the inception of the Constitution there was never an incentive for individuals to expressly pursue the vice presidency, and the Twelfth Amendment obviously reinforced the widespread aversion to seeking the second office.

Certainly Elbridge Gerry should be included among those disinclined to pursue the vice presidency. As James Madison recorded in 1787, there was no doubt where Gerry stood on the matter: "He was against having any vice President."[51] In the course of the Federal Convention proceedings, Gerry voiced objections to various provisions of the Constitution, but it was unease with the vice presidency that ensured the absence of his signature on the completed document.[52]

Considering his view of the office, Gerry's eventual election to the vice presidency was all the more remarkable because he had made it there on account of his comparative youth. Even though Gerry was sixty-seven when he was nominated in 1812 to be James Madison's running mate, his selection came about only after the first nominee, John Langdon, cited his own advanced age of seventy as reason to refuse a spot on the ticket.[53]

In his time as vice president, Elbridge Gerry presided over the Senate without incident, appears never to have cultivated a meaningful association with President Madison, and left the institution unchanged and unimproved. Gerry served less than two years as vice president, his death in 1814 serving as the final rejection of the office he had so vigorously opposed from the beginning. But if Gerry's tenure as vice president was brief and of no significance, his earlier, creative redistricting work from when he was the governor of Massachusetts inadvertently set his place forever in political lore. As such, Gerry's name entered the lexicon of politics and elections with the art of redrawing electoral districts that defy logic in their contours, but always make sense for the political party in power. The practice initiated by then-Governor Gerry, known as gerrymandering, has since eclipsed any recollections of Vice President Gerry.[54]

Elbridge Gerry's death left the vice presidency vacant—this time for close to three years—but there were no repercussions, and the nation and the government moved on, seemingly unaware. And yet, when the 1816 caucus of Democratic-Republicans met, they would have been remiss if they had ignored a fleeting, but disturbing pattern: two consecutive selections for vice president had died of old age while holding the post. Nominating elderly politicians for vice president, too old to later run for their own term as president—as had occurred with the nominations of George Clinton and Elbridge Gerry—was a deliberate move meant to ensure a lock on the presidency for Virginia's Democratic-Republican elite.[55] However, the deaths of Vice Presidents Clinton and Gerry, one after the other, were an unfortunate outcome of this strategy. As a result, and in stark contrast with prior well-aged vice presidents, forty-two-year-old Daniel Tompkins was nominated as the intended successor to Gerry.

Daniel Tompkins was the immensely popular governor of New York and the favorite of many Democratic-Republican partisans for the presidency. There are conflicting views on how the governor ended up James Monroe's running mate; what is certain is that every scenario involved internal divisions in New York politics, and the influence of future vice president and president Martin Van Buren.[56] Whatever the case, Tompkins simultaneously won election to the vice presidency and to another term as governor. New York state law in the 1800s permitted Tompkins to serve in both positions, but he opted exclusively for the national executive, resigning his post as governor one month prior to taking the oath of office as the sixth vice president of the United States.

If George Clinton and Elbridge Gerry contributed age and wisdom to the American vice presidency, Daniel Tompkins offered neither. While Tompkins might have been a tolerable presiding officer, he was in the Capitol building so rarely that his record in the chair remains incomplete. One legitimate explanation for his frequent absences was his preoccupation with allegations of financial impropriety leveled against him from when he was governor during the War of 1812.[57] As a result, Tompkins spent the better part of his vice presidency struggling to repair his reputation, the stress of which contributed to an increasing reliance on alcohol and the disrepute that came with such a habit.[58] In due course, Tompkins was cleared of any wrongdoing and his heirs were later compensated in a partial settlement of his affairs; still, his mental and physical health declined precipitously, as did the vice presidency.[59]

By the time President Monroe and Tompkins were elected to a second term in 1820, the vice president was so unessential to the administration that when he skipped the inaugural ceremonies it was hardly noticed.[60] If Tompkins took some satisfaction in being reelected, it was of no consequence, for his vice-presidential legacy was damaged even further as his second term unfolded. In this vein, a rare biographer of Tompkins has suggested that the vice president

> notoriously ignored his duty to preside over the Senate. [And] his second term proved to be even worse. As his health declined and his financial obligations continued to be a nagging worry, Tompkins spent less and less

time in Washington, more and more time in New York. Besides, his purely vice-presidential activities did not really interest him, while participation in the public life of his state did.[61]

Colleagues of Tompkins were familiar with his disengagement, and his wearied condition was obvious to all. John Quincy Adams, for one, made note of Tompkins, and his state of mind, after conferring with him on one of his intermittent visits to the capital. Adams documented that Tompkins "told me that he had recovered his health, with the exception of sleepless nights, and that he was relieved from all his embarrassments; that he had no intention of being a candidate either for election to the Presidency or for re-election as Vice-President. All he wanted was justice."[62]

Possibly Tompkins would have added more to the growth of the vice presidency were he not so consumed by financial troubles. But he never had the opportunity to display the promise he once enjoyed when New York's governor. Illustrative of this decline, one contemporary of Tompkins described the vice president, following a rare stint presiding in the Senate chamber, in this way: "The Vice President left this [city] yesterday. I dont [sic] think he was perfectly sober during his stay here. He was several times so drunk in the chair that he could with difficulty put the question. I understand he will never return here."[63]

Prior to winning the vice presidency, Daniel Tompkins had earned the trust and esteem of the Virginia presidential dynasty; served as the governor of New York for ten years; sought and gained a progressive law for reducing and eventually eliminating any vestiges of slavery in New York; and worked as a lawyer, legislator, and justice on the New York Supreme Court.[64] However, for such a rising political figure, attaining the office that was the logical precursor to the presidency unfortunately signified a considerably different outcome. For the vice presidency, figuratively and literally, was the beginning of the end for Daniel Tompkins. And nothing confirmed this more than his premature death coming just three months from his leaving the office he never coveted, rarely attended to, and was miserable occupying for the sum of his tenure.

THE VICE PRESIDENCY SERVED: BY AGITATOR, ANOMALY, AND ABSTENTION (1825–1841)

Daniel Tompkins and John Calhoun were dissimilar on most accounts; what they did have in common was unsatisfying tenures as vice president. Calhoun even tried the vice presidency under two different arrangements and still found the post wanting of satisfaction. But, similar to George Clinton, Calhoun does have the distinction of serving as the vice president for two presidents; at present, it is a mark only they have met.

Calhoun's first term came by way of the election of 1824 and his selection as the second to John Quincy Adams, son of the nation's first vice president. The pre-election machinations of 1824 were unusual in that all the major contenders were drawn from the ranks of the sole national party still standing—the Democratic-Republicans—yet there was no formal, partisan congressional caucus to nominate a party standard-bearer.[65] Instead, a number of state nominating conventions were used to indicate preferences, thus whittling away at the field of potential candidates who might stand for the presidency, including Calhoun.[66] With the contest being an entirely intra-party affair, Calhoun unexpectedly found himself holding the advantage for the vice-presidential nomination, as supporters of the two strongest candidates—Secretary of State John Quincy Adams, and Senator Andrew Jackson—all came to regard Calhoun as the running mate of their candidate.[67]

Eventually the informal Adams-Calhoun ticket won the election. However, Adams's clinch on the presidency was complete only after Jackson bested him in the popular vote but failed to gain a majority of the Electoral College vote. Because no single winner emerged from the Electoral College, per the design of the Constitution, a vote of the House of Representatives was required to settle the election. Almost certainly it was another defeated presidential candidate from that year, Henry Clay, who engineered the victory Adams achieved in the House. For his efforts, Clay was then rewarded with a cabinet seat in the Adams administration.

It was the collusion of John Quincy Adams and Henry Clay that incensed John Calhoun from the start. Because Adams nominated Clay for secretary of state, and because serving in the post was then antecedent to gaining the presidency, Calhoun surely recognized his best chance at the presidency was slipping further from the realm of possibility.[68] Calhoun therefore opted to align himself with Andrew Jackson on the assumption that his own presidential designs were more likely to be realized with the new political party starting to coalesce around Jackson.[69] As it stood, Calhoun spent his term with Adams openly suspicious of the president and biding his time, with the principal highlights of his first term being an intrusion into the selection of Senate committee members and his support of measures limiting the power and tenure of the president he was elected to serve with.[70]

Calhoun's subsequent reelection to the vice presidency in 1828, this time with Andrew Jackson, returned him to an office that gave him no satisfaction. Yet when he presided in the Senate, Calhoun had a platform from which he was able to advance his personal ambitions. More precisely, Calhoun took full advantage of the vice president's tie-breaking vote, using this constitutional prerogative to exasperate President Jackson. In the words of one observer, being posted in the Senate, wielding his vote whenever he could for his own ends, Calhoun had the means "which he sought ... to assert his spite against Jackson."[71] In all, Calhoun was able to take advantage of his tie-breaking vote twenty-eight times, second only to Vice President John Adams.[72]

Without doubt, the most damaging vote John Calhoun cast when he was vice president was to have a greater impact on his own career than it did on President Jackson, or even on the actual object of Calhoun's malice, Martin Van Buren. Jackson had appointed Van Buren minister to England during a congressional recess. Not waiting to gain the necessary confirmation of the Senate, Van Buren set sail for England. Once there, he was promptly engaged in diplomatic matters; meanwhile, back in the United States, Calhoun and his allies in the Senate had different plans for Van Buren. Calhoun deftly orchestrated a tie vote on Van Buren's confirmation, with the vice president opting to vote in opposition to the direct wishes of the president.[73]

As a result of Calhoun's vote, Van Buren was compelled to return to the United States without ever having earned his ministerial appointment. Of even more importance though, the episode guaranteed that Jackson and Calhoun's association was finished. From that point forward, Jackson was determined to rid himself of Calhoun at the next election, preferring to replace his recalcitrant vice president with an individual he could trust, and who was certain to be loyal to him; fittingly, the individual Jackson had in mind was Martin Van Buren.

From Van Buren's perspective, the vote of the Senate, coupled with Calhoun's decisive negation of his ministerial appointment, gave him just cause to stand for the vice presidency at President Jackson's side. Of the situation, Van Buren avowed that

> they have sought to bring discredit upon the act of the President, and to disgrace me personally in the eyes, not merely of my Fellow citizens but of foreign nations. If the [Democratic-] Republicans of the U. States think my elevation to the Vice Presidency the most effectual mode of testifying to the world their sentiments with respect to the act of the President and the vote of the Senate, I can see no justifiable ground for declining to yield to their wishes.[74]

Regrettably for Andrew Jackson, the vice president is the single member of the executive branch the president is powerless to fire, so, unless John Calhoun committed an impeachable offense or died, Jackson was bound to a patently hostile vice president until another presidential election was held. As it turns out, Jackson did not have to wait for Calhoun to self-destruct—as was the case with Aaron Burr—or to die in office—as had George Clinton and Elbridge Gerry. Instead, Calhoun made history, becoming the first vice president to resign from office.

By his abandonment of the vice presidency, Calhoun had tacitly signaled the futility of retaining an office that denied him active, substantive participation in the affairs of either the executive or the legislative branches of the government. His want for a meaningful role in public affairs was further evinced by his willingness to stand for an open Senate seat while still the vice president, subsequently choosing to return to the Senate as a voting member of the chamber, and in lieu of fulfilling his second term as vice president. Besides, in acting the part of irritant to President Jackson, Calhoun was unmistakably marked as an outlier in the administration, with his isolation exacerbated by his proclivity for sectional politics. Accordingly, with his second stint as vice president coming to a close, Calhoun found himself in an untenable position that ultimately jeopardized his viability for the presidency.[75]

John Calhoun's service as agitator to the president diverges considerably from conventional notions of the American vice presidency. If the historical view of the vice presidency has emphasized its futility, a companion view has persisted that vice presidents are reliable and willing to loyally support their president and the administration to which they are attached. Yet once in office, Calhoun refused to act the part of faithful vice president to either of the presidents he had been elected with. Alas, it was Calhoun's defiant character that distinguished his tenure from that of his successor, Martin Van Buren.

Amidst the numerous unremarkable vice presidents of the 1800s, Martin Van Buren was an anomaly. This was not a matter of his possessing an outstanding mind or notable education, nor was he venerated by much of the electorate; instead, it was Van Buren's close association with President Jackson that proved the exception. This aspect of the Jackson-Van Buren union is striking when compared to the presidents and vice presidents who preceded them in office, as well as in contrast to many of those who followed.

By some measure, Van Buren owed his elevation to the vice presidency to John Calhoun's vindictive, deciding vote against his ministerial nomination. But Van Buren surely would not have made it so far had President Jackson not insisted on him for a running mate.[76] Prior presidents had made clear their preferred successors, but Jackson's strong advocacy for Van Buren was the first instance when a presidential candidate overcame partisan and sectional leaders in naming his preference for vice president. At any rate, 108 years would pass before a presidential nominee again exercised such control over the vice-presidential nomination—a practice that today is accepted as a matter of course.[77]

Van Buren was in equal measures protégé and confidant to President Jackson. Having worked to ensure Jackson's election in 1828, Van Buren then served as secretary of state for the first two years of the administration. Jackson confided in Van Buren frequently, consulting with his secretary of state on matters of politics and policy as the two men rode horses across the hills and woods that were then contiguous to the nation's capital.[78] Jackson chose one such ride to express his disenchantment with Vice President Calhoun, suggesting that if he ran for a second term, he planned to replace Calhoun with Van Buren; then, once elected, Jackson claimed he would retire within the first year of his second term, paving the way for Van Buren to ascend to the presidency.[79] While presidential succession had yet to be tested, Jackson apparently was certain the vice president was the designated successor to the president if the president should resign. Although Van Buren did make it to the vice presidency, Jackson never resigned; either way, it was widely acknowledged that Van Buren was Jackson's intended heir to the presidency.[80]

In satisfying the duties of his office, Van Buren was always deferential when presiding in the Senate. Unlike John Calhoun, Van Buren did not assume that his position gave him license to agitate. He was mindful of the unusual juxtaposition of the vice president having been chosen by the people but then, in his words, having been "made the presiding officer of the Senate without any agency on its part, [and] differing in that regard from the Speaker of the House."[81]

Van Buren's disquiet with the vice president's place in Congress was evident in his willingness to relinquish certain prerogatives of his office, if and when he felt not doing so would make the vice president too much a part of the legislative branch. For instance, at that time Senate committees were selected prior to Congress formally convening, but, adhering to the rules of the Senate, the president of the Senate was the one set to determine the makeup of the committees. Consequently, the committees were fixed intentionally in the absence of the vice president.

In Van Buren's first year in office, due to a host of procedural and political matters, the president pro tempore had not made the committee selections before the vice president's arrival in the capital. As a result, the entire chamber was expected to vote for each committee member, and for each chairman, one after the other; it was a process that was sure to be protracted. Because adversaries to the second Jackson administration outnumbered its supporters in the Senate, it was assumed that the vice president planned to stack the committees as favorably to the administration as possible. But when senators took up the matter, Van Buren purposely exited the chamber, compelling the appointment of a pro tempore presiding officer, and thus ensuring that an elected senator oversaw the committee selection process.[82]

Undoubtedly Martin Van Buren's most challenging time presiding in the Senate arose when the Senate demanded information from President Jackson regarding actions he planned to take against the Bank of the United States. Jackson declined to divulge the information to Congress on constitutional grounds, so the Senate, in response, decided to censure the president.[83] Because the vice president is not permitted to participate in the debates of the Senate, Van Buren was unable to actively defend Jackson, though he did compose a speech justifying the actions of the president, and then recruited a sympathetic senator to deliver the speech as his proxy on the Senate floor.[84] When the episode culminated in the censure of the president, Jackson wrote a forceful exposition arguing for expansive presidential prerogative; however, he later tempered his arguments on the advice of the vice president.[85]

The historical record of Van Buren's vice-presidential tenure is rightfully characterized by the unusually close association between himself and President Jackson. Their relationship was unquestionably marked by the considerable sway Van Buren exercised in his dealings with the president; it was a level of influence not found in any prior executive pairings, and one rarely matched in the nineteenth century.[86] And finally, by winning the presidential election of 1836, Van Buren inadvertently set another mark. It would be 152 years before another vice president moved directly from the vice presidency to the presidency, without succession coming into play.

Although Martin Van Buren should be credited for adding to the incremental development of the vice presidency, his running mate and successor, Richard Mentor Johnson, merely added to the historic disdain for the second office. Andrew Jackson had dictated the choice of Johnson for Van Buren's running mate in a move he hoped might keep southern, slave-holding Democrats in step.[87] In the main, Jackson's choice was not well received, and the ensuing election did not go exactly as the retiring president had hoped.

When the election was over, and despite having more electoral votes than the opposition candidates, Johnson had failed to garner a majority of the Electoral College vote for vice president. But any uncertainty about whether Johnson would eventually take office was outweighed by the awkwardness of his not having secured the electoral vote in the first place. In the event of such an outcome, the Constitution is unambiguous: the winner of the vice presidency is resolved by a vote of the Senate. In due course, Johnson was voted into office by the Senate, making him thus far the only individual to win the vice presidency in this way.

Within weeks of the 1837 inauguration, Johnson lost interest in presiding over the Senate and gladly relinquished the duties of presiding officer to the president pro tempore. And because Van Buren decided not to emulate with his own vice president the intimate association he had shared with President Jackson, Johnson was decidedly expendable to the president and to the Van Buren administration.[88] Indeed, for the duration of their time in office, Van Buren never once asked for Johnson's advice or assistance with any administration business.[89]

Bereft of any substantial responsibilities, and therefore having time to fill, Vice President Johnson took advantage of his circumstances by running, in person, an inn and tavern in his home state of Kentucky. If being an entrepreneur in the hospitality industry was not enough, Johnson also devoted his attention to the operation of a for-profit school that aimed to refine the assumedly crude deportment of its Native American students.[90] But in greater measure, Johnson's frequent absences from the capital were due to the burdens of his romantic life. Plainly, Johnson was occupied with his African American mistress, a woman rumored to actually be his third wife and the sister of his unfortunate second wife, whom Johnson had sold back into slavery as a result of alleged indiscretions.[91]

Johnson endured the indignities, rumors, and lack of engagement with his elective position, in no small part because expectations for the vice president were virtually nonexistent. Incredibly, prior to the 1840 election, Johnson toured the country, testing the waters for a possible bid for the presidential nomination; however, when his prospects for winning the top spot on the ticket did not appear promising, he decided he would settle for the vice-presidential nomination again.[92] The only catch was that an offer of the nomination was never extended to Johnson. When Democrats met for their national nominating convention, party elites were unwilling to chance keeping him on as vice president.[93] Johnson was not, however, entirely without supporters, and so, from the clash of those who wished to retain him on the ticket, and those who wanted anyone but him, a compromise emerged from the convention: there would be no formally nominated Democratic candidate for vice president in 1840.[94]

The decision by Democrats to leave the vice presidency to the discretion of the Electoral College proved irrelevant, since the voters chose to retire Van Buren and Johnson by means of the election of 1840. A year prior to the election, Andrew Jackson had written to Van Buren and warned him, presciently so it would seem, that if Johnson were "the nominee it will be dead weight to you as it was before."[95] Surely Jackson was overstating the impact a nineteenth century vice-presidential nominee might have in an election. In the end, neither Van Buren nor Johnson was able to sufficiently turn the electorate away from the Whig Party candidates for president and vice president. Afterwards, Johnson drifted further into obscurity, eventually ending his political career, and his life, as a Kentucky state legislator. On the whole, Richard Johnson's vice presidency was no more than a footnote in history, and then only because he came to the office unlike any other before or since.

SUCCESSION AND THE PRECEDENT (1841)

John Tyler will always be conspicuous among vice presidents. Not because he was an exceptionally brilliant or talented individual, and surely not because he achieved a great deal in his time as vice president. For that matter, he barely had time to make a mark, serving only one month under President William Henry Harrison. What makes Tyler noteworthy is his place as the first vice president in American history to succeed to the presidency. That this honor landed on Tyler was obviously a fluke—at the time, some referred to the newly elevated president as "His Accidency"—but Harrison's demise, and Tyler's subsequent rise to the presidency, proved significant in establishing the vice president as the acknowledged successor to the president.[96]

Among others, John Quincy Adams appreciated the historic singularity of what was transpiring in the wake of Harrison's death. Adams, who had already served a term as president, was then a member of the House of Representatives. On April 4, 1841, the day Harrison died, Adams transcribed this in his diary: "In upwards of half a century, this is the first instance of a Vice-President's being called to act as President of the United States, and brings to the test that provision of the Constitution which places in the Executive chair a man never thought of for it by anybody. The day was in every sense gloomy—rain the whole day."[97]

Having never before been confronted with the death of the president while in office, there was no obvious precedent to follow. Tyler found himself in unexplored territory that presented several challenges; paramount among these was deciphering the intent of the Framers in the Constitution, specifically with regard to the replacement of the president. Determining the plan for presidential succession was not an easy task, nor was the constitutional ambiguity made any clearer by examining the proceedings of the Federal Convention, since the record of the Convention on presidential succession plainly added to the uncertainty.

On the matter of succession, historian Arthur Schlesinger Jr. once observed that the "Convention did not resort to the Vice Presidency in order to solve the problem of succession," and had recommended instead to have the president of the Senate— presumably whomever the Senate had selected for that position—assume the powers and duties of the president, until the election of a new president.[98] Furthermore, the Convention delegates were inclined to have the legislature choose "what officer of the U.S. shall act as President in case of the death, resignation, or disability of the President and Vice-President; and such officer shall act accordingly until the time of electing a President shall arrive."[99] And yet, James Madison countered that the foregoing, "as worded, would prevent a supply of the vacancy by an intermediate election of the President," and he suggested altering the language so as not to prevent having the successor serve only until a new election for president might feasibly be held.[100]

Clearly there were alternate perspectives on how best to resolve the succession question; it is apparent that the Framers anticipated that, at some point, the nation would find itself confronted with the circumstances of 1841. Undoubtedly it is why they included the death of the president in the list of vacancy-inducing possibilities for the office. Yet even if the death of the president is a contingency addressed in the

Constitution, how the transfer of power was meant to proceed is only marginally hinted at. In Article 2 of the Constitution it states:

> In Case of the Removal of the President from Office, or of his Death, Resignation, or Inability to discharge the Powers and Duties of the said Office, the Same shall devolve on the Vice President, and the Congress may by Law provide for the Case of Removal, Death, Resignation or Inability, both of the President and Vice President, declaring what Officer shall then act as President, and such Officer shall act accordingly, until the Disability be removed, or a President shall be elected.[101]

From this passage it is clear as to the power of the Congress to replace both the president and vice president—on those occasions when there is a double vacancy—but it is less obvious what is to happen to the vice president once the president is no longer in office. In delineating that "the Same shall devolve on the Vice President," the Framers embraced nuanced language to convey their intent, whatever that might have been. Consequently, it was evident that the powers and duties of the president were meant to "devolve" onto the vice president. But were the devolved powers and duties temporary, meant only to last until a new election? President Harrison's cabinet apparently took this view, when they decided in the immediate aftermath of Harrison's death that John Tyler should be addressed as "Vice President, acting as President."[102]

Was President Harrison's cabinet misconstruing the plan of the Framers? If the Framers intended the vice president to assume all of the powers and the duties of the president, did they expect the arrangement to stand for the remainder of the president's term? Tyler deemed the answer to be yes. His read of the Constitution was fairly simple: the vice president was not meant to be a transitory replacement for the president. From Tyler's standpoint, the death of the president meant that the vice president assumed the presidency and everything that came with it, including the nearly four years remaining in Harrison's term.

What made Tyler's approach to presidential succession so successful was the alacrity with which he acted. Within hours of being notified of President Harrison's death, Tyler made his way to the capital city; once there, he convened a meeting of Harrison's cabinet—all of whom he decided to keep in his own administration—and then he was sworn in to office, making him the tenth president of the United States. Taking the oath of office was an additional precedent that Tyler reluctantly established; it was his interpretation of the Constitution that, with the death of the president, it was preordained that the vice president was the new president—sans any oath—because he had already taken the same oath when he was inaugurated as the vice president.[103] Nonetheless, Tyler took the oath of office again, in the words of one writer, "to remove any doubt about his status."[104]

The choices John Tyler made institutionalized the mechanics for filling vacancies in the presidency. Had Tyler been less assertive, and simply acquiesced to being the "Vice President, acting as President," then the office of vice president would surely have been more repellant than it already was at that time. Still, Tyler's ascension from vice president to president did more than set the precedent on presidential succession; it created yet another vacancy in the vice presidency—but few, if any, seemed to care.

INTERLUDE OF IMPORT (1845–1849)

In assessing the historical trajectory of the American vice presidency, it is clear that the imprint of certain vice presidents has been greater than others. At times, when words or deeds augmented the growth of the institution, those words and deeds were routinely overlooked and swiftly forgotten. The eleventh vice president, George Mifflin Dallas, who had come to office on a ticket with James Polk, might be located in that arc of history with the Senate debate over the Tariff of 1846. If the specifics of the Tariff of 1846 are inconsequential today, the rationale Dallas offered for why and how he planned to vote if the Senate should find itself equally divided merits reevaluation.[105]

The tariff legislation was strongly supported by President Polk; to a certain degree, then, Dallas was acting the part of myrmidon to the president he served. But Dallas took the position that he, like the president, was merely a bystander when it came to crafting or influencing legislation. In remarks delivered to the Senate during the debate on the tariff, Dallas described the legislative role of the vice president as one whereby he was "excluded from any participation in forming or modifying the bill, [therefore] I am bound to sanction or condemn it exactly in the shape in which it stands. The responsibility is deeply felt. It belongs, however, to the office assigned to me by my fellow citizens, and will be assumed with frankness, and, I hope, not unbecoming firmness."[106]

In continuing to address the assembled senators, Dallas alluded further to the conundrum fixed to an institution that hovers between the executive and legislative branches. Of more significance was the proposition Dallas advanced that, in being the president of the Senate, the vice president has the power to affirm or veto legislation on those occasions when the vote of the Senate is tied. And yet, whichever way his vote should fall, by his way of thinking, it was inappropriate for the vice president to disregard the will of the people. To this end, Dallas declared: "Peculiarly situated as I am in my relation to the national legislature, these impressive facts cannot be overlooked. In a case free from constitutional objection, I could not justifiably counteract, by a sort of official veto, the general will."[107]

Dallas was well aware that many in his home state of Pennsylvania were opposed to the proposed tariff bill, but the vice president was certain his mandate exceeded the citizens of Pennsylvania.[108] The argument he made was that the vice president is a nationally elected official; therefore, like the president, the vice president has a constituency that extends far beyond any specific city, district, or state. Dallas put it this way:

> In strict concord with the letter and spirit of the Constitution, the Vice President of the United States, now called upon to act, is the direct agent and representative of the whole people. In advance, and dependent upon

contingent results, it is perfectly competent to this, his national constituency, to give instructions, and to receive pledges for their execution.[109]

Besides this sweeping view of the vice presidency—as a hybrid executive-legislative
institution, as the presiding officer in possession of a distinctive check on legislation,
and as an elected representative for the entire nation—George Dallas, when isolated
amongst nineteenth century vice presidents, was ahead of his time. He was, though
for different reasons, a forerunner of all that modern vice presidents now embody. For
example, despite Dallas and Polk not having met prior to their winning the election,
once in office, the president routinely sought the counsel and support of the vice president. Moreover, Polk took advantage of the ties Dallas maintained within the halls of
Congress, using his connections to advance the objectives of the administration and
even, on occasion, enlisting the vice president's assistance when composing presidential addresses.[110]

The diary James Polk kept during his single term in the White House is replete with
entries on meeting with Vice President Dallas. Now and again, the two men conferred
on matters before the Senate; while other times they met to discuss foreign affairs or
the ongoing expansion of the United States; and from time to time, the president and
vice president were brought together for purely social engagements.[111] Although Polk
occasionally recorded disapproving observations of various political figures of the era,
the notations in his diary concerning Dallas were always respectful and expressed his
high regard for the vice president. Comparable associations between earlier presidents
and vice presidents—such as Jefferson and Burr or Monroe and Tompkins—are difficult to imagine.

By all indications, George Dallas played a valuable role in the Polk administration.
Yet, the extent of any vice president's inclusion in the affairs of the government was
always a judgment made by the president. Such an arrangement is apposite to every
president-to-vice president relationship, as it should be, and so it is because of Polk
that Dallas should be remembered. And for Polk there was an advantage to keeping
Dallas content and loyal to the administration: the vice president's tie-breaking vote
was critical in the upper chamber of the legislature, where the president lacked majority support.[112]

By some measure, the four years Dallas served as vice president were similar to
Martin Van Buren's time in the office, for both men experienced relatively anomalous
tenures when compared to the records of some of their predecessors and successors. At
the same time, the Dallas vice presidency also epitomized what it was like to be the vice
president in the eighteenth and nineteenth century. For instance, even when he was the
second-highest elected official in the nation, Dallas continued to practice law for the
entirety of his time in office.[113]

Ultimately, the tenure of Vice President Dallas was defined by President Polk. It was
because of the president that Dallas publicly supported the Tariff of 1846, an unpopular
position in his home-state of Pennsylvania that helped to erode his support there and
subsequently extinguished any chance he had for someday reaching the presidency.
And it was Polk who frequently allowed Dallas into the highest councils of the executive

government, in the process reserving a minor spot for him in the annals of presidents and their vice presidents.

THE VICE PRESIDENCY SERVED: BY WHIG, DEATH, AND REBEL (1849–1861)

For every vice president like John Tyler—who initiated the precedent on presidential succession—or for a vice president like George Dallas—who had occasion to play a substantive role in the Senate, while sustaining a notable association with the president—an individual has landed in the office, leaving barely a trace of their service. Such was the case with the vice presidencies of Millard Fillmore, William Rufus DeVane King, and John Breckinridge.

When President Zachary Taylor died and Vice President Millard Fillmore succeeded to the presidency—at that point, only the second vice president to do so—Fillmore was guaranteed a place in history as the thirteenth president of the United States. Otherwise, had Taylor lived to fill his presidential term in its entirety, Fillmore probably would have been remembered as one of many insignificant vice presidents, distinguished more by the oddness of his name than by any contribution he made.[114]

Due to the precedent set by fellow Whig John Tyler, Fillmore's rise to the presidency went unquestioned. And since there was still not a constitutional remedy for filling vacancies in the vice presidency, the post remained open for the entire two and a half years that were the Fillmore administration. Further adding to the unease with presidential succession, the vice president who followed Fillmore, William Rufus DeVane King, died slightly more than one month after he took the oath of office. With King's death, the vice presidency again went unoccupied, this time for three years, ten months, and fourteen days.

William King was a rare politician for his era; he openly aspired to be vice president. During the twenty-nine years he was a senator from Alabama, King prepared for the job in the only way possible, by repeatedly seeking and winning the post of Senate president pro tempore. Finally elected vice president in 1852, on a ticket with Franklin Pierce, King was not the first choice of Democrats that year. He had won the nomination only after his close friend James Buchanan failed to earn the presidential nomination and, in turn, rejected the opportunity to be Pierce's running mate, insisting that King get the vice-presidential spot instead of himself.[115]

The friendship of King and Buchanan has long been the subject of speculation. Both men were committed bachelors, and when they served together in the Senate they shared living quarters in the capital city for several years. This arrangement provoked suggestions of a relationship defined more by intimacy than by collegiality.[116] To these allegations, a biographer of Buchanan has noted that her subject was "so intimate … with the handsome Alabama senator, who was known as a dandy in his home state and an 'Aunt Fancy' in Washington, that one congressman referred to the two men as

'Buchanan & his Wife' in a reference to their bachelor status, which also hinted at their homosexuality."[117] Regardless of the whispers and sexual innuendo, the nature of King's relationship with Buchanan will remain a mystery for the ages, a mystery made even more compelling when—four years after the death of Vice President King, and on the occasion of Buchanan's election to the presidency—nearly all the correspondence the two men shared was deliberately and inexplicably destroyed.[118]

The nomination for vice president came to King even though he was visibly ailing and was subsequently diagnosed with tuberculosis. Not surprisingly, he was never able to participate in the campaign of 1852. The loss of King from the campaign trail was significant in that vice-presidential nominees were expected to campaign for the ticket in lieu of the presidential nominee. As a result, the Democratic ticket of 1852 was devoid of an active candidate for vice president, with a minimalist candidate aspiring to the presidency. All the same, Franklin Pierce and the fading William King were elected and set to be inaugurated the following March.

In the interim, King sailed away from the United States, seeking relief for his medical condition in Cuba. Once there, it was soon obvious that sunshine and respite were not going to change the inevitable outcome of King's condition, nor would he survive long enough to be inaugurated with Pierce.[119] Therefore, with the required approval granted by a special act of Congress, King took the oath of the office he had long coveted on the island of Cuba. Because of this, King remains the only vice president in United States history to be sworn in to office beyond the nation's borders. King did live just long enough to return to his home in Alabama, but he died before he was ever able to complete a single act as vice president. For the duration of his term of office, Franklin Pierce served without a vice president.

When William King's friend James Buchanan made it to the presidency—four years after the election of Franklin Pierce—he arrived with John Breckinridge as his vice president. Breckinridge was chosen to run with Buchanan for the balance it was assumed he brought to the ticket, a balance achieved because Breckinridge came from the slave state of Kentucky and Buchanan hailed from the free state of Pennsylvania.

From the start, Breckinridge was destined to serve as a neglected and forgotten vice president, set apart by virtue of his being the youngest elected vice president in history, and the first not made to share office space in the Capitol building.[120] Still, apart from an enhanced working environment, the Buchanan-Breckinridge pairing was fundamentally futile. This, of course, came as no surprise because there was no expectation, as there is today, for the president and vice president, who are elected as a team, to work together like a team once they are in office. Writing of Buchanan and Breckinridge, one historian aptly captured this quandary, emphasizing that it was "by tradition, [that] vice presidents were not involved in policy. Buchanan accepted the custom without question. He never was close to Breckinridge and avoided him as much as possible. Breckinridge had no private interview with the president in over three years."[121]

To his credit, Breckinridge served well, absent notoriety, for the sum of his term. As the United States began to slowly break apart in the run-up to the 1860 election, and President Buchanan floundered about, losing any chance for retaining office for another four years, Breckinridge's availability for the presidency was known. In 1860, the Democratic Party nominating convention split over the slavery question. Later, primarily northern delegates reconvened for a second convention and nominated Senator Stephen Douglas for president and the former governor of Georgia, Herschel Johnson, for vice president. Their platform supported the prerogative of Congress and the Supreme Court to make determinations on slavery. Finally, a third Democratic convention was held, mainly with delegates from the South. At that convention, delegates nominated Vice President Breckinridge for president and Senator Joseph Lane of Oregon for vice president. The platform of the third Democratic nominating convention of 1860 supported slavery in the territories of the United States.[122]

Although Breckinridge was only thirty-nine at the time of the election, and was by no means an established national figure, the Breckinridge-Lane ticket managed to place third in the national balloting, just behind Douglas and Johnson, garnering nearly 900,000 votes. As a consequence, Breckinridge subsequently left the executive branch a losing candidate for the presidency, never having been brought into the confidence of President Buchanan.

John Breckinridge's later public career would eclipse his time as the vice presiden of the United States. In due course, he left the capital and moved back to the South. Gaining the confidence of a different president, Breckinridge served first as a solider and then as the secretary of war for President Jefferson Davis and the Confederate States of America. When the Confederate States eventually lost the Civil War, Breckinridge was charged with treason. He fled the United States, living the life of a fugitive in Cuba, Europe, and Canada for over four years. It was an unusually precipitous decline for any ambitious politician—even for a former vice president.

LINCOLN'S VICE PRESIDENTS (1861–1865)

Abraham Lincoln and his first vice president, Hannibal Hamlin, sustained a close association that has generally gone unrecognized. In part, this is attributable to the assassination of Lincoln and the subsequent succession to the presidency by his second vice president, Andrew Johnson. Had Johnson not replaced Hamlin on the Republican ticket in 1864, then there would have been a President Hamlin, and the political landscape of the nineteenth century would surely have looked quite different. Then again, some of Hamlin's critics at the time could have claimed, with Hamlin next in line for the presidency, that Lincoln's safety was ensured. Either way, the striking disparities that defined and distinguished Lincoln's two vice presidents—in their character and in their respective associations with the president—were emblematic of the dichotomous nature of the American vice presidency.

Lincoln and Hamlin had never met before their victory in the election of 1860. It defies modern sensibilities that a team of presidential and vice-presidential candidates could seek office and not meet until the election was settled. The first contact between the president-elect and vice president-elect occurred several days past their victory at the polls; it was a telling encounter in that neither man appeared troubled by the absence of any prior meeting. According to the account Hamlin gave to his family, the meeting went like this:

> "'Have we ever been introduced to each other, Mr. Hamlin?'
> 'No sir; I think not,' replied the Vice-President elect.
> 'That is also my impression,' said Lincoln."[123]

This commonplace start to the Lincoln-Hamlin association is indicative of the routine disregard for the vice presidency found in the mid-nineteenth century, as well as to the nature of presidential politics of that era. Quite simply, vice-presidential nominees were of almost no concern to the presidential nominees or to a majority of the electorate, and once elected, the vice president was rarely viewed as an officer of the government critical to its functioning.

But the impetus for Lincoln's initial conference with Hamlin makes their pairing unique to the development of president-to-vice president relations. What drove Lincoln to meet Hamlin went beyond common courtesy. Lincoln was seeking advice on the composition of the cabinet, and so he had turned to the vice president-elect, who possessed considerably more experience in the national government than did the newly elected president.[124] Lincoln even went so far to as to give Hamlin, till then a senator from Maine, exclusive rights to the choice of a token cabinet member drawn from one of the New England states.[125]

In the four years Hamlin was vice president, he routinely met with President Lincoln, offering advice whenever asked, particularly on the conduct of the Civil War. Hamlin recounted that "with Mr. Lincoln it was very easy. We had intimate relations, and he often consulted me. I was more radical than he. I was urging him; he was holding back on his problems, and he was the wiser probably, as events prove."[126] Lincoln also requested that Hamlin "become a consulting member" of the president's cabinet, but Hamlin had determined—despite his occasional attendance at meetings of the cabinet—that because the vice president did not lead one of the executive departments, and was therefore different from a cabinet secretary, merely being the vice president did not merit his presence in the formal council of the executive government.[127]

One anecdote, especially enlightening to the nature of the Lincoln-Hamlin association, concerns the Emancipation Proclamation. After Lincoln composed a preliminary draft of the document, he met alone with Hamlin, telling the vice president: "Mr. Hamlin, you have been repeatedly urging me to issue a proclamation of emancipation freeing the slaves. I have concluded to yield to your advice in the matter and that of other friends,—at the same time, as I may say, following my own judgment. Now listen to me while I read this paper. We will correct it together as I go on."[128]

It is extraordinary that it was Hannibal Hamlin whom Abraham Lincoln chose to first read the storied document to, and then Lincoln even asked for advice from the vice president on how to improve the text. To this, Hamlin later asserted he did offer "three suggestions, two of which Mr. Lincoln accepted."[129] Of equal significance, the greatness of Lincoln, coupled with the momentous place the Emancipation Proclamation holds in American history, makes such an encounter not just historic, but unique to the story of presidents and their vice presidents.

Hamlin's influence on President Lincoln did not stop with the issuance of the Emancipation Proclamation. This was apparent with his eventual success in convincing the president to enlist and arm free blacks in the ranks of the Union Army, an objective he had repeatedly pressured Lincoln on.[130] At the same time, when it came to the mundane details of the war effort, Lincoln apparently depended more on Hamlin than he did on one of his own executive departments. John Hay, one of Lincoln's two personal secretaries, noted in his diary that Lincoln "had just written a letter to Hamlin, requesting him to write him a daily letter in regard to the number of troops arriving departing or expected each day. He said that it seemed there was no certain knowledge on these subjects at the War Department, that even Genl. Scott was usually in the dark in respect to them."[131] The vice president complied with the president's request.

Unfortunately for Hamlin, the record of his tenure emphasizes the regularity with which he fell asleep when presiding over the tedium of the United States Senate, resulting in the caricature of a bored and ineffectual vice president. Adding further to the broad dismissal of Hamlin's service, as well as to the tendency to overlook the depth of his association with Lincoln, are the circumstances surrounding his absence from the Republican ticket in 1864—circumstances that, when reviewed, raise more questions than answers.

Foremost among the questions to arise is this: if Abraham Lincoln was at ease with Hannibal Hamlin, and relied on the sagacity of his vice president, why then was Hamlin denied re-nomination? The answer, in part, is that in the 1800s decisions on vice-presidential nominees were made at political party conventions by party elites, and in the waning hours of the convention proceedings. In 1864, the consensus of the Republican leadership was that the addition of a southern Democrat, loyal to the Union, and affixed to the bottom of the ticket, was the best assurance for reelecting the Republican president.[132] It has likewise been proposed that this strategy for victory was supported by Lincoln. Conversely, Lincoln approving of Hamlin being dropped from the ticket has been disputed by, among others, Hamlin himself.[133] Furthermore, John Nicolay, Lincoln's other secretary, insisted that the president had made it clear that he would be happy with the same team in 1864 as there was in 1860.[134]

It is impossible to determine how the vice presidency, the presidency, or for that matter the United States, might have been altered if Hannibal Hamlin, instead of Andrew Johnson, had been vice president when Abraham Lincoln was killed. As to the vice presidency, in fairness to Johnson, a mere forty-three days separated his inauguration as vice president and his succession to the presidency. Johnson could scarcely leave his mark on an office he barely occupied on his way to the White House. And yet, Johnson's record as president does exist; hence, it is difficult to imagine Hamlin being an inferior president to Johnson.

If assessments of Andrew Johnson's presidency will forever be framed by his impeachment, then his vice presidency will always be colored by the spectacle of his inauguration. On the day before the ceremony, Johnson drank heavily; then, in the hour prior to his inaugural, Johnson consumed a bottle of brandy in the vice president's office, while the soon to be former vice president, Hannibal Hamlin, watched in alarm.[135] Leaving the vice president's office, Hamlin assisted an intoxicated Johnson to the front of the Senate, whereupon Johnson launched into an incoherent inaugural speech, took the oath from the outgoing vice president, and then proceeded to slump down in a chair, unable to complete his first task as vice president—the swearing in of newly elected senators.[136] It was an inauspicious beginning to one of the most ephemeral vice presidencies in history and presaged one of the least successful presidencies to date.

THE VICE PRESIDENCY SERVED: BANALITY REIGNS (1869–1897)

Andrew Johnson's ill-fated start as a national executive was in many ways a poignant indication of the condition of the American vice presidency at that time. Clearly the vice presidency could be occupied by competent individuals of stature, as evidenced by men such as John Adams and Thomas Jefferson. Still others seized opportunities, and then set precedents, for the institution, like John Tyler had done. Similarly, experience had shown that certain vice presidents might serve, to varying degrees, as a reliable confidant to their president, with Martin Van Buren, George Dallas, and Hannibal Hamlin matching that description. But individuals and scenarios like those just cited were exceptions, and although each incrementally contributed to the growth and in-stitutionalization of the vice presidency, their contributions—with the exception of the succession precedent—rarely carried forward to the next occupant of the office.

Most of the vice presidents after Andrew Johnson failed, like he had, to raise expectations of what role the vice president might play as an elected officer of the fed-eral government. Of the four vice presidents to follow Johnson in the second office—Schuyler Colfax, Henry Wilson, William Wheeler, and Chester Arthur—only Arthur is remembered, and that is simply because he succeeded to the presidency upon the assassination of President James Garfield. Arthur also stands out due to his place in the debate on presidential inability, and because of the ambiguity that surfaced on account of Garfield having survived for seventy-nine days following the assassination attempt.

Schuyler Colfax was the first of Ulysses S. Grant's two vice presidents. He was also the first Speaker of the House of Representatives to be elected vice president, thus adding a measure of stature to the office by virtue of his experience leading the other chamber of Congress.[137] But Colfax was not intended to lead in the Senate, as he did when he was the Speaker; therefore, he went about his business, obsequiously fulfilling his official duties.

On seventeen occasions, Colfax was called upon to exercise the vice president's tie-breaking vote. Generally, when the Senate was equally divided, it came about on measures that were contentious because of regional or factional differences, and not necessarily when a matter of national principle was at stake; on these occasions, the vice president simply settled the matter with his vote. However, there were times that Colfax was able to use his vote to make known where his values lay. For instance, he voted in the affirmative on an amendment to a bill that would have broadened the rights constitutionally sanctioned for African Americans in the aftermath of the Civil War. Although the amendment was eventually stripped from the bill, Colfax later defended his vote by proclaiming that "we should either acknowledge that the Constitution is a nullity or should insist on that obedience to it by all, and protection under it to all which are alike the right and duty of the humblest as well as the most influential throughout the land."[138]

In addition to consistently presiding and sporadically voting, Colfax was witness to a fleeting, but earnest attempt to alter the manner in which the president is elected. In this instance, a joint resolution was put forward to provide for the direct election of the president by a vote of the people.[139] Naturally, if the resolution had passed both houses of Congress, the prescribed method for amending the Constitution would have then commenced. Of the numerically ordered lines in the resolution, Colfax would have been particularly interested in the last two. Line eighty-four called for the abolishment of the office of the vice president and line eighty-five gave senators the power to choose their own presiding officer.[140] No doubt the resolution gave Colfax pause—both over the futility of the position he held and the uncertainty of the institution enduring.

Without question the most excitement to come to the Colfax vice presidency occurred when he was presiding from the rostrum of the Senate and was unexpectedly struck with an intense case of vertigo, subsequently collapsing before the members.[141] The next day Colfax sent a letter to the chief clerk of the Senate stating: "I do not expect to occupy the chair during the remainder of this session."[142] With that, the vice president was gone for the session, and a president pro tempore was installed in his place.

Apart from the preceding incident, Colfax routinely presided in the Senate, on the whole attending to his duties there more faithfully than many of his contemporaries. At the same time, the vice presidency was not so demanding that it kept Colfax from traveling the lecture circuit, collecting honorariums along the way. Nor did his regular job prevent him from a prolific writing career.[143] The value in Colfax's speechmaking and writing was twofold: first, it allowed him to supplement the paltry $5,000 annual salary then paid to the vice president—a figure which paled when compared to the $25,000 paid to the president each year. And second, it provided Colfax a means otherwise unavailable to vice presidents in the nineteenth century for boosting his preferred political agenda while keeping his name before the public.

Curiously, with two years still remaining in his term, Colfax publically declared his intention to retire from government service and likewise announced that he had no interest in seeking the vice-presidential nomination for another term; besides, he assumed the Republican Party would prefer, for a second to President Grant, an individual who came from a different region of the country than he did.[144] What motivated Colfax to retire in the midst of a successful political career, and abandon what looked like the most linear course for making it to the presidency, is open to conjecture. It is unlikely that he had ever anticipated a substantial role in the Grant administration or was thus disappointed when that did not happen. And the president apparently held him in high enough regard that, at one point, he recommended that Colfax take the secretary of state posting when the position was thought to be opening.[145] But Colfax disavowed any interest in entering in the cabinet and turned the president down.

Whatever reasons Colfax genuinely had for prematurely leaving politics, his announcement was to have a profound impact on his future. Initially it was suspected that he could be encouraged to change his mind about retirement and run for reelection in 1872 with President Grant; then later, a quiet movement arose to replace Grant with Colfax at the next Republican nominating convention.[146] Of the preceding two points: Colfax did reverse his decision on not seeking the vice presidency again, but the move to substitute him for Grant waned as quickly and as quietly as it had begun. By the time Colfax actively sought the vice-presidential nomination for a second time, it was too late.[147] The president and the party had taken him at his word and Colfax was effectively retired from elective office.

Near the end of his uneventful tenure, Colfax was accused of having received railroad stock, on top of bribes, when he was still a member of Congress. He vigorously denied the charges before a congressional committee, only to have his testimony summarily discredited.[148] Predictably, Colfax's connection to scandal guaranteed that the Republican Party looked elsewhere for a running mate for President Grant when he stood for reelection in 1872. That year, Republicans gave the nomination instead to Henry Wilson.

Wilson represented Massachusetts in the United States Senate and had been linked to the same stock scandal as Colfax—just not to the degree that he was deemed unworthy of the vice presidency. Once inaugurated, Wilson suffered a stroke within two months of his taking the oath of office, and though he resumed his duties presiding, he did so partially paralyzed.[149] In the end, Wilson failed to raise the standing of the institution, serving slightly over two years of his term. He did earn a place in the history of the American vice presidency, however, as he remains the only vice president to have died, literally, in the vice president's Capitol office.

Because a constitutional means for filling vacancies in the vice presidency was nonexistent in 1875, the demise of Henry Wilson meant there would be no sitting vice president until the next presidential election was conducted—an election that subsequently brought Rutherford B. Hayes to the White House and Congressman William Wheeler to the vice presidency. Like many vice presidents and presidents of their era, Wheeler and Hayes were not acquainted when they were put together on the electoral ticket. Yet despite their unfamiliarity with one another, Hayes had promptly integrated Wheeler into his social circle, making the vice president an almost daily visitor to the White House, and the president and vice president eventually became close friends.

As it turned out, their association was kept exclusively social, with Vice President Wheeler's counsel on politics and policy never sought by President Hayes, and therefore he remained detached from all the important business of the administration for the four years he held office.[150] Certainly the lack of substantive participation in the administration characterized the tenure of many vice presidents before Wheeler; unfortunately, he would not be the last vice president so grossly underutilized.

In 1880, Rutherford B. Hayes chose not to seek a second term as president and the Republican Party chose not to nominate William Wheeler to replace him. Sitting vice presidents were not then the logical successor presidential nominees; that would not become the norm until much later, in the mid-twentieth century. Instead, the

Republicans retained control of the executive branch when James Garfield and Chester Arthur were elected president and vice president, respectively. As for Wheeler: two months after he left the vice presidency, he was a candidate for a vacant Senate seat from New York, but was defeated, thus ending his political career. Wheeler died six years later, perhaps the most enigmatic vice president in history—a title he will likely always hold.

William Wheeler's successor, Chester Arthur, was in many ways the perfect fit for the office, for Arthur's persona and career epitomized the state of the American vice presidency in the latter part of the nineteenth century. Arthur was a stock party and patronage man, and he had never been elected to any public office prior to winning the vice presidency. At present—when experience is so heavily emphasized as a requisite for higher office, and a lack of experience is subject to scorn, though clearly not cause for outright denial of a vice-presidential nomination, as John Edwards and Sarah Palin proved—it is still difficult to fathom an individual rising from the appointed position of collector of the port of New York to win the vice presidency, and then succeed to the presidency less than a year later. Nonetheless, this was precisely the trajectory Arthur followed in his swift ascent to the apex of the American political system.

In the expansive sweep of vice-presidential history, Arthur's transitory tenure shall be appended to the dilemma of presidential inability and the ambiguity of response that characterized those occasions when the situation arose. As noted previously, nearly three months elapsed from the time President Garfield was shot until his death. During that time, Garfield's condition fluctuated dramatically; at times he was lucid, yet at other times he was disoriented.[151] As a consequence, for the period of time Garfield lay dying, the nation went without a functioning president.

Garfield's precise condition was problematic in that the Constitution was vague when it came to managing a crisis of presidential inability. Put another way, the Constitution did not demarcate a clear-cut method for determining when inability begins and ends, nor was it indicated anywhere in the Constitution who was expected to make such a determination. Similar to the uncertainty John Tyler faced when he was the vice president, Chester Arthur was treading untested waters. Indeed, presidents had died while in office—Harrison, Taylor, and Lincoln—but none had lingered on, as Garfield did, perilously hanging onto life.

From the moment Garfield's assassin fired at him, Arthur was a model of restraint. He was careful never to appear as if he were anticipating the president's death, although he did confer with the president's cabinet, and he continued to stay in close contact with administration officials throughout the ordeal.[152] Curiously, when Arthur arrived at the White House—where Garfield was taken following the assassination attempt— and had then asked to visit with the president, Garfield's doctors refused to let the vice president near.[153] Regardless of the reasons given at the time, the vice president was simply not considered worthy of a conference with the dying president. This was in stark contrast to various members of the president's cabinet, several of whom, after a time, were allowed to visit Garfield, provided that they would not bother the president with government affairs.[154] As it stood, from the time Garfield was shot until he finally perished, he met just briefly with any of his cabinet, and he was responsible for only a single executive action.[155]

For his part, Arthur attempted to transcend the predicament of presidential inability, possibly with the aim of being more than a footnote in the debate. In each year of his presidency, Arthur reproached the Congress, insisting on some recourse to the uncertainty that presidential inability provoked. Because Garfield's condition had oscillated so greatly, it raised more questions than it might have otherwise.

For example, what if the inability of the president was only temporary? Assuming Garfield eventually was well enough to resume work, would he have simply regained leadership of the government? And what was to become of the vice president? In the Garfield situation, what if Arthur had gone forward and exercised executive authority, as some in the cabinet suggested he should? In the interim, if Garfield's health had improved, would Arthur have been compelled to hand the reins of government back to the formerly incapacitated president?

This was the nature of the questions President Arthur posed to Congress, first in 1881 and then in each of the three remaining years of Garfield's term that he fulfilled.[156] In the end, Arthur was unsuccessful in this endeavor, and Congress failed to confront presidential inability during the time he was president, finally settling on a remedy eighty-six years after Garfield's death. And yet, the Congress did not bother to find a solution to the problem of vice-presidential vacancies. It therefore remained, until 1967, that if under any circumstances the vice presidency became vacant the incumbent president was missing the service of a vice president for the remainder of their elected term.

After Chester Arthur, the next three individuals to inhabit the office of vice president served with neither merit nor malfeasance. Thomas Hendricks was the first to follow Arthur and the first of Grover Cleveland's vice presidents. Once in office, Hendricks was transparently hostile to Cleveland's aversion to patronage politics, though, ultimately, this conflict between the president and vice president was for naught, since Hendricks died after serving barely eight months of his term.[157]

Cleveland was defeated for reelection in 1888, but he would return to the presidency four years later with a new vice president. In the interim, Levi Morton claimed the vice presidency, having been elected to the post as Benjamin Harrison's running mate. Morton had squandered the first opportunity he had to seek the vice presidency, when eight years prior to his election with Harrison he had rejected an offer to run on the ticket with James Garfield and, as events turned out, missed what was his best opportunity to realize a Morton presidency.[158]

Like Thomas Hendricks had done earlier, Morton did not consistently support the program of the president he served, working instead for the interests of those who had advanced his nomination.[159] Morton indolently presided over the Senate for an uneventful four years, only to be bypassed by the Republican Party for nomination to a second term. By one account, President Harrison "seemed unnecessarily callous toward Morton" and also "disliked" the vice president's "rulings" and "lethargy" when presiding over the Senate—all of which was cause to deny the hapless Morton nomination for a second term.[160] Whether Morton's presence on the Republican ticket a second time would have made the difference in President Harrison's bid for reelection is open to speculation. In any case, Harrison lost and Grover Cleveland returned to the White House, this time with Adlai Stevenson for his vice president.

The vice-presidential nomination had been extended to Stevenson not because of an established relationship with Cleveland, as there was none, nor was it offered to him for the vigor he might bring to the office and to the government should he be elected. Instead, like practically every other vice-presidential nominee before him, Stevenson was granted the nomination for what he presumably brought to the electoral ticket. For Stevenson, this meant his position on the debate over currency backed by silver or gold as well as his record for being a party stalwart, willing to reward any Democrat with a job, irrespective of merit or skill.[161]

On the whole, Stevenson's time presiding over the Senate passed free of significance. The rare exception was when President Cleveland advocated for the repeal of the Sherman Silver Purchase Act. When a bill reached the Senate floor proposing repeal of the Act, Vice President Stevenson did nothing to dissuade a filibuster of the legislation; he was clearly unwilling to fight for the bill, in spite of the president's expressed wishes that he do so.[162]

Ironically, in what might have been the most critical period of Stevenson's vice presidency, he was purposely kept uninformed. This arose during the first year of the second Cleveland administration, when the president was diagnosed with cancer of the mouth. Fearing that news of an illness might cause economic instability, Cleveland made certain that information regarding the precise nature of the disease was kept secret.[163] Covertly boarding the yacht of a friend, the president cruised up and down the Long Island Sound for several days, ostensibly for a break from life in the capital. However, not long after beginning the trip, the left side of Cleveland's upper jaw was completely removed and then replaced with a crude prosthetic jaw piece made of rubber.[164] Throughout the entire ordeal, Vice President Stevenson was unaware of the president's affliction and obviously had no idea about the risky surgical procedure, either. What is more, if there had been an international or domestic crisis at any point during the lengthy surgery, or in the several days of recuperation Cleveland required, the president would have been incapable of responding effectively.

The aforementioned episode was symptomatic of the irrelevance of vice presidents in the nineteenth century. Hence, it was considered more important to conceal the president's illness than to inform the vice president of the temporarily leaderless government. Apparently President Cleveland deemed it unnecessary to prepare Stevenson for the likelihood of his ascending to the presidency. But withholding information about Cleveland's health crisis from Stevenson was not just an error in preparation, it was also a poignant reminder that the president and vice president were not intimate and that their association was anemic, at best. This type of arrangement would not be echoed by the next president and vice president.

Brief Interlude (1897–1899)

Much in the way that Abraham Lincoln's two vice presidents epitomized contrasting notions of the vice presidency, so it was with William McKinley and the two individuals who served at his side. McKinley's first vice president, Garrett Hobart, proved to be an exceptional example of what the vice president could be. And though McKinley and Hobart were familiar with one another when both were nominated and then elected, they were by no means close.[165] Even so, the commencement of the new administration marked the onset of a unique collaboration; it would become a personal and political friendship unmatched by any prior president and vice president.

For the duration of his tenure, Vice President Hobart visited the White House regularly, advising as well as socializing with the president. The frequency with which McKinley consulted with his vice president elevated Hobart's stature within the exclusivity of the capital city; likewise, there was a parallel broadening of the public's awareness of the vice-presidential institution, causing some to describe Hobart as the "Assistant President."[166]

When presiding in the Senate, Hobart was instrumental in advancing the McKinley administration's agenda, and his influence with Congress was no doubt enhanced by broad recognition of his closeness to the president. Here too, the ostensible deputation of the vice president by the president underscored the value in using the second officer of the government within the legislative branch; it was a practice that marginally aligned with the Framers having made the vice president the president of the Senate.

When Garrett Hobart died after only two years in office, President McKinley freely acknowledged the impact the late vice president had on him, on the office, and on administration policy. McKinley had occasion to speak about Hobart not long after his death. The gist of McKinley's remarks and emotions were captured well by Charles Dawes. Dawes worked in the McKinley administration and became an intimate of the president, who subsequently mentored the younger man in his political career. Dawes, who went on to be elected vice president with President Calvin Coolidge, described the scene as follows:

> After dinner the President spoke at length and with feeling of his regard for the Vice President and of the fact that of many popular Vice Presidents, Hobart was the one who was powerful as well. Popularity with the Senate could be easily attained by a kind Vice President, but Hobart attained an influence which made him one of the great factors in the fierce struggles in the Senate incident to the carrying out of the President's policy in the last two years.[167]

In the end, the two-year McKinley-Hobart association was notable because it expanded on the potential of the vice presidency and because it demonstrated that the vice president did not have to be an unwanted appendage to the president. And if McKinley and Hobart were initially brought together for political expediency, as was then the norm, their pairing confirmed the possibility of the vice president serving as both adviser and friend to the president.

RETURN TO FORM (1901–1921)

The death of Garrett Hobart meant that President McKinley held office for two years without his trusted vice president and confidant. Over the course of time when McKinley was serving alone, speculation was rampant as to who should replace Hobart when the president stood for reelection in 1900. The answer to McKinley's dilemma—or more accurately, the dilemma of the Republican Party—was a reluctant Theodore Roosevelt, then governor of New York. Roosevelt was accorded the nomination, like many of the nominees before him, because of the balance he conceivably added to the ticket. But there was another reason the nomination went to Roosevelt. Simply put, the political bosses of New York wanted a rising, independent political figure like Roosevelt out of the state, and they had decided that the vice presidency was the best place to end the young governor's political career.[168]

As for Roosevelt, in the months leading up to the nominating convention, he was unequivocal about his disinterest in the nomination for vice president. In a letter written to New York political boss Thomas Platt, Roosevelt complained: "I can't help feeling more and more that the Vice-Presidency is not an office in which I could do anything and not an office in which a man who is still vigorous and not past middle life has much chance of doing anything … Now, as Governor, I can achieve something, but as Vice-President I should achieve nothing."[169]

Roosevelt's natural restlessness made him ill-suited to the unassuming life and work of the vice president of the United States, and particularly to the tedium of presiding over the Senate.[170] Yet because of his innate vigor, Roosevelt surely would have had an indelible, distinguishing influence on the office if he had served there longer. This had been the case throughout his public life, a life that already tallied an impressive breadth of experience for a man who was just forty-two when he was installed in the vice presidency. Still, and despite his earlier protestations, at his inauguration Roosevelt feigned gratitude for having reached such an august place in the government, declaring: "Most deeply do I appreciate the privilege of my position; for high, indeed, is the honor of presiding over the American Senate at the outset of the twentieth century."[171]

Having never coveted the vice presidency, and certain that he was fated for utter boredom in exercising the responsibilities of the position, Roosevelt was determined to put the anticipated idle time to good use. To this end, he decided to study law at Washington Law School, in conjunction with his service as the vice president. Roosevelt had even queried the sitting Chief Justice of the Supreme Court, Edward White, for recommendations for a suitable reading list to aid in his studies.[172]

A few years earlier, when working as the city police commissioner for New York, Roosevelt had written an article about the vice presidency and the candidates standing for election to the post that year. In the article, Roosevelt reflected on the dichotomy of the institution, emphasizing that the American vice president

> is an officer unique in his character and functions, or, to speak more properly, in his want of functions while he remains Vice-President, and in his possibility of at any moment ceasing to be a functionless official and becoming the head of the whole nation. There is no corresponding position in any constitutional government. Perhaps the nearest analogue is the heir apparent in a monarchy. Neither the French President nor the British Prime Minister has a substitute, ready at any moment to take his place, but exercising scarcely any authority until his place is taken.[173]

Less than five years after Roosevelt composed the preceding passage—and one hundred and sixty-five days after becoming vice president—the assassination of President McKinley would take Roosevelt from being "a functionless official" and make him "the head of the whole nation."

With the ascension of Theodore Roosevelt to the presidency, once more the vice presidency had been vacated, with no constitutional means for filling the position before the next presidential election. This meant that the office of the vice president was unoccupied for three years, five months, and eighteen days. For a man who never saw any value in the vice presidency, Roosevelt was surely content with the office going unoccupied. Yet when he chose to run for his own term as president, he was forced to yield to tradition and the Constitution. Eventually, when Roosevelt appeared certain of success at the Republican convention, the leadership of the party gave the vice-presidential nomination to Charles Fairbanks, a senator from Indiana.

The staid Fairbanks was the ideal contrast to the ebullient Roosevelt. From top to bottom, Fairbanks was the model of what, at that time, the vice president was supposed to be: inconspicuous, banal, and of modest talents. One early biographer and friend to Roosevelt captured the Fairbanks persona best, describing the vice president as "tall and thin and oppressively taciturn ... and who was not less cold than dumb, so that irreverent jokers reported that persons might freeze to death in his presence if they came too near or stayed too long."[174]

Having already worked as a senator, Fairbanks was comfortable in the upper chamber and presided soundly. It was fortunate for Fairbanks that he had responsibilities in the Senate, because Roosevelt gave his vice president nothing else to do. In the aforementioned article penned by Roosevelt, he had suggested ways to make the vice president a more useful and empowered officer of the government. And yet, having moved up to the presidency, Roosevelt no longer showed any inclination for expanding the responsibilities of the vice president, and he was steadfast in excluding Fairbanks from any significant role in the administration.[175]

There were two outcomes of Theodore Roosevelt's absolute neglect of Charles Fairbanks. The first was that the president publicly snubbed the only other nationally elected officer of the government for four years, thus undercutting the strides made by Garret Hobart. And second, Roosevelt's treatment of Fairbanks incrementally weakened the vice president's prospects for gaining the Republican presidential nomination in 1908. As the election approached, however, Roosevelt did manage to promote his personal choice for successor, the secretary of war, William Howard Taft.[176] Taft went on to win the presidency, bringing a new vice president with him and consigning Charles Fairbanks to political obscurity.

The new vice president arriving with Taft was James Sherman. Prior to his victory with Taft, Sherman had been elected to eight terms in the House of Representatives, representing a district in upstate New York. Sherman was not Taft's first choice for a running mate; however, after two well-regarded political figures had declined the opportunity to run for the second-highest office in the land, Sherman's supporters pressed for his nomination, arguing that he added the necessary conservative ballast to the more progressive Taft.[177] Besides, there no doubt was apprehension among some Republicans, who had grown weary of Roosevelt, that the former president would exercise too much influence on his protégé if Taft won.[178]

Much to the chagrin of Sherman's detractors, the vice president succeeded in gradually drawing Taft away from the progressive wing of the Republican Party, although he never became an intimate adviser to the president.[179] As to the four years Sherman was the Senate's presiding officer, his service was adequate, but hardly noteworthy; it is recalled most, if at all, for the three tie-breaking votes he cast on one day, and within thirty minutes.[180] It is a record that stands, but it is of dubious importance today.

At the 1912 Republican Party convention, President Taft and Vice President Sherman were nominated, again, to vie for another term in office. Sherman's nomination was notable because it represented the first time in eighty years that an incumbent vice president was nominated to run for a second term. Taft and Sherman then stood for reelection, facing three viable sets of opposition nominees: Democrats Woodrow Wilson and Thomas Marshall, Theodore Roosevelt and Hiram Johnson of the Progressive Party, and Socialist Party candidates Eugene Debs and Emil Seidel.

Although their reelection bid ended in resounding failure, anything Sherman might have done for the ticket was not to be realized. From the outset of the campaign, it was acknowledged by all that Sherman was too ill with heart disease to engage in electioneering.[181] For that matter, Sherman never should have been nominated, given that the 1912 election transpired in an era when vice-presidential candidates were expected to take on the bulk of the requisite traveling and speechmaking for the ticket, while presidential nominees had a nominal role in the campaign. Regardless, the incumbent vice president's campaign activities would have proved futile. On the day of the election, James Sherman's name was listed on the ballot in every state, but the vice president had been dead for not quite a week.

A sufficient number of the electorate chose to retire Taft and Sherman, either by voting for the winning candidates, Woodrow Wilson and Thomas Marshall, or because their votes went to the second-place team of Theodore Roosevelt and Hiram Johnson. It is the only time in American election history that a third party presidential ticket has bested at least one of the major political parties. Of course, coming in second in a presidential election does not win the White House, and so Roosevelt and Johnson were relegated to a footnote in electoral history, while Wilson and Marshall came to power.

The victors were an improbable pair. Thomas Marshall was a simple person, known for his wit and earthiness, whereas Woodrow Wilson was recognized for being cerebral and aloof. But they were not put together in order to construct a harmonious executive team. Plainly, Marshall was added to the ticket because he came from Indiana and Wilson hailed from New Jersey. Giving a measure of balance to the ticket, as always, transcended any consideration of skill, intellect, or qualifications. Not that Marshall was entirely unqualified for the vice presidency or the presidency. If presidential candidates were judged solely on their time in elective office, then Marshall should have topped the Democratic ticket with his term as the governor of Indiana having been longer than Wilson's fleeting governorship of New Jersey.

If, at the onset of his new administration, Wilson failed to initiate a new approach to the vice presidency, Marshall should not have been surprised. Wilson had written a comprehensive text on the United States government, first published twenty-seven years prior to his winning the presidency. Wilson's *Congressional Government* outlined the ways in which the House and the Senate, as well as the executive, functioned independently and as interrelated branches of the national government. Yet when it came to the American vice presidency, he devoted just a single paragraph to it. Wilson's contempt for the number two office was palpable; he claimed that

> there is very little to be said about the Vice-President of the United States. His position is one of anomalous insignificance and curious uncertainty ... It is one of the remarkable things about him, that it is hard to find in sketching the government any proper place to discuss him ... He is simply a judicial officer set to moderate the proceedings of an assembly whose rules he has had no voice in framing and can have no voice in changing ... His chief dignity, next to presiding over the Senate, lies in the circumstance that he is awaiting the death or disability of the President. And the chief embarrassment in discussing his office is, that in explaining how little there is to be said about it one has evidently said all there is to say.[182]

The first years of the Wilson administration were eventful, although not for Thomas Marshall. The vice president was more akin to an elected bystander than an active participant in the executive government; hence, Marshall was of scant value to the administration. It was an arrangement that continued for the entirety of Marshall's time as vice president, and one that was not enhanced by Wilson's attitude of indifference. This was manifest in that Wilson rarely met with the vice president, including him only sparingly in government business.

But Marshall did have his responsibilities in the Senate. In his capacity as the presiding officer, he oversaw debate on countless matters, including the entrance of the United States into the First World War, the Treaty of Versailles, the League of Nations, and the struggle over extending the suffrage to women. Of the latter issue, Marshall was opposed and later suggested that the proposed "amendment really was submitted to the people in self-defense, to get rid of these women in order that some business might be transacted."[183]

Marshall interjected himself in the proceedings of the Senate infrequently and generally appeared amused by the office he held. Likewise, he understood that when it came to the vice presidency, the broader public seemed bemused. He once described the public perception of the vice president in this way: "The Vice-President's Chamber is adjacent to the Senate Chamber, and so small that to survive it is necessary to keep the door open in order to obtain the necessary cubic feet of air. When the vice-president is in the room these guides go by with their guests, stop and point him out, as though he were a curiosity."[184]

There was one milestone Marshall did reach when he was vice president. This came about with his re-nomination and subsequent reelection in 1916, making him the first vice president in eighty-eight years to be reelected. Not since John Calhoun's victory in 1828 had a vice president achieved this distinction. Then again, Marshall's reelection had portent beyond his personal gain, for his return to office augured a newfound prominence for occupants of the vice presidency. Specifically, although James Sherman lost his reelection bid, and died while trying, he nevertheless had gained a second nomination, as did Marshall immediately after him. This then was the beginning of the pattern of the incumbent vice president being the presumptive nominee for a second term. It is a pattern that has been disrupted only one time since, and naturally it mirrors the pattern that had begun earlier, and continues to this day, for all incumbent presidents.

Even if Thomas Marshall did not appear to be awaiting the death or disability of Woodrow Wilson, as Wilson foretold when writing of the vice president, he did have to face the uncertainty that arises when a president is rendered disabled. It was a protracted affair that, to a great extent, defined his eight years as vice president. In brief, in 1919 President Wilson suffered a stroke. Following the stroke, uncertainty prevailed as to who was running the government. The accepted narrative is that Edith Wilson, the president's second wife, and Joseph Tumulty, his personal secretary, were filtering the specifics, as well as the scope, of information Wilson had access to, and, of greater consequence, who in the administration was allowed to meet with the president.[185]

As time and events moved forward, and it became evident that Wilson was mentally and physically compromised, perhaps severely, the discussion among the cabinet turned to Vice President Marshall and the prospect of his assuming the executive responsibilities of the president. Robert Lansing, who was then secretary of state, argued that the Constitution gave Marshall the authority to act in the place of Wilson—specifically the proviso on presidential inability, wherein the powers and responsibilities of the president are intended to devolve to the vice president—and that indeed, Marshall's position superseded that of Edith Wilson or Tumulty.[186]

Lansing's overtures on behalf of Marshall—in conjunction with the former having convened informal cabinet meetings several times during the president's controlled isolation—led to a series of provocative written exchanges between President Wilson and Lansing, and only concluded when Lansing resigned from office.[187] There is no question that Lansing was the author of his letters to the president; however, whether or not President Wilson, during this period, was actually writing the letters that bore his signature—to Lansing and to others—remains undetermined.

The reluctance on the part of Wilson, his wife, and his secretary, to allow Marshall to manage the executive branch during the president's protracted illness does not add up. For instance, at Wilson's request, the vice president had conducted cabinet meetings when the president traveled overseas.[188] Granted, it was primarily a symbolic gesture by Wilson, but it did bring Marshall into the executive councils of government, albeit provisionally. However, what was equally striking was that in the aftermath of Wilson's stroke it was obvious to those who saw the president that he was severely debilitated, and yet the vice president failed to rise to the challenge. Certainly Marshall should be commended for not tastelessly seizing power when he might have, but he was much too passive in response to the crisis then gripping the executive branch.

Similar to the situation Chester Arthur had faced, Thomas Marshall was unable to turn to precedence for guidance, and the Constitution was vague, at best, on the procedures for handling presidential inabilities. In all likelihood, the history of the last years of the Marshall vice presidency would read differently if Vice President Arthur had not exercised restraint. Still, Arthur did engage the heads of the executive departments over the course of Garfield's ordeal, and he likewise kept abreast of the affairs of state. Conversely, Marshall was idle and knew no more about President Wilson's condition, or the operation of the executive government, than what he read or heard second-hand. At this critical time in Marshall's life, and in the life of the nation he served, he chose inaction, muddling on, until his term in office came to a close.

The end of Thomas Marshall's vice presidency marked the end of his political career; it also signaled the commencement of a new era for the American vice presidency. After Marshall, the vice presidency started to change; it was an incremental transformation, both aided and hindered in its progress by presidents, as well as by the caliber of individuals who held the second office. But when the American vice presidency finally began to morph into a modern political institution, it was never to return to its earlier, insignificant form.

4

THE MODERN VICE PRESIDENCY

FROM COOLIDGE TO JOHNSON

While I was Vice President, Roosevelt used me in a way
which made the office for a time a very great office.
–Vice President Henry A. Wallace

It would be more straightforward to embark on a consideration of the modern American vice presidency with the first elected vice president of the twentieth century. Such a demarcation would perfectly bracket the century, beginning with the first year of the century and the election of one of the most colorful political figures ever to hold the office, Theodore Roosevelt, and culminating with the close of the century and the tenure of one of the most substantial vice presidents to date, Al Gore. Further underscoring the preceding framework, Gore's successor and the first vice president elected to serve in the twenty-first century was Dick Cheney. Although proving less colorful than many of his predecessors, Cheney became one of the most influential and powerful vice presidents in the history of the institution. Alas, the modern vice presidency did not take shape within a perfect framework, nor did it initially emerge in the form of a visionary and vigorous individual; instead, the least likely of political leaders was in place for the transformation of the institution.

ONSET OF THE MODERN INSTITUTION (1921–1929)

For many, the name Calvin Coolidge evokes the image of an unusually taciturn president who spent much of his tenure napping and detached from the collapsing social and political world outside of the White House. If the preceding is an apt description of Coolidge as president, it is a caricature equally suited to many of his predecessors in the vice presidency. More to the point, if Coolidge was a reticent and ineffective president in the six years he held the office, the two years and six months that he served as vice president offer an entirely different portrait of the man, as does much of his pre-White House experience.

To a certain degree, Coolidge was the ideal choice for vice president. He had come to the office well prepared and thoroughly engaged by public administration and policy formulation. Having first served in local government, Coolidge had steadily moved up the elective office ladder, with the work of each new position adding to his political deftness. As a Massachusetts state senator, Coolidge was elected president of the senate by his colleagues and was recognized for being a talented parliamentarian, proficient in working with all parties.[1] At all times he exhibited a predilection for activist government and progressive political views, often supported labor unions, repeatedly backed the democratization of electoral processes, and consistently advocated for consumer protections.[2]

From the state senate, Coolidge was next elected lieutenant governor. As was already detailed, lieutenant governors of the colonial period were the source from which the position of the vice president was drawn. Because there was generally satisfaction with the colonial lieutenant governors, there was less resistance than there might otherwise have been to incorporating the vice presidency into the Constitution. For Coolidge, besides his relinquishment of the presiding officer's position in the senate, serving as the lieutenant governor of Massachusetts gave him nearly commensurate experience to that of the nation's second-in-command. This was rather ironic in that the lieutenant governor, at least in Massachusetts, was not the designated presiding officer of the state senate, therefore differing from the vice president on this one account. In Massachusetts, the lieutenant governor was intended to be a genuine deputy to the state's governor. Coolidge, who as a state senator had greatly valued the time he spent presiding in the senate, but gave it up for the lieutenant governorship, later described his great satisfaction with presiding in the upper chamber of the national legislature.

Calvin Coolidge was definitely an ambitious politician, and yet he accepted the inherent limitations to the position for which he had been elected. Coolidge described his notion of the second-in-command in this way:

> I apprehend that I was elected by the people of Massachusetts to a definite job, second in the administration, a long ways behind the first. I accepted the office and my duty is perfectly clear—to back up the administration to the limit, whether I like it or do not like it. If this position should ever be so bad that I positively cannot do this, then my duty is equally clear—to keep my mouth shut.[3]

Coolidge had articulated a well-defined idea of the rightful role for the lieutenant governor; nonetheless, his sights were definitely set on the governorship. Hence, after twice winning reelection as lieutenant governor, he attained the governor's job in 1918, just two years before he earned the vice-presidential nomination. Even if Coolidge's tenure as Massachusetts's chief executive was brief, it was long enough to launch a national political career. Based primarily on the strength of his stern rebuke of Boston's striking police union, the Coolidge brand was established: cool in the face of adversity, an advocate for law and order at any cost. There was an ancillary benefit to Coolidge's management of the situation, as it put him in good stead with the growing conservative wing of the national Republican Party. Even with his relatively progressive record as a state legislator, lieutenant governor, and governor, Coolidge's response to the strikers created the common perception that he was indeed a conservative.[4]

The nomination of Coolidge for vice president came after a movement to make him the presidential nominee failed to materialize in the months prior to the national convention and when a fleeting convention-based candidacy for the nomination fizzled out as well.[5] Such was not the case for the eventual Republican nominee for president, Senator Warren Harding. Harding was the archetypal party man and was never cited for his unconventional way of thinking. Still, Harding did possess rather remarkable ideas about the vice presidency. At the outset of the general election campaign, Harding had this to say about the vice presidency and Calvin Coolidge:

> I think the Vice-President should be more than a mere substitute in waiting. In reestablishing coordination between the Executive office and the Senate, the Vice-President can and ought to play a big part, and I have been telling Governor Coolidge how much I wish him to be not only a participant in the campaign, but how much I wish him to be a helpful part of a Republican Administration. The country needs the counsel and the becoming participation in government of such men as Governor Coolidge.[6]

Harding's public pronouncement on the way in which the vice president would best fit in the administration presumably meant that the utility of the office would be increased, and he had chosen Coolidge to make it happen. The most promising manifestation of this was in Harding's pre-election suggestion for Coolidge to regularly attend meetings of the cabinet. It was an offer Coolidge accepted when Harding formally reiterated the plan after their mutual inauguration.[7] By this act, Harding had made the vice president a de facto member of the group.

As the first vice president to routinely attend cabinet meetings, Coolidge was, if not always a vital participant in the cabinet's discussions, at the very least an undeniable figure in the executive government. However, Coolidge's presence at meetings of the cabinet signaled something much more profound. By inviting the vice president into the cabinet, Warren Harding set in motion the modern American vice presidency; it was the single most substantial act of Harding's presidency. And it was an act that, besides one unusual exception, set a precedent for all successive vice presidents.

It had always been a paradox that the vice president, as one of only two nationally elected executive officers, had never been considered part of the executive branch of the government. Intrinsically, this then meant that the vice president lacked parity with the heads of the executive departments, all of whom sat in the president's cabinet. Additionally, and up to the time of Coolidge's election with Harding, as the constitutionally designated president of the Senate, the vice president was identified almost exclusively with the legislative branch. But inclusion in the president's cabinet marked the vice president as a tangible member of the executive branch.

By most accounts Coolidge was less a contributor to cabinet meetings than he was an observer.[8] Either way, Coolidge was convinced of the advantage in having the vice president in the cabinet, and after leaving public life he had this to say about it:

> If the Vice-President is a man of discretion and character, so that he can be relied upon to act as a subordinate in such position, he should be invited to sit with the Cabinet ... He may not help much in its deliberations, and only on rare occasions would he be a useful contact with the Congress, although his advice on the sentiment of the Senate is of much value, but he should be in the Cabinet because he might become President and ought to be informed on the policies of the administration ... But he will hear much and learn how to find out more if it ever becomes necessary. My experience in the Cabinet was of supreme value to me when I became President.[9]

When it came to his service as the presiding officer of the Senate, Calvin Coolidge was an anomaly among vice presidents. This was because Coolidge, unlike most of his predecessors, did not find the upper chamber of Congress at all tedious. Writing about that period, six years after leaving the vice presidency, Coolidge claimed that "presiding over the Senate was fascinating to me. That branch of the Congress has its own methods and traditions which may strike the outsider as peculiar ... It may seem that debate is endless, but ... I was entertained and instructed by the debates."[10]

Then again, and notwithstanding his fascination with the Senate, Coolidge did add one caveat to his admiration for the upper chamber. He later claimed he had "intended to become a student of the Senate rules and I did learn much about them, but I soon found that the Senate had but one fixed rule, subject to exceptions of course, which was to the effect that the Senate would do anything it wanted to do whenever it wanted to do it."[11]

Nor did Coolidge find the position of presiding officer wholly lacking in power. To his way of thinking, the mechanics of presiding allowed the vice president to retain a measure of power over one half of the legislative branch of government. Hence, Coolidge suggested that "the President of the Senate can and does exercise a good deal of influence over its deliberations. The Constitution gives him the power to preside, which is the power to recognize whom he will. That often means that he decides what business is to be taken up and who is to have the floor for debate at any specific time."[12]

Calvin Coolidge's view on the vice president in the legislature was expansive; it suggested a larger role in determining what the Senate attended to than was the reality before, then, or since. Still, regardless of the relative power of the vice president over the Senate, in the course of the nearly three years Coolidge was the presiding officer, he dedicated more time to the daily drudgery of the proceedings than did the lot of his predecessors. Even Thomas Jefferson, just ten days into his vice-presidential term, had excused himself from the chair for a brief respite at his home, Monticello; it was a liberty Coolidge would never have dreamed of taking.[13]

There were other ways Coolidge confirmed the arrival of a different and more notable vice presidency. For instance, he seemed to enjoy the social perks that came with being the vice president of the United States. Writing in his inimitable and understated style, he reflected at length on the benefits in being the second-highest-ranking government official in the nation:

> Very much is said and written concerning the amount of dining out that the Vice-President does. As the President is not available for social dinners of course the next officer in rank is much sought after for such occasions ... When we first went to Washington Mrs. Coolidge and I quite enjoyed the social dinners. As we were always the ranking guests we had the privilege of arriving last and leaving first, so that we were usually home by ten o'clock. It will be seen that this was far from burdensome. We found it a most enjoyable opportunity for getting acquainted and could scarcely comprehend how anyone who had the privilege of sitting at a table surrounded by representatives of the Cabinet, the Congress, the Diplomatic Corps and the Army and Navy would not find it interesting.[14]

Coolidge's recognition of what he viewed as the exalted status of the vice president did not end with his appreciation for social engagements and prestigious dinner companions. Like those who served in the office before him, Coolidge was compelled to locate and provide for his own housing for the duration of his term in office. Housing for the vice president was the concern of every vice president, beginning with John Adams. Yet by the time Coolidge arrived in the capital, the vice president was still not considered worthy of publicly financed housing. To Coolidge, this was a situation peculiar and unbefitting for a public official ranked as high as the vice president; he therefore posited:

> But my experience has convinced me that an official residence with suitable maintenance should be provided for the Vice-President. Under the present system he is not lacking in dignity but he has no fixed position. The great office should have a settled and permanent habitation and a place, irrespective of the financial ability of its temporary occupant. While I was glad to be relieved of the responsibility of a public establishment, nevertheless, it is a duty the second officer of the nation should assume. It would be much more in harmony with our theory of equality if each Vice-President held the same position in the Capital City.[15]

Today, Coolidge's observations on the lack of adequate housing for the vice president might seem trivial. But when he wrote of his concerns on this matter, he had already served as vice president and president and was retired from public life; still, the former chief executive thought enough of the topic to ruminate on it in his memoirs. With hindsight as his guide, Coolidge was aware that the office of vice president continued to be dismissed. As one who had held the office, he knew all too well that the American vice presidency was a vastly underappreciated institution of the government, and yet he seemed to understand that, quite possibly, the institution had finally arrived.

From his attendance in the cabinet, to his overstated view of the role of the vice president in the Senate, Coolidge saw great value in being the second-in-command. If he found certain aspects of the vice presidency wanting—particularly the absence of a permanent residence—his take on the office was that it was time for the vice presidency to be recognized for what it was: a nationally elected office of the government, second only to the presidency.

In the months leading up to the 1924 presidential election, there was well-founded speculation that Coolidge would be dropped from the ticket.[16] Coolidge was never an intimate of President Harding, and many of the president's closest advisers presumably would have been content to drop him from the ticket in 1924. Moreover, progressive Republicans had made gains in the 1922 midterm elections. Movement in this direction was substantial enough that Harding and Coolidge possibly would have faced challenges from within their own party, putting both men on the defensive; it was a predicament which no doubt would have been compounded by the scandals of the Harding administration that later surfaced.

The premature death of President Harding in August of 1923, however, thrust Coolidge into the presidency instead of off the ticket. At the time, Coolidge was out of the capital, spending the entire summer at his father's country home in Vermont. The ritual of Coolidge's ascension to the presidency was later recreated in a painting that has since become a staple of political Americana.[17] The painting depicts Vice President Coolidge taking the presidential oath of office from his father—who was a public notary—in a small room in the father's house. The room appears to be illuminated solely by a kerosene lamp; on a nearby table the family's "Bible, the Revised Laws of Vermont and a catalogue of farming tools" are discernible.[18]

Besides capturing a moment in history, the outwardly simple scene is telling in that presidential succession had obviously advanced since John Tyler ascended to the presidency upon William Henry Harrison's death, eighty-two years earlier. In the years that separated Tyler and Coolidge, four vice presidents had risen to the presidency because of the death of the president, and with each, any uncertainty about their right to assume the presidency had whittled away, giving in to ritual solemnity. And so, Vice President Coolidge, woken in the middle of the night with news of the president's passing, simply claimed the presidency to be rightfully his.[19]

In 1923, the Constitution still lacked a method for replacing the vice president. As it stood, President Coolidge, the government, and the nation were without a vice president until the next election was held—fifteen months hence—and only then after the new vice president was inaugurated in March of 1925, four months past the election. Fortunately Coolidge appeared to be healthy at the onset of his presidency, so there was no readily apparent cause for concern about the vacancy in the vice presidency. Besides, the Presidential Succession Act of 1886 was in place; if something happened to Coolidge, the secretary of state would have moved into the White House. All the same, Coolidge managed to complete the remaining year of Warren Harding's term, minus a vice president.

It was a given that delegates to the 1924 Republican convention would again make Calvin Coolidge the nominee of their party, except on this occasion, he would be at the top of the ticket. The real question that year was who the nominee for vice president might be. Coolidge had indicated his preference for Senator William Borah, a westerner who provided ballast to Coolidge's New England roots, but Borah had no interest in the nomination.[20] Another possibility was former Illinois governor Frank Lowden. Lowden actually won the nomination, but refused to be a candidate.[21] With Lowden's disavowal of the nomination definite, the convention next turned to and nominated Charles Dawes. Dawes was formerly the comptroller of currency in the McKinley administration, an adviser and close friend to President McKinley, an officer in the First World War, and the first director of the federal government's Bureau of the Budget in the Harding administration. Remarkably, when Dawes received his party's nomination for vice president, he had run for elective office just once before, and lost.

Dawes initially achieved popular acclaim for his actions during and after the First World War, commencing with an extraordinarily swift rise in rank—from lowly Army bureaucrat in purchasing, to brigadier general—in one year. In the post-war years, President Harding recruited Dawes to oversee the Allied Reparation Commission, a group convened solely to develop a scheme to hold Germany accountable for its part in the war. The resulting plan, irrespective of the involvement of the other commission members, was promptly labeled the Dawes Plan.

In addition, Dawes earned a reputation as an outspoken political figure for his blunt testimony before a congressional committee that was scrutinizing the price he had paid for supplies during the war. It was his explicit choice of words when testifying that earned him the sobriquet that was attached to him from that day forward: "Hell and Maria Dawes." This was more than a colorful nickname, as the expression warned all that Dawes was verbose and aggressive, a combination that made him the prototype for confrontational vice-presidential candidates. Indeed, by his incessant electioneering for the Coolidge-Dawes ticket—in sheer miles covered, speeches delivered, and the occasionally strident tone of his rhetoric—Dawes served as the blueprint for future vice-presidential nominees on the campaign trail.[22] His influence and unique style was later noticeable in the tenor and the tactics adopted by several vice-presidential nominees, including Henry Wallace, Richard Nixon, Spiro Agnew, Sargent Shriver, Robert Dole, Dick Cheney, and Sarah Palin.

Despite Dawes not being Coolidge's first choice for a running mate, their relationship had begun satisfactorily. Well prior to the 1924 nominating convention, Coolidge had reached out to Dawes in the weeks following the death of President Harding. At that time, Coolidge gave every indication that he valued Dawes and that he hoped to retain the latter man's connection to the new administration.[23] But when personal tragedy befell President Coolidge, not quite a month after the convention, the part Dawes played in the subsequent campaign assumed greater import.

In the summer of 1924, Calvin Coolidge Jr., the younger of Coolidge's two sons, had played a spirited tennis match on the White House grounds. Playing in shoes without socks, Calvin Jr. induced a blister on one toe which rapidly developed into critical blood poisoning, killing the president's son within eight days. In the months and years to come, Coolidge's profound grief adversely defined his presidency. What is more,

Coolidge's depression over his dead son was to have a reciprocal, albeit passing, effect on the modern American vice presidency.[24]

The earliest manifestation of Coolidge's grief was his complete withdrawal from the 1924 general election campaign. He later acknowledged this, stating that he "did not attend any partisan meetings or make any purely political speeches during the campaign ... My own participation was delayed by the death of my son."[25] Dawes too accepted it was not Coolidge, but he, the candidate for vice president, who "was expected to bear the burden so far as activity" in the campaign.[26]

Apart from the unfortunate tragedy prompting Coolidge's disengagement, the arrangement actually suited the innate qualities of the two nominees. Where Coolidge was aloof, Dawes was gregarious. And if Coolidge was generally mute, Dawes was perpetually loquacious. In this way, the Coolidge-Dawes pairing offered contrasting symmetry in style; it likewise proved a winning combination, with the ticket capturing over 50 percent of the popular vote and 382 of the 531 votes of the Electoral College.

With the glow of their victory still bright, Dawes let the president know that he preferred not to be included in meetings of the president's cabinet. Dawes wrote in his journal of the rationale behind his decision:

> I have always sensed the inherent embarrassments involved in the plan of having the Vice President sit in the Cabinet, as Coolidge did under the Harding administration. After my election, not knowing how Coolidge felt about it, I wrote him stating my views on the subject.
>
> This was done to relieve him—if he shared my views—of any embarrassment, if he desired to carry them out, notwithstanding the fact that he had accepted Harding's invitation. Again I did not want to do him the discourtesy of declining a possible invitation, and I thus avoided any necessity for such a course, however remote.[27]

The problem was that Coolidge never extended any such offer to his own vice president, and the presumption on Dawes's part rankled Coolidge. It is quite obvious from his autobiography that Coolidge saw the advantage in having the vice president in the cabinet. He appreciated the preparatory value afforded by such inclusion, and he was grateful to Harding for the gesture. Perhaps Coolidge never reconciled himself to what he took to be an affront by an immodest Dawes; if so, it might explain why Coolidge, years later when he composed his autobiography, omitted any mention, by name, of his own vice president.[28] Or, quite possibly, Coolidge ignored Dawes in his memoirs because he was similarly irked by other, subsequent actions of Vice President Dawes.

Of the sum of his tenure, the day Dawes was sworn in as the vice president is the one most commonly recalled. After taking the oath of office, Dawes launched into an inaugural address wherein he confronted the Senate membership for its arcane practices, chastising what he viewed as the exploitation of the filibuster.[29] The speech did nothing to change minds, nor rules; instead, it made the vice president, who was not a member of the chamber, look the part of usurper in the tradition-bound institution. With his rebuke of Senate practices on record, his relations with its membership were tainted for the remainder of his time as presiding officer. Never one to wilt from confrontation, Dawes pursued his argument outside the Senate. He took his cause to the people, traveling across the country, delivering a stock speech on the flaws of the United States Senate.[30]

But his time in office was further undermined by an incident which colored the public perception of vice presidents in general and of Dawes, specifically. Unlike his controversial inaugural remarks before the Senate, in this instance he did not come across as one who challenged institutional traditions; instead, he appeared merely to meet the low expectations the broader public maintained for the vice president. When President Coolidge's appointment for attorney general faced unexpected opposition in the Senate, the tie-breaking vote of the vice president was essential if the president's choice was going to gain a seat in the cabinet. At the critical moment, when the vice president might have exercised one of the only constitutionally provided prerogatives of the office, Dawes was napping in a hotel suite a few blocks from the Capitol. By the time the vice president was awakened and was hurried to the Senate, the vote had already been recorded and the president's nominee for attorney general rejected.[31]

Neither his reprimand of a long-held Senate prerogative, nor his slumbering away from the Capitol when he should have been presiding, represented a complete retreat from the advances made during the Coolidge vice presidency. It is true that Dawes was not, as Coolidge had been, in attendance at meetings of the cabinet; likewise, he was never the obsequious presiding officer Coolidge was when in the Senate. But Dawes did bring sorely needed gravitas to the vice presidency when he won the 1925 Nobel Prize in Peace, for his earlier work on the German reparations plan.

Now and again Dawes was instrumental in the foreign policy of the Coolidge administration. For two reasons this was a critical, as well as an appropriate, place for his involvement. To start, Dawes was known on the international stage, primarily from his leadership on the Dawes Plan and for the Nobel Prize that followed. Such recognition also made Dawes an anomaly for a vice president of the United States in the nineteenth or early twentieth centuries. And because it was plain to most that President Coolidge was not going to be an especially extroverted and adventuresome president—at home or abroad—then it was important that a known commodity in the administration partook, on some level, in the diplomatic sphere, although in Dawes's case, such a role was discreet and generally escaped notice. For instance, at one point Dawes deliberately met with an administration supporter away from the capital to encourage him to accept a diplomatic posting to Mexico, an endeavor that subsequently led to significant policy advances in the region, which otherwise would not have been achieved.[32]

On the domestic front, Dawes sometimes charted his own course. On one occasion, he was an unofficial mediator for a farm bill passed by the House but stalled in the Senate. Dawes eventually affected consensus on the bill and it was sent to the president for his signature, though Coolidge ultimately negated his vice president's actions by vetoing the bill.[33] Dawes played, as one writer noted soon after his leaving office, a "deeply-hidden but nevertheless potent role in legislative affairs."[34] In the preceding case, and in a smattering of others, Dawes took the initiative, using his position as an executive of the national government to shape administration business when he could, and usually without the president noticing.

The personal tragedy Calvin Coolidge endured had an impact on his governance, on the policy agenda of his administration, and even on the American vice presidency. As such, Charles Dawes is an outlier in the trajectory of the modern vice presidency, in that President Coolidge was disconnected from his job, and he therefore neglected to involve numerous members of the administration, not the least of whom was his vice president. Had Coolidge not been depressed and detached, Dawes likely would have been one of the more effective twentieth century vice presidents. He certainly brought qualities and experience complimentary to the modern institution: intelligence, international recognition, self-assured independence, and formidable powers of persuasion. One historian described both the promise and the predicament the character of the thirtieth vice president presented, suggesting that because of "his bull-like integrity Dawes was to become recognized as one of the few outstanding Vice Presidents, but for the same reason he was as often to hamstring the Administration as he was to help it."[35]

In the aftermath of his youngest son's death, Coolidge was a different man and thus a different kind of chief executive. The puzzle of the Coolidge-Dawes relationship, then, is this: Coolidge's vice-presidential tenure marked the onset of the modern institution, yet when tragedy struck the Coolidge family, the Dawes vice presidency suffered, making his tenure an ephemeral return to a bygone era. Still, Dawes left enough of an imprint, and was a significant enough public figure, that the modern vice presidency began to recover soon after he left office.

BACK IN THE CABINET (1929–1941)

It is unfortunate that Charles Dawes was not used to better advantage by Calvin Coolidge. He came into the vice presidency familiar with the executive councils of government from his work in the McKinley and Harding administrations. And he was certainly capable of competently and vigorously completing any assignment Coolidge might have given him. If Dawes squandered a measure of his usefulness as a liaison between the administration and the Senate, thus not fully participating in the legislature in the manner Warren Harding had proposed for the vice president, Coolidge still should have made better use of his vice president when advancing the administration's policies in Congress.

At any rate, Coolidge chose to overlook Dawes while both were in office, and as the next quadrennial election approached, the president never entertained the idea of Dawes for a successor. Coolidge did make his choice for the 1928 election known, although it was not the front-runner for the nomination, the commerce secretary, Herbert Hoover. Choosing to look outside of his own administration, Coolidge settled on the Senate's majority leader, Charles Curtis, for his preferred successor.[36] Nevertheless, when Coolidge's preference for president did not resonate with the nominating convention, and Hoover subsequently captured the nomination, Curtis ended up the Republican nominee for vice president instead.

In every respect, Charles Curtis was a languid political figure. His childhood and early adulthood, however, were far from dull, and for that reason his life made for a great campaign biography.[37] Curtis was a native of Topeka, Kansas and was descended on his mother's side from a Kaw Indian chief. For part of his formative years, Curtis lived with relatives on a federal reservation, and for a time he earned a living as a jockey on the Midwest racing circuit. But it was his Native American ancestral connection that was the principal identifier for Curtis throughout his lifetime, and for that reason, he never missed an opportunity, especially when he was vice president, to advertise his unique bloodline.

After serving in the House of Representatives, Curtis moved up to the Senate, where he eventually rose within the ranks of his party to serve as Republican majority leader. His rise did not come about because of his modernism or his vibrant personality; instead, he achieved success in the hierarchy of the Senate as an outcome of his profound conservatism, and because of his deference to those who had inhabited the institution the longest.

By the time of the 1928 Republican Party convention, Curtis was an entrenched member of the Republican political establishment. At that point, he already had served in the Congress for thirty-four of the previous thirty-five years, and he was therefore a distant contender for the presidential nomination; still, his attempt to win the nomination proved futile and he watched as the more charismatic Hoover surpassed him to take the top spot.[38] With Hoover in place, and President Coolidge implying that he would be insulted if Vice President Dawes was returned to the second office—and after Theodore Roosevelt Jr. had "groveled" in a failed attempt to reclaim the vice presidency for his family—Republican leaders turned to the steadfast Curtis.[39] Left, then, without the presidential nomination, and even with his previous disavowal of any interest in the second office, Curtis accepted the vice-presidential nomination. And in so doing, Curtis chose to trade the tangible power of the majority leader for the transparent powerlessness of the vice presidency.

By acquiescing to be a candidate for vice president, Curtis unintentionally initiated a pattern of vice-presidential nominees coming from the leadership of Congress. Hence, when either of the major political parties sought nominees for vice president over the course of the twentieth century, both regularly turned to the highest ranks of Congress. In addition to Curtis, the list of congressional leaders willing to accept the second spot on the ticket includes John Nance Garner, Joseph Robinson, Charles McNary, Alben Barkley, Lyndon Johnson, and Hubert Humphrey.[40]

Going to the ranks of the congressional leadership for nominees confirmed that the Congress harbored a pool of experienced political figures. But it also indicated that a higher caliber of elected official was amenable to relinquishing the recognized power of a leadership position in the legislative branch for the often dicey chance at election to the vice presidency. Alas, on both occasions Curtis stood for national office, he faced Democratic nominees for vice president who held the top leadership positions in the Congress.[41] For Curtis, the job of vice president probably seemed a poor trade for that of the majority leader. Then again, four vice presidents had succeeded to the presidency since his birth, so he may have concluded that the vice presidency was his best shot at the presidency.

As it turns out, Charles Curtis made a fortuitous decision by accepting the nomination for vice president, for he and Herbert Hoover handily won the 1928 election. Although their victory was evidence of a successful electoral team, Curtis and Hoover were of dissimilar personalities and political experiences, and from the outset they maintained an uneasy partnership. In part this was from residual anger Curtis held for having lost the presidential nomination to Hoover; however, in the main it was founded on the stark differences that defined each man. Curtis was the personification of the elder, rigid member of Congress—a total creature of the legislative branch—and was fifteen years senior to Hoover, as well. Conversely, Hoover's reputation was for energy and productivity and his political experience was entirely in executive and administrative government. Still, irrespective of all that separated the two men, Hoover reinstituted the practice of the vice president sitting with the cabinet; in effect, the president chose to bring the vice president back into the executive councils of the government.[42]

Why Hoover decided to include Curtis in the cabinet is difficult to determine. When Hoover wrote a three volume memoir, nearly twenty years after he and Curtis left office, he never makes note of Curtis in the cabinet, nor does he make any reference to the vice president's performance during the time they were in office.[43] For that matter, Hoover alludes to Curtis just three times in the entirety of his memoirs. But in bringing Curtis into cabinet meetings, it is possible that Hoover was inspired by serving in the Harding cabinet with Vice President Coolidge, and from that experience thought it was an appropriate place for the second officer of the nation. If Curtis was not an overly active participant in the cabinet, his presence there implied inclusion in the highest consultations of the executive branch; it was a step in the right direction for such a beleaguered institution of the government.

From a purely aesthetic perspective, three formal portraits of the president and the cabinet, in three different administrations, are illuminating to the state of the modern vice presidency at different junctures. In the photo of the Harding cabinet, Vice President Coolidge sits at the end of a long table, far removed from President Harding. And the photo of Coolidge's cabinet is notable for the conspicuous absence of Vice President Dawes. However, in the formal photo of the Hoover cabinet, Vice President Curtis sits on the president's immediate right. Hoover had facilitated the return of the vice president to the cabinet, as well as to the official photo of the group.

In the Senate, Curtis competently managed his responsibilities, and he proved, as Charles Dawes once described him, that he was "a fine presiding officer."[44] Mostly Curtis presided with dignity and fairness, yet more times than not his fierce partisanship influenced his rulings from the chair. What Curtis added most to the modern vice presidency, however, was a sense that the institution had arrived. In both his behavior and in his attitude, and even when he was gallingly portentous—which he often was from the moment he repeated the vice-presidential oath of office—Curtis signaled that the vice president was second to just one.[45]

Much of what Curtis brought to the vice presidency is overlooked. Perhaps this is because the influence and scope of the vice presidency, as it now stands, contrasts so glaringly with where the institution was in the earlier decades of the twentieth century. Besides, the nature of the Hoover-Curtis association barred the vice president's involvement in much beyond the symbolic. As a result, Curtis tended to emphasize the ephemeral and aesthetic aspects of the office he held, giving added weight to concerns of minimal importance today.

Although there was a dose of mockery to it, one of Curtis's contemporaries captured the essence of what the modern American vice president had become—at least as personified by Curtis—claiming that formality and aplomb "oozes from his every pore, and he has set himself to the heroic task of making the Vice-Presidency a potent estate."[46] And when it came to the décor of the vice president's office, supposedly Curtis's offices were "one of the most lascivious sights of Washington" and included Native American memorabilia, as well as a desk chair with a plaque attached to it that read: "The Chief."[47] If some of his predecessors in office "had luxurious quarters," apparently it had been Curtis "who conceived the idea of blocking up a whole corridor to make a throne room and of fitting it out with such regal magnificence."[48]

By the time of their 1932 reelection campaign, Charles Curtis was seventy-two years old; he had never become an intimate of President Hoover, and for many Republicans at the nominating convention that year, he was the second choice for the second spot on the ticket, gaining the nomination only after his predecessor in office, Charles Dawes, declined another run.[49] In fairness to Curtis, he was a member of the administration that was in place for the implosion of the nation's economic system; it is unlikely that Hoover could have found any running mate to save the ticket.

When Hoover and Curtis were defeated by Franklin Roosevelt and John Nance Garner, the Curtis vice presidency was over; it would be up to the next president to determine where the institution stood. As for Curtis, he left office the first, and thus far only, vice president of Native American ancestry. But of more importance, Curtis reclaimed a visible place for the vice president in the executive branch. Even though President Hoover had opted not to seek Curtis's counsel, the stage was set for Curtis's successor to extend the boundaries of the institution even further, if the next president allowed.

John Nance Garner was in many ways the antithesis of his predecessor. At his best, or worst depending on one's view, he was the epitome of the back-slapping, salty talking, deal-making congressman. Moreover, he was a conservative southerner and the Speaker of the House of Representatives. Garner only agreed to be a candidate for vice president when his own presidential prospects diminished at the nominating convention. In consenting to be on the ticket with Roosevelt, he assumed he would prevent a divisive split in the Democratic Party.[50] And for a party stalwart like Garner, party unity was paramount.

Garner was the first of three vice presidents to serve with Roosevelt. All three were nominated for specific reasons, and all three held distinctive places in the Roosevelt epoch. Roosevelt certainly had different expectations for his trio of vice presidents, and therefore each was as useful to the president as he permitted them to be. As to Garner specifically, in conjunction with the southern advantage he brought to the electoral ticket, his utility to the president was mainly evident in his association with Congress. With his congressional career tied completely to the House of Representatives, Garner brought thirty years of legislative experience to the administration, including two years as minority leader and the same as Speaker. Plainly, Garner's ties to the Congress were strong, and in the eight years he was the vice president he cultivated valuable relations with members of the House and of the Senate.

The proposition has been made that within the power structure of the Congress, "the Vice-President, as presiding officer of the Senate, is more likely to be merely tolerated than looked to as a party leader."[51] Yet, because of Garner's heightened familiarity with Congress, and in light of his continued fraternization with its membership, he was, in the main, successful in marshaling his party for or against Roosevelt's proposals—employing the latter tactic frequently during their second term together.[52]

Garner respected the confines of the office he held, and therefore he was mindful of the limits to the power he possessed. He knew his was not a power derived from the Constitution, but was power based on who he was. To this idea, Garner explained that, as the vice president, he possessed "no arsenal from which to draw power. He has no offices to bestow or favors to extend. He can make power for himself sometimes by his personality and ability. Only if by his association with men they come to have friendship for him and faith in and respect for his judgment can he be influential."[53]

As their first term in office together played out, President Roosevelt sought Garner's counsel on domestic as well as foreign affairs, and the vice president was a vocal member when in gatherings of the cabinet.[54] Even when Garner privately disagreed with the president, he publicly worked for passage of Roosevelt's progressive agenda. But it was against type for Garner to subsume his conservative ideology to the president's liberalism for too long, and it was there that they eventually parted ways. Undeniably, Roosevelt was a practitioner of activist executive governance, and he was equally an advocate for broad government intervention in the social and economic life of the nation; it was a style and approach alien to Garner.[55]

It was after their lopsided reelection, in 1936, that Garner began to exhibit transparent opposition to Roosevelt's agenda.[56] Though there was divergence between the two men on several fronts, four specific cases arose which permanently ruptured their relationship. The first occurred a few weeks after the election and involved the tactical use of sit-down strikes by Michigan auto workers. Garner viewed the striking unionists as no more than lawbreakers doing the bidding of corrupt union leaders. In contrast, Roosevelt was sympathetic to the demands of the auto workers, and he hoped to settle the strike amicably, without bloodshed and by not acting directly against the striking workers.[57] Naturally Roosevelt prevailed, but not until after he and the vice president had, according to Garner, "the hottest argument we ever had."[58]

The second major conflict between Garner and Roosevelt surfaced when Roosevelt pushed forward with a plan to alter the composition of the Supreme Court. His proposal, if it had been passed by Congress, would have increased the number of sitting justices from nine to fifteen, thus allowing the president to refashion the top court in the land in his own ideological image. In an uncharacteristic move—at least for that point in their relationship—Roosevelt neglected to consult Garner about the merit, form, or feasibility of the proposal; therefore, the vice president was privately opposed to the plan from the moment the president blindsided him with it.[59] Garner was initially bound by loyalty to Roosevelt to support the court-packing plan. And later, when defeat of the proposal appeared certain, the president recruited Garner to craft a compromise plan. Nonetheless, it was all for show; it was widely understood the vice president opposed the president on the matter.

The third action by Roosevelt to severely strain his relations with Garner was his attempt to purge the Congress of Democratic members who were not steadfast supporters of the New Deal agenda. Roosevelt's scheme unfolded during the campaign that led to the 1938 midterm election and included appearances by the president in Democratic primaries, wherein he campaigned against incumbent Democrats who were inconsistent with their loyalty to him. Such an approach was anathema to a man as steeped in the Democratic Party as was Garner, and he conveyed his disapproval of the strategy to Roosevelt in no uncertain terms.[60]

The fourth break in Garner and Roosevelt's relationship was founded on a simple premise: Garner was opposed to Roosevelt seeking a third term as president. From Garner's perspective, no president should stay in office for three terms; it was an argument based on history, as well as on the notion that the two term presidency was by then an institutionalized practice.[61] At the same time he was making this case against Roosevelt's reelection, he advanced another argument for turning Roosevelt out of office. By Garner's way of thinking, two terms served in the vice presidency were ample preparation for his own term in the White House. Therefore, Garner suggested that he was the best alternative to Roosevelt for the Democratic nomination for president.[62] In the end, it was a futile bid by the vice president to gain the presidency and it guaranteed his absence from the Democratic ticket of 1940.

John Nance Garner's experience reaffirmed one of the paradoxes of the American vice presidency, and one that holds true to this day. The vice president is as essential and effective a member of the administration as the president permits. And though the vice president, like the president, is voted for by a national constituency, for all intents and purposes, the vice president serves at the president's discretion. For this reason, when Garner was no longer of use to Franklin Roosevelt, the president cut the vice president out of any substantive role in the administration. Garner continued to attend cabinet meetings, just as he had over the course of his tenure, but the last year of his second term was devoid of a single private meeting with Roosevelt.[63] Even when dealing with the Congress, where Garner had put his parliamentary skill to the advantage of the administration's agenda, Roosevelt forged ahead, sans Garner, using the power of the presidency instead of the legislative know-how of his first vice president.

At the 1940 Democratic convention, Franklin Roosevelt demonstrated his absolute control of the nomination process of his party. Apart from his own unprecedented nomination for a third term, Roosevelt engineered the replacement of John Nance Garner on the ticket. In a bold move, one that threatened to disrupt the Democratic Party, Roosevelt rebuked entrenched party leaders and staked his own candidacy, forcing his personal choice for the vice-presidential nomination: Henry A. Wallace.[64]

Not since Andrew Jackson insisted on Martin Van Buren for his running mate in 1832 had a president so completely dictated the selection of a vice-presidential nominee. In part, Wallace was chosen by Roosevelt in reaction to Garner. Of greater consequence, Roosevelt knew that he had found in Wallace the ideal modern American vice president.

ARCHETYPE FOR THE MODERN, SEMI-AUTONOMOUS VICE PRESIDENT (1941–1945)

In the fall of 1920, the *Saturday Evening Post* published an article written by that year's Democratic nominee for vice president, Franklin Roosevelt, titled "Can the Vice President be Useful?" As referenced earlier, in the article Roosevelt emphasized the value in making the vice president a more utilitarian member of the government than was previously the case. Roosevelt claimed,

> there is hardly any limitation upon the ways in which the Vice President might be of service to the President. He might serve as an executive aid to the President, and in that capacity could … exercise considerable influence through his close relationship with the President … He could, at the request of the President, serve in relation to the determination of large matters of policy that do not belong in the province of a member of the President's cabinet. He might serve as a kind of liaison officer to Congress and aid perhaps in carrying the large burden of interpreting administration policies to Congress and to the public.[65]

Franklin Roosevelt did not win the vice presidency in 1920, but he did, as president, augment the responsibilities of the vice president; as a result, he raised the expectations for the office and for whomever might hold it. In John Nance Garner, Roosevelt had the liaison to Congress that he had proposed when writing of the second office. And with his choice of Henry Wallace, Roosevelt gained a confidant and vice president who could be assigned wherever needed. But of greater significance, Roosevelt had found in Wallace a highly cerebral philosopher for his administration.[66] Wallace had served as Roosevelt's secretary of agriculture for eight years, proving to be the most effective department head in the executive branch. It was no surprise then, as the Wallace vice presidency moved forward, that Wallace personified the vice president as administrator.

As vice president and board chief, Wallace's ample skills as a public administrator, economist, and advocate for social justice were utilized in directing a considerable share of the government's domestic war preparation. Wallace understood the depth of his usefulness to the president, but he was equally aware that he was moving in a direction unfamiliar to the vice presidency. Along these lines, Wallace later observed that, while I was Vice President, Roosevelt used me in a way which made the office for a time a very great office. As is true with the Vice President when he is used in this way, and is true also of Cabinet officers, the importance depends on the will and desire of the President. My position to some extent was weak because there was no historical precedent for what Roosevelt did in precipitating me into key positions in the war effort.[67]

It was as the chief administrator of the Economic Defense Board (EDB), and for the expanded and renamed Board of Economic Warfare (BEW), that Wallace was put to work by Roosevelt in a way that no vice president before him ever had. In particular, in the time period leading to the Second World War, and then after the United States formally entered the conflict, Wallace efficiently managed several government entities with myriad responsibilities, nearly all of which fell under the umbrella of either the EDB or the BEW. Among the agencies Wallace commanded were the Office of Exports, the Office of Imports, and the Office of Warfare Analysis. The latter of the preceding three agencies was especially vital in the war effort; its principal mission was to choose what foreign targets should be bombed based on the economic value to enemy nations of those targets.

Wallace succeeded on many levels during his tenure running the BEW. At the same time, his objectives were oftentimes undercut by the enmity and competitiveness that frequently arises amongst competing bureaucratic organizations. Most notably, Roosevelt's secretary of the commerce, Jesse Jones, was an ideological adversary of Wallace and would prove to be a habitual antagonist to him for most of the four years he was vice president.[68] Jones had controlled the Reconstruction Finance Corporation (RFC) since the Hoover administration; it was a federal corporation mandated to borrow and disburse money to other federal agencies. As such, much of Wallace's far-reaching vision for the United States and for the world once the war was won, and that he hoped to implement via the work of the BEW and its sub-agencies, depended on the cooperation and largesse of the RFC—but only if Jones approved funding.

Today the specifics of the conflict between Wallace and Jones are not relevant. Frequently their disputes were petty, yet more times than not their clashes were fueled by conservative Democrats who had an ally in Jones and who were fixed on derailing Wallace's political career.[69] What is important is that the episodic infighting between Wallace and Jones threatened to destabilize the domestic wartime objectives President Roosevelt had set for the two men, their respective subordinates, and the government agencies they oversaw. Roosevelt was known to loathe when members of his administration competed against one another, and with the Wallace-Jones conflict increasingly being waged in public, the president was put in an untenable position.

Underscoring Roosevelt's predicament was that he alone was responsible for putting the vice president in command of a unit of the executive branch. Since it was an unprecedented assignment for a vice president, when it went awry, there was no ready solution. What Roosevelt chose to do was to relieve both Wallace and Jones of their respective assignments where they intersected. Therefore, the BEW was jettisoned for a new federal agency, the Office of Economic Warfare (OEW), and Wallace was not put in charge. Similarly, the authority Jones once had at the RFC was turned over to the new chief of the OEW.

Because Jones was a member of the cabinet, he was totally dependent on the president for his employment; for this reason, relieving him of certain responsibilities was straightforward for Roosevelt. In contrast, Wallace was an elected officer of the government and was not easily dismissed. But because the nature of the president-to-vice president arrangement always tilts toward the president, at any point Roosevelt could take back whatever authority he had previously granted Wallace. For Wallace, what mattered was not the loss of control of a bureaucratic organization by the vice president; what mattered was the perception of his having temporarily lost the confidence of the president he served. In this instance, although Roosevelt continued to rely on Wallace for the remainder of the term they shared, he demonstrated the advantage presidents hold over vice presidents. For when events were not going as Roosevelt wished, he simply pulled back on the expansion of the vice presidency.

Wallace also devoted his formidable intellectual and physical energies to planning for the improved world he hoped could be fashioned after the war was won. It was in this area that Wallace planned to implement the liberal philosophy of Franklin Roosevelt's New Deal, or, as Wallace conceived of it, the advent of the century of the common man.[70] On a practical level, Wallace was advocating the use of modern technology for the eradication of poverty, which, in his view, ultimately made for a better and more just society for all of humanity.

But Wallace went beyond planning for a future, idyllic world. He also made speaking tours across North and Central America, addressing anyone willing to listen, thus ensuring that the causes he advanced were heard of well beyond the insular political world of the nation's capital. Wallace likewise authored a series of books while he was part of the Roosevelt administration. This gave the vice president another means for articulating and disseminating his worldview; it was a worldview made plain with titles like *New Frontiers, Statesmanship and Religion, Paths to Plenty, Christian Bases of World Order, The Century of the Common Man, Sixty Million Jobs*, and an economic treatise, *Toward World Peace*. To those who admired Wallace and his work, he was a visionary and modern philosopher, yet to others, Wallace appeared to be a zealot, a mystic, or worse.[71]

From the start of Wallace's vice presidency, President Roosevelt insisted that Wallace be included, when practical, in all policy spheres of the administration. This contributed tremendously to the broad efficacy of Wallace's four years in office; it also made him the most fully engaged vice president to that point. Wallace's access to the power centers of the executive branch was truly unique when juxtaposed against Roosevelt's first and third vice presidents. In no other instance was this more glaringly obvious than by the exclusion of Wallace's—and Roosevelt's—immediate successor, Harry Truman, from critical government intelligence. Specifically, in 1941 Roosevelt assembled a select group to covertly meet on the development of an atomic weapon; Wallace was one of just five individuals designated for the project.[72] As the project moved forward, and therefore demanded the involvement of additional members of the government, Wallace was consistently briefed on its progress.

In contrast to Wallace, over the eighty-three days that elapsed from Truman's inauguration with Roosevelt to the occasion of Roosevelt's death, the president never bothered to inform his third vice president of the capacity of the United States military to build and use atomic weapons. In fairness to Truman, his vice presidency was among the briefest in history. Still, Roosevelt's keeping Truman uninformed of such a momentous development in science and warfare, and with the country embroiled in a world war, made it evident that Roosevelt was prepared to constrain the modern vice presidency if doing so met his immediate needs.

When it came to Wallace, however, President Roosevelt set no boundaries for what he thought the vice president was capable of, and this included enlisting him in foreign diplomacy. Although Roosevelt had sent Vice President Garner on a ceremonial trip across Asia in 1935—making Garner the first vice president to travel abroad while in office—he had more substantive objectives set for Wallace. The first opportunity for Roosevelt to use Wallace in this manner arose in the weeks immediately following the 1940 election, when he chose the vice president-elect to represent the United States at the inauguration of the Mexican president, Manuel Avila Camacho.[73]

This seemingly innocuous trip was crucial to the interests of the United States, chiefly because Mexico's commitment in the battle against international fascism, and against Germany specifically, was not then assured. And, since Mexico's place in the growing world conflict had been an issue in its presidential election, Wallace's presence, in lieu of the president, symbolized the value the United States placed on the prevailing political milieu of its neighbor.

For Wallace, the trip to Mexico was a personal and diplomatic triumph. He not only discharged his formal obligations with aplomb—at one point delivering a speech in Spanish before Mexico's Congress—but he also deliberately reached out to the citizenry of the nation. Wallace wandered among the throngs of people who trailed him, greeting and speaking to the people in their native language, thus greatly contributing to the ensuing cooperation between the two countries on a host of fronts. Yet the significance of Wallace's trip goes beyond any transitory benefit from improved ties between the United States and Mexico. What Wallace did, with the full support of President Roosevelt, was to introduce the vice president into a realm of policy long off limits to all but the president and the secretary of state.

As the uniqueness of Wallace's assignment in Mexico confirms, the vice president as a participant in foreign policy was not expected. This makes sense, for the Constitution does not invest in the vice president, as it does the president, the authority to seek the opinion of the heads of the executive departments, one of whom is the secretary of state. Not only does the secretary of state manage the primary department charged with implementing the nation's foreign policy, but the individual appointed secretary has, in practice, been the principal agent of diplomacy for the government as well.

Furthermore, in the earliest years of the nation the secretary of state was widely viewed as the most prestigious cabinet position, as well as the ideal spot from which to move to the presidency. That is why Thomas Jefferson, James Madison, James Monroe, John Quincy Adams, and Martin Van Buren all accepted the job on their way to the presidency.[74] Although for Jefferson and Van Buren, the vice presidency temporarily obstructed their climb to the top. And in Jefferson's case, serving as secretary of state to George Washington would have been the surest means to succeeded Washington, were it not for the election of 1796 and his defeat at the hands of Vice President John Adams.

Surely Roosevelt was not attempting, by his use of Wallace in foreign diplomacy, to supplant the secretary of state with the vice president; however, Wallace's inclusion in the foreign policy of the administration did further the idea of a utilitarian vice president. Moreover, choosing the vice president to visibly represent the United States at the inauguration of a coveted ally was tantamount to Vice President Coolidge's appearances at meetings of the cabinet. Or, to underscore the point in another way: with Coolidge in the cabinet, at the insistence of President Harding, and with Wallace the designated emissary abroad for President Roosevelt, it did not matter what either of the vice presidents did—what mattered was that they were there.

To Wallace's advantage, Roosevelt made it clear from the beginning that advancing Wallace within the administration was a priority. For instance, when Roosevelt initially insisted on making Wallace the vice-presidential nominee, he signaled sureness in his own judgment, as well as his confidence in Wallace as an individual. But of equal importance, Roosevelt indicated in his words and by his actions that Wallace was an intimate who was to serve, in effect, as a proxy for the president.

After his expedition to Mexico, Wallace repeated his distinctive diplomatic approach on additional trips abroad, including excursions into the Soviet Union and China in the latter part of his term of office.[75] In preparation for his trip to the Soviet Union, Wallace diligently studied the history, culture, and languages of the region; he even attempted to speedily master the complexities of Russian. True to form, upon landing in Siberia Wallace spoke the language, far from fluently, to any person he was given access to. And similar to his appearance before Mexico's Congress, Wallace opted to deliver the few formal addresses he made in the host country's language.[76]

Particularly vexing to Wallace were indications that Soviet scientists were nearing parity with American scientists in the field of atomic energy research.[77] Having worked as a scientist, as well as being one of the few individuals privy to his own government's atomic program, Wallace was keenly aware of the implications of the Soviet atomic program, both scientifically and politically. But this too is where Wallace differed from practically every major political figure of his time. According to Wallace's orientation, science and technology should be harnessed to improve the lot of humanity, not to intimidate or to destroy.[78]

When in China, Wallace had been tapped by President Roosevelt for a diplomatic mission that typically would have been the province of the secretary of state. Among the delicate tasks assigned to the vice president were mediation of existent tensions between the two nations, his direct intercession in the internal Chinese conflict between Chang Kai-shek and the communist insurgency, and an attempt by Wallace to influence, if possible, the currency exchange rate with China.[79]

It should be emphasized that Wallace's trips abroad were not devoted exclusively to cultural enrichment and populist diplomacy. Each time he left the country he traveled as the vice president of the United States, sent by the president on an explicit mission. This was the case when he went on a tour of South and Central America in 1943.

Ostensibly the trip was about maintaining strong ties with neighboring countries, but in reality Wallace was sent by Roosevelt to assess the mass production of goods the United States required for the ongoing war effort.[80]

Wallace was certainly familiar with many of the operations he inspected—in places like Costa Rica, Panama, Columbia, and Peru—because of his time directing the BEW. And yet, his concerns went well beyond the interests of the United States and the war at hand and extended to the impoverished people he encountered in the streets and in the countrysides he traversed. Later, based on his assessment of the economic plight of the nations he visited, Wallace procured private and public funding to expand domestic production in the southern hemisphere and to increase the yield of the native farmers. Ironically, Wallace was aided in this particular mission by the generosity of the Rockefeller Institution and a man who would later serve as vice president, Nelson Rockefeller.[81]

Besides the positive, practical outcome to Wallace's tour of South and Central America, there was an additional, overt benefit to his visiting that hemisphere of the world. By the use of personal diplomacy, in tandem with his undeniable popular appeal, Wallace was able to recruit several of the nations he visited to the Allied cause. By one account, because of Wallace's direct involvement in the region, "twelve Latin American countries had declared war on Germany and a total of twenty had broken diplomatic relations with Axis nations. On a few occasions this was done as an immediate result of his visit."[82]

Although Wallace attained greater progress in some spheres of government than he did in others, his presence in foreign diplomacy was unprecedented, and it marked the entrance of the American vice president on the world stage. What is more, because he was the second-highest elected officer of the government, and because it was widely understood that when he spoke, he spoke for President Roosevelt, Wallace was uniquely positioned to represent his nation and his government to the governments and the citizens of the world, and at a level the secretary of state could not match.

When it came to the vice president's constitutionally enumerated responsibilities in the Senate, Henry Wallace's performance contrasted considerably with that of his performance in executive administration. This was not a case of Wallace being an unskilled presiding officer; it was simply that the rigid proceedings of the United States Senate were contrary to his very nature; hence, spending his days ruling on points of order and the like plainly squandered his intellect and his talents.[83]

The clubby atmosphere of the Senate never sat well with Wallace either, nor did Wallace sit well with most senators. Harry Truman, who was serving as a senator from Missouri when Wallace was the presiding officer of the Senate, later claimed that Wallace "was a damn poor Vice President. Why, hell, he'd been there presiding over the Senate for almost four years, and I'll bet there weren't half a dozen Senators who'd call him by his first name. He didn't have any friends in the Senate, and that's the way things get done in the Senate."[84] Yet, what Truman fails to note is that if Wallace was to behave in the converse, thus acting the part of an overly active vice president within the walls of the Senate, then more than likely he would have been rebuked for being an interloper in a legislative body of which he was not an elected member.

Clearly, when thrust among those in Congress, Wallace stood apart. He was not a politician—particularly when using the descriptor pejoratively—and so he was resistant to the comportment, and the mindset, of a conventional politician. Instead, Wallace was occupied by the intellectual and spiritual dimensions of those areas that captivated him wholly: science, religion, and the land. As it stood, he was indifferent to the hyperbole that typified much of the discourse of the United States Senate. Alben Barkley, the majority leader of the chamber when Wallace was vice president, captured the essence of the latter man, emphasizing that

> Mr. Wallace had many other interests besides being Vice President. He was writing articles, and he was conferring with people everywhere about different things, he was interested in a lot of social welfares and programs of all kinds, and ... he did not devote that acute attention to the routine job of being Vice President that Vice President Garner had done.[85]

In every way, Wallace distinguished himself from those individuals to have previously served as vice president, and this extended to the uniqueness of his political career as well. Before the election of 1940, he had never run for an elective office, and yet over time he had managed to cultivate a political constituency of his own, apart from President Roosevelt. It was his eight years as secretary of agriculture—where he gained numerous admirers of his work—followed by four years in the vice presidency that made his reputation and added to the political capital he accumulated. From his combined twelve years in the executive government, Wallace proved to be a stalwart of progressive, New Deal promise, and one of the highest ranking liberals in the Democratic Party. For these reasons, Wallace was eventually viewed as a threat to the political legacy of the president he served.

As the 1944 election approached, and where it concerned Wallace's possible repeat candidacy for vice president, President Roosevelt was ultimately swayed by a cabal of conservative advisers and Democratic Party leaders, all of whom were wary of Wallace. To this group, Wallace was a bulwark of liberalism, a characterization accentuated by the vice president's outspokenness on civil rights and women's rights, as well as his unfailing advocacy for unions and his promotion of the common man.[86] Roosevelt was equally attentive to the power of southern, conservative Democrats in Congress, many of whom had never forgiven the president for discarding John Nance Garner for Wallace in 1940.

But Roosevelt should have ignored the Democratic leadership and instead taken note of impartial polling done the week prior to the Chicago nominating convention. Had he done so, Roosevelt would have known that the preference of 64 percent of rank-and-file Democrats was for Vice President Wallace's return for a second term, with his nearest competitor for the nomination, Senator Alben Barkley, polling a dismal 14 percent.[87] Still, the transparent resistance to Wallace in certain quarters, combined with Roosevelt's legitimate concerns about the reaction to his own bid for a fourth term, led to his caving to pressure to drop Wallace from the ticket. When, on the first balloting for the vice-presidential nomination, Wallace gained more support than any other candidate, though not a majority, Roosevelt must have wondered, at least for a moment, if his desertion of Wallace had been wise.[88]

The specifics of Vice President Henry Wallace's tenure matter. His legacy, however, is defined by the ways in which he, with the unequivocal support of President Roosevelt, expanded the utility of the American vice presidency. Wallace left the vice presidency a considerably stronger political institution than it had been when he took the oath of office. And by his activism on multiple fronts, he validated the efficacy of employing the vice president in any capacity the president chose. More importantly, Henry Wallace's service demonstrated that the vice presidency was at last a truly modern institution, one that should never be neglected or overlooked.

EXPANSION BY STATUTE (1945–1953)

Harry Truman was a throwback to vice presidents of an earlier era. In part this may be attributed to the underlying cause for Truman's nomination as Franklin Roosevelt's third running mate. Because Truman was not Henry Wallace, and because he came from a Midwest, border state, he was acceptable to conservative southerners. Nominating Truman, then, was a matter of political expediency. Besides, Truman was a Democratic loyalist and therefore he was the choice of party leaders who, mindful of Roosevelt's by then rapidly declining health, knew that in settling on a vice-presidential nominee, they were actually selecting the next president.

There has long been uncertainty with regard to Roosevelt's complicity in the substitution of Truman for Wallace. Certainly in the prelude to the nominating convention, Roosevelt sent mixed signals. To some advisers, Roosevelt suggested that if Wallace were re-nominated it would lead to an irreparable rupture within the Democratic Party, and probable defeat in the election.[89] At the same time, Roosevelt told the vice president privately, even if "I cannot put it just that way in public, I hope it will be the same old team."[90]

What finally assured Wallace's fate at the convention was that unlike the scenario in 1940, in 1944 President Roosevelt did not insist on Wallace for the nomination for vice president.[91] What Roosevelt did do after the nomination went to Truman was to offer Wallace his choice of any cabinet position except secretary of state. Even if Roosevelt would not keep Wallace in the vice presidency, he seemed determined to keep Wallace nearby. To this point, Roosevelt told the vice president prior to the convention that no matter what happened there, "we will have a job for you in world economic affairs."[92]

After the Roosevelt-Truman ticket successfully captured the nation's top two offices, Wallace settled for the secretary of commerce position. Poignantly, Vice President Truman devoted a considerable share of his fleeting tenure attempting to get his predecessor confirmed by a broadly antagonistic Senate membership.[93] Initially, President Roosevelt had hoped to make Wallace both the commerce secretary and the federal loan administrator—replacing Wallace's longtime nemesis, Jessie Jones, in the two positions the latter man held—but Truman "knew the Senate would never sit still for that."[94] As it was, Truman had his hands full trying to get Wallace back into the cabinet. According to Truman, "Henry was not at all liked in the Senate. And I had to break two ties to get the son of a bitch confirmed. I didn't want to do it, but if that's what the old man wanted, I did it."[95]

Regardless of the brevity of the Truman vice presidency, it was during this time that the office was further institutionalized. This came about when Truman became the first vice president to have a military aide included among the nominal staff then accorded to the office. Since the United States was thoroughly involved in the Second World War, it made sense to link the vice president, by some means, to the military establishment of the nation. In addition, for the first time in the history of the second office, the vice president was deemed worthy of the protection of a single Secret Service agent.

Without a doubt, times had changed; no longer was the vice president immune from the threat of violence. In good conscience, Truman could not refuse a measure of the protection afforded the president—granted, by absurdly reduced numbers, but protection nonetheless. By 1945, it seemed almost quaint that Vice President Thomas Marshall, during the First World War, had once chastised a police officer for protectively shadowing him. Marshall had made light of any peril coming to a vice president, telling the police officer that "nobody was ever crazy enough to shoot at a vice-president. If you will go away and find somebody to shoot at me, I'll go down in history as being the first vice-president who ever attracted enough attention even to have a crank shoot at him."[96]

Since Truman was vice president for such a short period of time, it is impossible to know how Franklin Roosevelt planned to use him. Because Truman came to the office from the Senate, his vice presidency, in all likelihood, would have focused on advancing the administration's legislative agenda. What is known, however, is that Roosevelt assigned Truman the chore of getting Henry Wallace confirmed by an unfriendly Senate and failed to enlighten the new vice president on the development of the atomic bomb; with the exception of a few cabinet meetings, the two men met on just two other occasions before Roosevelt's death on April 12, 1945. This lack of interaction with the president, in tandem with Truman's ignorance of the most important state secret of the century, surely influenced Truman once he succeeded to the presidency. From that point forward, Truman was resolute on the vice president never again being so utterly outside of the executive branch.

Harry Truman's ascension to the presidency created a protracted vacancy in the vice presidency, lasting three years, nine months, and eight days. Truman eventually filled the void by the only means available to him: in 1948 he was elected to his own term as president with a new vice president, Alben Barkley. Barkley, a senator from Kentucky, had been, depending on the electoral fortunes of the Democratic Party, either the majority or minority leader for twelve years. Once in office, Barkley reinstituted the practice of the vice president operating as a broker between the administration and the Congress, having formerly participated in the fusion of the executive and legislative during the Roosevelt-Wallace years. At that time, Barkley was the Senate majority leader, and with his counterpart in the House, he had attended weekly meetings with the president, the vice president, and the Speaker of the House to coordinate the administration's legislative program in Congress.[97] The Senate was clearly where Barkley was most at home, and, by one account, he chose to preside anywhere from "fifty to seventy-five percent of the time," always holding firm to "his concept of how it [the Senate] ought to be run regardless of the precedents."[98]

Although Barkley was satisfied by his work with the Congress, President Truman made certain that the vice president was integrated into the executive branch. As indicated before, Truman had learned from the deficiencies of his too brief association with President Roosevelt. According to Barkley, "Truman knew how little opportunity had been given in the past for Vice Presidents … to acquaint themselves with the job they might have to take over, and he wisely set out to rectify this situation."[99] To this end, Truman insisted that Barkley participate in the cabinet, and, of enduring consequence, Truman initiated and signed the National Security Act of 1947, making the vice president a permanent member of the National Security Council. He also issued an executive order for a coat of arms, seal, and new flag for the vice president.[100] Truman personally oversaw the redesign of the flag, which initially was conferred on the second office by President Franklin Roosevelt. These were among the few formal adornments attached to the vice president, and though they were symbolic in nature and of mostly aesthetic value, there is no question that such visible signs of the office contributed to the further institutionalization of the vice presidency.

And because Barkley had the time, he also began the practice of traveling across the country promoting the policies of the administration, at the same time hoping to distill for the citizens he encountered what it was their government was actually doing.[101] By Barkley's own admission he was figuratively going where no vice president had gone before. Put another way: of his own initiative, Barkley opted to communicate with the public in a fashion previous vice presidents had never attempted; in so doing, the vice president became an accessible, familiar voice and face for the Truman administration. It was a novel practice, but on a practical level it made sense for the vice president to do what the president surely did not have the time to do.

In all, Alben Barkley succeeded in the vice presidency in ways that some of his recent predecessors had not. Whereas John Nance Garner was primarily occupied by the legislative nature of the office and Henry Wallace had been a vocal partner in executive administration, Barkley was able to effectively straddle the executive-legislative conundrum of the vice presidency. In this manner he made the vice presidency responsive to the unique, inherent duality of the institution. And in doing so, Barkley demonstrated that the modern vice presidency possessed features—constitutional, statutory, and symbolic—that would make it attractive to even the most ambitious politicians.

THE POLITICIAN AS VICE PRESIDENT (1953–1963)

In 1952 the Republican Party candidates for president and vice president, Dwight Eisenhower and Richard Nixon, respectively, captured the two nationally elected offices. Their victory ended twenty years of uninterrupted control of the White House by the Democratic Party and commenced a new era for the modern vice presidency. Specifically, by taking the apolitical Eisenhower and then pairing him with the epitome of the professional politician, Nixon, expectations for the vice president—first as a candidate, and then upon taking office—were redoubled.

Nixon was just thirty-nine years old when he was offered the Republican nomination for vice president. Too often nominations for vice president had gone to political has-beens, or to defeated contenders for the presidential nomination. But Nixon was different; he was blatantly ambitious and fiercely partisan, and his career was going nowhere but up. Nixon, unlike the lot of nominees before him, actually seemed to want to run for vice president. By one account, he favored a run for the vice presidency because there was "nothing to lose from defeat and everything to gain from victory."[102] Furthermore, Nixon was undeniably aware of the broader utility of his most recent predecessors, so Eisenhower's insistence on the vice president being an informed and prepared member of the administration must have resonated with him.[103]

True to his word, Eisenhower brought Nixon into the government wherever possible. This included the vice president's active participation in the cabinet and his membership, by law, in the National Security Council. In addition, he was assigned the chairmanship of an assortment of policy groups and commissions, all of which were established by the president. This included the President's Committee on Government Contracts—aimed at excising racial and religious discrimination by businesses receiving federal contracts—as well as the Cabinet Committee on Economic Growth and Price Stability, from which Nixon helped to coordinate the administration's proactive and reactive economic policies.

With these expanded administrative tasks, Nixon's vice presidency took shape. In turn, Nixon came to represent, and more so than either Henry Wallace or Alben Barkley, the model of the utilitarian vice president. What is more, the emphasis placed on public administration was beneficial to both Nixon and Eisenhower, filling a gap in the vice president's résumé and concurrently meeting the needs of the president.[104]

Even though Nixon came into the Eisenhower administration principally as a practitioner of domestic politics, President Eisenhower continued to build on the foreign policy portfolio of the vice president, going beyond what President Roosevelt had done for Henry Wallace. By giving their vice presidents foreign policy assignments, Roosevelt and Eisenhower raised the visibility of the institution while taking advantage of a latent use of the individual then holding the office. This set in motion the incremental encroachment by the vice president into an area that was historically the purview of the secretary of state. It was a notable advance for the vice presidency, made even more striking since not even the president had traveled abroad before Theodore Roosevelt did so in 1906.

For Nixon, foreign affairs was both fascinating and challenging, and he quickly established himself as the traveling vice president. At Eisenhower's behest, Nixon undertook several transcontinental missions; ultimately, when he was vice president, he would visit sixty-one countries and log nearly 160,000 miles.[105] Initially prompting Nixon's extensive excursions overseas was an innocuous question Eisenhower posed in their first term in office. With Congress usually out of session for the better part of summer, and the rest of the government equally quiet, Eisenhower had queried Nixon on his plans for the summer.[106] With the vice president traditionally the least occupied officer of the government, Nixon would have been hard pressed to answer the president with any response besides his complete availability; as such, he jumped at the chance to be of use, even if it meant working outside the country.

But Nixon's trips were not nearly as perfunctory as might be assumed, and he took the assignments seriously, preparing for whatever might come his way with thorough briefings on the culture, politics and politicians of every region and country on his itinerary.[107] Of all the regions of the world, Asia probably interested Nixon the most. Asia was certainly a part of the world he eventually became an authority on; so much so that one author has posited that in the years Nixon was vice president and president, he was perhaps "the most important American politician in Asian affairs."[108]

As the vice president, Nixon's forays into foreign diplomacy were quite different than those of the secretary of state. Whereas the travels of the secretary of state are meant to be about diplomacy, Nixon's excursions outside his home country were decidedly political. Nixon was able to infuse politics when traveling abroad in two ways. First, he made certain that wherever he traveled, his formal, diplomatic activities did not preclude his meeting citizens outside of government, including workers in factories, shoppers in markets, and children in schools. Although Henry Wallace had done the same when he traveled outside the United States, Nixon added a distinctive campaign-like aura to his trips. One author, referencing a trip Nixon took to La Paz, Bolivia, described how the vice president "bounded around the city shaking hands, making speeches and joining native dances."[109]

And second, the political context of Nixon's travels was consistently ratcheted up by his unfailing arguments for the virtues of democracy versus the iniquities of communism. Conveniently, it was on the different continents that Nixon visited—such as Asia and South America—that he found his best opportunity to play the politician abroad. These regions were teeming, from Nixon's perspective, with too many nations at or near communist domination.[110]

The narrative of Vice President Nixon's involvement in foreign affairs is filled with anecdote, though certain parts of the story have greater meaning than others. Some aspects, like his celebrated face-to-face debate with Soviet Premier Nikita Khrushchev, were simply posturing on the world stage, meant to build political capital at home, and surely of token value to the foreign policy of the United States; whereas, Nixon's substantive, long-term association with President Eisenhower's secretary of state, the legendary John Foster Dulles, was essential to his intellectual growth. For years he cultivated a relationship with the older, internationally experienced Dulles, eagerly playing the part of understudy to the secretary of state.[111] By Nixon's telling: "many nights I would have cocktails or dinner with him [Dulles], and then we would sit for hours talking our way around the world. It was an incomparable opportunity for me to learn from one of the great diplomats of our time."[112]

Besides attending to politics, administration, and foreign travel, Nixon added to the modern vice presidency in another way—though surely it was in a way neither Nixon nor Eisenhower would have chosen. In 1955 Eisenhower suffered a heart attack;

it was the first in a series of illnesses for the president. Eisenhower's age and health greatly shaped the remaining years he held office and were critical to his decision, after getting approval from his doctors, to seek a second term in 1956. Furthermore, because Eisenhower's health issues were widely known, Nixon's behavior during each episode influenced the public's perception of the vice presidency, broadly, and of Nixon, specifically.

In Eisenhower's case, having arrived in the presidency with a military record that included commanding Allied forces in the Second World War, he could not help but have an acute sense of his own mortality. Perhaps because of that wartime experience, Eisenhower seemed to appreciate to a greater extent than had any of his predecessors the necessity of preparing the vice president for succession. Eisenhower was dismayed by what he saw as Harry Truman's ignorance of government affairs upon ascending to the presidency; therefore, he was set on not repeating what he considered Franklin Roosevelt's error in keeping the vice president in the dark.[113]

To this end, Eisenhower insisted well before winning the 1952 election that he wanted to make Nixon more than "'a figurehead,'" and he was equally committed to having the vice president be an informed "'member of the team ... able to step into the presidency smoothly in case anything happens to me.'"[114] As a result, when Eisenhower was struck with his first heart attack, Nixon was equipped to take the reins of government. He was versed in the ways of the executive government, he had been carefully fostering relationships with the leaders of assorted foreign nations, and he had become a familiar, national political figure.

For the duration of Eisenhower's incapacity, Nixon's actions were an exercise in managed symmetry, balancing deference with firm control. However, despite outward appearances, Nixon was rattled by the prospect of succeeding Eisenhower, or so he claimed in a memoir he penned in 1962, which included the ominously titled chapter: "The Heart Attack."[115] Of this period, Nixon wrote: "I realized that my own position as Vice President had become extremely delicate; my every move during this period had to be made with caution, for even the slightest misstep could be interpreted as an attempt to assume power."[116]

Along with his concerns about appearing to be taking advantage of the president's condition, Nixon also was mindful of the legitimacy of the office he held. Later, in the same memoir, he argued that

> aside from the President, I was the only person in government elected by all the people; they had a right to expect leadership, if it were needed, rather than a vacuum. But any move on my part which could be interpreted, even incorrectly, as an attempt to usurp the powers of the presidency would disrupt the Eisenhower team, cause dissension in the nation, and disturb the President and his family.[117]

In all, Dwight Eisenhower suffered heart attacks, a stroke, and a major intestinal operation. From those experiences, he rightly concluded that the procedures in place for handling presidential inability were wholly inadequate. To rectify this, Eisenhower wanted to establish an appropriate response for contingencies similar to those which had arisen while he was in office. What he had in mind was a plan that would sustain the operation of government in a crisis, and in the absence of a healthy, functioning president. Eisenhower sought counsel and solutions from both the Justice Department and the Congress; however, a satisfactory remedy came from neither institution.[118]

Therefore, in 1958, with three years remaining in his second term, President Eisenhower composed an agreement between himself and Vice President Nixon, delineating a formal response to temporary presidential inability.[119] In this historic document, the president gave himself the authority to determine when an inability to execute the duties of his office was present, and when the inability was over. Eisenhower likewise conferred the same authority to Nixon, for those instances when the president was incapable of making the determination himself. Under those circumstances, the vice president was expected to resolve, "after such consultation as seems to him appropriate under the circumstances," if the president was able to fulfill his constitutional obligations.[120] And in each scenario, Nixon was expected to "serve as Acting President, exercising the duties of the office until the inability had ended."[121]

When Eisenhower released to the public his directive, it reinforced the impression that the vice president was becoming an indispensable part of the executive government. Clearly, even if the vice president's place in government continued to be inextricably tied to the fortunes of the president, there was no justification for excluding the vice president from the most important business of the administration. More than anything, what Eisenhower did was to create a framework that might lessen the confusion surrounding presidential inability. When Presidents Garfield and Wilson were subject to prolonged disabilities—which in Garfield's case ended in death—confusion reigned as to who was actually running the government.

By the era of the Nixon vice presidency, however, an enormous leap in perception had transpired. The public, as well as most individuals serving in the executive branch, including the cabinet, assumed Nixon was in charge. And though the agreement crafted by Eisenhower did not have the force of law, it served as a template for a similar agreement between President John Kennedy and Vice President Lyndon Johnson. Likewise, upon Johnson's succeeding to the presidency, and since he did not have a vice president, he employed a comparable arrangement with the Speaker of the House, John McCormick. Later, Johnson did the same with Hubert Humphrey upon Humphrey's election to the vice presidency in 1964.

Over the course of his vice presidency, Richard Nixon successfully raised the visibility and the viability of the institution. For these reasons, as early as 1956, when Eisenhower reportedly considered dropping Nixon from their joint reelection bid, the president was unable to force the matter.[122] This came about because Nixon operated as a fiercely partisan politician; he always framed his advocacy of the administration's policies and programs on purely political terms. Since Nixon had become so closely identified with the Eisenhower administration, any repudiation of Nixon by the president was by extension repudiation of the administration. Eisenhower even offered Nixon a cabinet post in lieu of the vice presidency, but Nixon knew that should he choose the cabinet over the vice presidency, he was less likely to ever make it to the presidency.[123]

By Nixon's calculations, he would either succeed to the higher office because of the president's poor health or, at the least, as a two-term vice president, he would be in the best position to capture the next presidential nomination; besides, in Nixon's words: "I knew I was acquiring executive and administrative experience in the various assignments given me by the President."[124] Sure enough, Eisenhower and Nixon triumphed in the 1956 election, making Nixon the first incumbent Republican vice president in history to win reelection; Eisenhower lived to finish his second term, and Nixon won the presidential nomination of the Republican Party in 1960. And by Nixon successfully capturing the presidential nomination of his party, he demonstrated that the vice presidency was no longer a political wilderness from which few emerge; it was instead a position that even a rising politician might aspire to hold.

Richard Nixon lost the 1960 presidential election, yet the transparent expansion of the vice presidency, coupled with Nixon's subsequent nomination for president, must have influenced his eventual successor when he agreed to run for vice president on the Democratic ticket that same year. That nominee was Lyndon Johnson, and like Nixon, Johnson was never immune to putting his political career above all else. Having lost the battle for the presidential nomination to John Kennedy, Johnson accepted the consolation prize. Perhaps Johnson, again like Nixon, assumed that the modern vice presidency held the best opportunity for reaching the presidency.

When Johnson was nominated for vice president, he was counted among the most powerful and persuasive Senate majority leaders on record; still, accepting the vice-presidential nomination was a sacrifice he was obviously willing to make. In some measure this was due to what the vice presidency had become by 1960. Yet, in equal or even greater measure, Johnson must have been influenced by the notion of what his job in the Senate would likely become if he did not accept Kennedy's offer. He was too smart of a politician to have not appreciated how his power in the Senate was sure to diminish if Kennedy went on to win the presidency without him.

The preceding potential scenario was conceivable to Johnson because of his experience in Congress when Dwight Eisenhower was in the White House. Specifically, during the latter part of the Eisenhower era, Johnson had possessed considerable leverage with the incumbent president, primarily on account of his selection as majority leader of the opposition party. By one senator's telling: "Johnson was the single most powerful person, even more so than Eisenhower. Johnson talked to Eisenhower on the phone regularly ... Eisenhower relied on Johnson much more than he did on his own Republican leadership. Johnson was it. He was totally it."[125] He was a shrewd political operator who played the power game at a level few in Congress could match; it would not have escaped him that a fellow Democrat occupying the White House would have made for an untenable power arrangement. In such a scenario, Johnson would have had few options but to defer to the de facto leader of his party, and president of his country.

Years later, when discussing why he thought a reluctant senator would ultimately accept an offer for the vice-presidential nomination, Johnson hinted at his own thinking in 1960, declaring: "Let me tell you something ... That's what they said about old

Lyndon Johnson in 1960. But when they lead you up on that mountain, and show you those green fields down below and that beautiful White House standing there—you know what you do? You take it. They all take it."[126]

If Johnson was disinclined to serve as vice president, he never indicated it publicly. Fortunately for him, John Kennedy seemed sympathetic to the record of neglected vice presidents. At one point, when he was still a senator, Kennedy had acknowledged the intrinsic awkwardness of the vice presidency, claiming "if my life expectancy was not what I hope it will be ... but that really is not ... an enviable prospect for the second man ... to exert influence in the course of events [only] if I should die."[127]

But in choosing Johnson for a running mate, Kennedy was motivated by more than confidence in his own mortality. Kennedy was cognizant that, even with the vast power and reach of the presidency, he would have minimal control over Johnson if the senator from Texas remained in Congress. Kennedy might be the president, and therefore have more leverage in the White House than Johnson would have in the Capitol, but Johnson could still do some damage to a young president from the well of the Senate. Kennedy acknowledged as much when, at the Democratic convention, he told an aide: "I'm thinking of ... the leadership in the Senate. If we win, it will be by a small margin and I won't be able to live with Lyndon Johnson as the leader of a small majority in the Senate. Did it occur to you that if Lyndon becomes the Vice-President, I'll have Mike Mansfield as the leader in the Senate, somebody I can trust and depend on?"[128]

Like other modern presidents, Kennedy contributed to the substantive portfolio of the vice president where he could and when he chose; thus, he gave Johnson a reasonably meaningful role in the administration. In addition to Johnson's participation with the cabinet and the National Security Council, Kennedy assigned his vice president the chairmanships of the National Aeronautics and Space Council and the President's Committee on Equal Employment Opportunity. It was all part of the president's effort to make the vice president useful. Of course, making the vice president useful to Kennedy did not include making Johnson an integral part of the president's inner circle. Nor did it mean, according to the chief administrator of NASA during the 1960s, that President Kennedy, by giving the vice president leadership of the space program, would not retain for himself "control [of] the agenda of the council, [and furthermore] that he wanted to determine those items on which he would seek and would accept advice."[129] There are always limits to how much control over a policy sphere any president will cede to the vice president.

Unlike Richard Nixon, Lyndon Johnson was an established political figure well before he won the vice presidency. Having been a member of the legislative branch generally worked to Johnson's advantage, especially in making him a viable candidate for national office. Yet when Johnson was inaugurated as the number two executive of the nation, he struggled with relinquishing the immense power he had possessed as the Senate majority leader. Initially, and to the consternation of many senators, Johnson tried to have it both ways. First, he wanted to lead the Senate Democratic caucus, and then he fought to keep the expansive offices in the Capitol that were reserved for the majority leader.[130] When both endeavors failed, Johnson had to settle for the presiding officer's chair, and a suite of offices in what was then known as the Old Executive Office

Building.[131] Indubitably, being the first vice president to have offices in the historic building, adjacent to the West Wing of the White House, was a minor consolation for a man with Johnson's outsized ego.

In light of his prior experience, Johnson was the logical choice to lead the New Frontier legislative program to passage by the Congress. Surprisingly though, Johnson was utilized inconsistently in this area by President Kennedy; the result was that many of Kennedy's plans stalled in Congress and were only realized after his death, when Johnson was the president. Moreover, because the vice president's efforts with the Congress were so sporadic, he could not gain a foothold there and so, after a time, it was futile for him to try.[132] Maybe Johnson could not have done as much with the Congress as was initially thought, for again it was in the Senate where he encountered the strongest resistance upon his assumption of the vice presidency. Quite simply, as vice president, Johnson was no longer a member of the club, even if, as the president of the Senate, he was the president of the club.

The area where Lyndon Johnson did leave an indelible imprint when he was vice president was in his work as one of the principal emissaries for the Kennedy administration overseas. When John Kennedy was a senator, he had diligently built-up his foreign policy expertise, whereas Johnson had focused his work in the Senate exclusively on domestic policy. Despite the dichotomy in their legislative experience, Kennedy readily sent Johnson abroad, for it was obvious that the vice president was frustrated by the traditional constraints of the job he held. For Johnson, this arrangement worked well. He was forever the complete politician, and so any opportunity to recast himself, far from the shadow of President Kennedy, was a welcome opportunity.

Johnson treated his trips abroad like frenetic campaign swings. He would wade into crowds, giving away pens and cigarette lighters, every item emblazoned with the official seal of the vice president's office.[133] Although Johnson's antics, at every level, were an exercise in excess, the impression he left, particularly in communist or allegedly communist-leaning countries, was the embodiment of the proud American. Set in the context of the ideological underpinnings of the era, foreign policy was waged equally by leader-to-leader diplomacy and rhetorical hyperbole. Hence, by his words and actions, and in being the second-highest ranking official of the United States government, Johnson was effective in imparting this message: democracy, and by extension robust capitalism, offered a life of abundance for the citizens of the world—an outcome that communism, according to Johnson, ostensibly could not produce.

On the whole, Lyndon Johnson's performance on the world stage owed a debt to Richard Nixon. Like Nixon, Johnson made foreign diplomacy as much about himself as he did about the specific mission the president had assigned to him. In so doing, he did not necessarily supplant the secretary of state, or for that matter the president, in conducting foreign affairs. What Johnson did, though, was to carve out a unique legacy, making the vice president a semi-independent political actor in foreign affairs. Surely, upon Johnson's return home, Kennedy could have ignored the vice president's assessments. But as a roving diplomat, Johnson was always center stage; it was not easy for Kennedy, or the world, to entirely dismiss the vice president's presence.

In the summer of 1960, when John Kennedy, by virtue of his own nomination for president, was confronted with selecting a running mate, he was dismissive of the vice presidency. At one point, Kennedy asserted: "I'm forty-three years old, and I'm the healthiest candidate for President in the United States ... I'm not going to die in office. So the Vice-Presidency doesn't mean anything."[134] Yet, because of events beyond his control, Kennedy's words belied the reality. In Lyndon Johnson's case, the vice presidency did mean something; it meant the presidency. Years later, looking back through a lens tainted by his own discredited presidency, Johnson claimed to abhor his time as vice president, telling one biographer that "the Vice-Presidency is filled with trips around the world, chauffeurs, men saluting, people clapping, chairmanships of councils, but in the end, it is nothing. I detested every minute of it."[135]

Johnson never could admit that the gamble he had taken in accepting the vice-presidential nomination had paid off. He had made it to the presidency because he was the vice president. Still, Johnson's vice presidency ended because of tragedy, and for that reason his presidency began amidst tragedy. It was poignant, then, that Johnson's presidency came to a close, five years after his assuming the office, while yet another tragedy unfolded.

THE MODERN VICE PRESIDENCY AND THE TWENTY-FIFTH AMENDMENT

FROM HUMPHREY TO QUAYLE

It's like being naked in the middle of a blizzard with no one to even offer you a match to keep you warm—that's the vice presidency.

– Vice President Hubert Humphrey

AT THE MERCY OF THE PRESIDENT (1965-1969)

If Lyndon Johnson's vice presidency ended due to tragedy and his presidency de-volved into tragedy, then it is sadly fitting that Hubert Humphrey's vice presidency unfolded as tragedy at the hands of Johnson. For Humphrey, there were signs of what was to come well before he was nominated as a candidate for vice president. In the nine months that elapsed from the assassination of President Kennedy to the Democratic nominating convention of 1964, President Johnson had turned his choice of a vice-presidential nominee into a game, whereby he dangled the possibil-ity of the nomination before every plausible contender. Yet Humphrey stood apart from other prospective nominees; he really wanted to be vice president.

Quite possibly, Humphrey's desire to be the nation's number two executive was a result of his yearning to be the chief executive. As a senator from Minnesota, he had pursued the Democratic nomination for president in 1960, and he was briefly con-sidered for the vice-presidential nomination that year, as he had been in 1956.[1] By 1964, Humphrey had already witnessed three vice presidents rise to the presidency because of the death of the president. Since Humphrey knew that Lyndon Johnson suffered from heart disease, morbid as it was, he surely could not help but wonder if the vice presidency might serve as his conduit to the White House. As it turned out, the man in the White House so rigidly delimited Humphrey's vice presidency that it ultimately stifled his best chance at winning the presidency.

After Johnson and Humphrey scored a significant victory in the 1964 election, they were able to use their mandate, in tandem with residual sympathy from the death of President Kennedy, to advance an ambitious legislative agenda. Although Johnson is rightfully acclaimed for shepherding the Great Society program through Congress, he also used Humphrey to great effect when the latter man was still in the Senate, and then after he became vice president, in seeking passage of the administration's domestic policies. On the domestic front, specifically, the list of legislative accomplishments attributable to Johnson and Humphrey during their time in office together is impressive, and included statutes extending voting rights, the creation of innovative anti-poverty and housing programs, the establishment of broad civil rights protections, and significant increases in aid to education.

In his work with Congress, Humphrey was able to draw on fifteen years of Senate service and an equally long history of advocacy for progressive causes; he was, for these reasons, ideally suited to the role of the vice president as legislative deputy to the president. In large part, Humphrey's success was because his actions and words were considered a legitimate extension of the president. All told, Humphrey took the modern vice presidency further into the legislative sphere than any of his predecessors ever did and, indicative of where the institution was heading, further than practically all who have followed him.

As was the same with Richard Nixon and Lyndon Johnson, Hubert Humphrey was given a foreign policy portfolio that was a healthy mix of substance and ceremony. Irrespective of the insignificance attached to some of his missions abroad, by Humphrey's time, a level of engagement in foreign affairs was becoming the norm for vice presidents. Furthermore, combining hands-on diplomatic experience with statutory membership in the National Security Council proved advantageous to the vice presidency, and the sitting vice president, in four ways. First, it made for a better prepared vice president in the event of succession to the presidency. Second, it conferred a higher degree of gravitas to the institution. Third, in handling assignments that previously were the primary focus of the secretary of state, the vice president was gradually being viewed as an equivalent member of the cabinet. And fourth, a foreign policy and national security portfolio gave the vice president an enhanced platform from which to seek a future presidential nomination.

Employing the vice president in world affairs was not done by President Johnson merely to make Humphrey look like a participant in that sphere of activity. To begin with, when Johnson was vice president, his trips overseas were among the most memorable highlights of his abbreviated time in the office. More importantly, Johnson could rely on Humphrey's blend of intellect and ebullience to leave a positive imprint wherever he might land. This was critical because the vice president, in Humphrey's words, was

> an elected official of the nation, second only to the President in personifying the nation, [and therefore] the Vice President can relieve the President of some ceremonial duties and responsibilities which, however trivial they

This item is due back on:

April 30, 2018

Please return to the main
library, library drop box or
street-side drop by the blue
USPS mail box.

Clackamas
Community College

;ual observer, signal to the nation and the world that the
ted to specific domestic and foreign policy objectives.[2]

president, Humphrey toured the world. But, according to
missions were more than ceremonial displays of American
hat Johnson regularly "sent me as goodwill ambassador to
. Goodwill is easy but, in each case, I was able to perform
antive nature."[3] Johnson likewise had occasion to use his vice
e international crisis situations, as he did when he tasked
ing, on behalf of the United States, in the 1967 Israeli-Arab

, yet telling, hole in Humphrey's foreign policy and national
m. And it was the divergence in viewpoint on the escalation
Vietnam that eventually made Humphrey's relationship with
e early stages of the conflict, when the involvement of the
United States military was limited, but beginning to escalate, Humphrey, in a private
meeting of the president's advisers, argued for a restrained response to an attack on
American forces.[5] What Humphrey did not know was that Johnson had already decided on the action he planned to take in this instance. Johnson immediately dismissed
Humphrey's dissent out of hand, taking it as a betrayal of the administration and not as
the offer of an alternative plan. From that moment forward, the president excluded the
vice president from any meaningful involvement in the conduct of the war.

Because Hubert Humphrey was vice president, and therefore a statutory member
of the National Security Council, President Johnson could not entirely banish him
from top level meetings on the war. What Johnson could and did do was to restrict
the information covered in those meetings, and then convene alternate, substantive
meetings, to which the vice president was not invited.[6] By withholding information
from Humphrey in this way, Johnson was playing a dangerous game with the man who
easily might ascend to the presidency. Fortunately there were some individuals in the
White House who made sure the vice president was kept in the loop; one adviser to the
president described it as "an open conspiracy to make certain he [Humphrey] was privy
to all that went on in the White House so he could at all times be armed with precious
information necessary to him and his future."[7]

Even if President Johnson made a point of keeping Humphrey from critical discussions on Vietnam, he continued to give the vice president substantive domestic
policy assignments. This included making Humphrey the chairman of the National
Aeronautics and Space Council, the Peace Corps Advisory Council, the Cabinet
Committee on Employment, and the Antipoverty Program Advisory Council. But
Lyndon Johnson was a complex man, and a difficult president to work for: one day he
would praise Humphrey for his work on a presidential commission, and the next day he
would relieve the vice president of any tangible authority over the same commission.[8]
By his use of duplicitous maneuvers, Johnson effectively constricted Humphrey's vice
presidency.

Clearly this state of affairs was frustrating for Humphrey; he was the second-highest elected officer in the nation, yet he was forever at the mercy of a capricious president. It was precisely this type of treatment of the individual holding the office that made the vice presidency such an awkward institution. Plainly, even with the vast expansion of the modern vice presidency, it is the president who decides what form the institution takes, as well as what satisfaction the occupant of the office does or does not achieve. Humphrey captured the essence of this best with his personal idiom, which went like this: "He who giveth can taketh away and often does."[9]

Hubert Humphrey was consistently a loyal vice president. But in the four years he was vice president, he suffered ongoing humiliation at the feet of Lyndon Johnson. The question then is this: why would Humphrey—who was an established political figure, and who was building a national constituency—stand for it? Quite simply, the answer lies in the duality of Humphrey's character. It was in his nature to remain steadfast in his commitment to the president. At no point in his career was Humphrey ever accused of betraying his colleagues or his friends. Conversely, like most politicians, he was ambitious beyond the pale. As such, Humphrey wanted Johnson's job.

Early on Humphrey appreciated the potential to affect the affairs of government by way of the modern vice presidency. He was similarly confident that it was the best position from which to earn the presidential nomination of the Democratic Party, and subsequently win the presidency as well. In this, Humphrey's judgment was correct on two counts: he utilized the increased institutional strength of the vice presidency to impact politics and policy, and he won the Democratic nomination for president in 1968. But on the third point, he failed.

Humphrey's loss in the 1968 election should be taken as considerably more than a failure to win the presidency. For the outcome of the election was emblematic of a fundamental tenet of the American vice presidency: the vice president is insuperably linked to the president. And it was Humphrey's incontrovertible connection to Lyndon Johnson that doomed his presidential bid from the beginning. By the time Johnson decided to not seek another term as president, the Vietnam War had consumed his presidency, as well as all of the goodwill Johnson had accrued in the wake of President Kennedy's assassination.

Being so closely identified with the Vietnam policy of the Johnson administration, Humphrey could only be hurt by the association when he ran for president on his own. Not surprisingly, data at the time indicated that 13.7 percent of major party voters were unwilling to vote for Humphrey because of his connection to Johnson, and 16.7 percent of independent voters cited the same rationale for their vote against Humphrey.[10] Considering that less than 1 percent of the popular vote separated Humphrey from his opponent, former vice president Richard Nixon, it is not unreasonable to suggest, in the end, that being Lyndon Johnson's vice president cost Humphrey the prize he had long coveted.

SUCCESSION, PRESIDENTIAL INABILITY, AND THE TWENTY-FIFTH AMENDMENT

Managing presidential succession, in addition to instances when the incumbent president became incapacitated for some reason, was problematic, and had been since the establishment of the Constitution. At the same time, vacancies in the vice presidency were consistently an auxiliary concern, although concern may be too strong of a term for the reaction to those occasions when the second office fell vacant. As was demonstrated by the earlier review of the string of succession laws, Congress, in tandem with specific presidents, repeatedly confronted equivocation on the subject within the Constitution. And though the Constitution did offer some direction for filling presidential vacancies—and John Tyler seized on the first opportunity to test it—the Constitution offered no guidance for replacing the vice president, should the vice president die, resign, or succeed to the presidency. Naturally, the main worry was not about finding a replacement vice president so the duties of the office could be satisfied; instead, the anxiety came from the absence of a ready successor, should a vacancy in the presidency occur again.

Because the deaths of Presidents Franklin Roosevelt and John Kennedy came within eighteen years of one another—making them the seventh and eighth presidents to die while in office—presidential succession was becoming an inescapable facet of the American political system. Moreover, with Roosevelt's death occurring when the United States was involved in a world war, and with Kennedy's assassination happening suddenly and violently, in the shadow of a nuclear showdown with the Soviet Union, the necessity of having a vice president in place to succeed to the presidency could not have been clearer. The vice presidency could no longer be neglected, nor could the office be left vacant for years at a time.

It was therefore in a climate of fear and uncertainty when the first steps were taken toward the enumeration of an orderly, constitutional method for managing presidential succession, as well as for handling when the president is incapacitated, and finally, for filling vacancies in the vice presidency. This all came about when Senator Birch Bayh of Indiana introduced Senate Joint Resolution 139, just twenty days after President Kennedy was killed; it was the precursor for what eventually became the Twenty-fifth Amendment to the United States Constitution.[11]

After countless hours of congressional debate, obtaining the support of two-thirds of both chambers of Congress, and gaining passage by three-fourths of all the state legislatures in the nation, the Twenty-fifth Amendment was ratified on February 23, 1967. The Twenty-fifth Amendment unequivocally demarcates presidential succession, declaring in the first section that should the president be removed from office, die, or resign, "the Vice President shall become President."[12] Finally, any residual ambiguity on the vice president rightfully succeeding to the presidency was put to rest.

In the third and fourth sections of the amendment, the framework for dealing with presidential inability is delineated, including provisions for when the president may declare an inability exists, or when the vice president and a majority of the cabinet assert the same on the president's condition. Under either circumstance, the vice president assumes the presidency and "the powers and duties of the office as Acting President" until it is confirmed by the president, vice president, and the cabinet, that an inability no longer stands.

One scenario the succession provision of the Twenty-fifth Amendment does not directly address is managing the remote possibility of a double-vacancy in the executive offices, though the absence of direction made sense. If it should occur, the Presidential Succession Act of 1947 would take effect. Under the Succession Act, the Speaker of the House of Representatives is the first in the line of succession, meant to discharge the duties and responsibilities of the president for the remainder of the current presidential term, and until an election is held.[13]

It was the second section of the Twenty-fifth Amendment which was put in practice twice in the 1970s. That section defines how vice-presidential vacancies are to be filled, giving the president the power to "nominate a Vice President who shall take office upon confirmation by a majority vote of both Houses of Congress." Obviously this gave the president a strong hand in choosing a potential successor and, assuming that the vice president served ably and without scandal, aided that individual in gaining a future presidential nomination.

Additionally, by granting the president the means for choosing a replacement vice president, the political party in control of the executive branch had a better chance for maintaining control. Without fail, the earlier debates on the different succession laws had gravitated to an unwelcome prospect. If the vice president was to succeed to the presidency and then die, resign, or be removed from office, and the opposition party was in control of Congress, then the will of the majority of the voters would be overturned.

More challenging than having the losing political party in the presidential election take over the executive branch via succession was the selection of a replacement vice president, essentially by presidential fiat, and devoid of the direct consent of the voters. Such a process created, historian Arthur Schlesinger Jr. once noted, "a unilateral presidential appointment subject to congressional confirmation."[14] Hence, if the Twenty-fifth Amendment solved, among other concerns, the quandary of filling vacancies in the vice presidency, it did so by a method that was outwardly contradictory to the spirit of democratic ideals. Then again, in all likelihood the Framers never meant for the selection of the president and vice president to be grounded in democratic idealism. Returning to Schlesinger, in order to rectify that flaw in the amendment, the simplest way would be to "adopt a constitutional amendment abolishing the Vice Presidency, an office that has become both more superfluous and more mischievous than Hamilton could have imagined ... and then provide for the succession ... through a congressional statute reestablishing the principle of special presidential elections."[15]

The alternative to vice-presidential succession—special presidential elections— would provide a valuable dose of direct participation by the electorate, yet this method does not account for the immediacy of succession. In other words, succession by the vice president to the presidency has occurred eight out of nine times because of death. The ninth instance of succession came about when President Richard Nixon resigned from office, following a protracted struggle by Nixon to remain in office. Aside from the Nixon case, as well as the lengthy death watch following the shooting of President James

Garfield, the circumstances prompting succession have been abrupt. What matters, then, is that in each instance when the vice president has succeeded to the presidency, and despite the alacrity of events, the transition of power has been seamless.

Here too the sagacity of the Framers is evident in that succession was provided for, even if imprecisely. The powers of the presidency, absent a president, were meant to devolve to the vice president, and such powers were to rest with the vice president until an election for president was held. It was James Madison who, at one point at the Federal Convention, proposed drafting alternate wording for how and when to fill such vacancies. Madison's disquiet was based on the absence of any provision for "an intermediate election" to choose a new president. Madison won his point, but the wording of that part of the Constitution was indefinite. Was the vice president meant to serve as president until the traditional quadrennial election was held? Or was Congress meant to determine a date and time for an intermediate election of the president? Over the years, when presidential succession was prompted, and the vice president was compelled to fulfill the remainder of the president's term of office—thus avoiding a rushed, intermediate election—propinquity, continuity, and stability have underscored the entire process.

Finally, the effectiveness of the Twenty-fifth Amendment is patently manifest in the reduction in time the vice presidency remains unoccupied after the office becomes vacant. As supported by the data in Table 1.1, prior to the adoption of the Twenty-fifth Amendment in 1967, the vice presidency fell vacant on sixteen occasions, and since 1967, the office has been unoccupied just twice. Of the first sixteen vacancies, seven were due to the vice president dying in office, one vacancy came about with the resignation of the vice president, and eight of the vacancies were initiated when the vice president succeeded to the presidency. Of the two vacancies post the Twenty-fifth Amendment, one occurred when the vice president resigned, and the second was prompted by the only resignation of a president, thus far, and the subsequent succession to the presidency by the first appointed vice president in history.

Remarkably, prior to the Twenty-fifth Amendment, the vice presidency was regularly left unoccupied for considerable periods of time. For example, in the nineteenth century the vice presidency was vacated eleven times. Of those eleven vacancies, on five occasions the office remained unoccupied for three years, and of those five cases, three times the office was vacant for almost four years. In addition, with two of the vacancies to occur in the twentieth century—both of which occurred prior to 1967, and each due to the vice president succeeding to the presidency—the office went unoccupied for well over three years.

Since the Twenty-fifth Amendment was incorporated in the Constitution, providing a systematic means for filling vacancies in the vice presidency, the amount of time the office was left unoccupied diminished precipitously. For instance, when Vice President Spiro Agnew resigned in 1973, merely one month and twenty-six days elapsed from the time President Richard Nixon submitted his choice to succeed Agnew, Gerald Ford, and Ford's confirmation by Congress. Subsequently, when Ford moved from the vice presidency to the presidency, and then named his own successor to the second office, Nelson Rockefeller, there was a vacancy gap of just four months and eight days.

By most measures the Twenty-fifth Amendment has been a success. The time that the office stands vacant has been lessened because the president now has the authority to locate, nominate, and replace the vice president within a brief period. This is important because modern vice presidents are considerably more utilitarian than vice presidents in earlier eras; intrinsically, the vice president is of greater value to the president, to the administration, and to the nation, than has ever been the case.

The Twenty-fifth Amendment, however, has not escaped criticism.[16] It has been put forward that in allowing the president to choose a replacement vice president, the president is doing much more than filling a vacancy in an otherwise elective position. When selecting a nominee for vice president, the president does so without the appreciable input of the electorate. In theory, this then gives a single individual the authority to choose the second-highest-ranking officer of the United States government.[17] Still, even when acknowledging the validity of the preceding objection to the Twenty-fifth Amendment, the more significant outcome is that the amendment reduces the probability of overturning the mandate of the electorate, as would happen if circumstances dictated and the Succession Act of 1947 was implemented.

THE VICE PRESIDENCY SERVED: BY RESIGNATION AND PRESIDENTIAL SELECTION (1969–1977)

Hubert Humphrey's successor, Spiro Agnew, was not the most likely candidate for the vice presidency. When Richard Nixon selected Agnew for a running mate in 1968, Agnew was then governor of Maryland, having served in the position for less than two years. His only previous government experience, aside from the governorship, amounted to three years as the elected chief executive of Baltimore County. It was a thin résumé, to be sure, but Agnew more than compensated for it with audacity. Curiously, the narrative of Agnew's life—he was the son of Greek immigrant parents, and he had worked his way through law school—augured a different, more humble persona than the one the electorate grew to know. In the summer of 1968 few could have foreseen just how ill-suited Spiro Agnew was for the vice presidency or presidency.

Nixon bore sole responsibility for the selection of Agnew; it was from the outset a mystifying choice. At the Republican convention, after winning his own nomination for president, Nixon met with an assortment of Republican stalwarts throughout the evening and well into the next morning.[18] Having weighed the advantages and disadvantages of several potential vice-presidential nominees, the group came up empty-handed. At that point, it was Nixon who first suggested Agnew for a running mate, but he was unknown to most of Nixon's intimates, and even Nixon had only met with him on a few prior occasions, and then just briefly.

Whatever it was Nixon saw in Agnew was enough to convince him that Agnew was the one. But that too is odd in light of the pool of quality candidates Nixon could have picked from, including Governor Nelson Rockefeller of New York, Senator Mark

Hatfield of Oregon, Governor Ronald Reagan of California, and New York City Mayor John Lindsay. Later, Vice President Hubert Humphrey insisted that of all "the able Republicans Nixon might have chosen ... Agnew's record and character had little to recommend him."[19]

Ultimately, doubts about Agnew's experience and fitness for higher office were inconsequential, since the prerogative of the presidential nominee is paramount in choosing the vice-presidential nominee. If Nixon wanted him, any opposition to the choice was incidental to the selection process. And Nixon did want Agnew for the ticket, irrespective of his own unfamiliarity with the Maryland governor. Yet the mystery surrounding Agnew's selection went beyond Nixon. This was apparent following the introduction of the vice-presidential nominee to the nation when, fittingly, politicos and the press posed a question that resonates to this day: "Spiro who?"

This much is irrefutable: the selection of Spiro Agnew was a throwback to an earlier era of politics, when mediocrities were turned to for the vice-presidential nomination. What made him an especially odd choice for the office was Nixon's own success serving as vice president to President Dwight Eisenhower. By all rights, Nixon should have chosen an ambitious, experienced, and industrious vice-presidential running mate—a candidate with attributes reflective of his own, and one who, once in office, would be a useful vice president. But from Agnew, Nixon instead got ambition and little else. When it came to electoral politics, Nixon was a utilitarian; he had an explicit use for Agnew in his own campaign for the White House—after that, he would have no need for a working vice president. Indeed, it was likely because Agnew was so unspectacular that Nixon sought him for the ticket; Nixon could only shine next to a man like Agnew.

A decade after the 1968 Republican nominating convention, writing as a former vice president and president, Nixon revealed a cavalier attitude with respect to who the vice-presidential nominee was and how the nominee choice had been determined. Nixon wrote: "Ted Agnew placed my name in nomination. [John] Mitchell had asked him if he would like to have the assignment and had suggested that, if he did a good job, he would be among those considered for the second spot on the ticket. To that extent, at least, Agnew's speech was an audition."[20] Apparently, in Nixon's mind, a good speech outweighed fitness for the vice presidency or presidency.

During the 1968 campaign Nixon used Agnew shrewdly, much in the way Nixon was used by Eisenhower in the 1952 and 1956 campaigns. It was Nixon the candidate for vice president who eagerly descended into harsh partisan attacks on the opposition, while the candidate for president stayed far above the political fray. And it was Nixon who was once described by a journalist as "the knife" of the Eisenhower administration, cutting his way through the political fray at any cost.[21]

Even if, as the nominee for president, it was impossible for someone like Richard Nixon to stay completely out of the campaign trenches, Spiro Agnew proved to be in a class by himself when it came to vitriolic electioneering. Given that there was an unusually viable third party ticket for president and vice president that year—a ticket which appealed primarily to angry white voters—Agnew was the perfect lure for attracting the same constituency, and then he could serve as a necessary counterweight to the opposition.[22] Still, whatever appeal Agnew might have had was almost certainly of less consequence than the presence of a third party ticket competing for the top executive offices. That pair, Alabama Governor George Wallace and his running mate General Curtis LeMay, drew just enough support away from the Democratic ticket, Vice President Hubert Humphrey and Senator Edmund Muskie, to allow Nixon and Agnew to eke out a victory.

When Spiro Agnew was sworn in to office on January 20, 1969, becoming the thirty-ninth vice president of the United States, he came to the nation's capital after serving exclusively in state government; he never had been an elected member of the legislative branch. Agnew's background contrasted sharply from his most recent predecessors—Humphrey, Johnson, Nixon, and Barkley—who shared a combined total of sixty-nine years of legislative experience prior to their stints as vice president. No doubt conscious of this deficiency in his political career, when Agnew won the vice presidency, and by extension became the president of the United States Senate, he was determined to master the constitutional responsibilities of the job. To this end, Agnew initially met on a regular basis with the Senate parliamentarian to "discuss parliamentary procedures and practices and precedents of the Senate, for anywhere from an hour to two hours each day."[23] In turn, Agnew gained satisfaction from presiding in the Senate, and so at the outset of his first term he spent an ample measure of time presiding in the upper chamber.[24]

But Agnew's experience with the Senate was eventually tainted by a breach in protocol. The mistake he made was that he dared to venture onto the Senate floor, and then he tried to persuade a senator to vote with the administration on a specific piece of legislation. The view of the typical United States senator toward such behavior has always been rather provincial: since the vice president is not an elected member of Senate, then the vice president has no place on the chamber floor. Clearly Agnew was unaware that his presence on the floor was, in practice, forbidden. From his perspective, he was the vice president of the United States and the presiding officer of the chamber; it made sense for him to be there. Either way, the damage was done and Agnew was effectively ostracized from the Senate. And the senator in question, Len Jordan of Idaho, claimed that if Agnew ever tried to coerce his vote in the future, on principle and without reservation, he would vote contrary to the vice president's wishes.[25]

Agnew's excursion to the floor of the Senate, and his alleged offense while there, seems petty today, yet it underscored the awkwardness of ever designating the vice president the presiding officer of the Senate. It is worth recalling that it was precisely because of the vice president's attachment to the president that some delegates to the Federal Convention were bothered when the vice president was included in any capacity in the legislative branch. For those delegates, doing so violated the principle of a separation of powers and was tantamount to placing the president "at head of the Legislature."[26] Poignantly, Agnew's predicament symbolized the long-standing underutilization of the office in its most logical and practical capacity—as a conduit for executive-legislative relations.

On the executive side of the vice presidency, Agnew hardly fared much better than he had on the legislative side. Ironically, when Richard Nixon was the Republican candidate for president in 1960, he had indicated that if he was elected, his preference was for a proactive and engaged vice president to serve with him. Such an arrangement was manifest in Nixon's proposal for the vice president to lead an executive board charged with reorganizing and coordinating the work of various agencies of the executive branch.[27] Of course, Nixon and his choice for vice president in 1960, Henry Cabot Lodge, failed to win the election, so it is unclear if Nixon would have acted on his plan, but suggesting a role of this type for the vice president was a significant acknowledgement by Nixon that the office could be better utilized.

When Nixon finally won the presidency in 1968, he seemed to be trending again toward making the vice president a more substantial player in the government. To this end, Nixon gave Agnew an office in the White House, making him the first vice president in history to have an office there.[28] Although Nixon's gesture turned out to be purely symbolic, meant only to make the vice president appear integrated within the executive operation, it did allow Agnew, for a time, to get closer to the locus of power than many of his predecessors.

Apart from the close proximity to the Oval Office Agnew briefly enjoyed, he was never included in the president's inner circle, and it was not long before he was working primarily out of the Old Executive Office Building, among his own staff and advisers. Agnew later lamented his treatment, claiming that if Nixon "had picked up the phone and asked me to come in and work with him, I would have … But he never did. Our only interchanges came at the staff level."[29] The deliberate exclusion of the vice president from important Oval Office deliberations was especially acute on account of the coterie of sycophantic aides Nixon kept; however, Agnew's dilemma was not an unfamiliar one.

Always, the staff of the vice president will put their principal first; it is a phenomenon even more pronounced with the president's staff. For instance, several years after serving as vice president, Henry Wallace noted the innate rivalries and pettiness which typically characterize relations between the White House staff and the vice president. Wallace, a vice president denied a second term in office primarily because of the covert maneuverings of zealous presidential advisers, asserted that "there is always likely to be a palace guard which will be jealous of anyone whom the President builds up. It doesn't make any difference who is President."[30]

Although Agnew was hardly built up by Nixon, he did owe his place in the national government entirely to Nixon's benevolence; it was an arrangement which did not go unnoticed by overtly hostile White House intimates. In time, Agnew acknowledged that the signs of his exclusion from the administration were apparent from the outset, stating that he "first began to feel isolated from the really important Nixon decisions after our 1968 election victory."[31]

Regrettably, even with the vastly improved relations evidenced between every president and vice president since the end of the Nixon era, the competition between those close to the president with those who are near to the vice president has been exacerbated by the growth of the modern vice presidency. Put another way, as the institutional resources and power of the vice presidency have increased, so too has the assumption that the vice-presidential institution is now competitive with the presidential institution.

Eventually one of Nixon's top aides asked Agnew to relinquish the historic first office for a vice president in the White House, citing a need for "more space in the West Wing."[32] By first giving, and then taking away, valuable White House office space, President Nixon delivered a setback to the modern vice presidency—a temporary one, but a setback nonetheless. The treatment of Agnew by Nixon and his staff was emblematic of the oddness in ever having put the two men together on the same electoral ticket. Moreover, when Nixon had been vice president, President Eisenhower made use of his talents in ways that extended expectations for the office and contrasted with the way many previous vice presidents had been used. Yet when Nixon had the opportunity to do the same, he opted to ignore his own vice president.

As for Agnew, he did not blame the failures of his vice presidency on his own limitations; instead, he placed the blame squarely on Richard Nixon's character. Because Nixon was president, he could make or break the vice presidency. Along these lines, Agnew asserted:

> I really would have enjoyed serving in the vice-presidency with Lyndon Johnson, because if anything had gone wrong, probably he himself would have picked up the phone … Unfortunately, I could have no such man-to-man talk with President Nixon. Absolutely none. I was never allowed to come close enough to participate with him directly in any decision. Every time I went to see him and raised a subject for discussion, he would begin a rambling, time-consuming monologue. Then finally the phone would ring … and there would be no time left for what I really had come to talk about. He successfully avoided any subject he didn't want to be pinned down on. He preferred keeping his decision-making within a very small group. I was not of the inner circle.[33]

In the aftermath of Nixon and Agnew's successful reelection campaign, the vice president found himself the presumptive Republican nominee for the next presidential election.[34] To a certain extent, this may be attributed to the four years Agnew already had campaigned on behalf of Republican candidates across the country. But in greater measure, by 1972 the growth of the vice presidency was undeniable; it had become the logical political institution to draw presidential candidates from. What is truly remarkable is that the inevitability of Agnew's candidacy arose despite the best efforts of the Nixon White House to exclude the vice president from vital administration business. From Agnew's standpoint, though, "there was no chance that a Vice-President would be overlooked as a candidate [for president] and, in my case, my popularity in the party was recognized by all."[35]

If Richard Nixon had been a different type of person, and therefore a different type of president, Spiro Agnew's years in the executive branch would have signaled another step forward for the modern vice presidency. It did not matter, though, as Agnew's own failings got the better of him, and a web of corruption charges eventually devoured his vice presidency. All the charges against him originated from his time in Maryland politics, implicating him in bribery and extortion schemes, as well as in accepting payoffs inside the vice president's White House office. Although he denied wrongdoing for the rest of his life, in 1973 Vice President Agnew pled no contest to a charge of income tax evasion. In addition to his plea, Agnew agreed to resign from office, thus avoiding possible time in prison and making him only the second vice president in American history to resign from office.

It was Spiro Agnew's theory that Richard Nixon, and those closest to the president, actively promoted his ouster because the vice president had become an unpleasant, though at times welcome, distraction.[36] Nixon was increasingly embroiled in the Watergate scandal, and he could scarcely expend time or political capital defending his vice president. With Agnew's resignation there was the chance that those who were bent on holding Nixon accountable for Watergate might relent, satisfied by having forced the vice president from office. Perhaps Nixon held that view too. Agnew certainly thought so, complaining that "Nixon naively believed that by throwing me to the wolves, he had appeased his enemies and they would stop clamoring for his blood. But he had merely whetted their appetite for more."[37]

Apart from their penchant for aggressive campaigning and sometimes unlawful conduct, Agnew and Nixon had little in common. They were not close personally, and Nixon clearly had no use, nor respect, for Agnew. Furthermore, Nixon never bothered to seek or to take his vice president's advice, their relations contrasting sharply with the association Nixon had enjoyed when he was vice president to President Eisenhower. By a neat twist of fate, the one occasion when Nixon probably should have listened to Agnew was when the infamous Watergate tapes first came to light and the vice president told him to destroy the recordings.[38]

But the weakness of their relationship was never more apparent than when the fury over the alleged crimes of both men was reaching a peak. At that time, Agnew attempted to leverage an offer of a public defense of Nixon, if the president would simply agree to meet with him. Nixon was astounded, writing in his diary:

I received a rather astonishing message … from Agnew to the effect that he would speak up on Watergate, but only at a price and that was that he would have to see the President. I told Ehrlichman to pass the message … that I didn't want under any circumstances to ask Agnew to do something that he was not convinced he ought to do on his own, that under the circumstances he should just chart his own course and of course I would chart my own course.[39]

In the end, even if the pairing of Nixon and Agnew is deemed a failure, Nixon's treatment of Agnew did succeed in reinforcing the conventional wisdom of the vice presidency being only what the president allows it to be.

Spiro Agnew's resignation from office was effective on October 10, 1973. The vice presidency was again vacant. With Agnew gone, it was never more apparent how fleeting the stature and presumed power of a political life may be, even for the vice president, and the certainty of this was captured ably by Nixon's acting chief of staff, General Alexander Haig. With the advantage of hindsight, Haig confirmed that "Agnew's departure showed how right Nixon had been about the effect of his resignation. He was forgotten instantaneously by the public and the press, and I do not recall ever hearing his name mentioned in the White House again."[40]

Although Agnew's exit marked only the second time a vice president relinquished the office in such a manner, it set in motion the first occasion for the Twenty-fifth Amendment to the Constitution to be put in use. Wasting no time, President Nixon immediately initiated the formal process for selecting a new vice president. Nixon was exercising a new power of the presidency; he was no doubt aware that he held a power with considerable portent for his personal and political future. In effect, Nixon was acting as a proxy for the nation's electorate, for he, not the voters, was set to choose one of the two nationally elected officers of the government.

Nixon's preference to replace Agnew was the former Democratic governor of Texas, John Connally.[41] In the early 1970s, Nixon had appointed Connally treasury secretary, and Connally had switched his political affiliation soon after. Always one to advance political calculations first, Nixon was confident that Connally was the most viable candidate for the Republican Party to field in the presidential contest of 1976.[42] It then followed that should Agnew be replaced by Connally, the latter man would have a better shot at keeping the White House under Republican control.

What was problematic for Connally was that he was too fresh a convert to the Republican Party; as such, members of his new political party were restrained in their enthusiasm for him. Likewise, those in his former political party could not help but view him as an opportunist. This partisan conundrum went beyond electoral calculations; it also made the odds of Connally winning the requisite confirmation by the United States Congress uncertain, at best.

Because John Connally was unlikely to win confirmation on his own merits, and since Nixon was lacking the requisite political capital to compel the Congress to accept a controversial nominee, Nixon instead turned to a congressman from Michigan who also happened to be the minority leader of the House of Representatives. That member of the House was Gerald Ford, and he appeared to be the nominee who was least likely to cause controversy, and for that reason, most apt to be confirmed.[43]

Before deciding on Ford, Nixon had already eliminated two other contenders, both governors, because one, Nelson Rockefeller, was undeniably too liberal for many Republicans in Congress, and the other, Ronald Reagan, was surely too conservative for the moderate-to-liberal wing of the Republican Party to give its consent.[44] Also, working against Rockefeller and Reagan was that each came from a state Nixon could call home—New York and California. In settling for a nominee who was ideologically and geographically adequate, Nixon had reverted to traditional notions of filling the vice presidency. By no means was Ford lacking the necessary political and governmental experience to serve as vice president—by 1973, he had been a member of the House of Representative for twenty-five years—nor was he ill suited in any way to hold either of the nation's top two executive offices. But in every way, Ford was well suited to bide his time, innocuously holding the second spot in the government until the next election.

When Richard Nixon introduced Gerald Ford as the first individual ever to be nominated by a president to fill a vacancy in the vice presidency, he delineated what the nominee should bring to the office. Nixon asserted that "above all, the individual who serves as Vice President must be qualified to be President," and then he added that the vice president should likewise "be an individual who can work with members of both parties in the Congress."[45]

By including the preceding two points among the other conditions he listed, Nixon shielded himself in four ways. First, if something were to happen to Nixon, Ford ostensibly was well prepared to step into the presidency; therefore, Nixon could not be accused of dereliction in meeting a fundamental expectation for any vice-presidential nominee. Second, being a creature of the House of Representatives, Ford could win confirmation fairly easily, so Nixon would not have to fight Congress to have his choice. Third, because Ford came from Congress, his selection might temper some of the fervor the Watergate scandal had generated to rid the executive branch of Nixon. And fourth, despite the tandem Agnew and Watergate scandals engulfing his administration, Nixon, because the Twenty-fifth Amendment gives the president the constitutional authority to nominate a replacement vice president, continued to have a significant impact on, and control over, the broader political landscape.

Of the foregoing four points, the last is the most intriguing, mainly in light of the political predicament Nixon was in when he offered the nomination to Ford. At that time, remarkably, Nixon was able to extract a pledge from Ford that he would not seek the Republican nomination for president in 1976. In Nixon's words, "John Connally is my choice for 1976. He'd be excellent."[46] Although an embattled president, clearly Nixon maintained a substantial degree of leverage over other political actors.

But the nomination of a new vice president was not entirely at the discretion of the president. Ford had to endure a congressional confirmation process, including an extensive investigation of his personal and public life, as well as hearings conducted by both the Senate and the House. Ford's confirmation hearings are a matter of public record and it is plain from the transcripts that they were relatively benign affairs.[47] In many respects, Ford was akin to the classic nineteenth century vice president: he was bland, a loyal partisan, and refused to upstage the president. By his estimation: the vice presidency "was going to climax my political career."[48] It was an ending familiar to many of his predecessors.

To appreciate Ford's view, it is essential to understand that he was one of the rare members of Congress who did not dream of becoming president. Ford's overriding ambition had always been to be elected the Speaker of the House, nothing more, and so he had told his wife that after twenty-five years in the House, his service as vice president would be the pinnacle, as well as the end, of his political career.[49] Still, Ford had accepted Nixon's offer, persuaded by the idea that his vice presidency might differ from others who had served in the office before him; he believed that what Nixon expected from him was an ally and advocate for an administration facing an increasingly hostile Congress.[50] Ford could be that for Nixon, but he did not anticipate being much more.

Gerald Ford was sworn in as the fortieth vice president on December 6, 1973. Ford had requested to have the ceremony held in the House chamber he had inhabited for so long. Not since John Nance Garner's first inauguration in 1932 had the vice president taken the oath of office inside the Capitol building. Afterwards, the new vice president spoke to those assembled, and to those watching on television. Noting the historic first application of the Twenty-fifth Amendment, Ford went on to define himself for a nation to whom he was broadly unfamiliar, proclaiming: "I am a Ford, not a Lincoln."[51] Perhaps Ford was acknowledging more than his own limitations; perhaps he was stressing that, as the vice president, he would always be second best.

The arrangement Nixon and Ford agreed on, naturally, did not play out as planned, and Nixon dictated the terms of Ford's service for the duration of their time together.[52] Furthermore, Ford's position was not helped by the obsequious staffers surrounding the president, who saw in the vice president a reliable, but expendable appendage.[53] It was, according to one account, as if Nixon's White House staff "wanted Ford to be a mouthpiece for the president and nothing more."[54] As for Ford, his relationship with the president soured about a month after he took the oath of office. Around that time, Ford had the audacity, from Nixon's outlook, to stray from the official line on Watergate, suggesting in an interview on national television that Nixon could reach an agreement over materials sought in the Watergate investigation and, in effect, should "compromise."[55]

Ford's veracity did him in. He had broken one of the cardinal rules adhered to by all vice presidents and presidents: the vice president should never publicly disagree with the president. Hubert Humphrey had framed it in this way: "If a Vice President doesn't like the way he is treated or disagrees violently with a policy, he could make an open break with the President, fighting it out on an issue. He would lose."[56]

In Humphrey's case, no doubt he was referring to his failure to part ways publically with President Johnson over the war in Vietnam, as it was his loyalty to Johnson which likely cost him his own term in the White House. Yet Humphrey's theory is likewise applicable to Ford's public divergence with Nixon, since from that point forward, Ford was treated with indifference, and his usefulness to the president was marginal. And because Ford's association with Nixon was weakened so soon after his taking office, the Ford vice presidency simply, and swiftly, slipped into irrelevance. As it stood, Ford would spend the entirety of his vice presidency in a holding pattern for the presidency.

Obviously only Richard Nixon knew precisely the extent of his involvement in the Watergate affair. It was therefore impossible to predict how he would respond to the pressure. But there was one certainty: Nixon's presidency was indisputably doomed in the weeks and months following the onset of the Ford vice presidency. While Ford endeavored to maintain loyalty to the president who picked him, he made certain he was ready to take over for Nixon if the outcome of Watergate made it so.

To prepare for his probable ascent to the presidency, Ford regularly conferred with Nixon's national security team, met with members of the cabinet, and was kept abreast of the economic and budgeting policies of the administration.[57] And so, on August 9, 1974, when Richard Nixon became the first president in American history to resign from the nation's highest elective office, Ford was standing by, set to take the reins of government. Even though the transition of power was smooth, the circumstances under which the transition unfolded were wholly anomalous. For unlike every other vice president to have made it to the top spot in the United States government, Ford was the first individual in history to make it to the vice presidency, and then to the presidency, without the nation's electorate ever having had an opportunity to vote for or against him.

It was oddly appropriate that among the myriad critical tasks facing President Ford, the first order of business was the selection of a nominee for vice president. Just as Nixon had done before him, Ford committed himself to nominating an individual "fully qualified to step into my shoes should something happen to me."[58] To this end, aides to Ford reviewed potential nominees for "their national stature, executive experience and ability to broaden ... [Ford's] political base, [then] assigned them points and ranked them numerically."[59] He was next presented with the names of five individuals and their total scores. Of those five—including George H.W. Bush and Senator William Brock—Ford eventually settled on Nelson Rockefeller. As it turns out, Rockefeller was the one individual Nixon had recommended Ford choose on the eve of his resignation from the presidency.[60]

Nelson Rockefeller's service in the federal government went as far back as a stint in the third administration of Franklin Roosevelt. His career continued with appointments to different administrative posts made by Presidents Truman and Eisenhower. Moreover, Rockefeller had been one of the longest serving governors of New York—in office from 1959 to 1973—and he was a nationally recognized political figure in his own right. Just how well established and attractive within the world of politics Rockefeller was could not have been any more apparent than in 1968. In that year, Rockefeller was a contender for the presidential and vice-presidential nominations at the Republican Party convention, and then later he was covertly approached by Vice President Hubert Humphrey to join the Democratic Party ticket.[61] Even Ford viewed Rockefeller for his potential as a vice-presidential candidate when, despite his earlier disavowal of any plans to run for president in 1976, he admitted that in choosing Rockefeller, the strengths of a future Ford-Rockefeller ticket had been persuasive.[62]

If Rockefeller never aspired to be vice president, he did want to be president, and he was a candidate for the office more than once. He had also made the short-list for vice president on more than one occasion, but Rockefeller was unaccustomed to answering to anyone and once proclaimed that he "never wanted to be vice president of anything."[63] Nevertheless, when Ford offered him the number two spot, Rockefeller accepted. It was a decision Rockefeller more than likely regretted, primarily because he was put through a grueling confirmation process that made Ford's confirmation a year earlier, for the same office, look effortless. The Rockefeller confirmation hearings were an ordeal which would have made lesser individuals retreat from consideration.

Over the course of the confirmation process, there appeared to be more concern with the Rockefeller family, and the wealth which came with the name, than any other aspect of the nominee's life.[64] Rockefeller's qualifications for the vice presidency, and quite possibly the presidency, were secondary concerns. This was not a case of those in Congress shirking the constitutional responsibility entrusted to them by the Twenty-fifth Amendment. Assessing and investigating Ford's chosen successor for vice president was unequivocally the central mission of the Congress; it was just that Rockefeller's fame and fortune made him an unusually ripe object of curiosity. Either way, from the outset of the hearings there was no denying that the nominee was a remarkable individual with a singular political career.

When opening the hearings, Congressman Peter Rodino, chairman of the House Committee on the Judiciary, juxtaposed the unusual background of the nominee for vice president with a dose of hyperbole on the office he was intended to hold. But perhaps Rodino's comments were not so much overstatement as they were an acknowledgement of how far the second office had come, and of the necessity to be cautious in filling the position, particularly by a means which entirely bypassed the direct input of the national electorate. Rodino asked,

> what does it mean to wed great, indeed immense, personal wealth to the awesome powers of the American Vice Presidency and Presidency?

> We would do a great disservice ... if we established a principle that money, either too much of it or too little of it, disqualifies a man from service in high public office. But it has been said that the wealth of the Rockefellers is more than just another large fortune; it is an unusual aggregation of immense private economic authority. It creates a diversity of complex relationships and interrelationships, and Congress has a responsibility to address the ramifications of these issues forthrightly and honestly.[65]

By delving deeply into Rockefeller's financial holdings, and even deeper into his personal, political, and business associations, dual objectives were satisfied. For those observers merely curious about the Rockefeller fortune, there was some degree of satisfaction, as heretofore unknown investments and financial holdings of the Rockefeller family were publicly divulged. And those parties seeking elucidation on Rockefeller's philosophy, personal interests, and political associations, would likewise find answers, and possibly some reassurance, in Rockefeller's testimony.

The vice-presidential nominee confirmation process, as Nelson Rockefeller experienced it, was arduous and exhaustive. It lasted almost four months to the day from his formal nomination, and it came on the heels of Gerald Ford's abrupt move to the White House. Documentation of just the hearings before the House Committee of the Judiciary ultimately totaled 1,455 pages.[66] But more importantly, the overlap of Ford's transition to the presidency with Rockefeller's protracted battle to win confirmation influenced the form, and the outcome, of the Rockefeller vice presidency.[67] While Rockefeller expended critical time and energy appearing before Congress, explaining why he would be an ideal vice president, the inevitable palace guard, of which Henry Wallace spoke so knowingly, had erected barriers which bounded the vice president's future utility to the president.

When Rockefeller was duly confirmed by the Congress—first by a vote of the Senate, and then nine days later by a vote of the House—he finally took the oath of office on December 19, 1974, within hours of the House vote. That evening, Rockefeller was poised to become the most thoroughly modern vice president to date, bringing to the office an extraordinary measure of stature, the likes of which had not been approached in close to two centuries. Not since Thomas Jefferson's tenure did an individual arrive in the vice presidency with such a well-earned national reputation and personal following. For sure, like Jefferson, Rockefeller had admirers and detractors in equal measure; however, in contrast to a vice president like Spiro Agnew—who was an unknown commodity upon his inauguration in 1969—there were few Americans who did not know of Nelson Rockefeller and the famous family he hailed from.

Because Rockefeller was Rockefeller, from his first day in office he garnered a level of respect and attention rarely accorded a vice president. Furthermore, the incremental expansion in the scope of power, and in direct responsibilities, of the office of the vice president made the institution of enough substance and significance that Rockefeller had been willing to take the job. It is quite possible that he was swayed by what had happened to the vice presidency over the course of the twentieth century. For starters, the office had become a reliable springboard to the presidency, whether it was by way of succession or, since 1960, as the logical precursor to a presidential nomination. Indeed, when it became apparent that Vice President Agnew was going to have to resign, Rockefeller considered actively campaigning for the spot on the assumption that the vice presidency offered the best route for him to finally gain the presidency.[68]

In addition, Rockefeller must have been encouraged that the institution, by 1974, had become transparently integrated into the broader operations of the executive branch. Hence, Rockefeller could count on a seat in the cabinet, membership in the National Security Council, chairmanships of a number of high profile commissions, should he so desire, and inclusion in the decisional framework for foreign policy and national security concerns; also, initially with Ford's concurrence, Rockefeller was set to formulate and implement the administration's domestic policy agenda.[69]

Notwithstanding the improved condition of the vice presidency, much of Rockefeller's tenure proved to be an exercise in futility. What hampered his quest for a fully functional vice presidency, however, was not President Ford. The two men had a mutually respectful relationship, and they worked well together, particularly when they met alone. During their service together, they initiated the practice of meeting privately each week in the Oval Office; it is a custom every president and vice president to follow them has imitated.[70] The weekly luncheon meetings were initially suggested by Rockefeller, and agreed to by Ford, when they first discussed Rockefeller's expected role in the administration. It was unprecedented to set aside time for the president and vice president to meet alone, and it gave Rockefeller exclusive and unparalleled access to Ford.

From his experience as a state chief executive, Rockefeller undoubtedly understood the value in meeting alone with the president—absent jealous, competitive White House staffers. Fittingly, it would be political maneuvering at the staff level that eventually caused Rockefeller the most grief when he was vice president. More precisely, White House staffers deliberately thwarted many of Rockefeller's initiatives, and there is considerable anecdotal evidence of the obstructionism that plagued his vice-presidential tenure.[71]

While some members of Ford's staff were adverse to Rockefeller personally, there were also partisan staffers who were wary of the vice president's assumed deep liberalism. For example, when Ford put together a campaign organization for the 1976 presidential election, the campaign chairman, Howard "Bo" Callaway, was certain that

Rockefeller's liberalism would handicap Ford's run for his own term. By Ford's telling, Callaway tried to distance the president from Rockefeller in the belief that doing so would "extend an olive branch to conservatives."[72]

Of equal significance, the increased influence and resources of the institutional vice presidency contributed to the soured environment, fostering conflict and rivalry between the staffs of the president and the vice president.[73] The prospect of the vice president and his staff having responsibilities for specific policy spheres, as Rockefeller envisioned it, was likely viewed by those working in the White House as an unwelcome encroachment of their authority and prerogative.

To better understand why White House staff and advisers may have felt threatened by the prominence of the corresponding office and staff of the vice president, it is instructive to briefly reexamine the expansion of the institution, and the accompanying increase in resources available to the vice president. For instance, when Henry Wallace was vice president-elect and traveled to Mexico at the behest of President Franklin Roosevelt, Wallace did not travel by plane, nor did a large entourage accompany him. Instead, Wallace traveled in the company of his wife and three other individuals, making the entire trip by car. In contrast, by Rockefeller's time in office, Air Force Two or Marine Two—essentially any government aircraft used by the vice president, as well the president, but renumbered accordingly—were available to fly the vice president anywhere, anytime.

Similarly, when Richard Nixon was elected vice president, he was allotted $47,970 for his staff, a considerable drop from when he served as a United States senator, and his budget for staff totaled $70,000.[74] But when Rockefeller landed in the vice presidency, he was allocated over two million dollars for a staff of more than seventy. Granted, Nixon's staff consisted of just a handful of individuals, most of who came with him from the Senate, but the contrast to Rockefeller, in terms of budget and personnel, is nonetheless striking.

The perceptible manifestations of institutional resources, such as access to government jets, an extensive staff, and an ample office budget, symbolize power and influence. Whether power and influence are realized is of course another story, depending entirely on the level of either feature a specific president permits. Nevertheless, the vice president's access to a wide range of institutional accouterments definitely benefits the perception of a substantial vice-presidential office.

As referenced previously, Rockefeller had suggested, and Ford had insisted on, the vice president taking on the direction of the administration's domestic policy agenda.[75] It was obvious in the Ford administration that foreign policy was the exclusive dominion of Henry Kissinger, though to Rockefeller's advantage, he had a longstanding, mentoring relationship with Kissinger; as such, he offered counsel to Kissinger throughout the time they shared working in the Ford administration. Years later, in one of his many memoirs, Kissinger affirmed that, when he was secretary of state and Rockefeller was vice president, "Nelson provided me with invaluable moral support and practical advice in trying times."[76]

Regardless of how much he claimed to rely on Rockefeller, Kissinger was an assertive secretary of state, skilled at statecraft, and he proved invaluable to Ford. Of equal importance, Kissinger had emerged untainted by the scandals of the Nixon administration; his continued presence therefore signaled continuity and stability in the foreign policy of the government. This was especially relevant in the aftermath of President Nixon's resignation, since the circumstances which had devoured the Nixon presidency made only passing sense to observers outside the United States. As such, because of Kissinger's specific area of expertise and control, if Rockefeller was to have a sizable impact within the Ford administration, it would have to come on the domestic policy front.

From the outset, Rockefeller believed that the ideal way to take charge of the administration's domestic policy agenda was to commandeer the principal policymaking unit in the president's office, the Domestic Council. To this end, and in the face of strong opposition from Ford's chief of staff, Rockefeller placed one of his own advisers as the director of the council, and then took the vice-chairmanship for himself.[77] Yet Rockefeller's triumph essentially ended there. He did recommend a number of ambitious domestic enterprises—including a national health care plan and a proposal for massive outlays in government loans for independent energy initiatives—but none of the preceding was ever implemented. Surely frustrating for Rockefeller was that during this time the most tangible accomplishment he could point to was his decision to redesign the official flag of the vice president's office.

The burden of Nelson Rockefeller's ineffective vice presidency does not lie with him. Nor should his failures in office be attributed, as was the case for so many of his predecessors, to the intrinsic deficiencies of the vice-presidential institution. Instead, Rockefeller's tenure should be viewed a casualty of a coup d'état of the modern vice presidency. Or, if not a coup, at a minimum a deliberate campaign to impede the increasing influence and power of the institution, as well as that of the occupant of the office. Irrespective of how it is framed, unwavering opposition to the idea of a powerful vice president existed in the Ford White House. And leading that opposition was Ford's chief of staff, Donald Rumsfeld.

Gerald Ford and Donald Rumsfeld first met when they served in the House of Representatives together. Rumsfeld later worked for the Nixon administration in the Office of Economic Opportunity, then as the United States ambassador to the North Atlantic Treaty Organization, before finally joining Ford's White House staff. By some accounts, when Ford ascended to the presidency, and was therefore required to fill the vacancy in the vice presidency, Rumsfeld had coveted the second spot which, to his disappointment, went to Rockefeller.[78] Then again, if Rumsfeld was aiming for the vice presidency, it was surely a pretense masking his presidential ambitions. Yet when Rockefeller landed the nomination for vice president, Rumsfeld had no choice but to take a different route to influence and power in the White House.

Well before Nelson Rockefeller's confirmation was granted by Congress, Rumsfeld had laid the groundwork to undermine the former governor of New York. This came about by Rumsfeld's positioning of key staffers who were loyal foremost to him, then to Ford, and never to Rockefeller. Consequently, when Rockefeller's confirmation finally came through, Rumsfeld had already established a level of access and influence that the new vice president was unable to match, even though he was, ostensibly, second in command.[79]

Paradoxically, what deepened the quagmire Rockefeller found himself in was the national visibility he brought to the office on day one. This alone made Rockefeller unique among vice presidents. But of greater importance, Rockefeller's political future was considerably less tied to the president than for others who had previously held his position. Being such, those closest to Ford almost certainly feared from the outset that Rockefeller was destined to serve as an uncommonly strong, independent vice president. Were that to happen, then Rockefeller would be a threat to Ford's political future, and by extension a threat to those working closest to the sitting president.

Of those individuals nearest Ford, none appeared more concerned with the efficacy of Rockefeller's tenure, and therefore the political future of the president, vice president, and himself, than did Rumsfeld. Relentless is possibly the adjective that best characterizes the manner in which Rumsfeld went about destabilizing Rockefeller's position in the Ford administration. Each time Rockefeller put forward a new policy proposal, Rumsfeld interceded.[80] Time and again he stifled the vice president's agenda, engendering a hostile environment in which Rockefeller seemed to be on the outside of the White House, unable to get inside.

According to Ford, Rumsfeld was not acting on any malice for Rockefeller when trying to restrain the vice president's frequently complex and expensive proposals; instead, as Ford recounted, Rumsfeld was worried that Rockefeller had too many other obligations to attend to, and besides, "the Vice President, [as] Don pointed out, had to preside over the Senate."[81] Apparently Ford and Rumsfeld were among the rare few in government who considered presiding in the Senate a vital responsibility of the vice president.

If Rumsfeld was the architect of Rockefeller's failure to gain a foothold in the Ford administration, then Rumsfeld's assistant, Dick Cheney, was the engineer who facilitated Rumsfeld's plan. And though Cheney worked under Rumsfeld, he was not averse to challenging Rockefeller by his own volition. For instance, at one point Cheney suggested that there were two appropriate responses to the policy proposals of the Domestic Council: "consider doing nothing … and also the possibility of doing less."[82] Later, when Ford moved Rumsfeld to the cabinet, Rumsfeld could rest easy knowing that Cheney, who was duly moved up to replace him as chief of staff, was a reliable conduit for his continuing influence in the White House.

On the whole, Rockefeller's experience was the consequence of a White House staff aligned in opposition to a potentially influential and strong vice president. Rockefeller was in a difficult position that was further eroded by a president who was far too complacent. Sadly, at any point Ford could have regained control of the situation and stood by the man he had asked to be his number two. Ford was, after all, the president. As it seems, the modern vice presidency, with its enhanced visibility and institutional resources, remained at the mercy of the president and those who comprised the palace guard.

After being subjected to an entire year of obstructionist political gamesmanship, primarily at the behest of President Ford's chief of staff, Vice President Rockefeller resigned from the Domestic Council. When he finally relinquished control of what was supposed to have been his primary vehicle for influence in the Ford administration, he dispatched a lengthy missive to the president. In the document, Rockefeller delineated the unfailing sabotage of his work on behalf of the Domestic Council, directing his severest criticism at Donald Rumsfeld and Dick Cheney.[83]

As for Rockefeller's political future, the damage was done. In the lead up to the 1976 presidential election, the vice president's standing within the administration had been so irreparably compromised that his placement on the ticket with Ford proved untenable. Still, from Ford's point of view, Rockefeller's tenure was something of an unnoticed and underappreciated success; he chose to blame low performance polls of the vice president on conservative Republicans who had never warmed to Rockefeller.[84] Whatever the cause, a smattering of negative poll numbers on Rockefeller obviously gave Ford pause. Recognizing the ascendancy of conservatives within the Republican Party, Ford told Rockefeller that he was less likely to win his party's presidential nomination if Rockefeller was considered to be a potential running mate, whereupon Rockefeller agreed to take himself out of the running for vice president.[85] Ford later described his own behavior in the incident as cowardly, and Henry Kissinger stated flatly that "dropping Rockefeller still strikes me as the single worst decision of Ford's presidency."[86]

Even if Rockefeller failed to fully realize his vision of a vice president charged with formulating and advancing domestic policy, at the end of the day he could take consolation in his role as a respected confidant to the president. Besides his regular private meetings with the president, Rockefeller was integrated into all national security deliberations, and Ford valued the vice president's advice on a number of critical problems, with Rockefeller becoming, in the words of Kissinger, "an indispensable personal adviser to the President."[87]

Surely because of who he was, and with what he brought from the outset to his vice presidency, Rockefeller would have been a more significant political actor in foreign policy and national security were it not for the brevity of his time in office and the near dominance of those fields by Kissinger. Still, Ford confronted a number of problems beyond the borders of the United States with Rockefeller at his side. These included development of an evacuation plan for American civilians and military personnel who remained in Vietnam as late as 1975.[88] And on another occasion, Rockefeller worked in concert with the secretary of state and other top national security advisers to the president in coordinating an appropriate response to the seizure of the United States freighter *Mayaguez*, near the Cambodian coast, by a group of rogue belligerents.[89]

In addition to the preceding concerns, as well as numerous others not addressed here, President Ford appointed Rockefeller to head a commission tasked with comprehensively reviewing the clandestine activities of the Central Intelligence Agency (CIA), specifically where the agency was involved on the domestic front. Founded in a similar vein to the numerous commissions and councils typically assigned to modern vice presidents, the Rockefeller Commission had the potential to generate favorable attention for Rockefeller and was likewise perfectly suited to the vice president's considerable skills as a public administrator.

Unfortunately, during much of the time the Rockefeller Commission spent fulfilling its charter, there were two ongoing congressional inquiries into the CIA as well. The Church Committee in the Senate and the Pike Committee in the House not only matched the Rockefeller Commission's mission, but both of the congressional panels were afforded sweeping investigatory powers that went well beyond those given to the vice president. After devoting considerable time to conducting a comprehensive, detailed analysis of the CIA, the Rockefeller Commission released its final report to negligible effect.[90]

In the long run, the level of success Rockefeller encountered in advancing various policy objectives should not be the metric used for his vice presidency. Nor should his tenure be defined by his participation in the accustomed activities of the vice president—infrequently presiding in the Senate, delivering partisan speeches, and making ceremonial appearances on behalf of the president—because he met, and then exceeded, those expectations. What should be noted, however, is the tripartite of dynamics that distinguish the Rockefeller vice presidency.

First, the collegiality of Ford and Rockefeller's relationship established an expectation that the vice president could, and should, be treated by the president with a measure of deference. In this way, Ford and Rockefeller's relationship rivaled the pairings of Andrew Jackson and Martin Van Buren, James Polk and George Dallas, Abraham Lincoln and Hannibal Hamlin, and in the twentieth century, Franklin Roosevelt and Henry Wallace. Naturally, in each of the preceding cases it was explicitly understood that the president and the vice president were not equals, per se. And yet, by facilitating an arrangement in which the vice president was patently included among the highest counselors to the president, the value of the vice president to the president and to the broad efficacy of the executive branch was immeasurable. For these reasons, the collegiality underscoring Ford and Rockefeller's time together became the norm, and it has since been reflected in every ensuing president and vice president pairing.

Second, the visibility of the vice presidency was further enhanced by Rockefeller's tenure. He was a prominent politician and elected executive of a large and important state; he therefore would have commanded attention regardless of the position he held in the national government. At the same time, serving as the vice president of the United States, Rockefeller benefited from the myriad resources the institution had accrued since its inception; he was then able to build the institution further, from the vantage of his long and storied political career. In the process, all of this made the vice-presidential institution even more widely visible and thus a more valuable institution to succeeding vice presidents.

Along these lines, Rockefeller at one point decided to organize a series of public forums across the nation to promote his domestic policy priorities.[91] There were no reservations about the vice president's prerogative in the matter, nor was there any doubt that he would command a national audience for his policy odyssey. What is most telling about this is that Rockefeller was able to initiate the forums, in essence making himself envoy for the administration's domestic policy agenda. He then utilized staff resources for extensive preparation, and finally, when the time came to start the tour, the vice president commandeered a government jet to take him across the country. In this,

Rockefeller was not simply promoting a domestic policy agenda; he was promoting the notion that it was appropriate for the vice president to perform such a conspicuous role for the administration.

Although Rockefeller's tour went off as planned, and he did draw considerable attention at every stop he made, because of deliberate, covert maneuvering by White House staffers, much of what the vice president was proposing was never included in the president's projected federal budget. Still, the assumption that Rockefeller could embark on such a high profile venture, and of his own volition, would have been inconceivable just two years prior when Spiro Agnew was the vice president.

The third distinguishing dynamic manifest in Rockefeller's tenure was the breadth of resources at the vice president's command by the time of he was confirmed by Congress. In this vein, the organization of the office of the vice president was starting to take shape in a form remarkably similar to that of the office of the president.[92] As such, assigned specifically to the office of the vice president were special assistants for legislative, domestic, international, and military affairs, including military aides; a press secretary; a legal counsel; liaisons dedicated exclusively to state and local governments, the state department, and the executive branch; a coterie of administrative assistants charged with managing the vice president's appointments, scheduling, research, and media affairs; and naturally, a chief of staff. In addition, Rockefeller employed a special assistant devoted solely to the vice president's work as the presiding officer of the Senate.[93]

The preceding list is far from inclusive, and while it does account for many of the staff positions paralleling those in the president's office, then and now, the numerous assistants and staff members allotted to the vice president for each of the councils President Ford designated Rockefeller to oversee are not recorded. The problem for Rockefeller, and one which future vice presidents subsequently accommodated for, was having his staff operate in isolation. Consequently, competition between the vice president's staff and that of the president overrode any meaningful cooperation between the two offices. This was not only inefficient and led to unnecessary duplication of certain tasks, it also engendered a further diminishment in the perceived utility of the vice president and his staff.

Because Ford did nothing about the strained relations between his White House staff and Rockefeller's staff, nor did he restrain, as he could have, transparently ambitious and vindictive personnel, it appeared as if he condoned the situation. Hence, the limitless potentiality of the Rockefeller vice presidency was hindered; as a consequence, the modern vice presidency was put on hold until the next vice president was inaugurated.

The best lesson to take from the Rockefeller vice presidency is that life and politics are cyclical. Accordingly, whether it is attributed to design or to a quirk of fate, twenty-four years after Rockefeller's exit, Donald Rumsfeld and Dick Cheney returned to prominence and power in the executive branch and, poignantly, a complacent president once again lived in the White House. But upon their return, Rumsfeld and Cheney were no longer set on destroying a vice president; instead, Rumsfeld was back in the same cabinet position he had held under Ford, and Cheney was the vice president.

Contrary to Rockefeller's experience, Cheney's subsequent tenure in the second office indicated a vast expansion in the reach and power of the modern vice presidency. Indubitably, credit for the growth in the institution from Rockefeller's time forward does not belong to Cheney alone, as an intervening four presidents and their vice presidents contributed to a greatly augmented American vice presidency.

THE VICE PRESIDENT IN THE WEST WING (1977–1989)

Nelson Rockefeller's unsatisfactory experience as vice president was as much about a White House staff determined to curb the vice president's influence in the administration as it was about a president incapable of restraining his staff. For these reasons, the Ford-Rockefeller partnership was—even with the distinctiveness accorded it by the Twenty-fifth Amendment—in certain respects, rather typical. President Ford had indeed agreed to conditions that should have resulted in a productive vice presidency for Rockefeller, and yet he never exercised control over his own White House staff, nor did he ever defend Rockefeller's position or advocate for a strong vice-presidential institution once Rockefeller was installed in office.

If at any point Gerald Ford had chosen to put his presidency on the line—as Franklin Roosevelt did for Henry Wallace in 1940—in all likelihood, Rockefeller would have had a satisfactory experience when he was vice president. Rockefeller then might have been named Ford's running mate in 1976, and quite possibly, he could have provided the boost Ford, as it turned out, desperately needed in the election. But because the president always delimits the vice president, and because Ford took the approach he did with his own number two, Rockefeller's tenure will be recorded as not only a disappointment, but as a missed opportunity for the president and for the nation. Fortunately for those who followed him in the office, Rockefeller's experience turned out to be a transitory setback to the institution, as Ford's challenger and successor, Jimmy Carter, proved to be the foremost facilitator of the modern vice presidency.

Jimmy Carter's contributions to the vice presidency began even before he was elected president. During the latter part of the 1976 presidential primary season, when Carter appeared to be the inevitable presidential nominee of the Democratic Party, he began considering possible running mates in earnest. Then, as time for the Democratic nominating convention neared, Carter undertook a calculated process for vetting potential vice-presidential nominees, and in doing so, he built a selection model which has since been employed by several presidential nominees. In approaching nominee selection in the manner he did, Carter added a level of forethought and transparency to the process which had never existed before. For Carter, the immediate outcome of his approach was that he had isolated a competent running mate, and for the long-term, he had put in motion a collegial partnership that would flourish over the next four years.

Carter's choice in 1976 was Minnesota's senior United States senator, Walter Mondale. Oddly enough, Minnesota's junior senator was former vice president Hubert Humphrey. Humphrey, who had returned to the Senate two years after leaving the vice presidency, had long been a mentor to Mondale, so when it looked like Mondale had a shot at the vice-presidential nomination, Humphrey supported the idea without reservation.[94] Humphrey encouraged Mondale to pursue the nomination, telling him that despite his own frequent disappointment while serving in the office, "if you really care about public policy, you'll get more done there in a day than you'll get done in the Senate in a lifetime."[95]

Since Carter was a governor from the South and was widely perceived to be a conservative, the choice of Mondale, a liberal senator from the Midwest, made sense. Furthermore, by then Mondale had already served in the Senate for nearly eleven years. He had been an effective senator, sponsoring progressive legislation and engaging in critical Senate investigations on national security, and his Washington experience gave Carter a much needed insider's perspective in what would be an otherwise outsider administration.

Jimmy Carter permitted the Mondale vice presidency to take the form that it did. Yet, befitting the nature of their partnership, Mondale was equally responsible for engineering the direction in which the institution moved. To this end, after defeating President Ford and his running mate, Senator Robert Dole, at Carter's request the vice president-elect delineated a set of proposals for making the vice presidency meaningful; it was, in Mondale's words, "historic ... Nothing like it had ever been done before, and it led to a redefinition of the vice president in modern American government."[96]

To Mondale's credit, Carter agreed to every suggestion.[97] But in trying to rectify many of the inadequacies that plagued the vice presidency since its inception, Carter and Mondale first had to confront the principal, intrinsic contradiction of the institution. As Mondale described it, "the only role the Constitution assigns the vice president is to preside over the Senate and break a tie when necessary. In a strange way, since the vice presidents were in both branches, they historically had been treated as though they were in neither."[98]

Induced by the strength of Mondale's blueprint, Carter was resolute on the vice president to "truly be the second in command, involved in every aspect of governing."[99] This, by Carter's interpretation, meant that Mondale "received the same security briefings ... was automatically invited to participate in all ... official meetings, and helped to plan strategy for domestic programs, diplomacy, and defense."[100] Of particular note, Carter also made sure that the vice president was given a private office in the West Wing of the White House, just a few doors down the hall from the Oval Office. The location of the vice president's office was important to Mondale, and for the institution, because previous vice presidents were only allocated office space scattered across the capital city, and not in the White House. Because of this logistical arrangement, "the vice president ... was usually uninformed, uninvited, and often unwanted by the White House."[101]

In contrast to Nelson Rockefeller's experience as vice president, Mondale did not encounter challenges to his authority from within the White House. Carter let Mondale select personnel for several key positions, including prime postings on the National Security Council and the Domestic Council, as well as in the Office of Management and Budget. Additionally, Carter facilitated the assimilation of Mondale's staff with his own, making the vice president's staff, both in theory and in practice, equal to the White House staff. Still, as Mondale pointed out, "all of this would merely have been symbolic if I didn't have a concrete role backed by the president."[102] Critical then to the effectiveness of Mondale's tenure was Carter's declaration to every person working in his administration that, regardless of their title, it was to be understood that when the vice president spoke, "they should assume they were hearing from the president."[103]

Prior to Walter Mondale, most vice presidents worked reactively—responding to political opponents, defending administration policies, following the president's orders—but Mondale was a decidedly proactive vice president, based on the Henry Wallace mold, if any. On a number of occasions, Mondale interceded when he thought it was necessary, and without prompting from the president. For instance, at one point in the opening year of the Carter administration, an affirmative action case was before the Supreme Court. When the administration decided to file an amicus brief in the case, Mondale discovered that the initial brief would have put the federal government on the side of ending affirmative action. Mondale was committed to the notion that he and Carter were elected to defend and sustain civil rights initiatives, not to allow the successes of the movement to diminish. With the tacit support of the president, Mondale worked alongside others in the executive branch to construct a stronger brief for preserving, and in essence improving, existent affirmative action programs.[104]

The Supreme Court subsequently supported the arguments of the Carter administration in the case. Mondale's involvement was highly unusual for a vice president, but it was emblematic of his proactive posture within the Carter administration. Moreover, by Mondale taking the initiative, after having reviewed the administration's initially weak argument in the case, and then rewriting and strengthening the administration's response, he demonstrated that the vice president could and would venture into new realms of policy and politics. More importantly, Mondale knew he could take the initiative because of the full support he received, at all times, from the president he was elected with. Although he was referring broadly to his time with Carter, and therefore not specifically to the preceding example, Mondale later emphasized that in every instance

> the president's support made it possible for me to advise and push and reach over and between high officials in our government to force needed decisions. Under Carter, for the first time, the one other elected national figure became an engaged participant in all the important issues confronting the president.

> This had both strategic and historic consequences. Strategic because a vice president, with his special stature, has a potentially powerful voice. And historic because the model we put in place was followed by future administrations, and, I believe, will be followed in the future.[105]

But Mondale's service, in essence as an extension of the president, went beyond domestic concerns. When Mondale traveled overseas, naturally he represented the foreign policy objectives of the administration; however, the strength of his association with Carter was widely recognized, and therefore their particular arrangement meant that when the vice president met with foreign heads of state, the meetings were, for the most part, equivalent to meetings with the president.

One of the earliest manifestations of the Carter-Mondale approach in foreign affairs came just four months after their inauguration. On this occasion, Mondale traveled to the neutral location of Vienna, Austria to meet with the prime minister of South Africa, John Vorster.[106] This offered an early opportunity for Mondale to display his diplomatic skills, while simultaneously introducing the Carter administration to the world. And, of more significance to the vice presidency broadly, by sending Mondale out so quickly, President Carter was signaling to other nations that his vice president was as much the face of the administration as he was.[107]

Conversely, since Carter came to office unusually inexperienced in foreign affairs, at least for a modern president, there was great value in having the vice president be the first to test the diplomatic front. If Mondale stumbled at diplomacy on the world stage, any deleterious outcome would be lessened since he was merely the vice president. On the whole, it was a win-win situation for Carter: if the vice president were successful, the president and the administration would profit and the president would accrue additional accolades for his wise choice of a partner in governance. But if the vice president failed, on almost any level, ample distance could be placed between the president and his number two.

On the occasion of Mondale's meeting with Vorster, he was given an assignment that would have been a challenge even for a seasoned diplomat. Among other concerns, Mondale was expected to confront the prime minister about his nation's dismal record on human rights. Suggesting how any sovereign nation should conduct its internal affairs is dicey at best, but confronting the leader of a country which, for most of the world, embodied all that was reprehensible about apartheid, was sure to be a losing proposition, politically and diplomatically.[108]

Being the second-highest elected officer of the United States government afforded Mondale greater distinction than most diplomats, yet the political environment of South Africa was too inextricable, having been shaped over the course of many years; as it was, there was only so much any outsider could do. Regardless, Mondale gingerly managed the difficulties of his assignment, putting human rights and political equality at the forefront of the discussions, while acknowledging that the historical record of the United States in the same realm was far from unblemished.[109] If not for an importunate reporter—who extracted a public commitment from Mondale, and presumably from the United States government as well, to the idea of universal suffrage for all of the people of South Africa—then the vice president's mission would have finished as a broad success.[110]

Even as President Carter progressively became more self-confident on the international stage, he continued to use Mondale when circumstances dictated that intercession by the vice president might be advantageous. Such was the case at the historic Camp David summit Carter hosted for the leaders of Egypt and Israel, Anwar Sadat and Menachem Begin. Mondale joined in the weeklong series of meetings, and at one point, when negotiations started to veer off track, Carter engaged Mondale as an intermediary in the process, having the vice president convey his personal directives to the two opposing leaders.[111]

On another occasion, when Indochinese refugees from Vietnam, Cambodia and Laos were being set adrift in the South China Sea and the Gulf of Siam, most to die, Carter designated Mondale the administration's spokesman before a conference of the United Nations, convened in Geneva, Switzerland, which was devoted specifically to the refugee problem. Once there, Mondale delivered an impassioned speech, equating the absence of a substantial international response to the refugee problem with a similarly inadequate response to the expulsion of Jews from Nazi Germany in the 1930s.[112] What seemed to be an intractable crisis was eventually addressed by dozens of nations, in no small part because the vice president of the United States had made such a strong argument for action over inaction by the international community.[113]

The uniqueness of the Carter-Mondale partnership was unprecedented and, critical to their success, it was entirely by design. From the outset, Carter saw the advantage in making Mondale broadly useful in more and different ways than previous vice presidents had been used. As far as Mondale was concerned, he was willing to do whatever Carter asked of him, knowing his own political future was tied to Carter's success or failure; it only made sense to make it work. Still, the key to their partnership was found in the president's willingness to let it happen. By all indications, Carter did not view Mondale as a rival or a threat to his power or legacy, nor did he see the vice president as an unwanted appendage of the government. After leaving office, Carter wrote of the anomalous, exceptional quality underscoring his and Mondale's service together. Writing with hindsight, Carter stressed that in their

> four and half years together, I never for a moment had reason to doubt his competence, his loyalty, or his friendship.

> This harmony had not existed between many of my predecessors and their Vice Presidents. Most chiefs of state had ignored their partners, did not completely trust them, or felt threatened by the obviously strong character or stature of some of them. Often, the partnership had been a "forced marriage" arranged at a national convention, where trading for delegate votes or regional influence had taken place.[114]

In large part, by his words and by his actions, Carter was conceding that the modern presidency had become too much for one person to manage. It was for just that reason that the Hoover Commission—among the earliest efforts to systematically assess and recommend ways to reorganize the federal government—suggested that part of the solution to an overloaded presidency was the addition of a second, exclusively administrative vice president.[115] Carter likewise went to great lengths to ensure that the vice presidency, as an institution of the government, was reflective of the era in which it operated. To this end, Carter made the vice president second in the military chain of command and likewise insisted that Mondale gain a comprehensive understanding of nuclear weapons.[116]

Carter was plainly cognizant of the imprudence shown by prior presidents in their failure to prepare the vice president to manage a national security crisis. Along these lines, and before either Carter or Mondale was sworn in to office, Carter insisted that Mondale be included in an intensive series of exercises meant to simulate how a president might best manage a nuclear exchange. Clearly Carter expected presidents to be prepared for any and all contingencies; however, he could not understand how the vice president could be left so ill-informed, claiming he "was astounded to learn that former Vice Presidents had never been involved in this process. It was obvious to me in a nuclear exchange, the president might well be incapacitated, and the Vice President, as the *new* Commander in Chief, had to be fully qualified to assume his duties."[117]

As noted throughout this text, there were presidents who came before Carter who delegated greater responsibilities to their vice presidents, so Carter did not necessarily reinvent the vice presidency; instead, he augmented the expansion of the institution, building on the incremental growth which was taking place since the time of Warren Harding's presidency. But, in stark contrast to some of his predecessors—in particular Franklin Roosevelt, Lyndon Johnson, and Richard Nixon—Carter never retracted any of what he gave to his vice president. Nor did President Carter ever express any disdain for Vice President Mondale—a feat which none of his predecessors could claim.

Of less consequence to Mondale's vice-presidential record, but still of some meaning, was that Mondale and his family were the first to reside in the official residence provided for the vice president. As referenced earlier, the house located at the United States Naval Observatory, which had been home to admirals of that branch of the military, was first made available for Vice President Ford, and then Vice President Rockefeller. Because of Ford's condensed vice-presidential tenure, and then by Rockefeller's choice, neither man occupied the vice president's house. But Mondale did; it was, in his view, the best house his family had ever inhabited.[118] Finally, and after only 188 years, the vice president of the United States resided in government housing.

When Jimmy Carter and Walter Mondale were defeated for reelection in 1980, Mondale's four-year stint as vice president stood beyond reproach. As it happens, there were many in the Democratic Party who would have preferred Mondale at the top of the ticket that year. Still, regardless of the preference of rank and file members of his party, and irrespective of the method by which a presidential ticket is selected, Mondale was the candidate for vice president, and in American elections, votes are recorded for president, not for vice president.

Aside from the Carter administration's mixed record in domestic and foreign policy, and while Mondale deserved credit for many of the successes, and could hardly be blamed for its share of failures, probably the greatest accomplishment of the four years Carter and Mondale served together was the impact the administration's two principals had on the vice-presidential institution. Mondale acknowledged as much when he reflected on the enduring dual narrative of the Carter-Mondale era:

> President Carter and I changed the model for future vice presidents in a fundamental way that has helped, and will help, future presidents better serve their country in an ever more complex world ... [And] I am very sure

that Carter was one of the most decent and able presidents in our history. I was proud to serve him. We never lost our trust in each other, even in the worst of days, and we remain good friends after all of these years—a rare accomplishment.[119]

If Jimmy Carter and Walter Mondale did not begin their relationship as friends, they nonetheless were not political opponents. The same cannot be said of their Republican opposition in 1980, Ronald Reagan and George H.W. Bush. Reagan had gained the Republican presidential nomination only after having survived an early, spirited challenge from Bush in the primaries. When it appeared that Reagan's capture of the presidential nomination was certain, Bush opted out of the primaries. Bush did this not only because he knew Reagan's strength precluded his own chance of winning the nomination, but because in ceasing with intra-party campaign rhetoric, he would make the political environment more amicable and, in the process, more conducive to an offer of the second spot on the ticket from Reagan.[120]

Later, at the Republican convention, Reagan did offer Bush the vice-presidential nomination, but only after an attempt to make Gerald Ford the candidate for vice president fell through. Reagan initially approached Ford with the idea, but when Ford appeared to be angling for a co-presidency, Reagan balked. If Reagan and Ford had reached some consensus on how their partnership would have worked, and if they had then won the election, Ford would have added another notch to his already complicated record, for he finally would have been elected to one of the two national offices he had previously held.[121]

George Bush brought a wide array of prior government experience to the vice presidency: congressman, ambassador to the United Nations, chairman of the Republican National Committee, chief of the Liaison Office in Beijing, China, and director of the Central Intelligence Agency. Since Ronald Reagan was a former actor with minimal government experience, consisting of just two terms as the governor of California, Bush filled the traditional balancing function of the vice-presidential candidate. Furthermore, Bush's work for the federal government qualified him as an elite Washington insider. Even though this was a benefit to Reagan's candidacy—as he had run for president as an outsider, bent on reforming the federal government—it was a bigger advantage for Bush, personally, for he returned to the executive branch knowing how to play the power game.

After the election, among the first moves Bush made was to engineer the appointment of his close friend and adviser, James Baker, as Reagan's first chief of staff. With Baker situated atop the White House staff, Bush had an individual he implicitly trusted, probably more than any other when it came to politics, overseeing the very people who might otherwise undercut the vice president. Baker's presence, coupled with the vice president's private office near the Oval Office, gave Bush a solid foothold inside the White House. Moreover, because Bush was once a member of the Ford administration, and because he was intimately acquainted with Donald Rumsfeld and Dick Cheney, he clearly understood what had happened to Nelson Rockefeller when he was vice president. As it was, Bush would not permit his vice presidency to suffer a similar fate.

Beyond the physical proximity to President Reagan in the White House, and the placement of key administration staff, Bush had an added edge when he took office. Since Carter and Mondale had worked so diligently at enhancing the vice-presidential institution, Reagan and Bush inherited a changed executive dynamic. The question then became whether they would replicate some, all, or nothing of the Carter-Mondale model. Yet even with the marked dichotomy in Reagan and Bush's strengths and weaknesses, it was most sensible to capitalize on the strides already taken by Carter and Mondale.

This was no more apparent than with foreign policy and national security, where from the outset Reagan pushed Bush to the fore. Along these lines, Bush traveled abroad, covering approximately 1.3 million miles in his eight years of service as vice president, and he continued to travel extensively even after Reagan grew comfortable, and quite adept, on the world stage.[122] In addition, Reagan insisted that Bush chair meetings of the National Security Council when he was absent. And, by continuing what President Carter started, he helped to institutionalize the placement of the vice president as second in the military chain of command. All of the practices just listed were intended to signify the vice president's presence in the executive branch. Furthermore, there was a value in confirming that the vice president was prepared to step in for the president whenever, and wherever, necessary.

Reagan likewise sanctioned a broad portfolio of substantive duties for Bush, including his use of the vice president as coordinator of multiple federal agencies that were simultaneously combating the importation of illegal drugs into the United States. This was a way to utilize the office of the vice president in the management of disparate bureaucracies, all of which were engaged in a similar mission but without any synchronization of the groups. In this area, Reagan exploited the visibility of the modern vice presidency to emphasize the importance he placed on fighting the drug war, as well as for centralizing command of the project. In doing so, Reagan was employing the vice president in a fashion similar to Franklin Roosevelt's use of Henry Wallace during the Second World War.

Bush was also asked to direct a task force charged with deregulating an assortment of programs administered by the federal government, as well as to function as the administration's point man with Congress. The latter was a particularly vital role for Bush to play since Reagan, other than wide familiarity with his ideological agenda, was an enigma to many of those working on Capitol Hill. Conversely, Bush was a fixture in the national government, and his experience was a boon to Reagan personally, and to the administration generally. Besides, since Bush was a product of the political culture of Washington, he did not incite the suspicions of insiders, as did Reagan. Ironically, Reagan had built his political career chastising the very people and institutions he was elected to lead.

Bush's status within the Reagan administration was enhanced considerably when an attempt was made on Reagan's life in the early months of their first term in office. The assassination attempt on the president, and the vice president's behavior in the aftermath of the incident, reinforced the supportive relationship that ultimately defined their shared tenure. From the moment Reagan was shot, Bush became the acting president, taking on all the responsibilities that came with the title. However, Bush never assumed that there was any permanency to his hold on presidential responsibility. This was evident when, upon returning to the capital on the day of the attempted assassination, Bush ignored the recommendation of his security detail to travel by helicopter to the White House grounds. Bush purportedly based his decision in elemental logic: he was the vice president and not the president; it would have been inappropriate for him to arrive by helicopter at the president's house.[123]

Throughout Reagan's recovery period, Bush went to great lengths to never appear the usurper, angling for the president's job. Hence, Bush conducted business entirely from his own White House office, and when he presided at meetings of the cabinet, as well as of the National Security Council, he did so from the vice president's chair, leaving the president's chair, for the time being, unoccupied.[124] In all, it was a seamless, transitory transfer of power in appearance and in substance.

Reagan, however, was not content having the vice president function merely as a stand-in for the president in a crisis—although there was certainly a benefit in Bush being prepared to do just that—and so Reagan took advantage of Bush's expertise in multiple ways. For instance, Bush was put in charge of the administration's drive to deregulate business and industry; it was a cause that had underscored Reagan's campaign for the presidency more than once.[125] Bush was subsequently given high marks for his work in this area, and in a telling gesture of the value he derived from the project, he assigned the same mission to his own vice president eight years later.

In a move that appeared perfectly in line with conventional notions of the modern vice presidency, Reagan committed to further extending Bush's presence in the affairs of national intelligence and security. Appended to his original directive on the vice president chairing meetings of the National Security Council when he could not be present, Reagan installed Bush as the head of a newly formed crisis management team which was, in essence, an extension of the Security Council. Initially there was some internal dissension over Reagan's decision, though it came almost entirely from General Alexander Haig, then the secretary of state.

Haig possessed an almost unmatched ego in a town teeming with ego; he also seemed to have, at some point, misread the Constitution and the Succession Act of 1947. This became apparent when, in the immediate aftermath of the assassination attempt on President Reagan, Haig asserted: "Constitutionally ... you have the president, the vice president and the secretary of state, in that order, and should the president decide he wants to transfer the helm to the vice president, he will do so. As for now, I'm in control here, in the White House."[126]

Far from being constitutionally in control, Haig was further down the chain of command than he seemed aware. More importantly, as Haig spoke the preceding words at a press briefing in the White House, Bush—who had been alerted of the shooting while aboard Air Force Two—was already on his way back to the capital to take control of the government, if need be. The protocol for such events was being followed and the vice president, as intended, was in charge. For that matter, it would have taken either the president himself, or the vice president and a majority of the cabinet, to declare that the president was unable to fulfill his constitutional duties, per the dictates of the Twenty-fifth Amendment. Only then would the vice president have been legally in charge. There were also contingencies in place if Bush happened to be incapacitated at the same time as the president. As was described in Chapter 3, under those circumstances the Succession Act of 1947 would be invoked and the Speaker of the House of Representatives, followed by the president pro tempore of the Senate, would be empowered to act as president—all before the responsibilities of the presidency would have fallen to the secretary of state.

For the sum of his vice presidency, George Bush epitomized the administrator as vice president, going about his work, generally unnoticed. Even his appearances presiding in the Senate were seldom and uneventful, yet the eight years he spent there totaled four more years than he had been a member of the House, and he did use his position there to marshal support for Reagan's agenda when he could. There was, however, one situation to arise when George Bush was Ronald Reagan's vice president that severely undercut the standing of Reagan in the eyes of the public, and threatened to drag Bush down, as well. The episode in question involved the clandestine effort by certain members of the Reagan administration to supply money and weapons to Nicaraguan rebels, or contras as they were known, who opposed Nicaragua's Sandinista government.[127] Via a complicated web of illegal weapons sales to Iran—ostensibly in exchange for American hostages being held in Lebanon—money and weapons were funneled to the contras.

The entire Iran-Contra affair revealed a great deal about how the Reagan White House operated and was likewise indicative of the dichotomy in approach to governance exhibited by Reagan and his vice president. As information regarding the affair surfaced, it exposed an executive government breaking the law—among other infractions, the sale of weapons to Iran was prohibited by congressional statute—and a White House environment in which presidential advisers seemingly operated of their own accord. The broad portrait to emerge was of a disturbingly disconnected president at the helm and of a vice president who claimed to be unusually ignorant of certain dubious activities going on in the West Wing.[128]

What was most peculiar about Bush's disavowal of any foreknowledge of the government's aid to the Nicaraguan contras was that foreign policy was his forte. Bush had landed in the vice presidency with greater foreign policy experience than any vice president since Martin Van Buren had come to the office not long after he had served as secretary of state in the first Jackson administration.[129] Besides, Bush consistently maintained that he was an integral member of the Reagan team, bragging to one interviewer, "I'm in on everything."[130] Yet, when it came to selling arms-for-hostages, and then redirecting part of the proceeds from the sale to provide resources to rebel fighters in Central America, Bush was curiously, in his words, "out of the loop."[131]

Later, when Bush ran for president, doubts about his veracity in the Iran-Contra affair followed him throughout the campaign. Obviously his involvement was not enough of a problem to dissuade too many voters, as Bush handily won the election. Quite possibly, Bush did the most damage to his credibility when, in the final days of his own presidency, he pardoned six individuals involved in the affair. At the time, Bush cited the investigation by the Independent Counsel's office and "the criminalization of the policy differences" as the principal reason for issuing the pardons.[132]

In all likelihood, the prospect of questions resurfacing about Bush's own involvement in the Iran-Contra affair weighed more heavily in his issuing the pardons than any factor having to do with defending the right for policy differences in the Reagan administration. Either way, when President Bush issued the Iran-Contra pardons, he stopped any further investigation of his role in the affair and summarily closed an unpleasant chapter of the Bush vice presidency.

Throughout their years of service together, George Bush was always deferential, as well as loyal, to Ronald Reagan. Moreover, a genuine friendship emerged between the two men, remarkable in itself, considering that they were once committed political opponents. The bond that developed between them did not stop Bush from reliably advocating for what he believed in; however, if Reagan decided otherwise, Bush suspended his own position and towed the line of the chief executive.[133] All the while, Bush carved his own niche within the administration, concurrently burnishing his credentials with the conservative wing of the Republican Party. This was imperative to Bush's political career because the more extreme conservatives in his party had always viewed him with apprehension; hence, with his aspirations for presidency never dimming, Bush knew conservatives held the key to any chance he might have for someday gaining the presidential nomination.[134]

In serving under Reagan, Bush was engaged in a perpetual political balancing act, always needing to convey his preparedness for the presidency, but never wanting to come across as too eager to take the office from a president whom the public was unusually captivated by. Such a balancing act could only succeed if Bush adhered to a routine of understatement in both words and deeds—never an easy job for an ambitious politician. Bush's challenge, though, was not unique to him, for every vice president faces the same, regardless of the era or the president they serve. Apart from the constitutional impossibility of Reagan seeking a third term, Bush's quandary remained: he was forever perceived as the understudy to the president he served.

Bush prevailed in the 1988 Republican primaries, eventually earning the nomination for president, and then winning the general election as well. During the long campaign season, he could plausibly argue that since his was a meaningful vice presidency, he was better prepared for the presidency than any opponent of any political party. This argument worked, first within the Republican Party, and despite the lingering reservations many conservatives continued to hold for him, and then later, in the general election against the Democratic nominee for president.

For nearly a year Bush ran as the most experienced and therefore, ostensibly, the most qualified candidate for president. With the eight years he had spent as vice president being the longest he had stayed in any government job, he could justly point to his own activist tenure, in the service of a frequently disengaged president, as the necessary preparation for the top job.

The Vice Presidency Served: A Caricature Restored? (1989–1993)

After George Bush was inaugurated president in 1981, he left the vice president's house for the White House. This was a significant move on two counts. As only the second vice president to have ever lived in the vice president's official residence, he was the first to live there for two terms. And, for the first time since the 1836 presidential election, a sitting vice president had won his own term as president. The vice president Bush replaced in the record books was Martin Van Buren. However, the parallels between the two did not end there, as both men were unable to retain the presidency for a second term. Furthermore, Bush and Van Buren both won the presidency with rather controversial running mates at their sides. In Van Buren's case, it was a slave owning, alcoholic senator, Richard Mentor Johnson, and in Bush's case, it was a young, able, and conservative senator from Indiana named Dan Quayle.

Quayle was not in the least bit like Martin Van Buren's vice president. He was, however, to some observers a startling addition to the Republican ticket, and, unhappily for Quayle, his vice presidency would be framed by the occasional missteps and gaffes he committed, in the main, during the early stages of the campaign. Quayle's selection also signaled a shift in the level of prior government service a vice president might bring to a new administration, which was dissimilar from the level of experience that characterized the vice presidents who served in the four administrations prior to the Bush administration. Whereas Gerald Ford, Nelson Rockefeller, Walter Mondale, and George Bush were established political elites when they came to the vice presidency, and all possessed considerable years of government service, Quayle was, in comparison, a novice. Again, this was not a wholly accurate portrayal in light of his eleven years in elective office, first as a member of the House of Representatives and then as a senator for eight years.

It was in his service in the upper chamber of Congress where Quayle steadily distinguished himself, and from where he had drawn the attention of then-Vice President Bush as a possible running mate.[135] Then again, it would have been hard for Quayle not to have been viewed as an upwardly mobile member of such a decidedly older body of legislators. Yet despite his comparative youth—for a senator—Quayle got along well with colleagues from both parties, crossing the aisle if necessary to gain traction for legislation he favored. With an aim to preparing for higher office, Quayle purposively immersed himself, as did Senator Al Gore before he ran for vice president, in military and foreign policy issues, principally from a stint on the Senate Armed Services Committee.

Quayle likewise drew attention on the domestic front, which no doubt helped him at home in Indiana. A case in point arose in the early 1980s when he went so far as to oppose the Reagan administration on a jobs training program that was slated to be abolished. On this occasion, he teamed with Senator Edward Kennedy to formulate and advance what eventually became the Jobs Training Partnership Act of 1982.[136] It was a rare instance of Quayle not towing the Republican line, but it did accord him a bit more cachet within the corridors of the Capitol. Furthermore, when he was vice president, Quayle's knowledge of individual senators, as well as his comfort with the sometimes arcane methods of the Senate, was invaluable to the Bush administration's legislative agenda.

What hurt Quayle the most was the characterization by the media that his youthful demeanor was akin to that of an overly excited adolescent.[137] Granted, he was only forty-one when he gained the vice-presidential nomination, but Quayle was the equivalent in age to Theodore Roosevelt upon the latter man's nomination for the same office—with Roosevelt turning forty-two four months after the Republican convention. Furthermore, Quayle was actually three years older than Franklin Roosevelt was when he too was nominated for vice president, and Quayle was two years older than Richard Nixon was when he was first nominated to run with Dwight Eisenhower in 1952.

In terms of years of public service, Quayle had held elective office longer than Theodore or Franklin Roosevelt and had been in Congress six years longer than Nixon was before being elected vice president. And though Theodore and Franklin Roosevelt both had served as the assistant secretary of the Navy, as well as governor of New York, neither man had ever served in the Congress, as had Nixon and Quayle. Nevertheless, by the end of the 1988 campaign, a caricature of Quayle would emerge and persist; it did not matter if it was inaccurate or not—Quayle would be marked as a lightweight who was allegedly unprepared for the vice presidency, let alone the presidency.

The preceding was an image of a candidate for vice president which disproportionately underestimated Quayle's potential. Still, notions of what Quayle supposedly was like were reinforced by the media over the course of the four years he was vice president. There is no question that this came about, from time to time, because of Quayle's own words and deeds, but on occasion the media unfairly emphasized minor slips by the vice president, pandering to the ease with which the public accepted a misrepresentation of whoever happened to be the vice president of the United States.

Happily for Dan Quayle, voters in 1988 cast their votes principally for the candidate for president, and not for the vice-presidential candidate; as a result, he emerged from a campaign of distortions of his persona as the forty-fourth vice president of the United States. Once inaugurated, Quayle profited from the many precedents established during the vice presidencies of Rockefeller, Mondale, and Bush. Recognizing that his job was much easier because his immediate predecessor was Bush, Quayle later remarked that he "had the good fortune to work with a former vice president."[138] In this regard, Quayle's experience was relatively unique: in the two hundred years preceding his tenure, only eleven of the forty-three individuals to precede him in office could say the same. And of those eleven, few if any could have honestly claimed, as Quayle could, to have been treated with a modicum of respect by the president under whom they served. As a testament to the strength of the Bush-Quayle partnership, past and present, Quayle has said that "it speaks volumes" about their relationship that they continue to have regular contact by phone or email, and occasionally meet in person.[139]

If Quayle misspoke on occasion, he was never derelict in the conduct of his duties, or in fulfilling specific assignments given to him by President Bush. In retrospect, Quayle cited his work chairing the Council on Competitiveness and the National Space Council as especially noteworthy facets of his vice presidency.[140] For the Council on

Competitiveness, Quayle managed a federal task force charged with minimizing, and whenever possible eliminating, government regulation of business. To do this, Quayle was given authority to intercede before federal regulations were issued, modifying the regulations to suit the agenda of the administration. According to Quayle's critics, this method violated the law requiring standard procedures, including the availability of a forum for public comment for all proposed federal regulations.[141]

The value for Quayle was that the outcome of the work of the Council on Competitiveness, by-and-large, was a boon for the business community—not coincidentally, a traditional constituency of the Republican Party. As a consequence, Quayle was able to foment increased deregulation of industries and businesses that could potentially underwrite a future presidential run by the vice president.

The prospect for earning political capital was a bit less promising with the Space Council than with the Council on Competitiveness, but undeniably there were opportunities to profit from the American public's long-time infatuation with space exploration. Hence, Quayle eagerly tackled the government's space program, attempting to streamline the bureaucracy of the National Aeronautics and Space Administration (NASA), with the intent of making it more economical. In this vein, Quayle directed, via the recommendations of the Space Council, a change in the top echelon of administrators at NASA, which subsequently led to a fundamental rededication of the agency's intuitional mission.[142]

In addition, Quayle was an activist on Capitol Hill, using whenever possible the network of relationships he had cultivated serving in the House and in the Senate. No doubt members of Congress were more aware than the general public that Quayle was indeed a close adviser to President Bush. This, coupled with Quayle's familiarity with the membership and the mechanics of Congress, worked to the decided advantage of the administration.

With the incremental increase in conservative Republican members of Congress—a trend which began in earnest during the Reagan years, and crested in 1994 when Republicans took back control of the House of Representatives after forty years in the minority—it was critical for Quayle to shore up support with members of his own party, many of whom continued to be uneasy with President Bush. In order to achieve this, Quayle worked in tandem with the White House's congressional liaison office on selling the administration's legislative program as a more conservative-friendly agenda than actually was the case.[143] It was a hard sell, particularly after Bush had vowed he would not advocate for new taxes, but then recommended a set of tax increases anyway.[144]

If Dan Quayle's vice presidency strayed at all in form or in function from his most recent predecessors, it was in the field of foreign policy. Yet even there it was a matter of degree, and he was not entirely absent from this sphere of activity. In large part, Quayle's restraint was prompted by the unusually engaged foreign policy role played by President Bush. In light of his earlier years of international experience, Bush was considered an authority in the field; for that reason he utilized Quayle less as a foreign policy surrogate than might have otherwise been the case. Notwithstanding Bush's stature in this area, Quayle managed to travel to forty-seven countries in his four years as vice president, engaging on a personal level with countless world leaders.[145] If sometimes these diplomatic missions were inconsequential, there was always an auxiliary benefit in the interests and influence of the United States being strengthened throughout the world.

It was in the fields of foreign policy and national security where Quayle confronted an age-old problem which arises near the presidency. As has been the case since the inception of the American presidency, and has been noted here before, coteries form around a president, erecting transparent barriers that diminish, or even completely deny, the influence of individuals outside of the group. With the power of the presidency on the ascent throughout the twentieth century, this phenomenon has become even more pronounced, and, irrespective of the corresponding growth of the modern vice presidency, the vice president has not been immune from such selective exclusion. In particular, when Calvin Coolidge, Henry Wallace, Lyndon Johnson, Hubert Humphrey, and Spiro Agnew served as vice president, they were all purposefully kept at bay, whenever possible, by intimates to the president.

Not having been a long-term adviser to President Bush, Quayle could only be viewed as an interloper by those closest to the president. This impression of Quayle as an outsider who inexplicably gained access and influence at the top of the executive government was accentuated by the seeming covertness of his selection for the vice-presidential nomination. Even though Quayle was put through a measure of a vetting process similar to some prior vice-presidential candidates, the relative quiet before he was selected, and Bush opting to keep the decision close to the vest, added further to the enigma of Quayle's place by the president's side.[146]

At no time was it more apparent that Quayle was on the outside than during the Persian Gulf War. Perhaps it was deliberate, perhaps not, but those closest to the president appeared to do what they could to keep the vice president on the periphery of the decision making process—in the prelude to the conflict, and then once it began to unfold.[147]

It did not help Quayle's position that Bush's secretary of state, James Baker, who was closer to the president than any other figure in the administration, was unhappy with the initial choice of Quayle for the second spot on the ticket and continued to doubt Quayle's abilities even after his becoming vice president.[148] In addition, those who were most involved in the conduct of the war—such as the secretary of defense, Dick Cheney, and the national security adviser to the president, Brent Scowcroft—were all well acquainted with the president, and many of them had served with Bush in the Ford administration. Surely Quayle was reluctant to admit to his exclusion in this area; he was, after all, the vice president, and Bush had encouraged him to "know everything that was going on in the Oval Office."[149] At the same time, it was clear that Quayle understood the boundaries that existed because he was not seen as part of the president's closest war counselors, offering that "if the president was in a one-on-one meeting with ... Brent Scowcroft, the secretary of state, or the secretary of defense, I would not bother him."[150]

For Dan Quayle, the vice presidency failed to be a successful launching pad for the presidency. After suffering defeat in their 1992 reelection bid, George Bush retired from public life, and Quayle strove to position himself as the loyal opposition to the new Clinton-Gore administration. In the lead up to the 1996 presidential election, Quayle campaigned across the country for Republican candidates and established an exploratory committee for a possible run for the presidency.[151] Nonetheless, it was all for naught, as the distorted and fundamentally erroneous image perpetuated by the media, of the Quayle vice presidency, persisted.

It was of no consequence the number of policy speeches Quayle made, or the countless campaign appearances he made on behalf of assorted Republican candidates; Quayle was simply unable to garner sufficient support for the idea of him as the president. In the long run, the successes Quayle achieved when he was vice president were not enough to shake the first impression he had made on the national stage, when he was merely a candidate for the second office. As it was, certain notions about him endured. Ultimately, Quayle's campaign for the presidency ended before it began. For Quayle, the vice presidency had become a political quagmire from which he could not entirely emerge; it would prove to be, as it had been for far too many of his predecessors, the highest and final rung on the political ladder.

Apart from of the public misperception of Dan Quayle's vice presidency, he should not be included with the scattered anomalies of the modern institution—like Charles Dawes, Charles Curtis, Harry Truman, and Spiro Agnew. For that matter, it was Agnew, the only one of the preceding group of vice presidents to resign from office, who was a complete outlier among the modern vice presidents isolated here. Ironically, Quayle was the beneficiary of a generous president who himself had once been vice president; therefore, Quayle's vice presidency, aside from a slightly less substantial role in foreign policy, met all the criteria of the expanded institution. And in the process, the Bush-Quayle partnership took the form the president allowed.

The American vice presidency only advanced toward a fully realized institution when President Warren Harding set it in motion by his invitation to his vice president to attend cabinet meetings. Was it an artificial gesture on Harding's part? Almost certainly so, but later, when Vice President Coolidge became president and the remnants of the Harding administration were engulfed in scandal, Coolidge was easily relieved of any wrongdoing, since he was never an intimate of Harding. Besides, he was only the vice president: how much could he really have known about the machinations of the executive government? And yet, there was an important advantage gained from Coolidge being in the cabinet. Cabinet attendance made the vice president appear tangibly linked to the executive branch for the first time in history.

After Harding's gesture to Coolidge, President Franklin Roosevelt went to great lengths to expand, and when it served his needs, contract the reach of the vice presidency. Of course, Roosevelt was coming from the unique vantage of defining the vice-presidential experience for three different individuals. In addition, by excluding his third vice president and eventual successor, Harry Truman, from knowledge of the program to develop the atomic bomb, Roosevelt unintentionally influenced the tenure of a fourth vice president, Alben Barkley. This came about because President Truman was determined never again to risk the security of the nation by leaving the vice president in the dark.

Truman, and then President Dwight Eisenhower, both accelerated the further modernization of the vice presidency, particularly in terms of involving the vice president in foreign policy and national security. From that point forward—and with a measure of restraint exercised, oddly enough, by two former vice presidents who later became president, Lyndon Johnson and Richard Nixon—each successive president added to the power, perks, and institutionalization of the modern American vice presidency. In so doing, the institution was set for the two most influential and powerful vice presidents to hold the office, thus far.

THE VICE PRESIDENCY AUGMENTED

THE CASE OF GORE

If you close your left eye and turn your head just right, the great seal of the vice president reads: President of the United States of America.

– Vice President Al Gore

Legend has it that Albert Gore Sr. always imagined that his only son and namesake would be elected president of the United States.[1] It was a dream which supposedly the son shared. Whether the shared dream was legend, and there is good reason to believe it is not, it is a reasonable assumption that neither Al Gore nor his father ever dreamed of his serving as the vice president of the United States. Put another way: the dream of any natural born citizen of the United States someday becoming president has yet to enter the popular imagination, as far as the American vice presidency is concerned. But Gore did win the vice presidency, twice, though he never won the Electoral College vote for the presidency. Gore's win of the popular vote in the 2000 election, but not the Electoral College vote, will forever link an asterisk to his name in the endnotes of history texts. Yet depicting Gore as simply another vice president who served with a healthy president, and therefore did not gain the presidency by succession, nor win his own term as president, unjustly delimits his contribution to the modern American vice presidency.

HOW AL GORE ARRIVED IN THE VICE PRESIDENCY

Analogous to every other individual to have served as vice president—aside from Vice President William King—Al Gore never intended for his political career to take him to the vice presidency. Gore envisaged himself winning the presidency, instead, and for this reason aspirations for the vice presidency would have been absent from his mind. For that matter, why would he want to be vice president? By and large, it is the rare occasion when an individual actively seeks to be second best. Equally, there is the practical mechanics of pursuing the vice presidency in the American system; mechanics that preclude much in the way of campaigning for the number two spot on the ticket. This has characterized the selection of the vice president since John Adams was first elected in 1789 and has continued with each shift in the nomination and election processes.

Irrespective of the mode used for choosing the vice president, the selection of the president always has been paramount and has come, figuratively and literally, first. This notion was captured well by Vice President Charles Dawes when he wrote of the impending 1928 presidential election. Dawes observed:

> The superficial attitude of indifference which many public men assume toward the office of Vice President of the United States is easily explained. It is the office for which one cannot hope to be a candidate with sufficient prospects for success to justify the effort involved in a long campaign. One's political availability for nomination to the position cannot be determined until the nominating convention has in effect decided upon the head of the ticket.[2]

It was fitting then that Al Gore had run for president before he ran for vice president, signifying where his genuine ambitions lay. Gore's initial foray as a presidential candidate had been in 1988, and though he was unsuccessful that year, his goal of attaining the presidency never dimmed—it was simply put on hold until the next election. Then, at one point in the intervening years—between the 1988 and 1992 presidential election seasons—Gore's only son was badly injured when he was hit by a car; it was an event that shook Gore, compelling him to rethink how family factored into the electoral equations of an ambitious politician. Accordingly, because of his family, and keeping in mind what a campaign for the presidency entailed, Gore decided, as far as the 1992 election was concerned, that he would not run for president.

By that time, Gore had served as a member of the House of Representatives for eight years and for an equal number of years in the Senate. Gore was young—he was only forty-four in 1992—yet the seriousness of purpose he exuded, which later provided ample fodder for comedians when he was again a presidential candidate, was already manifest in every word he uttered. If Gore's stiff intellectualism was off-putting for voters when they tried to visualize him as president, his persona, combined with his résumé, made it seem like central casting had stepped in with the ideal candidate for the role of vice president of the United States.

Indeed, Gore did appear to be the perfect choice for the vice presidency. In retrospect, it is evident from his earnestness, and surely based on his experience on Capitol Hill, that Gore was a necessary addition to filling out an electoral ticket with Bill Clinton at the top. Since Clinton was a governor, and Gore a senator, they could then claim to have experience with the national government, but still not be a part of it. Therefore, it followed that they were best equipped to fix the problems besetting the nation. Both Clinton and Gore were from the South, the former from Arkansas, the latter from Tennessee. This was an anomalous geographic pairing for a national ticket of either of the major American political parties, yet it worked well and contributed to the Democratic Party's recapture of parts of the South on the two occasions Clinton and Gore ran as a team.

In all probability, it was because the two men hailed from the same region of the country that their partnership quickly grew so strong. Not only did both men speak the same political language—and with virtually the same accent—they also shared a passion for the minutiae of policy. In Clinton's case, he was steeped in the intricacies of domestic policy, specializing at the micro level of policy formulation and implementation which was demanded of a governor of a small, rural state. In contrast, Gore's preferred policy genres were inclusive, encompassing the interwoven spheres of environmental, foreign, and military policy. It was crucial for a United States senator, let alone a potential vice president or president, to demonstrate mastery in these areas. That Gore actually grasped the preceding fields was telling about him as an individual, and correspondingly gave a boost to the Clinton-Gore ticket in an area that it needed it the most.

Because Clinton and Gore evidenced a shared heritage and political outlook, and because they were of the same generation, they formed an uncommon bond. When taken together, it plainly made sense for Clinton to ask Gore to be his running mate.[3] On Clinton's part, he certainly did not offer the second spot to Gore from a long-term working or personal relationship the two shared, since there was none; it was just a good fit. It also proved to be a polling phenomenon, as the announcement of Gore's selection immediately boosted Clinton's poll numbers by 10 percent.[4] By adding Gore to the ticket, Bill Clinton had set the stage for one of the strongest president-to-vice president associations in the annals of the two national executive offices.

THE CLINTON-GORE PARTNERSHIP

In Al Gore's first debate appearance as a candidate for vice president, he was asked a three-part question relating to the role he was expected to play as vice president, what his specific interests would be, and what qualified him to be president, should circumstances dictate he step up to the higher office.[5] Being, at his core, a politician, it was hardly surprising when Gore sidestepped the specific components of the question. In lieu of a direct response, Gore offered a brief description of what, over the course of the campaign, had already become the Clinton-Gore partnership, and would thus continue to serve as the underpinning of their tenure together. That evening Gore stated:

> Bill Clinton understands the meaning of the words teamwork and partnership ... Discussions of the vice presidency tend sometimes to focus on the crisis during which a vice president is thrust into the Oval Office, and indeed, one-third of the vice presidents who have served have been moved into the White House. But the teamwork and partnership beforehand ... how

you work together is critically important. The way we work together in this campaign is one sample.[6]

On the whole, Gore's response in the debate was remarkable, since from the onset of the campaign he evidently considered himself an equal, working partner with Clinton. What is more, he was articulating the outline for a considerably broader president-to-vice president arrangement than was the norm, and one which indicated that the vice president was meant to be less of an understudy to the president than a collaborator in governance. It was therefore clear, well before winning the election, let alone assuming office, that Gore did not anticipate his being merely a junior partner in the Clinton administration.

Unlike Gore's theory on teamwork, his opponent in the election and adversary in the debate, the incumbent vice president, Dan Quayle, described a structure emphasizing traditional conceptions of the vice president working as the principal surrogate for the president. In the debate, Quayle pointedly countered Gore's assertions on teamwork and partnership, remarking that either "may be fine in Congress, Senator Gore—that's what Congress is all about, compromise, teamwork, working things out. But when you're president of the United States or when you're vice president and you have to fill in like I did the night of the crisis in the Philippines, you've got to make a decision, you've got to make up your mind."[7]

What Quayle was referencing, albeit briefly, was an attempted coup of the Philippine government in 1989. On that occasion, Quayle was obligated to intervene for the president, George H.W. Bush, who was traveling overseas. Going with Quayle's narrative of events, he functioned primarily as a coordinator of the White House response, leaving the final decision on how best to handle the situation to the president.[8] The decision making model employed by Quayle in this instance was in keeping with the model Bush adhered to over the course of the eight years he was vice president to President Ronald Reagan. It was the apposite model to follow under the circumstances, grounded by a basic principle: the foremost use of the vice president was in a supporting and advising capacity to the president. In the end, as Bush himself had emphasized on a number of occasions, there must only be one president.[9]

If, at the time of the debate, Gore foresaw his occupying an expanded vice presidency with considerable power, as well as his having sustained, meaningful influence on the president, then the determining caveat was whether Clinton would actually honor the commitment to such an arrangement. Or, posed differently, once the pair took office, would President Clinton be receptive to sharing power with his vice president to the extent that Gore anticipated? Extending the idea even further, Gore must have wondered if Clinton would facilitate an arrangement wherein the vice president was appreciably more than just another elected officer of the government and was instead counted among the president's top advisers and confidants.

As time went by, it was clear that Bill Clinton never abandoned his commitment to Al Gore as his partner, nor to the American vice presidency as an institution. For obvious reasons Clinton's follow through mattered—to Gore, as well as to the vice presidency—but it is the overlooked, almost subtle, affect Clinton had on this front that necessitates an additional, nuanced appraisal.

To begin with, Clinton's choice of Gore represented the continuation of the practice of selecting vice-presidential nominees with experience in the national government explicitly because the presidential nominee had no experience there. In this way, the pairing of Clinton and Gore was no different than that of Jimmy Carter with Walter Mondale, or Ronald Reagan with George H.W. Bush. But when juxtaposed with Carter-Mondale or Reagan-Bush, Clinton and Gore demonstrated a degree of symmetry that neither pair of their predecessors could claim.

Because of the characteristics they shared—relative youth, deep roots in the South, unyielding ambition—and even in the ways they contrasted—an easygoing, empathetic personality for Clinton, and a rigid, at times cold, persona for Gore—they were peers in a way few, if any, of their predecessors could match. Clinton captured best the sense of equilibrium binding the two when he reflected on their working relationship, three years after leaving the White House. Recounting the simple, almost mundane routine they introduced at the beginning of their first term in office, and which they continued for the entirety of their time as president and vice president, Clinton maintained:

> Al Gore helped me a lot in the early days, encouraging me to keep making hard decisions and put them behind me, and giving me a continuing crash course in how Washington works. Part of our regular routine was having lunch alone in my private dining room once a week. We took turns saying grace, then proceeded to talk about everything from our families to sports, books, and movies to the latest items on his agenda or mine. We kept our lunch schedule up for eight years, except when one of us was gone for several days at a stretch. Though we had a lot in common, we were very different, and the lunches kept us closer than we otherwise would have been in the Washington pressure cooker, and eased my adjustment to my new life.[10]

Significantly, Clinton accorded Gore the latitude whereby he could provoke the president into action when the situation required his doing so. This understanding made a difference, since Clinton was renowned for vacillating when he needed to decide political, policy, and personnel questions. Illustrative of this, in an often cited encounter, Clinton was frustrated by a political environment he was unable to master, complaining unceasingly of his predicament; finally, yet irresolute as ever, he asked Gore for direction, to which Gore snapped at Clinton—"get with the goddamn program"—in effect insisting that the president commit to, and stick with, a decision—and in full view of a conclave of advisers.[11] Although it was a fleeting exchange, one would be hard pressed to find a similar confrontation, wherein the vice president challenged the president in this manner.

Because Clinton operated at the pinnacle of the American government and generally went uncontested—at least by those who populated the executive branch—there was added weight in any, even deferential, confrontations the vice president had with the president. This was not purely an indication of an assertive personality trait Al Gore possessed; instead, it was emblematic of Gore's confidence in the position he held in the government, and in the strength of his association with President Clinton. And yet the leeway Gore maintained with the president was unparalleled and indicated a paradigm shift in the American executive branch, though that outcome went largely unnoticed.

The absence of any real awareness of what was happening to the top two elective offices of the nation, and the vice presidency in particular, was not a matter of Clinton and Gore failing to focus publicly on it. Moreover, the shift in the president-to-vice president arrangement was not the product of a single, redefining moment or action, although, in isolation, the adoption of the Twelfth and the Twenty-fifth Amendments may be taken as distinct acts profoundly impacting the vice presidency. Instead, the shift in the president-to-vice president arrangement was, by the time of Gore's tenure, the culmination of incremental, sometimes profound, developments in the vice presidency as an institution, and to the advantage of each subsequent vice president as an officer of the national government.

If the origins for the transformation of the vice presidency are wide-ranging and sundry, with the enablement of change to the institution prompted by the words and deeds of several presidents, there are specific individuals and actions which merit reiteration. Hence, the inclusion of Vice President Calvin Coolidge in the cabinet, the assignment of Vice President Henry Wallace to coordinate multiple wartime bureaucracies, the addition of Vice President Alben Barkley to the National Security Council, the patent utility of Vice President Richard Nixon's service in the Eisenhower administration, the national stature Vice President Nelson Rockefeller brought to the office, and the placement of Vice President Walter Mondale in the military chain-of-command, as well as his acquisition of an office in the White House—all of these cases contributed to the augmentation of the American vice presidency.

Accordingly, as the last decade of the twentieth century unfolded, Al Gore took the helm of a vice-presidential office unmatched by prior manifestations of the office—in stature, resources, and influence—and then, with the backing of President Clinton, Gore proceeded to bring the vice presidency nearer to equipoise with the presidency. This came about as a result of the aforementioned shift in the way the president and vice president worked together, an alignment starkly dissimilar from the working relationships of presidents and vice presidents who have come before. For as the vice presidency developed over time, and regardless of how accommodating the incumbent president proved to be, there had been one constant: the president-to-vice president relationship was a vertical, hierarchical arrangement, transparently oriented from the president down to the vice president.

With the commencement of the Clinton-Gore era, the traditional arrangement flipped, structuring it closer to a horizontal, hierarchical setup. It should be understood, however, that in no way was there any blurring of the line of final authority. The consensus was that Clinton would have the final say, but typically only after the vice president had weighed in as well. To this point, it has been suggested that President Clinton never made a "major policy decision … without discussing it with the vice president."[12]

Since Gore clearly held substantial sway with the president, and he retained the clout to prod the president when need be, it necessarily followed that an expectation was set for future vice presidents to hold commensurate leverage with their president. Here again, Clinton offered testament to the experience and talent Gore brought to the administration, affirming from the outset that Gore was prepared on all of the issues "we'd have to deal with," and besides, "Al understood Congress and the Washington culture far better than I did."[13]

President Clinton's acknowledgment that his choice for vice president had been schooled in the ways of Washington, and was therefore able to inform him as well as to shield him from the political hazards awaiting all presidents, buttressed the increasing credibility of the vice presidency and further diminished any reservations about making the vice president a completely utilitarian officer of the government. There was an additional upside for Clinton in selecting such an able individual to join him on the ticket, as he improved his prospects for victory while reassuring wary voters about his own readiness for higher office. Later, the acuity of Clinton's choice was confirmed by the vice president's success in practically every assignment the president delegated to him.

When taken together, the outcome of the Clinton-Gore partnership made for a significant vice-presidential institution, actualized beyond any notions the Framers of the Constitution may have held for the second office of the land. Besides, it is improbable that any of the Framers envisioned a president and vice president maintaining the degree of equilibrium in their association as Clinton and Gore did. And yet, in light of the exponential growth of the American presidency over the course of the twentieth century, it made sense for the vice presidency to approximate keeping pace with the higher office.

By every measure, Gore was the appropriate fit for the vice presidency at that juncture in the trajectory of the institution's development. Of course, he benefited immensely by serving a president who chose to extend, and not retract, the prerogatives and responsibilities the office had accrued. To Gore's credit, he sustained the required balance of deference and influence with President Clinton. In this vein, Gore consistently made his political and policy ambitions secondary to those of the president. On any number of occasions he avowed to observe an unassuming, yet straightforward precept: do whatever necessary to achieve the goals of the president and, in the process, help to ensure that Clinton was, in Gore's words, "the best" president.[14]

Warren Christopher, who conducted the vice-presidential nominee search for Clinton and afterwards served as secretary of state for the first term of the Clinton administration, offered one of the better observations on the shared Clinton-Gore tenure:

> The partnership that began so auspiciously continued throughout my time in office. The way they worked together raised the office of vice president to a new level of public awareness. Gore became a full partner, not because Clinton made a formal commitment to make it so but because the president genuinely valued Gore's views and talents. They enjoyed each other's company, teasing and laughing in a natural way that bespoke friendship rather

than a number one/number two relationship. Time and again, I found that the president made his most important decisions only after talking privately with the vice president. Clinton's mantra—'It's all right with me, but let's talk it over with Al before we decide'—became familiar to every member of the cabinet.[15]

The effect of the Clinton-Gore association went well beyond the immediacy of their two terms in office; instead, the model Clinton and Gore established extended the president-to-vice president construct. The result of this, depending on one's point of view, was positive. Conversely, a feasible argument could also be advanced that what Clinton and Gore initiated went too far in setting precedents, while creating an opening for potentially unwanted outcomes for the vice-presidential institution and to the model for executive governance. Still, the advantages in how Clinton and Gore operated together were realized by the way executive responsibilities, as well as lines of authority, were shared. The answer to why this matters is deceptively simple: the American presidency of the twentieth and twenty-first centuries has become an enormous challenge for one individual to manage.

The Vice President as Chief Administrator

The expansion of the presidency is a phenomenon the Framers could not have foreseen when they were shaping the Constitution. Neither those who argued at the time of the Federal Convention for a strong chief executive nor those who warned against an omnipotent president could ever have predicted how robust the American presidency would become. Furthermore, and in light of the increased resources and staffing made available to the president—an expansion manifest during the eight years Woodrow Wilson was president, then redoubled over the course of Franklin Roosevelt's twelve years in office, and then augmented by each successive presidency—it is readily apparent that for modern presidents, meeting the obligations of the office necessitates all of the tools and resources the institution has amassed.

Additionally, the Executive Office of the President (EOP), formally established in 1939 at Franklin Roosevelt's behest, quickly became a centralized and potent locus of institutional resources and personnel, functioning entirely at the direction of the president. In conjunction with the wide scope of the EOP's power and resources, the trio of decades to close out the twentieth century saw the White House chief of staff assigned oversight of the sum of the EOP's day-to-day operations.[16] Over the years, the chief of staff position has typically been filled by assertive political operatives—individuals like H.R. Haldeman for President Nixon, Donald Rumsfeld and Dick Cheney for President Ford, Hamilton Jordan for President Carter, James Baker for President Reagan, and Rahm Emanuel for President Obama—all of whom have met the standard for a strong chief of staff.[17]

In recent administrations, conferring cabinet-rank status on the chief of staff has become standard protocol, thus highlighting the prominence of administration and personnel management in the operations of the executive government. Likewise, since the major units charged with domestic, economic, and foreign policy formulation are located under the aegis of the EOP, the chief of staff obviously has considerable influence in all these spheres. Of equal importance, nearly all those individuals designated chief of staff have performed a critical gatekeeping role. In being proactive here, the chief of staff has the twofold advantage of determining who has access to the president and what arguments the president hears. As it stands, the chief of staff is consistently, and rightly, viewed as one of the most conspicuous members of any administration. And, depending entirely on who is president, some who have been the designated chief of staff have exercised influence and power in excess of the vice president.

The regularity with which recent presidents have sanctioned appreciable levels of authority and influence for their chiefs of staff is problematic. To begin with, the chief of staff is appointed by the president, and as a consequence is not subject to the approval of the electorate. Granted, all the heads of the executive departments are similarly nominated by the president, as are federal judges and Supreme Court justices, but unlike the cabinet and the members of the federal judiciary, a prospective chief of staff does not have to endure the congressional confirmation process, by way of the advice and consent of the Senate.

Conversely, the vice president is initially selected by the presidential nominee, endorsed by a political party by winning the vice-presidential nomination, and then elected by the votes of the national electorate. The point then is this: the better part of the coordinating responsibilities, as well as the role of advisor, performed by the chief of staff may be fulfilled, instead, by a utilitarian vice president. A vice president, it should be emphasized, who has the added legitimacy of having been chosen by the presidential nominee for the vice-presidential nomination and then elected to office with the president. It therefore makes sense to augment the vice-presidential institution with a greater measure of the day-to-day oversight of the executive branch, generally, and the Executive Office of the President, specifically.

Having the vice president serve in a capacity similar to that of the modern chief of staff was in theory introduced when the Hoover Commission suggested a congressional statute for adding a second, strictly administrative vice president. The details of the Hoover proposal are many and expansive and are evaluated at greater length in Chapter 8, but at this juncture it is worth noting that if the broad goal of the Hoover Commission was to reorganize the executive branch, the underpinning of the enterprise was to relieve overly burdened modern presidents. Relevant to the consideration here, the Hoover proposal argued for Senate confirmation of the administrative vice president.

Additionally, perchance lately, vestiges of the Hoover recommendations infused the discussions that took place in the mid-1960s on filling vacancies in the vice presidency. At the time, Congress was deliberating on the proposed Twenty-fifth Amendment to the Constitution. One alternative to the amendment called for the addition of a second vice president to be elected with the president and slotted in the line of succession after the first vice president but before the Speaker of the House.[18] Clearly, in its final form, the foregoing option was not included in the Twenty-fifth Amendment, though the amendment did stipulate that the president's choice of nominee for vice president had to be confirmed by both chambers of Congress.

Under the preceding proposed structure there would be an executive as well as legislative vice president; the former would be first in the line of succession and "take on special assignments" delegated by the president; the latter "would hold the constitutional powers and duties" of the vice president, "serving as presiding officer of the Senate and breaking tie votes there."[19] The essential point for partisans was that the second vice president, having been elected with the president, would be drawn from the same political party; another layer would be added to the line of succession, in the process diminishing the chance of the opposition party taking the presidency from the rightful victors of the presidential election.

Irrespective of the vice president's place in the Constitution, by virtue of the elective status of the office, the individual serving as vice president is much more than what the Constitution delimited. At the same time, the vice president is definitely not a glorified public administrator because, again, the vice president is equivalent to the president in being a nationally elected officer of the government. However, dissimilar from the cabinet or the staff of the EOP, the vice president does not serve at the pleasure of the president.

Consequent of the foregoing points, the vice presidency would seem the logical institution to which to extend additional administrative responsibilities. While doing so would burden the vice-presidential institution more than it already is, it would correspondingly relieve a large share of the weight the presidency presently carries. One means for deciding if this is the ideal form and function for the vice presidency is to make a cursory evaluation of when this has already been put into practice. For example, it is no coincidence that an aggressive, autocratic chief of staff like H.R. Haldeman served President Nixon at the same time that a weak vice president like Spiro Agnew held office. Certainly this reflected Nixon's preference for how his administration was to function. But it was also further affirmation of his initial choice of a running mate. Plainly, Nixon never intended his vice president to be integrally involved in the administrative operations or policy formulation going on inside the White House.

Later, when Gerald Ford was the president, three men held the chief of staff position: first, General Alexander Haig, who was a holdover from the Nixon administration, next Donald Rumsfeld, and then Dick Cheney. Haig was in the position too briefly to merit comment here, but Rumsfeld and Cheney, as documented in Chapter 5, strong-armed Vice President Nelson Rockefeller whenever feasible and, as a result, made Rockefeller relatively inconsequential. President Ford's press secretary, Ron Nessen, described Cheney's time in the Ford White House in this way:

> There was no question that Dick Cheney was firmly atop the White House chain of command. Cheney had taken on more and more power until he was running the White House staff and overseeing the [1976] campaign in an authoritative manner—his easygoing style had disappeared. Although he kept

a low public profile, Cheney had accumulated as much control as some of the better-known chiefs of staff. Some reporters privately started calling him the Grand Teuton, a complex pun referring to his mountainous home state of Wyoming and the Germanic style of his predecessor, H.R. Haldeman.[20]

The preceding brief examples are meant merely to underscore a discernable commonality: when an aggressively domineering individual is vested with the powers of the chief of staff, then the vice presidency may be rendered a less essential institution, and the vice president will in turn be perceived as the less effective official of the two. Conversely, when the vice president is a strong presence in the daily operations of the White House—as were Walter Mondale, George H.W. Bush, and Al Gore—those who worked as chief of staff were less efficacious when attempting to control the functionality of the EOP, and subsequently, they were not as persuasive as the vice president when it came to prompting the agenda emanating from the White House.

Such was the situation even with President Carter's chief of staff, Hamilton Jordan, who had been an intimate of Carter's before coming to the West Wing. In the long run, it was Vice President Mondale who proved indispensable to Carter and exercised a larger share of influence with the president. Mondale's preeminence within the administration, and over Jordan, was established because it is the president who determines whether the chief of staff or the modern vice president is more essential to the administration. As a consequence, Carter's preliminary assurance to Mondale of significant involvement in the administration, in union with the wide spread recognition of his commitment to the vice president, ultimately defined the tenures of Mondale and Jordan.

But where Mondale and Jordan stood in the Carter administration went beyond personal relations or presidential pledges. Carter's extension of authority to the vice president was given additional legitimacy because of Mondale's election to the second highest office in the nation. As was indicated before, since the vice president is elected with the president, and even though voters in the United States do not cast separate ballots for president and vice president, elections nonetheless serve to legitimize governments and the officials who run them. For this reason, and by virtue of Mondale having been elected in the era of the modern vice presidency, from the moment he took the oath of office there was a presumption of his stature in the government.

As it was, and similar to the circumstances Walter Mondale enjoyed, Al Gore had not only his president's confidence and support, he had the electoral legitimacy every vice president gains when they are successful with the electorate, winning the popular vote as well the vote of the Electoral College. Yet, beyond the dual legitimacy the American electoral system accords the president and vice president, Gore further promoted his place in the administration by his active engagement in the transition process that commenced immediately after the 1992 election. How Gore made this happen says much about his drive to make the most out of a job that had been openly spurned for much of its history.

Upon winning the presidency, Bill Clinton returned to his native Arkansas to begin organizing for the transition—and the vice president-elect went with him. The time which elapses between the election of the president and vice president and their in-auguration is central to how the power dynamics of the administration play out over the ensuing four years. Intrinsically then, it is the first days and weeks following the election which are unusually critical to the transition.

For Al Gore, this was an especially opportune juncture in the transition, as he built on the strides Walter Mondale and George H.W. Bush had made when influencing the makeup of the Carter and Reagan administrations, respectively. Dick Cheney likewise seized on the transition period to solidify his standing well before the administration of George W. Bush took charge of the government. As will become evident in the fol-lowing chapter, Cheney's influence during the transition period surpassed that of all his predecessors. In all likelihood, much of what Cheney accomplished in this sphere might never have been realized were it not for Gore's extension of precedent. In other words, because Gore behaved as he did, Cheney's subsequent behavior was less likely to be questioned.

In the lead up to the inauguration, Gore's involvement in the selection of the cabinet, in league with his recommendations for filling positions in the Executive Office of the President, was an unmistakable manifestation of the vice president—or, in this case, the vice president-elect—integrating himself into administrative and personnel decisions, thereby underscoring the enhanced utility of modern vice presidents. Therefore, as the transition unfolded in Arkansas, Gore was continually at Clinton's side.[21]

Curiously, and despite the urging of the delegated transition coordinator, Warren Christopher, to do so, Clinton refused to anoint his chief of staff before filling the nu-merous openings in the White House operation.[22] Instead, Clinton relied on Gore, and the latter man's principal adviser, as well as a handful of intimates, including Hillary Clinton, to determine who would be working in the president's office. When Clinton eventually did name a chief of staff, he chose a long-time friend who proved no match for a Washington insider like Gore. In retrospect, Christopher suggested that "the comfort level between the president and his chief of staff is certainly a factor in making the choice, [but] it should not be the defining or even a dominant consideration."[23] What Christopher neglected to mention was that Clinton, by his selection of Gore, had found a collaborator who brought a measure of experience, advice, and support that most presidents would be hard pressed to find in their chief of staff.

During the transition, Gore participated in each interview Clinton held with prospective nominees for the cabinet. This was an important place for Gore to insert himself, as it gave notice to all of the eventual cabinet secretaries of the vice president's commitment to the policy direction of the future administration; it also indicated the certainty of his being an integral member of the cabinet. Gore's engagement was not, however, limited to determining the top postings of the executive departments, for he was consistently involved in vetting and recommending individuals for the innu-merable positions the president-elect is required to fill when piecing together a new administration.[24] Of greater import than any of the former points, Gore's ubiquity in the course of the transition period signaled his intent to be a constant at the future president's side. Indeed, by securing his proximity to the president, Gore was situated to be a full partner in the conduct of the executive government.

Although there are myriad examples of Al Gore's involvement in the administration of the executive branch in the eight years he was vice president, there was no project that defined his tenure to the extent that the reinventing government initiative did. Formally instituted in March of 1993 by President Clinton, the National Performance Review was led by Gore and commissioned to identify ways to streamline the federal government, specifically with regard to management, personnel, procurement, and budgeting. Although the project was clearly not as contentious as others advanced by the Clinton administration, it would prove to be a noteworthy success for Gore.[25]

Gore was the best choice for this assignment for a number of reasons, not the least of which was because the project was intended to be a prominent feature of the Clinton administration's maiden agenda. By signing on to the initiative, Gore was set to increase his own political capital, as well as that of the administration, and in the process broaden the portfolio of the vice president. This last point is particularly salient in that in each instance when the purview or resources of the vice presidency has increased, each then has become an established prerogative for the institution, and consequently has moved forward to the advantage of the next occupant of the office.

Naturally, any new president may decide not to extend the same responsibilities and assignments to their vice president and could even retract all the duties granted to the preceding vice president, apart from those prescribed by the Constitution. For that matter, the president could prompt, with the collaboration of willing members of Congress, legislation aimed at repealing earlier statutes granting the vice president specific prerogatives—like the vice president's permanent place on the board of the Smithsonian Institution or membership on the National Security Council—although pursuing such a course would be highly irregular, and somewhat suspect. But the preceding schemes stand merely as hypothetical constructs since the institutional vice presidency, at least since the Carter-Mondale years, and even in view of variations between individual vice presidents, has not regressed in form or in function. Furthermore, because successive presidents have facilitated an expanded institutional vice presidency, the fundamental dynamic of the president-to-vice president relationship has been profoundly, and permanently, altered.

Returning to the National Performance Review initiative and Vice President Gore, specifically, of the many pledges made by the Clinton-Gore ticket during the 1992 campaign, prominent among these was a commitment to reducing the size and inefficiency of the federal government. To reconfigure the federal bureaucracy, per se, is a daunting, though innocuous proposition, unlikely to raise the ire of most observers, and thus an attractive undertaking for any political figure. For all intents and purposes, having one half of the victorious electoral ticket spearhead the initiative lent distinction to a project that would undoubtedly be a boon to the Clinton administration, as well as to the vice president.

There was no uncertainty about Gore's suitability for the initiative. On the whole, he was atypical for a politician, in that he had always been comfortable immersing himself in the minutiae of politics and policy; it was no different for him when it came to reorganizing the federal bureaucracy. Gore was fine with non-glamorous tasks, working in the shadows, as it were; it was a rare trait he shared with his immediate successor, Dick Cheney. Nevertheless, on a tangible level, and in pursuit of the agenda of the National Performance Review, Gore took the vice presidency further into the cabinet by his interaction with, and dictates to, each cabinet secretary. This entailed the vice president's coordination of every department and agency in the federal government—from the leadership to countless midlevel public administrators—all with the intent of micro-evaluating, and then overhauling, every organization therein.

The outcome of Gore's effort was impressive: 100,000 federal government jobs were eliminated, federal regulations which had taken 16,000 pages of the Federal Register to delineate were made obsolete, and 10,000 pages from manuals for federal employees were discontinued.[26] And there were additional, equally noteworthy results. Later, Bill Clinton lauded the work of his vice president, claiming that the reinventing government project was "developed according to a simple credo: protect people, not bureaucracy; promote results, not rules; get action, not rhetoric. Al Gore's highly successful initiative confounded our adversaries, elated our allies, and escaped the notice of most of the public for the reason that it was neither sensational nor controversial."[27]

From an institutional perspective, President Clinton's selection of Vice President Gore to lead the initiative reaffirmed the standing of the vice presidency at that point in its history. In choosing the vice president to oversee the reorganization of the federal bureaucracy, of which the president is the chief executive, the place of the vice president was established squarely in the executive branch, thus lessening the ambiguity on what branch of the government the institution belonged to. The inference is not of the vice president's role in the legislative branch being incrementally erased by a commensurate increase in responsibilities in the executive government—nor could it, as presiding in the Senate was precisely where the Constitution sanctioned the vice president to be—but giving the vice president vast administrative oversight confirmed the station the office held within the executive branch.

In the long-term, the specifics of the National Performance Review are not nearly as important as was assigning the vice president to lead it. For on top of the accolades Gore's leadership accrued, his work in this area expanded on the concept of the vice president as public administrator. This was an auxiliary, but vital, outcome of Gore's success with the reinventing government project, as it contributed considerably to the form and substance of the vice-presidential institution. Why this mattered was simple: the imprint Gore left on the institution was sure to carry forward. Therefore, if history was indeed a reliable indicator, and previous augmentations to the institution did not occur in a vacuum, Gore's successors were bound to take over a substantial, multi-layered vice presidency.

VICE PRESIDENT GORE AND FOREIGN POLICY

Al Gore brought to the vice presidency a substantial level of experience with the most pressing foreign policy concerns of the United States government. Gore was well versed in the intricacies of arms control, nuclear weapons, and the global environment, but his knowledge of foreign policy did not end at these three subfields; it was instead wide-ranging and thorough. Gore's expertise in this realm was indispensable to President Clinton, initially because of the president's insufficient exposure to foreign policy before coming to office and later because Clinton encouraged the direct involvement of the vice president in foreign policy. Moreover, Gore was allowed to pursue multiple objectives—including face-to-face diplomacy and policy formulation and implementation—because of the acquiescence of the two individuals who served as secretary of state in the Clinton administration, and he did so at a level neither was able to match.

Cataloguing Gore's achievements in foreign policy is an undertaking better suited for a project devoted exclusively to it. As an alternative to such an enterprise, it is sufficient to examine a pair of examples which in isolation exemplify how vital Gore was in this area. By no means is this meant to diminish any of the extensive overseas traveling Gore undertook, some of which was closer to the traditional excursions expected of modern vice presidents.

Foremost among Gore's activities in foreign affairs was the relationship he developed with the prime minister of Russia, Viktor Chernomyrdin. A second, yet striking example was Gore's participation in the televised debate over the North American Free Trade Agreement (NAFTA), wherein he argued for passage of the agreement. Together, these two examples are instructive and accentuate the vice president's value to the president in unparalleled ways.

Unlike his involvement in the single, televised NAFTA debate, Gore's contribution on the diplomatic front, as it applied to relations between the United States and Russia, was an ongoing endeavor, lasting the better part of his vice presidency. In total, Gore was the co-leader of four distinct foreign policy groups.[28] Although all four groups were established with unique objectives, underlying all was a modest goal: to improve relations between the United States and the specific partner nation.

With respect to Russia, the formally titled Gore-Chernomyrdin Commission set about finding consensus on the reciprocal interests of the two nations, primarily in regard to space and energy policy. Unofficially, the outcome of the commission's work was largely the product of the uncommon rapport Vice President Gore and Prime Minister Chernomyrdin developed.[29] As their relationship deepened over time, Gore was responsible—with the collaboration of Chernomyrdin, and essentially under the radar of either of their nation's diplomatic corps—for a deal to convert Russian nuclear plants to civilian purposes, which in turn led to a reduction in stockpiles of obsolete, but still dangerous, nuclear weaponry housed in Russia.[30]

Select interpretations of Gore's vice presidency suggest that his prominence in foreign policy was fomented in equal shares by the president and by the two secretaries of state to serve under Clinton.[31] Without question, President Clinton had to sanction Gore's activism in foreign policy and diplomacy. On any front, if the vice president were to act without the president's support, the outcome would surely be negated, and in all likelihood there would be long-term repercussions on the efficacy of the vice president within the administration. In the case of Gore, he worked first with Warren Christopher and then with Madeline Albright, when each was secretary of state. Typically the secretary of state does not encourage an adventurous vice president in the conduct of the administration's foreign policy; at a minimum, approbation from the secretary is expected, without reservation, under every circumstance. But Gore was given a measure of autonomy in foreign policy that was unmatched by any of his predecessors.

Above all, Gore's stature and relative independence in foreign policy is attributable to the nature of the Clinton-Gore partnership. Explicitly, in terms of the president's behavior toward the vice president, Albright has commented on how Clinton "treated him like a full partner in policy discussions, so there was little sense of hierarchy."[32] Albright likewise made note of Gore's sizable presence within the foreign policy organization of the administration, suggesting that "Gore had a steadying influence on the rest of our team ... he also cared passionately about issues of justice and human rights."[33]

Perhaps the most telling indication of the sway Gore held over foreign policy inside the Clinton White House was when Albright was initially being considered for the secretary of state post and she was asked to meet alone with Gore first, and then with Clinton. In describing her "job interviews," Albright pointed out how the individual meetings "reflected the very different styles of the two men. Gore was earnest and specific, grilling me first about big issues, then about smaller ones. What did I think should be done in the Maghreb? What was my view about the problems in the Sakhalin Islands?"[34] It is not Gore's behavior that is important here; rather, it is that Clinton, in his second term in office, and ostensibly more comfortable in the world of foreign policy and diplomacy, felt it necessary to have the vice president so conspicuously involved in filling the secretary of state position.

As to the North American Free Trade Agreement: Gore's role in the passage of NAFTA should not be minimized. Free trade agreements were controversial with traditionally loyal Democratic Party constituencies, most notably minorities, low income workers, and labor unions. Pursuing an expansive free trade policy could be politically perilous. Still, if the Clinton administration was able to convince Congress to pass the agreement, and if its implementation proved to be an economic triumph, it was worth the risk of temporarily alienating the aforementioned constituencies.

In addition to the opposition NAFTA encountered from Democrats in Congress, loud disapproval of the plan was emanating from Texas businessman Ross Perot. If the portrait of Perot to emerge was of a cartoonish figure, his moderately viable third party candidacy for president in 1992 gave his political views cachet. Therefore, it was not an option to summarily dismiss him from the wider political discourse of the nation.

It was Gore's chief of staff who initially suggested challenging Perot on his criticism of NAFTA.[35] If there was some resistance, amongst advisers to the president, to the vice president setting himself up for a potentially spectacular public failure, Gore's confidence never wavered. And so, with Clinton's endorsement of the idea, Gore went on a nationally broadcast talk show and took on Perot.

From nearly all quarters, the determination of success in the debate was solid. Gore was roundly viewed as the winner in his debate with Perot. As a result, there was a transparent rise in his vice-presidential favorability scores, allowing Gore a fleeting, public emergence from the significant shadow of President Clinton.[36] He had staked passage of NAFTA on his ability to come across convincingly, conveying authority in a forum that, in the past, he had seemed uneasy taking part in. In this instance, Gore's studiousness was an asset. He had accomplished a feat that even his most noteworthy predecessors could not: in one evening, he had demonstrated that the vice president could be much more than a caricature. Moreover, in terms of the dynamics informing the president-vice president arrangement, Gore had, in a highly visible manner, succeeded in making the vice president the public face of the administration.

THE VICE PRESIDENT RUNS FOR PRESIDENT

Virtually from the moment he was sworn in as the forty-fifth vice president of the United States, and especially after being reelected to the office in 1996, Al Gore was the presumptive future presidential nominee of the Democratic Party. Obviously, this was a supposition based on the Twenty-second Amendment to the Constitution and its imposition of a two-term limit for incumbent presidents. In tandem with the Twenty-second Amendment, Gore's ambitions were contingent on Clinton having finished holding the office for the maximum period of time. Still, the inevitably of Gore, at a minimum, winning a nomination for president was the upshot of his being the incumbent vice president.

Because the impression that incumbent vice presidents are destined to be future presidential nominees has, in recent years, repeatedly been validated, the idea of the vice presidency as a springboard to the presidency is given added credence, while institutionalizing the office further.[37] In retrospect, it seems Bill Clinton was acknowledging, from his perspective and even before the Clinton-Gore ticket won their first term of office, that a would-be Vice President Gore was on the fast track to the presidency. In a sense, Clinton was advocating the objectives of having a competent successor, regardless of how Gore got there. Clinton asserted: "I thought he would be a good President if something happened to me, and I thought he'd have an excellent chance to be elected after I finished."[38]

Expressing the importance he placed on Gore's preparedness to step in if something were to happen to him, Clinton was also juxtaposing that idea with the notion of the vice president as heir apparent. By stating this, Clinton had included the obligatory qualification every presidential nominee deems necessary in the vice-presidential nominee, with the electoral calculation of Gore moving onward and upward to the presidency.

By pursuing the presidency for the second time in his career, Al Gore finally gained the presidential nomination of his political party. In reaching this milestone, he had earned entry into a relatively exclusive group, though this was not based solely on his status as a presidential nominee. Instead, the exceptionalness of what Gore had achieved was founded on his being the incumbent vice president at the time of his earning the presidential nomination. For observers of modern American presidential campaigns, Gore's success here might be looked at as almost commonplace, and yet, in actuality, the incumbent vice president gaining a presidential nomination has been an intermittent occurrence, at best.

John Adams, Thomas Jefferson, and Martin Van Buren all met the goal. But after Van Buren, there was a void of twenty-four years before another vice president, John Breckinridge, gained a presidential nomination. In Breckinridge's case, it was an anomalous election year in which he was the nominee of a splinter group of Democrats, with the official core of the Democratic Party choosing Stephen Douglas for their nominee. Either way, it was for naught; the Republican Party's candidates for president and vice president, Abraham Lincoln and Hannibal Hamlin, were the winners. Yet to the credit of Breckinridge and his running mate, Senator Joseph Lane of Oregon, they bested Douglas in the Electoral College tally.[39]

After Breckinridge, there was a 100 year gap before a sitting vice president was again the nominee for president of a major political party. This occurred in 1960 when Richard Nixon was the Republican nominee for president. Nixon's nomination was followed eight years later by Vice President Hubert Humphrey's, and then, twenty years past Humphrey, in 1988, Vice President George H.W. Bush achieved the same.

There was a companion concern to the phenomenon of incumbent vice presidents gaining the presidential nomination, thus putting them on track to succeed the president they serve. For after Gore became the Democratic Party nominee for president he was, quite simply, faced with this conundrum: his greatest asset, as a candidate for president, was the experience he had gained serving as a meaningful partner to the president, yet it was precisely because of his attachment to the scandal-tainted Clinton presidency that Gore's presidential bid appeared vulnerable.

Even if the Clinton presidency was predominantly defined by the words and actions of Bill Clinton, Al Gore's ties to him were irrefutable. There was a pervasive implication, one grounded in the quality of their association, of Gore having responsibility, as well as accountability, for a substantial share of the praise and the blame Clinton received. Hence, as the logical successor to Clinton, Gore was the recipient of all that came from his connection to the president; he could not deemphasize the strength of their association—the merits of which he and Clinton had been burnishing for eight years—when it was convenient to do so. For all intents, and barring the resignation or impeachment and then conviction of either man, they were indissolubly linked.

In the second year of the Clinton presidency, Gore characterized his experience as vice president as one wherein he was regularly exposed to the rigors of the presidency, asserting that because Clinton was "so generous in his definition of our partnership, I have gotten a pretty good taste of what that [the presidency] is really like. And on a daily basis."[40] Around the same time, Gore's chief of staff, Jack Quinn, underscored the vigor of the Clinton-Gore relationship. But Quinn foresaw an unusual outcome of the president-to-vice president association that Clinton and Gore maintained, claiming that if Gore were to run for president again, he would "do so with a very real record on which he will be judged, as opposed to" any of his predecessors in the second office.[41]

The preceding comments from Gore and his chief of staff raise some questions. If Gore worked in as close proximity to the president as all the evidence indicates, then how would he, as a candidate for president, distinguish himself from Clinton? Or could Gore, if his chief of staff was the more prescient, and if he was unlike previous vice presidents, run for the higher office on a record that stood apart from that of the incumbent president? If history is a reliable indicator, then Gore's chief of staff was bound to be off target and a bit too optimistic.

Clinton, as presidential nominee and then president, had approved and encouraged the positive, proactive form Al Gore's vice presidency took on, but he was inarguably responsible for encumbering his vice president with a sizable share of his own personal and political baggage. It is therefore suggested, here and elsewhere, that public opinion of any vice president is certain to be affected by the actions of their president; it is an inescapable condition of the American vice presidency.[42]

By any standard, the list of factors shaping public opinion of Clinton was extensive, and its bearing on Gore's candidacy is incontestable. But in facing this scenario, Gore was not alone. Vice President Hubert Humphrey too had sought, within reason, to disassociate himself from his president, Lyndon Johnson. By mid-1968, Johnson had been ostracized by the public and from the electoral process. Humphrey, in running for president, had the Herculean task of running as the best prepared candidate to take over for Johnson, all the while subtly distancing himself from a very unpopular war which, as vice president, he had steadfastly defended for four years on Johnson's behalf.[43] Even though Humphrey was not the architect of the Vietnam War, the failures of the conflict were so closely identified with Johnson that public opinion of Humphrey, as a candidate for president, was predominantly informed by his tangible connection to the administration.[44]

Even more than Johnson, Clinton's actions could not help but overshadow Gore. For that matter, besides Richard Nixon, no president other than Clinton had so pointedly and so unjustly eclipsed the public's view of the vice president—although in Nixon's case, prompted by his resignation, his second vice president, Gerald Ford, had already ascended to the presidency before making a run for his own term in office. Consequently, Ford was no longer the vice president when he became a candidate, as Gore was in 2000. Paradoxically, when Ford first moved to the Oval Office, he enjoyed a 71 percent approval rating; however, in the immediate aftermath of his pardon of Nixon, his approval rating crashed to 50 percent, and for the most part remained low, never to recover anywhere near his pre-pardon ratings.[45] Although Ford was personally popular, he could never entirely escape his connection to the man who had nominated him for vice president, and who had then stepped aside to make him president. In the end, the specter of the Nixon presidency contributed greatly to Ford's defeat in 1976.

Ironically, the impeachment of President Clinton, in conjunction with the scandals that plagued his tenure—specifically, the Monica Lewinsky episode—may have aided Gore in his quest for the presidency, albeit briefly, and only then at the margins.[46] Because the sordid details of Clinton's affair with Lewinsky were well documented, and because Clinton was impeached by the House of Representatives, though the Senate failed to convict the president of an impeachable offense, Clinton's standing with the American public was severely compromised. As it turned out, by the time of the 2000 presidential election, the alleged crimes and misdemeanors of Bill Clinton were seemingly working to the advantage of his partner, Al Gore. Advancing this idea further, one scholar has posited that the twin matters of the Lewinsky affair and Clinton's impeachment produced "an upswing in favorability toward the vice president, [which was] the opposite of the effect on presidential favorability."[47]

Perhaps it is axiomatic, but there are additional dynamics at play when running for president, even if the candidate is the incumbent vice president. Indeed, Gore's principal asset—that he was the vice president—and his, potentially, most significant liability—the troubles plaguing President Clinton—were not exclusive factors affecting Gore's candidacy for president, or the public's opinion of it. For instance, for the duration of his vice-presidential tenure, Gore had been accepted as a conceivable candidate for president; however, his formal entrance into the 2000 race instantly cast a different light on him.[48] In other words, there is a considerable difference between conjecture of a candidacy and an actual candidacy. From this perspective, as a stand-alone candidate for president, Gore was defined, at least temporarily, by his character, his experience, and notably, his substantive vice-presidential tenure.

By no means is it suggested here that Gore could ever have distanced himself far enough from Clinton to appear an absolute, independent political figure; he had been, after all, elected with the president. Gore had frequently defended the veracity of the president he served for eight years. He was facing a dilemma that any incumbent vice president running to succeed their president confronts: how to minimize the record, if need be, of the president, while expounding on their own, positive attachment to it.

The public's perception of vice presidents, and of the vice presidency, is indisputably impacted by the current occupant of the office. For Gore, this was not too inhibiting; generally, he was viewed as a substantial member of the Clinton administration, and he was by far one of the better known vice presidents.[49] As supported on the pages herein, the narrative of the American vice presidency, as well as that of the forty-seven individuals to hold the office, has been informed by limited accolades and abundant derision. Gore, as the Democratic nominee for president, was therefore challenged by this quandary: how could he rise above the history of an institution that, for a majority of the electorate, he embodied?

When it came to public opinion on the Gore vice presidency, a logical argument might be made that Al Gore had minimal cause for concern. In part this is explained by his performance as the number two executive in the national government. With the exception of an alleged ethical lapse stemming from his efforts to raise money for the Democratic National Committee in 1996, Gore was, across-the-board, a successful vice president.[50] By and large, it is reasonable to assume that public opinion of Vice President Gore was fairly positive. Of those who paid attention to the political scene, most had only fleeting curiosity about the vice president, and in the main Gore's activities while he held office were unlikely to adversely sway public opinion.

If the public's view of the vice presidency has been either uninformed or indifferent, there are two probable causes. Foremost of the two is the presidency. As the presidency grew incrementally in the eighteenth and nineteenth centuries, and then exponentially in the twentieth century, it did so at the expense of all other institutions in the American system. Commensurate to the firm establishment of the president as the premier elected officer of the nation has been the public's attachment to the presidency and presidents. For these reasons, emphasis has understandably been placed on the president, not the vice president.

The second reason the vice presidency has consistently been overlooked is derived from the first. Since the presidency so completely dominates the political system, and at the same time captivates the attention of the pubic, there has been less incentive to gauge the public's knowledge or curiosity about the vice president. Suggestive of this absence of interest, for many years, was the lack of public opinion polling about the vice president.[51] Plainly, there was not sufficient interest to warrant polling on the vice president, and since scientific polling is necessarily market driven, research into attitudes on the vice president and the vice presidency were minimal.

From the mid-point of the modern vice-presidential era, with vice presidents increasingly viewed as likely presidential candidates, it made sense to measure public interest and attitudes about the vice president. In sum, the earliest public opinion polling relating to the vice president indicates that prospective or actual vice-presidential candidates were routinely the topic of polling beginning late in the winter of 1939, in the lead-up to the 1940 presidential election.[52] Aptly, of the earliest polls taken, questions about vice-presidential candidates arose in union with questions about the presidential candidates with whom they shared the electoral ticket. This held too for surveys wherein the vice presidency was the focus, but the questions were still consistently inclusive of the presidency.

The early predilection for linking the vice president to the president in every sphere of public opinion polling included atypical questions, alongside the standard preference for questions related to elections. For example, in a survey taken during President Franklin Roosevelt's 1940 reelection campaign, likely voters were asked whether they would approve of the Republican Party taking Roosevelt as its presidential nominee—in tandem with his nomination by the Democratic Party—on the condition that Democrats accepted the Republican's nominee for vice president.[53] And away from measuring candidacies, a 1941 poll queried respondents on whether the president and vice president, upon leaving office, should become lifetime members of the United States Senate.[54] Finally, over the years, vice presidents have been the subject of a plethora of inane survey questions, not the least of which were random samplings of the public's knowledge of the vice president's salary.[55]

Not until the onset of the 1950s did polling organizations begin to conduct research on vice presidents, constructing survey questions meant to gauge public opinion of the vice president, apart from the president. Vice President Richard Nixon, for whom public opinion throughout his political career was always strongly expressed, one way or another, was the first incumbent vice president to be the subject of favorability polling.[56]

In the case of Al Gore, public opinion remained fairly steady throughout his time in office, occasionally rising or falling, outwardly contingent on the prominence of specific activities.[57] If favorability metrics on Gore, overall, were decent, there was a definite correlation between his becoming an official candidate for president and a subsequent decline in favorability scores.[58] Furthermore, even though it may not have any bearing on an actual decline in how favorably the public viewed Gore, there was a transparent spike in the sheer number of surveys conducted after the announcement of his second presidential candidacy.[59]

If attention on the incumbent vice president, expressed via public opinion polling, augmented the visibility of the institution, it likewise had the potential to undermine the candidacies of those vice presidents who choose to run for president. Greater attention focused on the vice presidency might help someone like Gore who was acknowledged for his competence and his utility to the president. By the same token, while polls that concentrated on Gore and the likelihood of his becoming president would certainly help promote his candidacy, in equal parts such polls would continue to remind the public of Gore's ties to President Clinton.

All this serves to further complicate the puzzle of the vice presidency. Candidates for vice president are always potential presidents, if only because of human mortality. And yet, as a rule, when voting for a presidential ticket the electorate tends to discount that they are actually voting for two prospective presidents. Put another way, those voters who cast their ballots for Bill Clinton and Al Gore in 1992 and 1996 were plainly voting for Clinton for president and Gore for vice president. Yet by extension they were confirming that a vote for Clinton for president was analogous to voting for Gore for president, as well, since Gore feasibly could rise to the presidency at any moment.

If the preceding theory holds, and a Gore presidency was conceivable for the eight years he was vice president, and likewise a plurality of voters affirmed such a scenario in 1992 and 1996, then why in the early stages of his presidential candidacy did Gore struggle to gain favor with the public? Initial public opinion surveys indicated a mixed reception to a Gore presidential candidacy, and in hypothetical matchups with then-Governor George W. Bush, Gore was routinely topped in the polls.[60] To some extent, Gore's candidacy was likely plagued by the historic misconception that, since the vice presidency was presumed to be a shallow institution, filled only by second-rate political figures, then in all probability he was not up to serving as president.

So what was Gore to do? He was the vice president, he had been fully integrated into the administration of the executive government, and for two terms in office he was, in the words of one of the earliest utilitarian vice presidents, Richard Nixon, getting "complete on-the-job training for the duties of the Presidency."[61] If Nixon was correct—though it is a disputable premise because without actually being president, it could never be quite the same—then it would be problematic for Gore to disavow the tutelage he purportedly benefited from when working by the side of President Clinton.

Despite Clinton's overly publicized personal failings, the economy had grown on his watch, and he consistently polled well for the work he did as president.[62] For Gore, the dichotomous cast to the Clinton presidency put him in an unusual position. Again, similar to when Vice President Hubert Humphrey was the Democratic nominee for president, Gore was affixed to a highly capable president who had accrued considerable liabilities. Moreover, Gore shared with Vice President George H.W. Bush the dilemma of seeking the higher office while serving with a president who surpassed him as a practitioner of the art of campaigning and connecting with the electorate.

Strategically, in his role of the candidate hoping to succeed his president, Gore had two options. He could try and make a clean break from Clinton and the scandals that shadowed the president, or he could tout the considerable successes of the Clinton administration and, in doing so, embrace the best of Clinton's legacy. In the end, Gore decided to employ the former approach and dismiss the latter.

There was an additional, periodic facet of presidential election years that would have some bearing on Al Gore's aspirations for the presidency. In the twentieth century, just four incumbent presidents—Dwight Eisenhower, Lyndon Johnson, Ronald Reagan, and Bill Clinton—were ending their political careers concurrent with their vice president actively attempting to replace them in office. In all four instances, the incumbent president was clearly in a position to affect the prospects of the incumbent vice president who had earned the presidential nomination of their party. All four of the presidents confronted with the preceding scenario were understandably mindful that history and fact are not always the same. If they could impact interpretations of their time in office, even if it came at the expense of their vice president, indubitably they would side with their own account of events.[63]

Eisenhower and Reagan both left office after eight years, old and beloved, their political careers effectively ended. Their vice presidents—Nixon and Bush—had the luxury of running for president on the record of the administration they were a part of. But the departure of Johnson and Clinton from their respective presidencies was complicated. Their vice presidents—Humphrey and Gore—had to straddle the awkward divide of loyalty to, and independence from, their principals. In essence, they were as much running from the incumbent president as they were running for the presidency.

In Johnson's case, he was leaving embittered and, in his mind, prematurely. Even though the specifics of the Twenty-second Amendment permitted his seeking another term, Johnson decided against it after winning the New Hampshire preference primary, but sensing that the results indicated his political fortunes were rapidly dimming.[64] Adding to the tenuousness of the Johnson-Humphrey association was the incongruence coloring their distinct approaches to the Vietnam War.[65] As for Clinton, the Lewinsky affair and subsequent impeachment ordeal had undermined his presidential legacy. This no doubt compelled him to try to perpetuate, at a minimum, the policies of his presidency, with Gore as the required conduit for achieving this goal. And for the long-term, Gore's candidacy presented Clinton with the opportunity to revise, with some limitations of course, the historical record of his tenure.

In many respects, Clinton's generosity towards Gore when the latter was running for president was on a par with his liberal promotion of an expanded vice-presidential institution for Gore to inhabit. Furthermore, Clinton was agreeable to campaigning for Gore, and when he did, to extolling the attributes of a vice president he knew would make a fine president. But in conceding the value he derived from Gore serving as his second, Clinton was unable to sever the tie that traditionally binds the vice presidency to the presidency.[66] To put it in another context: though Clinton rightfully deserved credit for allowing Gore's vice presidency to take the form that it had, his narcissism was such that he could not completely relinquish his claim to the presidency—even when it would have aided the electoral fortunes of his governing partner.

If the temptation is great to psychoanalyze Bill Clinton or Al Gore, it is a task better left to psychiatrists and the future. Suffice it to state that theirs was an unusually equitable president-to-vice president arrangement that bolstered Gore's argument, in the 2000 campaign for president, that he was better prepared to move up to the presidency than any opponent he faced. In the end, Gore chose not to highlight the merits of the president-to-vice president arrangement he had molded with Clinton, he opted out of campaigning in person with the president, and he decided to minimize his association with an administration that he had helped to staff and to manage.[67]

Even if Al Gore's partnership with Bill Clinton defined the better part of his bid for the presidency, he did retain one prerogative that was exclusively his. When Gore captured the presidential nomination of the Democratic Party, he had to make what is widely considered the first presidential-caliber decision every nominee makes: the selection of a vice-presidential running mate. If equating this quadrennial ritual to the level of presidential decision making is appropriate, the effect was particularly pronounced when an activist, substantive vice president such as Gore was in the position to select the vice-presidential nominee. Gore had participated in the executive decision-making process for the length of the Clinton presidency; he had also, on occasion, forcefully urged the president to make difficult choices, and to avoid, as was Clinton's want, to try and please everyone. Presumably, the aforementioned part Gore had played put him at an advantage when picking a potential vice president.[68]

As previously noted, Gore was in the unique position of simultaneously holding the titles of incumbent vice president and presidential nominee of a major political party. Due to this status, Gore could have ignored the standard criterion applied when presidential nominees select their running mate, while still heeding to certain parameters. But Gore's choice for the vice-presidential nomination, Senator Joseph Lieberman of Connecticut, correlated to all of the balancing variables that presidential nominees typically employ when making their selection.

For instance, Lieberman represented a New England state in the Senate, thus countering Gore's southern roots. Lieberman was viewed as slightly more conservative than Gore, though their ideological bearings were not overtly disparate. In addition, Lieberman was Jewish and Gore was Baptist, and the novelty of Lieberman being the first nominee for either of the nationally elected offices who was Jewish would be helpful in capturing a critical voting bloc in states where the Electoral College mattered: New York, California, Florida, and New Jersey. And finally, by Gore's stint as vice president, he could claim the mantle of administrator; therefore, Lieberman's presence, at the time of the election in the legislative branch, improved the attractiveness of the ticket overall.

Senator Lieberman was not chosen to run with Vice President Gore because he satisfied the preceding list of balancing variables. Lieberman was selected on the presumption that he was everything Bill Clinton was not. Intrinsically then, the Democratic nominee for vice president restored a moral fiber to the Democratic ticket that had been stripped from it by the actions of the president. Surely under different circumstances Gore could have sustained the ticket on his own, but his connection to Clinton made this impossible. As it were, he settled on a running mate whom the indiscretions of the president made mandatory. Far from unfettered by the legacy of

Clinton, Gore appropriately chose to counterbalance the president when constructing the Gore-Lieberman ticket.

The idiosyncratic nature of the 2000 presidential election has already produced countless competing interpretations of what happened.[69] There is no question that assessments in the vein of what Gore did or did not do right over the course of the campaign will continue to be advanced. It is equally assured that pessimists will continue to question the constitutionally sanctioned method used to conduct elections in the United States, and by which Gore and Lieberman were denied the presidency and vice presidency, respectively. But the outcome will remain the same. Until the Electoral College is abolished, and the Supreme Court recuses itself wholly from future elections, the system will stand, as is.

What matters is that Gore was the incumbent vice president, running for president on a record of accomplishment, founded on his deft management of a wide-ranging portfolio of traditional and non-traditional vice-presidential assignments. Gore was, in the words of his running mate, "the most effective vice president in the history of the United States."[70] And still, he lost the election. Was Lieberman's praise hyperbole? Categorically, yes, but at the same time, what he said was far from the overestimation of a candidate for vice president in the midst of a national campaign. In every sense of the word, Gore was an effective vice president. He had remained loyal to his president—the requisite expectation for anyone elected vice president—while further institutionalizing the breadth of responsibilities future vice presidents would be required to meet. This, then, will be Gore's legacy.

At this point, Richard Nixon holds the distinction of being the only incumbent vice president to have run for president, lost, and then returned to electoral politics to win the presidency. With the Gore vice presidency receding in the collective memory of the nation, it is obvious that he will never attempt to match Nixon's feat. By his failure to win the presidency in the 2000 election, Gore will remain second best.

On January 6, 2001, just three weeks after the Supreme Court returned its decision in the case of *Bush* v. *Gore*, thus resolving the 2000 election in a manner unparalleled for an American presidential election, Vice President Gore returned to Capitol Hill. He was there in order to fulfill one of the constitutional obligations of the vice president in the capacity of Senate president; he was there to announce the results of the Electoral College vote. This was one place where the Twelfth Amendment to the Constitution did not supersede the original plan for the election of the president and vice president. For this reason, after the electors in each of the states met and voted for president and vice president, the certificates recording the Electoral College vote were delivered to a joint session of the Congress. From there: "The President of the Senate shall, in the presence of Senate and House of Representatives, open all the certificates and the votes shall then be counted."[71]

In executing the preceding task prescribed for the president of the Senate, Gore joined a select group of vice presidents—John Breckinridge in 1861, Richard Nixon in 1961, and Hubert Humphrey in 1969—in having to announce their opponent the winner of the Electoral College for president. Of the four, Breckinridge was the only one who also had the uncomfortable task of swearing in his replacement in the vice presidency,

Hannibal Hamlin. But surely Breckinridge gained some satisfaction when Hamlin, as the new vice president, was then compelled to swear in Breckinridge as a returning United States senator from Kentucky.[72] For Gore, this quirk of the Constitution simply meant he had to announce that George W. Bush had defeated him for the presidency. And later, at the inauguration, he was just a bystander while his successor in the vice presidency took the oath of office.

The paucity of literature devoted to the Gore vice presidency is unfortunate, though not unexpected. He was, after all, only the vice president. As for Gore, he seems to be in no hurry to write his autobiography. If he adheres to the example set by some of his predecessors—like Walter Mondale, who waited thirty-one years to pen his autobiography, only to have it published to scant fanfare and minimal public interest—then it will be well into the twenty-first century before such a tome appears. For the most part, the lack of attention to the modern vice presidency is understandable, since those who have most recently held the office have not made it to the presidency; it is the presidency and presidents that garner the greatest interest and earn an established place in history.

But Al Gore should not be overlooked when evaluating the executive government. In many respects, he was the exemplar of the modern American vice president, and in being so, he embodied the best features of certain of his predecessors in the modern era. The utilitarianism of his approach was particularly reminiscent of Henry Wallace, Richard Nixon, and Walter Mondale, while the dual assets of loyalty and reliability he showed to his president matched those of George H.W. Bush and Dan Quayle. Likewise, Gore held his own when it came to the role modern vice presidents play in the rhetorical sphere of partisan politics. And like all his predecessors, beginning with Wallace, with the sole exception being Spiro Agnew, Gore brought the vice presidency the furthest, to that point, into the realm of foreign policy, and in the process, he advanced the ongoing displacement of the secretary of state.

If there was one modern vice president Al Gore resembled most, it was Henry Wallace. Wallace and Gore were enigmatic, and they shared an intellectualism that sometimes caused them to disconnect from ordinary people, despite their genuine concern for the citizens they sought to lead. Curiously, both men were faulted for being too cerebral. Wallace was frequently charged with mysticism and Gore was often mocked for his otherworldliness. Wallace and Gore seemed, when holding the vice presidency, and especially after leaving office, as if they did not belong in the eras in which they served. And both tried and failed to take their vision to the White House.[73]

The contributions Gore made to the domestic and foreign policy agendas of the Clinton administration are meaningful. Whether derived from his counsel, his leadership, or his active, hands-on participation, even a cursory delineation of Gore's accomplishments validates the wide-ranging influence of his vice presidency. This included Gore's role in the White House effort for passage of the Telecommunications Act of 1996 and the Family Medical Leave Act, his actions on behalf of expanded funding for Head Start, Pell Grants, and a program for increasing access to the internet in schools and libraries, and his activism for broad initiatives relating to improved air, water, and public health standards. Even if much of the preceding is standard fare for the policy agenda of a Democratic administration, the involvement of Gore in so many places, and at so many levels, spoke volumes about him, as well as about the depth of purpose the vice presidency, as an institution, had reached.

Notwithstanding the value in the foregoing achievements, why Al Gore matters is the influence he exerted on the vice presidency as an institution of the executive government. It was not that he was remiss in fulfilling the constitutional duties of the vice president, because when he presided, he did so ably. Still, in eight years he was called on to cast just four tie-breaking votes; therefore, it is a fair assumption that his presence was not essential in the day-to-day working of the Senate, nor was it ever expected to be.

Yet in making the vice-presidential institution better and more complete, Gore helped to make it indispensible. He had, by President Clinton's estimation, "a larger role substantively and more influence than any" of his predecessors ever had.[74] Working in unison, Clinton and Gore found a way to build on the template for a substantial president-to-vice president arrangement—the outline for which was first suggested by President Ford and Vice President Rockefeller, extended and practiced by President Carter and Vice President Mondale, and then facilitated by every succeeding president, making it the norm for every president-vice president team to follow.

All things being equal, Al Gore very well may have been the ideal vice president, yet the source of his power and prestige, President Clinton, may have hampered Gore's own rise to the presidency. The predicament Gore found himself in was neatly framed, nearly forty years earlier, when President Johnson had told an eager Hubert Humphrey that, by taking on the position of Johnson's second, their relationship would be analogous to "marriage with no chance of divorce."[75] Johnson may have been overstating his case, but, short of resignation, impeachment, or death, Humphrey really had no way out; he would forever be Johnson's vice president. In much the same way, Gore was bound to Clinton—for better or for worse.

When accounts of the Clinton era are written, it will always be in the context of President Clinton and his achievements and his failings. The irony here is this: as the vice president for eight years, Gore will share the burden of Clinton's legacy, good and bad, but the partnership he forged with Clinton, and the contributions both made to the institutional vice presidency, will be largely overlooked. For Gore, it is an unfortunate outcome of his never having made it to the presidency, for it is the presidency that is remembered, rarely the vice presidency. Perhaps of most consequence, Gore's concerted elevation of the office of vice president prepared the foundation for the ascension of the most influential vice president to date.

THE VICE PRESIDENCY UNBOUNDED

THE CASE OF CHENEY

Vice President Cheney has been the most dangerous
vice president we've had probably in American history.

– *Vice-presidential nominee, Senator Joe Biden*

January 20, 2009, was a stunning, cold day in Washington DC. On a platform erected to cover the steps of the Capitol building, built solely for the inauguration of the president and vice president, the vice president-elect, Joe Biden, was among the elected officials, families, and friends gathered that day. From Biden's vantage: he undoubtedly took note of the swarm of people filling the view; it was a crowd estimated to be over 1.8 million, and it stretched from the Capitol to the Washington Monument. The scene, aside from the larger than usual number of people gathered, was a familiar one for any American citizen who had grown-up in the twentieth and twenty-first centuries.

The inauguration of the vice president of the United States was not always such a transparently public affair. For 144 years, every vice president, except one, took the oath of office in the Senate chamber.[1] In addition, prior to the oath being administered to the winner of the presidency, the newly elected vice president was permitted a token address to those assembled. Over the years, the order in which the newly elected vice president spoke and was sworn in varied. For instance, Abraham Lincoln's vice presidents, Hannibal Hamlin and Andrew Johnson, spoke, even if briefly, before taking the oath, whereas Woodrow Wilson's vice president, Thomas Marshall, was sworn in and then delivered his inaugural remarks. Customarily the remarks were rarely more than a brief acknowledgement of gratitude on the part of the speaker for having been elected to such a noble office. And now and then, a newly elected vice president would publicly commit to mastering the presiding officer's duties. But for most, the inaugural remarks of the newly elected vice president marked the beginning of the end of their political career.

Perhaps Thomas Marshall captured best the perceived insignificance of the vice presidency in the epilogue to his inaugural comments. On the appointed day in 1913, Vice President Marshall mounted the Senate rostrum and proclaimed: "Here in this most sacred spot ... may one humble American express ... hope before he enters upon a four years' silence."[2] Even if Marshall was grossly overstating his impending predicament, the relative quiet of his job was genuine.

In contrast, when Joe Biden was sworn in to office, becoming the forty-seventh vice president of the United States, he was not tucked away, deep within the exclusivity of the Senate chamber; instead, Biden stood in the light of day. In 2009, the vice president was an equal participant in the pageantry accorded the president, with one exception. In 1937, when the inauguration of the vice president was brought outdoors with that of the president, the vice president's traditional speech of appreciation was omitted from the program.[3] At the quadrennial inauguration of the president and the vice president, only the president addresses those assembled.

Even if Vice President Biden became merely a spectator after taking the oath of office, he was poised to command a vastly different institution than Vice President John Adams had in 1789, when Adams became the first to hold the post in the new government. Undoubtedly Biden could have pointed to any number of his predecessors, particularly in the modern era, who had contributed to the enhanced prestige and scope of the institution. But there was no question that he must have realized that the vice presidency, and certainly the public's view of the institution, was heavily influenced by the outgoing vice president, Dick Cheney.

At the 2009 inauguration, Cheney appeared before the assembled crowds slouched in a wheelchair, unable to walk. Reportedly he had injured his back the night before, packing boxes of his private papers in preparation for his move out of the vice president's official residence. It was an inauspicious finish to a tenure in which Cheney had defined, for those Americans who took notice, what the modern vice presidency is today.

It was also a tragically ironic twist to the Cheney narrative, a narrative highlighted by a singular case of self-selection for the vice-presidential nomination, the thinly veiled, yet successful assimilation of the vice president's office into that of the Executive Office of the President, a concerted and vast expansion of executive powers, and the systematic deconstruction and reformulation of government policies—all of which left an attractive blueprint to follow, should any future vice president so choose. What is equally remarkable is that the preceding points are only part of the story of Dick Cheney's vice presidency. Ultimately, Dick Cheney's eight years of service holding the second-highest-ranking elective office in the United States, personified a matrix of executive governance unique to the American system: an acquiescent president, a fiercely ideological and secretive vice president, and the pursuit of expanded executive power which may well have set a perilous precedent for how the institutions of the American vice presidency and presidency function in the twenty-first century.

THE STRANGE CASE OF DICK CHENEY'S SELECTION AS GEORGE W. BUSH'S RUNNING MATE

When Texas governor George W. Bush formally announced his intent to run for president in 1999, he was making a career move that at the time seemed premature. Despite coming from a family grounded in politics and money, on his own he had never been proficient in either sphere. Before winning election as governor, his stabs at independence were most notable for minority ownership in the Texas Rangers baseball franchise. Eventually Bush embarked on a political career that saw him elected governor of one of the largest, most populous states in the country, on a résumé void of any prior government experience and with marginal political experience. Therefore, he acquired experience in government and politics in the six years he served as governor, augmenting his once skimpy résumé along the way; it would prove to be enough.

In the main, George W. Bush spent the entirety of his second term as governor planning for, and then running for, the presidency. Over the course of that preparatory period, it was readily apparent that Bush required, if he was to be a successful candidate for president, a means for countering the gap in national and international political experience he evidenced. Of greater import, Bush needed to effectually minimize the perception that he was a vacuous political figure.

The task Bush faced was made even more difficult because his Democratic opponent in the general election was sure to be the incumbent vice president, Al Gore. Gore's résumé epitomized everything that Bush's did not. Furthermore, Gore exuded an intellectualism that usually worked in his favor and contrasted sharply with the view held by some of Bush's alleged cerebral limitations. It was clear Bush had to counter the advantages Gore held. And so, when it became obvious that Bush would gain the presidential nomination of his party, he opted to correct the public perception of his inadequacies, in part by way of his vice-presidential nominee.

Generally, once a presidential candidate appears certain to gain their party's nomination, they will undertake a systematic process for winnowing the field of potential vice-presidential nominees. It is the type of deliberative process Jimmy Carter introduced in 1976 and which proved to be a sound method for choosing a vice-presidential nominee. Therefore, in the spring of 2000, George W. Bush began such a process, but he did not do this on his own, and curiously, the process was absent significant involvement by his own circle of political intimates. Bush decided, instead, to rely on a friend and one time colleague of his father to administer a thorough vetting process for suitable candidates for the vice-presidential nomination. That family friend was Dick Cheney, and he was to become the chief engineer of Bush's vice-presidential nominee selection process.[4]

In concert with the trust his connection to Bush's father engendered, Cheney was the ideal individual to assess prospective nominees for vice president. The sum of his government service was beyond competitive, having worked under Presidents Nixon and Ford in administrative and policy positions, then later having held a post in the cabinet of the elder Bush. What is more, Cheney's government service was not exclusive to the executive branch, for he had spent ten years in Congress representing the state of Wyoming as its lone member of the House of Representatives.

Accordingly, Cheney brought a breadth of experience that was essential to determining the ways Bush's candidacy needed shoring up if he was to have a realistic shot at winning the election. Yet of equal importance, Cheney had to calculate what a future Bush presidency would require if the candidate was successful in the impending presidential contest. As it was, Cheney oversaw what was by all appearances a rigorous search for the appropriate running mate to join the presidential candidate on the electoral ticket.

Cheney's mission began with a listing of individuals ostensibly worthy of more than a perfunctory appraisal. Next, he subjected those who made his list to a meticulous financial background check. Then, for those potential nominees who made the first cut, Cheney sought responses from each individual to an exhaustive questionnaire he had constructed. Finally, of the individuals to emerge from the vetting process unencumbered by anything too salacious from their past or present, each was then summoned to Bush's Texas ranch for a personal interview with the presidential candidate.[5] Of the preliminary pool of possible nominees, only a smattering actually made it to Texas; it would prove not to matter.

The interviews Bush conducted were meant to test his comfort level with each of the individuals he might tap for the vice-presidential nomination. This was a critical exercise in that whomever Bush chose would share with him the burden of campaigning for national office. Of greater import, if Bush and his running mate were successful in the election, they would serve in the government together for the ensuing four years. In light of the close associations of more recent presidents and vice presidents—particularly Jimmy Carter and Walter Mondale, and later Bill Clinton and Al Gore—establishing a comparable association between Bush and his future running mate was essential.

Nevertheless, there was no opportunity in these sessions for the type of one-on-one interaction that might have allowed Bush, as well as his potential running mate, to gauge their compatibility. The reason for this was simple: Cheney joined every meeting. Plainly this impeded the prospect of Bush being alone with any of the contenders for the vice-presidential nomination. When contrasted to the several hours Clinton and Gore spent alone—when the two men exchanged ideas on politics and policy prior to Clinton offering the nomination to Gore—the difference with what transpired in Texas is striking.

The manner in which the Bush-Cheney vice-presidential nominee selection process played out was emblematic of how the Bush presidency was destined to function. It is now evident that Dick Cheney's direction of the entire process was the precursor to how he would, after being installed in the vice presidency, exert considerable influence over the affairs of the executive government, while President Bush would at times come across as an innocuous observer of events.

With the outcome of Bush's vetting process for a vice-presidential running mate now known, the entire process looks as if it was a pretense for what was a foreordained selection. Put another way: it is unlikely that Dick Cheney did not have himself in mind when he initiated and then conducted the search for the right addition to the Bush ticket. In light of that, once Bush decided that Cheney was the best individual to run for vice president, three tasks remained in order to make him the certified Republican vice-presidential nominee.

First, because the Constitution explicitly forbids the president and vice president from being residents of the same state, Cheney was forced to switch his legal residence from Texas to Wyoming. He had only moved to Texas in order to work in the oil industry, so when the vice-presidential nomination came his way, and because he owned a vacation home in Wyoming, it was an easy fix to reregister in the state he had once represented in Congress.

Second, Bush had to make a public announcement of his preference for the vice-presidential nomination. He therefore called a press conference and, with Cheney at his side, announced what many had suspected all along. Maybe it was the Texas heat, but Bush claimed to have had an epiphany after meeting with Cheney to review possible running mates, remarking at the press conference that it was then that he realized "the best candidate might be sitting next to me."[6] And when Cheney's turn at the microphone arrived, true to form, his statement was sparse. He offered platitudes to Bush, and then concluded by noting that "big changes are coming to Washington and I want to be a part of them."[7]

And third, delegates to the Republican Party nominating convention had to confirm Bush's decision to give Cheney the second place on the presidential ticket. This came about when the Republican convention met in Philadelphia and subsequently affirmed Bush's pick for a running mate, just seven days after his press conference. This process was of course just a formality; not since Democratic presidential nominee Adlai Stevenson opened the choice of the 1956 vice-presidential nominee to the convention floor have delegates had any say in the selection of the vice-presidential nominee. It is a given that the presidential nominee's preference stands unchallenged.

Having easily dispatched of the prerequisites to making Dick Cheney the vice-presidential nominee, the campaign commenced for the Bush-Cheney ticket. In light of the integral, domineering part Cheney played during the course of the eight years that were the Bush administration, his activities on the campaign trail personified the candidate as minimalist. It was not a question of whether he participated in the campaign—he did—what was striking was the incongruity in his involvement over the course of the campaign, when compared to his immersion, once in office, in every facet of the executive operations of the Bush administration.

Cheney spent the better part of the campaign season traveling to out of the way locations, where he was guaranteed friendly, conservative Republican crowds.[8] In taking this approach, he put in motion a two-pronged electoral strategy, one uniquely suited to his predilections. Preeminent in this approach was Cheney's execution of the customary chore of the vice-presidential candidate acting as an overtly aggressive member of the ticket, thus providing him numerous opportunities to intensify partisan rhetoric and attack the opposition ticket. In itself, this was not unusual. Beginning with the 1924 candidacy of Charles Dawes, vice-presidential nominees routinely, and for the duration of the campaign, have kept a combative posture, making statements and claims that, as a matter of course, presidential nominees are reluctant to make.[9] It has therefore become a fundamental expectation for all candidates for vice president to campaign in such a manner; at the same time, presidential nominees remain, comparatively, dispassionate.

The secondary but no less important component of Cheney's strategy was that when he went to remote locations he spoke almost entirely to the faithful and he stayed beneath the radar. Not only did this make sense due to his long-time aversion to being in the spotlight, but it also meant that his words and actions, no matter how provocative, generally escaped wide public notice. In the context of any campaign for elective office, Cheney's scheme would seem counterproductive; it is a given that candidates want and need public and media attention. His goal, apparently, was not to draw attention to the words and actions of a candidate for vice president; his aim, evidently, was to invigorate party loyalists and hopefully convert a few uncommitted voters along the way.

When the election was finally held, and before the result was final, Dick Cheney embarked on an extraordinary journey; it was a journey that had been in the making for nearly twenty-three years. As it happens, Cheney was on a quest of epic proportions, for he appeared determined to rebuild and restore the presidency. In doing so, Cheney would refashion the American vice presidency as well.

Dick Cheney and the Assimilation of the Vice Presidency into the Presidency

The official result of the 2000 election was not ascertained until thirty-six days after voters had cast their ballots. Dick Cheney, however, acted as if he never questioned whether he and George W. Bush had won the election. This was most evident in Cheney's move to McLean, a suburb of Virginia, approximately twenty miles from the nation's capital, not quite two weeks before the Supreme Court handed the White House to Bush. The stated purpose of Cheney's preemptive relocation was to direct the transition from the Clinton administration to an impending, hypothetical Bush administration.[10] Assuming control was a bold move, to say the least, especially in light of the lingering inconclusiveness of the election.

Cheney's actions during this interlude did not go unnoticed. The storyline of his domination of the Bush campaign organization, in essence arrogating the customary prominence of the presidential candidate in the lead up to the inauguration, had already begun to take hold. Indicative of this was when Cheney convened a press conference to announce the location of the temporary Bush transition headquarters, and he was asked how it was possible to "avoid the appearance that he's [Bush] retreated to his Texas ranch while you take charge."[11] Cheney brushed aside such criticism, asserting that it was "perfectly appropriate for him to spend time on his ranch and to continue to spend time in Texas."[12] Along the same lines, a reporter then questioned whether he was concerned about the impression that "in the post-campaign ... you are overshadowing" Bush, to which Cheney casually responded: "I don't worry at all" about it.[13]

From the would-be vice president's perspective, it seemed the unusual events of the 2000 election, as well as the indeterminate status of the election at that point, were subordinate concerns to initiating the transfer of power. Addressing this point, Cheney unequivocally, although possibly not intentionally, admitted that he had wrested an additional responsibility for himself that was unparalleled in the tasks delegated to candidates for the vice presidency. With the election still undecided, Cheney declared that "my job is to get an organization [established] ... I've got a job to do."[14]

Even when it came to the practical mechanics of funding the transition, Cheney took matters into his own hands. Normally presidential transitions are the financial concern of the federal government's General Services Administration (GSA). Prudently, the GSA was waiting for a conclusive resolution of the election before it commenced with the standard protocol for the transition from one administration to another. On Cheney's direction, the Bush-Cheney campaign had applied with the Internal Revenue Service for non-profit status, whereby they could collect private donations to fund their transition, confident of the GSA eventually reimbursing their endeavor.

Apart from the audacity of Cheney's actions on this front, his role as the chief coordinator of the transition of power was unprecedented on two counts. Never before had a vice-presidential candidate, in the throes of a contested election, assumed to be the victor before the Electoral College vote had been tallied. And as was just indicated, it was anomalous for a candidate for vice president to oversee an enterprise as vast as the transition from one government to another. But Cheney's assumption of control, and his subsequent vigorous exercise of authority, eventually distinguished all dimensions of his vice-presidential tenure.

It was in the midst of the transition period that Cheney shrewdly set in motion the assimilation of the vice presidency into the presidency. This was a different product of the Bush-Cheney association than has been suggested elsewhere. For instance, in recent years it has been argued that what Bush and Cheney implemented was analogous to a "co-presidency."[15] This proposition is problematic because the term co-presidency implies that presidential powers are divisible and shared executive governance is feasible. For that matter, where political systems are concerned, examples of legitimately shared, or collegial, executive arrangements are few and not enduring.[16] Of necessity, all plural executive arrangements are characterized by countervailing dynamics, with one executive having a modicum of an advantage over the other; were it not so, definitiveness on policy questions would routinely be elusive.

As a practical matter, hierarchical arrangements are just that—hierarchical—and thus a top-down format is necessary to reach, if not consensus, conclusion. Granted, in a presidential system, like the one found in the United States, which has a trifold balance of power, the executive is subject to specific veto options delegated to the legislative and judiciary by the Constitution.[17] The caveat here is that over time the American presidency has unquestionably gained strength at the expense of the legislative and judicial branches of the government, thereby moderating the effectiveness of the checks the two countervailing branches hold on the executive branch. Then again, in acknowledging the checks of the legislature and of the judiciary, with no less than the Supreme Court atop the latter branch, the president has commensurate checks on each, compounded by the legitimacy of being elected nationally—a claim no other officer in the system, besides the vice president, is justified in making.

Yet, in the midst of a transition of his making, Dick Cheney did claim to be legitimately elected, if not by a majority of the nation, then with enough evidence to satisfy him. And when the Supreme Court's decision in the 2000 election was announced in his and George W. Bush's favor, Cheney worked the opportunity he had been given, taking his new executive position past notions of a shared presidency. In retrospect, it was as if Cheney was bent on absorbing control of the transition from the president-elect—specifically in terms of filling cabinet posts, as well as securing the top-level positions responsible for formulating the domestic and foreign policy agenda of the impending administration—knowing it would set the tenor of the ensuing four years.

In deconstructing Cheney's plan, it is clear that he succeeded in partially blurring the divide between the president and the vice president, as well as the respective formal organizations that heretofore separated the two institutions. Hence, to a certain degree the vice-presidential and the presidential institutions coalesced and took the form of a single political institution with, in practice, two concurrently elected executive officers.

When evaluating Cheney's actions on this front, it is important to recognize that the vice presidency continues to be viewed by the broader electorate as a sinecure filled by politicians who were not of presidential caliber, but who would be fine as the vice president. What Cheney accomplished, with Bush's compliance, was to take an institution like the vice presidency—which had benefited from precedent and statute and likewise had acquired abundant institutional resources—and integrate that institution into the presidency, while making himself indispensible to the president he was elected to serve under.

Moving forward, it is worthwhile to revisit Woodrow Wilson's observations on the nature of institutions, introduced at the outset in Chapter 1. Wilson's interpretation was simple: institutions were "an established practice, an habitual method of dealing with the circumstances of life or the business of government."[18] But Wilson offered another proviso with respect to institutions; it symbolized the president-to-vice president arrangement that Cheney encouraged and was therefore apropos to the assimilation of the lesser institution into the greater that he helped to carry out. Wilson had presciently declared this: "There may be firmly established institutions of which the law knows nothing."[19] To paraphrase Wilson, Cheney helped to reinvigorate an institution which most of the American public, then and now, knew nothing of.

In his drive to remake the presidency, which in turn transformed the vice presidency, Dick Cheney was largely repeating the absorption of White House operations he had observed, and then participated in, when he was an apprentice to Donald Rumsfeld in the Ford administration. As reviewed previously, Rumsfeld was a holdover from the Nixon administration who, at the request of President Gerald Ford, restructured White House operations for Ford when he moved there from the vice presidency. It was during the transition period that Rumsfeld implemented a scheme to control the day-to-day functions of the Executive Office of the President (EOP) and, pointedly, the selection of personnel to staff the EOP.[20] Later, Cheney reinstituted Rumsfeld's model to a greater extent when he too seized a large measure of control over the affairs of the White House.

Apparently when Cheney was given the chance to replicate Rumsfeld's scheme, he was prepared to do so. He had witnessed the efficacy in curtailing Vice President Nelson Rockefeller's attempts at establishing a substantial policymaking role in the Ford administration.[21] Rockefeller had endured a lengthy and difficult confirmation process, giving Rumsfeld the necessary time to place his own people in the best positions. Then, once Rockefeller was installed in office, the White House staff was structured in a manner to limit the vice president's access to President Ford. Of equal importance, in his capacity as the White House coordinator, Rumsfeld tightly controlled the flow of information Ford received, deliberately and routinely circumventing Rockefeller in the process. Cheney had observed Rockefeller's experience and applied the same obstructionist tactics against him as Rumsfeld had when the latter man eventually left White House operations for the cabinet.[22]

By gaining control of the transition from a Clinton administration to a Bush administration, Cheney used the gap between the election and the inauguration to his benefit. During that time he enlisted White House staffers who were tied more closely to the future vice president than they were to the future president. Cheney's aim then was the inverse of Rumsfeld's, since the preferred outcome was a decidedly strong vice president who would be well situated to filter what information reached the president. This too would afford Cheney the best vantage from which he could manipulate the policy direction of the Bush administration. Furthermore, in addition to stocking the White House with his preferred personnel, the future vice president was instrumental in filling more than one cabinet position. Not the least of these was the return of his former mentor, Rumsfeld, to lead the Department of Defense for, figuratively, a second tour of duty.

Cheney's proactive placement of key personnel was a critical move with long-term implications, and it augmented the access points the vice president was bound to have within the White House. It also meant that the vice president was ubiquitous; he could influence the president by way of well-placed surrogates without appearing solely responsible for the advancement of a specific agenda. Ultimately, Cheney's position in the administration was broadly enhanced by the multiple proxies he had placed throughout the executive branch.

With the benefit of hindsight, Dick Cheney's strategy now seems deceptively simple. He had served in the Nixon, Ford, and George H.W. Bush administrations; therefore, he had seen the rewards of physical proximity to the president, surely cognizant that such proximity was vital to agenda setting, policy advancement, and the exercise of raw power. Consequent of the preceding experiences, at the commencement of the first term of George W. Bush's presidency, Cheney was situated so that he would have a singular hold at the highest reaches of the executive government, unmatched by any previous vice president. It was a scenario made even more profound because Cheney, unlike Al Gore, was the second to a more malleable president.

On top of having an ally commanding the Department of Defense—which, because of Donald Rumsfeld's long-term connection to Cheney, gave the vice president an atypical, added influence in the conduct of any future military affairs—Cheney also placed a long time confidant, I. Lewis Libby, as an assistant to the president and national security adviser to the vice president. In addition, Libby was appointed the chief of staff for the vice president's office and served as the most intimate counselor to Cheney. It was Libby's job as national security adviser to the vice president that allowed him to attend all meetings of the president's staff devoted to this policy realm.[23] This also provided Cheney—on the off chance he was not present at a meeting of the president's national security team—a constant place at the table.

In the time that Libby worked for the vice president, he proved willing to do the bidding of his boss. It was Libby's unwavering loyalty to Cheney that compelled him to follow the instructions of his boss, which then concluded with his conviction, in 2007, on perjury and obstruction of justice charges. Aside from Libby, the most effective placement Cheney made was that of the chief legal counsel to the vice president, David Addington. Addington would later double as chief of staff when Libby was forced to resign that post.

If Libby and Addington turned out to be unusually conspicuous postings, they are nonetheless useful appointments to mention, even in brief, as their selection was illustrative of Cheney's use of classic patronage politics for an explicit purpose. In this, he was exercising a perk of the vice presidency which had been extended, in greater or lesser degrees, to all his predecessors. The difference, though, between Cheney and earlier vice presidents, was that when patronage was dispensed by the vice president, generally it was based on rewarding stalwarts for their electoral support. Or, particularly in the eighteenth and nineteenth centuries, patronage was used to meet regional considerations which, again, were founded on satisfying supporters of the vice president who, more times than not, were having to be placated after their preferred presidential candidate landed the second spot on the ticket.

In putting Libby and Addington at the apex of executive branch operations, Cheney had placed two talented political operatives who shared his values, and who were categorically loyal to him over President Bush. But Cheney's purpose in bringing Libby and Addington on board went beyond their unwavering dedication to him. They, as well as several other key appointees, abetted Cheney in a mission to expand and further establish the supremacy of the national executive.

It is now clear that when Cheney was organizing the transition for the impending Bush administration, and by his securing key positions on the White House staff and in the vice president's office for his personal choices, the result would be the assimilation of the vice presidency into the presidency. And because the vice presidency has always been something of an outcast among the branches of government, it was improbable that Cheney would not find a suitable home, finally, for the office he held. Scheming to bring the vice presidency further into the executive branch than ever before must have made sense to Cheney, as his sights always seemed set, one way or another, on accessing and exercising executive power and prerogative.

Cheney had observed the perks and the perils of executive power up close. He had watched the Watergate affair, in conjunction with the alleged crimes of Vice President Spiro Agnew, gradually undermine the Nixon presidency. Yet Cheney never came to view the downfall of either Nixon or Agnew as a consequence of the abuse of executive powers. Instead, as an assistant to Nixon's hand-picked successor, Gerald Ford, and then, for a time as the White House chief of staff to Ford, Cheney had despaired as Congress endeavored to reestablish the balance of power between the executive and the legislative branches of the national government.[24]

Dick Cheney plainly regarded the actions of the Congress as an unjustifiable incursion of the legislative branch into the conduct of the executive branch. From where he stood—with legislation like the War Powers Act of 1973, the Budget Impoundment and Control Act of 1974, and the Federal Election Campaign Act of 1974—Congress was overreaching in reaction to an "imperial presidency," historian Arthur Schlesinger Jr.'s seminal descriptor for the office in the latter part of the twentieth century.[25] Predictably, Cheney held a perspective contrary to that of Schlesinger; from his angle, the theory of an imperial presidency was a "myth."[26] By his rationale, the presidency was not imperial enough.

The American presidency was a sacrosanct institution to Cheney's way of thinking. From his standpoint, Congress appeared bent on tearing down the executive institution. Along these lines, Cheney later described what he saw as a dark era for the presidency. In his words, it was

> a period of time when Congress sought repeatedly to impose its will on the President, to move, if you will, the balance from the strong executive concept to which we adhered very faithfully from F.D.R. thru Kennedy, to a situation in which the Congress was predominant; where the number one concern on the part of those who were involved on a day-to-day debate over the presidential power and authority was not how to help presidents accrue power in the White House—so that they could achieve good works in society—but rather how to limit future presidents so that they would not abuse power in the past—specifically, Lyndon Johnson and Richard Nixon.[27]

On the whole, Cheney appeared to take the attempts by Congress to restrain the reach of the presidency as almost a personal affront, motivated principally by partisanship. But was he far astray in thinking partisan politics fueled the moves by Congress to recover its share of the balance of power? Since the investigation into the Watergate affair was prompted by Democratic members of Congress, who controlled the legislative branch at the time, his interpretation of the situation was not completely amiss. Undoubtedly there were some Democrats who relished the idea of disposing of the Republican president and vice president in a clean sweep of the executive branch—an option available to them by means of a double-impeachment. Although Spiro Agnew spared the country of that spectacle with his preemptive resignation, the simultaneous impeachment of the president and vice president does present an intriguing scenario worth contemplating.

Theoretically, if a double-impeachment had occurred within a condensed time frame—with Agnew going before Richard Nixon, and then Nixon having insufficient time to initiate a nomination for vice president, as demarcated by the Twenty-fifth

Amendment to the Constitution—then, under the Succession Act of 1947, the Speaker of the House at that time, Carl Albert, a Democrat from Oklahoma, would have lawfully succeeded to the presidency. The rise of Carl Albert under these circumstances would have facilitated the takeover of the White House by the Democratic Party; more importantly, moving the Speaker straight to the White House would have effectively overturned the ballots of the 47 million voters who had supported Nixon and Agnew in 1972. If such a transition of power had transpired smoothly, it would have exemplified the stability of the constitutional design in place in the United States; unfortunately, it also would have undercut claims to democratic legitimacy in presidential elections.

But the future vice president, Dick Cheney, appeared unable to reconcile himself to the reasonable concerns of the Congress. Based on his writings about the topic, it is a fair assumption Cheney was convinced that the Democrats in Congress were pursuing a partisan vendetta, bent on enervating the presidency. That Congress might have been compelled by a different aim—for example to reestablish equilibrium in the national government—would have been anathema to Cheney's theory, challenging his belief in an executive institution dominant over two necessary, but inferior institutions of the government. For this reason, from the time Gerald Ford failed to win his own term as president, and Cheney was likewise out of a job, the latter seemed determined to return to the executive branch. In retrospect, there is every indication that Cheney was fixed on one goal: to restore the power and the glory of the presidency no matter what the cost. If doing so meant bringing the vice presidency along for the ride, so be it. And if he happened to be the vice president at the time, and he was able to assimilate the vice-presidential institution into the presidential institution, his task would be virtually seamless.

VICE PRESIDENT CHENEY AND THE QUEST FOR EXPANDED EXECUTIVE POWER

To understand the type of vice president Dick Cheney became, all one has to do is review remarks he made in the vice-presidential debate. It was the first debate Cheney participated in as a candidate for vice president, held a few weeks before the 2000 election, and if he did not reveal a great deal in the course of the debate, there were clues to what qualities and qualifications he believed he might bring to the number two position in the national government. In response to a question from the debate moderator, in which Cheney was expected to qualify himself in contrast to the opposition candidate for vice president, Senator Joseph Lieberman, Cheney stated:

> Clearly we're both in the positions we're in because of our personal relationships with our principals. I think the areas that I would bring are the things that Governor Bush emphasized when he picked me. That I have been White House chief of staff and ran the White House under President Ford. Spent

ten years in the House, eight of that in the leadership. Served as secretary of defense, and then had significant experience in the private sector. I think that is where there are differences between Joe and myself in terms of background and experience. I clearly have spent a lot of time in executive positions running large organizations both in private business as well as in government. And that is a set of qualifications that Governor Bush found attractive when he selected me. I'll leave it at that.[28]

What is most striking about Cheney's comments is this: he claimed that because of his involvement in running the White House, and due to his time in a leadership position in the Congress, and from his service as the top executive of a department of the federal government, as well as of a private corporation, he was supremely qualified to serve as vice president of the United States. At face value, he was offering an unusual interpretation of what career experiences might be useful for a future vice president, particularly on account of the vice presidency being devoid of any constitutionally granted executive responsibilities or powers. Hence, his response was not at all about the vice presidency; it was as if he was describing the qualifications and skills that would make for a good president. By Cheney's metric, he was obviously the best equipped candidate for the top job, and evidently his running mate was satisfied with this understanding.

In the eight years Dick Cheney served as vice president, his mission to expand the power and the reach of the top two executive offices of the United States government was relentless. Cheney had indicated in the 2000 vice-presidential debate that it was best to be an executive, the person in charge. This applied when he was in Congress, as well, for he plainly thought he could do more in the leadership than as Wyoming's solitary representative in the House. Yet being in charge for Cheney was about unfettered control, and much less about working with others toward consensus. It was as if the lesson he learned from President Nixon's downfall was that the executive was in all instances nonpareil. And if executive supremacy is threatened, never back down as Nixon did by resigning. Restated: Cheney's quest to expand the reach of the chief executive officer of the government was informed by his confidence that, in the beginning, Nixon was right to affirm the preeminence of the president in relation to the legislative branch of government.

Since the Supreme Court presumably tilted toward the preferences of the Bush administration, the only obstacle for Vice President Cheney in reclaiming and expanding the executive branch appeared to be the United States Congress. Fortunately for Cheney, during much of his vice presidency Congress was controlled by the Republican Party, and on occasion the Senate was equally divided, so there was potentially value in his vice-presidential tie-breaking vote in those sessions. Besides, the Congress that Cheney confronted in the twenty-first century was less assertive when it came to oversight than had been the case in the 1970s, when Richard Nixon was the president. On those rare occasions when Congress tried to reassert itself, Cheney, and thus President Bush as well, claimed a disproportionate level of sovereignty for the executive branch amongst the three, allegedly coequal branches of the United States government.[29]

Although Cheney's conduct synchronized perfectly with his disdain for the balance of power—a fundamental tenet of the American constitutional system—it was his transparent insolence when dealing with Congress that struck many as puzzling. Among those who found Cheney's approach to the legislative branch disconcerting was retired vice president Walter Mondale. Thirty years after taking the vice-presidential oath of office, Mondale went public with his appraisal of Cheney. Specifically, Mondale contrasted the incongruity of Cheney's decade of service in the House of Representatives with the arrogance he exhibited toward Congress while he was vice president. Mondale described what he considered inconsistencies in Cheney's behavior in this way:

> I've never seen a former member of the House of Representatives demonstrate such contempt for Congress—even when it was controlled by his own party. His insistence on invoking executive privilege to block virtually every congressional request for information has been stupefying—it's almost as if he denies the legitimacy of an equal branch of government. Nor does he exhibit much respect for public opinion, which amounts to indifference toward being held accountable by the people who elected him.[30]

Understanding Dick Cheney's attitude when dealing with Congress presents a conundrum: since the vice president is the constitutionally designated presiding officer of the Senate, it follows that the vice president will, even if it is only on occasion, have contact with at least one chamber of Congress. Besides, vice-presidential nominees are frequently selected for the bridge they may represent, once they are in office, between the executive and the legislature. Most often this is the case when the candidate for president is primarily associated with the executive branch, as was George H.W. Bush, or in those instances when the presidential nominee has served as a governor—as did Jimmy Carter, Ronald Reagan, Michael Dukakis, Bill Clinton, and George W. Bush. Indeed, when it came to reviewing potential running mates, some presidential nominees, like Carter, Dukakis, and Clinton, looked only to members of Congress.[31]

In the case of Dukakis: his plan, if he had won the election, was to have his running mate, Senator Lloyd Bentsen, synchronize the administration's relations with the Congress. Dukakis later asserted that he "undoubtedly would have asked Senator Bentsen to take responsibility for our congressional relations, particularly given that my experience was largely at the local and state level ... he would have provided great leadership in that area."[32]

Still, the role of the vice president in the Senate is pointedly less important in the modern era than it ever was in the past. While the duties vested in the vice president by the Constitution have not been altered in any manner—the vice president is still the presiding officer of the Senate, allowed to vote only when the membership is equally divided—any emphasis on the vice president's presence in the chamber subsided long ago. As a rule, many early vice presidents took their cue from Thomas Jefferson, frequently excusing themselves from the presiding officer's chair, and then retiring to less staid surroundings, sometimes hundreds of miles from the Capitol building.

In this respect, Dick Cheney was not unusual when compared to other vice presidents; he evidently preferred to excuse himself from the overtly public function of presiding. Reflective of how inconsequential presiding in the Senate has now become, during the 2004 Bush-Cheney campaign for reelection, Cheney confirmed that in his "capacity as vice president, I am the president of the Senate, the presiding officer. I'm up in the Senate most Tuesdays when they're in session."[33] Dismissiveness aside, as a transparently powerful vice president, Cheney never failed to use his leverage when dealing privately with members of Congress.[34]

Cheney's patent indifference toward Congress was not exclusively the concern of former vice presidents; instead, it was an outlook shared by some in Congress, and even by members of his own political party. Senator Chuck Hagel, for one, has commented that Cheney and the Bush administration, "viewed Congress as an appendage, a nuisance. Clinton was just the opposite. Reagan was the opposite. Bush's father was the opposite. They understood the value of making the Congress their ally."[35] Hagel also pointed out Cheney's consistently mute presence at weekly meetings of Senate Republicans, commenting that "by his very lack of engagement or even giving us the courtesy of saying something … they [gave the impression they] could care less about us. Except when he wanted us to do something: 'Vote this way.'"[36]

One of the better examples of Vice President Cheney maximizing executive power came about by means of executive signing statements. Specifically, executive signing statements are added at the time the president signs legislation and serve several purposes. In theory the statements are intended as a way for the president to articulate any doubts about the constitutionality of specific legislation passed by Congress. Additionally, signing statements provide for presidents a supplementary means for expressing views on public policy that might not otherwise be included in the language of the legislation, while offering a way to integrate various provisos favored by the president that are then realized in the final interpretation of the legislation. As such, signing statements are a convenient tool for sanctioning a president's decision to ignore specific parts of legislation and, with the greatest implication, may be used in lieu of vetoing legislation in its entirety.

When there is an excessive use of signing statements by any president, the effect is pushback against the balance of powers intrinsic to the Constitution. This is because the constitutionally guaranteed power of the Congress to formulate, amend, and adapt legislation—with the objective of making the legislation satisfactory to the president in order to then gain the president's signature—is essentially arrogated from Congress by the use of executive signing statements. Since the constitutionally delegated legislative authority of the president is to either sign or veto legislation, nothing more, executive signing statements purposefully increase the president's participation in the legislative process, in the end making the president the primary crafter and interpreter of laws.

None of this is meant to suggest that President Bush was the first president to utilize executive signing statements. Still, the use of signing statements to deliberately subvert the intent of the legislative branch of government was practiced by Bush, and frequently at the vice president's behest, more often than in any prior administration.[37] Historically, the exercise of executive signing statements may be traced back to

President James Monroe, and it was then carried forward by a number of succeeding presidents, including Andrew Jackson, John Tyler, Ulysses Grant, James Polk, and Franklin Pierce.[38] Notwithstanding the foregoing examples, there is no evidence that any of the preceding presidents, or any of the twentieth century presidents who have made use of signing statements, served with a vice president who played a minor, let alone an integral part in the repeated use of such statements.

Even though the vice president, per se, is not responsible for deciding when to use executive signing statements, Dick Cheney demonstrated his resourcefulness time and again when pressing for this action from the president. Above all, he did this by a circuitous, but nonetheless effective method, wherein legislation pending the signature of the chief executive was directed first to the vice president—an officer of the federal government vested with absolutely no executive authority.[39] Once Cheney had the legislation in hand, his legal counsel, David Addington, masterfully deconstructed the legislation, first isolating and then excising those parts objectionable to Cheney, and finally writing the statements in preparation for the president's signature.[40]

Over two terms, the use of executive signing statements emanating from the Oval Office helped President Bush and Vice President Cheney to further solidify the authority of the executive branch. Nevertheless, the superfluity of signing statements was in some ways an unexplainable phenomenon of the Bush years. As noted before, during their joint tenure Bush and Cheney maintained an advantage in the power struggle between the executive and the legislative branches due to the Republican Party's frequent control of Congress. Logically, it would follow that President Bush and the Republican majority in Congress should have held a shared policy agenda; it is also appropriate to suggest that the president and vice president should have been willing to emphasize their policy goals without the use of signing statements, and yet the opposite occurred. This was because signing statements allowed the president, and by extension the vice president, to shape legislation to their liking, while bypassing the otherwise certainty of a presidential veto. It was the check of the veto that was the traditional means for the president to show disapproval of legislation; however, obviously Bush favored imposing his legislative preference with signing statements. This was evident when comparing his use of vetoes to the lot of his predecessors, as Bush used the veto just twelve times in eight years.[41]

The central concern here is the unprecedented intrusion by the vice president into legislating, coming via a plethora of executive signing statements that signaled Cheney's influence. Moreover, he succeeded at affecting the specifics of the signing statements through his ideological and practical proxy, Addington, and with the complicity of his constitutional chief, President Bush. Cheney had extended the reach of the vice presidency by gaining, at least during his tenure, a check for the vice president on the legislative branch which, by any metric, is unequivocally an executive function.

In context, what Cheney had pulled off was the implementation of vice-presidential prerogative in the legislative process; it was, to a certain extent, the realization of assertions made by one of his nineteenth century predecessors, George Mifflin Dallas. As detailed in Chapter 3, it was in 1846 when Vice President Dallas suggested that his constitutional power to break a tie in the vote of the Senate gave the vice president a check over the legislature that was analogous to a presidential veto. Yet in Cheney's case, it was executive signing statements that accorded the vice president a form of veto. That signing statements were closer to a line-item veto was not important; what mattered was that signing statements were being used by Cheney to interpose the vice president in the legislative process.

When the Framers crafted the Constitution they never sanctioned any executive authority for the vice president. In this regard it is only the president who has the constitutional authority to issue executive signing statements. And even though the vice president was deliberately placed by the Framers in the legislative branch—and given the authority to preside over the Senate, but denied a regular vote or any part in making legislation or participating in the debates of the chamber—most of those who held the office did not feel at home there. For these reasons, Dick Cheney's activism on this front is rife with irony. He had managed, by his own devices, to straddle the executive-legislative divide of the vice presidency, and then have this accomplishment certified by his president's signature.

THE VICE PRESIDENT AS POLICY CZAR: THE ENERGY TASK FORCE

Across the board, Dick Cheney put his unique imprint on the modern vice presidency and the way in which the executive branch did business. There were no exceptions to this, but there were certain policy spheres that Cheney seemed to find more engrossing than others, and to which he devoted considerable thought and time. From the outset, having the vice president occupied by policy formulation dovetailed perfectly with the Bush-Cheney governance model.

In practice, their governance model deviated from the arrangement expected for a presidential system and instead was closer in form to the executive model found in a parliamentary system.[42] In a conventional parliamentary system, the head of state is principally tasked with the ceremonial obligations of the government and typically is represented in the guise of the monarch, whereas the head of government is the political and administrative chief of state, devoted to the business of running the government, and usually designated the prime minister or chancellor. Fittingly, a parliamentary system has also been characterized for being one part "dignified," the other "efficient."[43]

Alternatively, in presidential systems the president acts as both head of state and head of government. To be sure, there are deviations within the structural facets of presidential systems, depending on the nation employing the system. Moreover, a pair of scholars has posited that fusion between presidential and parliamentary systems has from time to time occurred, outlining systems they describe as "premier-presidential-ism" and "president-parliamentary."[44]

Not every nation with a presidential system in place includes a vice president. Yet besides the disparagement the American vice presidency has suffered over time, and despite the enigma of the office to many, most citizens in the United States would find the omission of the vice president from the system anomalous. Either way, abiding by the preceding definitions of systems, President Bush performed his job as the head of state—though he did tend to important business, he likewise exercised a considerable degree of ceremonial duties—while Vice President Cheney worked as the head of government—predominantly behind the scenes, recasting the form, the function, and the outcome of federal policies.

When Dick Cheney arrived in the vice presidency, he was unwavering in his drive to initiate new policies, in conjunction with vigorous movement towards the deregulation of the existing practices of the government. More times than not, he pursued an ancillary goal of clearing the way for unfettered commerce. In no policy sphere was this more apparent than with Cheney's consistent intercession on behalf of those corporate interests impacted by the environmental policies of the federal government, in particular the regulation of energy resources.

For the most part, Cheney's involvement in formulating a national energy policy escaped the attention of the public. Perhaps Americans were simply becoming accustomed to activist vice presidents. All three of Cheney's immediate predecessors were involved on multiple fronts, although they clearly maintained a larger presence in certain areas than they did in others: Walter Mondale in foreign affairs, Dan Quayle with the Council on Competitiveness, Al Gore and the reinventing government initiative as well as in foreign policy. But Cheney exercised greater and wider influence on the formulation of government policy than any vice president before him. The difference, however, was that Cheney never appeared to relish the spotlight, as did Mondale, Quayle, and Gore. Frankly, it seemed that Cheney preferred to work in the shadows. In many ways this was fitting, since from its inception the vice presidency always seemed a shadow institution, with the presidency forever the more tangible of the two.

When Dick Cheney first ran for vice president, he bemoaned the lack of a national energy policy. He liked to lay blame on the Clinton-Gore administration for what he saw as too much restraint, specifically when it came to expanding the domestic production of oil; it was a point he made repeatedly on the campaign trail, as well in his debut appearance in a vice-presidential debate. Although Cheney preferred to deliver speeches to friendly audiences in out-of-the-way venues, the two vice-presidential debates he took part in provide scattered, yet invaluable glimpses of his beliefs and of his attitude. Simply put, since the single debate held for vice-presidential candidates has become a staple of presidential campaigns, Cheney had little choice but to participate. The debates therefore represent the two times in eight years that he was compelled to abandon his steadfast reticence and publicly answer questions.

Throughout the first vice-presidential debate, Cheney exhibited the single-mindedness that would characterize his behavior for the whole of his tenure, offering curt, unequivocal responses on complex topics. For instance, when asked about the fluctuations in oil, natural gas, and electric prices, and how the government, by allowing market instability, was not doing enough to protect the American people, Cheney briefly delineated the failure of the Clinton administration to foster energy production in the United States. He then concluded by suggesting, "it's important that senior citizens don't suffer this winter, but we need to get on to the business of having a plan to develop our domestic energy resources in producing more supplies."[45] It was a terse and not too subtle indication that expanding the business of energy production was a priority for the prospective vice president.

In retrospect, Cheney's comments in the vice-presidential debate do not seem especially noteworthy, since his subsequent actions on energy policy—specifically his chairmanship of the National Energy Policy Development Group (NEPDG)—are now, in part, public record. Appropriately, the preceding task force devoted to creating the Bush administration's energy policy came to symbolize the Cheney vice presidency in its entirety: the expansion of executive power, the collusion of government and business, and the complete, imposing, and unprecedented presence of the vice president.

Eight days after Dick Cheney took the vice-presidential oath of office, NEPDG was established by President Bush. Immediately referred to as Cheney's task force on energy, the group was instructed to formulate "a national energy policy designed to help the private sector, and government at all levels, promote dependable, affordable, and environmentally sound production and distribution of energy for the future."[46] In addition to the vice president, the task force included four senior officials of the Bush administration, nine cabinet-level officials, assorted support staff, an interagency working group, and public administrators from various federal agencies.[47]

There was a parallel group of individuals who met with Cheney about the direction of the Bush administration's energy policy who were never accounted for in any organizational chart. The composition of these unofficial counselors to the vice president and the extent of their influence in the formation of the administration's energy policy would in time become one of the more mysterious elements of the inner workings of the Cheney vice presidency. For the vice president to meet with a group of energy industry leaders, in addition to government officials, was not unusual, nor was it unexpected. After all, Cheney had been a chief executive of a major corporation immersed in the business of energy. The president too had worked in the same industry, though the vice president was markedly more successful when he was in the business world than was his boss.

Poles apart from his mid-1970s approach to policy formulation in the executive branch, Dick Cheney was determined to keep matters of policy within the vice president's office. There was no need for a Domestic Council, per se, as the vice president, and those working closest to him, kept their own counsel. And because President Bush by most accounts appeared disengaged with the details of governance, Cheney had no need to wrest control of the public policy agenda from the president.[48]

But what made Cheney's actions with the energy task force germane to a broad review of his vice presidency was that all the components underlying his theory of executive preeminence coalesced. This included the vice president holding meetings on the nation's energy policy in secret and with anonymous attendees; the assertion of executive privilege for the vice president, thus setting precedent; the cooptation of cabinet secretaries, in this case affecting those individuals heading the Department of Interior and the Department of Energy; and challenging the principle of congressional oversight, therefore repudiating the system of checks and balances implicit in the United States Constitution. In the end, Cheney achieved the outcome that had underscored his every move when he was vice president: he had helped to restore the power and supremacy of the presidency in the American constitutional system.

DICK CHENEY AND THE ALTERED AMERICAN VICE PRESIDENCY

There is no question that the record of the Cheney vice presidency will be exhaustively assessed, well into the future. What will be revealed will of course vary from one account to another, hence offering contrary impressions of the same individuals and events, and resulting in sometimes starkly different portrayals of the Cheney era. Still, when the empirical evidence has been evaluated, and after scores of memoirs by participants, both major and minor, in the events of the Bush administration, have been published, the paramount question about the Cheney vice presidency will likely remain unanswered. And if the question is as simple as it is complex, the outcome of Cheney's tenure will reverberate in American politics and government for years to come. The question, then, is this: why does the Cheney vice presidency matter?

The Cheney vice presidency matters because it signaled the arrival of the American vice presidency as a fully realized political and government institution. In part, this came about because, by the time Dick Cheney was inaugurated the forty-sixth vice president of the United States, the institution was poised for an ambitious and assertive executive vice president—precisely what Cheney became. Moreover, the nature of the working relationship President Bush and Cheney kept indicated a fundamental shift in the balance of power between the president and the vice president. Only time and future presidential elections will determine if a similar setup will resurface in the executive government; nonetheless, that such a shift has happened at all is profound.

If the president-to-vice president arrangement Cheney helped to engineer was the culmination of 212 years of incremental institutional growth, prompted by the actions of presidents and vice presidents alike, the Bush-Cheney partnership seems equally to have been fashioned on a once-proposed electoral ticket of Ronald Reagan and Gerald Ford.[49] The template for a Reagan-Ford ticket was developed, in the main, at the Republican Party nominating convention of 1980. Even though the ticket never materialized, it bears further examination for four reasons.

First, the potential pairing of Reagan and Ford has rarely been appraised, and as that time period recedes further into political history, it is less likely that it ever will be; however, the extraordinary implications for the presidency and vice presidency intrinsic to the deal are of value to the canon of executive scholarship, and therefore it merits a further, cursory look.[50] Second, that Reagan, the presumptive Republican presidential nominee in 1980, was in a position to offer the vice presidency to a former president reinforced the notion of presidential nominees unequivocally determining the choice of their running mate, sans the concurrence of party leaders. Third, Ford's willingness to consider the deal signaled the immense potentiality of the American vice presidency, even then, and equally indicated how the presidency might someday be refashioned. And fourth, there are a number of correlations between what might have been a Reagan-Ford administration and what the Bush-Cheney administration became.

In brief, by 1980 Gerald Ford had already served as vice president and president of the United States. Having been defeated for election to his own term as president in 1976, Ford retired from public service. When Ronald Reagan was poised to take the 1980 Republican Party nomination for president—a title he had battled against Ford to hold, just four years before—he approached Ford with a unique proposition. Reagan wanted to know: would Ford consider running on the ticket with him as the nominee for vice president?

Originally, Reagan had offered the vice-presidential slot to Ford far in advance of the convention, but Ford had resolutely declined, suggesting George H.W. Bush would be a good compromise choice.[51] At the time, Reagan rejected Ford's recommendation of Bush; then, once he arrived at the convention, he reiterated his offer to Ford. Ford's reluctance faded as pressure mounted for him to accept Reagan's proposal. There was also intense media speculation that the two men might join forces. Combined, this then set in motion a series of negotiations to determine specifically how an individual who had already served as both president and vice president would function if voters returned him to the second office.

One of the accomplices involved in bringing Reagan and Ford together was Alan Greenspan. Greenspan was a friend and adviser to Ford, and he had been a colleague to Cheney when both were part of the Ford administration. In Greenspan's retelling, Reagan's offer to Ford was historic since

> a former president had never served as vice president, [therefore] they were envisioning an expanded role that would make the job attractive and appropriate for Ford. In their proposal, Ford would be the head of the president's executive office, with power over national security, the federal budget, and more. In effect, while Reagan would be America's chief executive officer, Ford would be its chief operating officer.[52]

Making the offer to Ford was a highly political calculation on Reagan's part; it was founded on the premise that having Ford on the ticket would improve the odds of defeating the incumbent president, Jimmy Carter.[53] And for Ford, his willingness to run for national office again was more than likely based on the satisfaction he would gain in helping to defeat the man who had taken the White House from him. All the same, and whatever their motivations may have been, if the electoral alignment Reagan and Ford contemplated had been implemented, they would have upended 191 years of the way in which the presidency and the vice presidency had coexisted.

Gerald Ford's shot at a second vice presidency ended at the 1980 Republican Party convention, but the intended outline for it did eventually arrive by way of the Cheney vice presidency. On all accounts, what Ronald Reagan offered to Ford was put into practice when Dick Cheney took the vice-presidential oath. Naturally, neither President Bush nor Cheney have ever suggested that the understanding they came to on how they would operate once in office was based on any prior model. For that matter, their arrangement was unlike that of any other president and vice president in the history of the two offices, so there is not an easily analogous pairing from which to draw comparisons.

Dick Cheney was at the 1980 convention, however, and he was one of several influential Republicans who made a concerted effort to bring Ford on board with Reagan.[54] Hence, the parallels between the Bush-Cheney administration and the theoretical Reagan-Ford ticket correlate too strongly to dismiss out of hand, even if the latter pact failed to coalesce. And far too many of the principals involved in the Reagan-Ford negotiations were connected, then and now, to George H.W. Bush. Indeed, it is only because the Reagan-Ford deal imploded that Ronald Reagan moved swiftly in his selection of the elder Bush for a vice-presidential running mate.[55]

What Dick Cheney put in motion when he was vice president, again borrowed from Reagan's offer to Ford, skirted the objectives of the Framers when they structured the presidency and vice presidency at the Federal Convention of 1787. By the same token, it diluted a substantial measure of the hegemony the president historically retained in relation to the vice president. Many of the valid concerns that were raised about the type of vice presidency Gerald Ford was to have were centered on critical questions about the constitutionality of what Ronald Reagan was offering. Despite these concerns, a similar association reappeared in the Bush-Cheney union.

The principal question for Reagan, and ostensibly for George W. Bush, twenty years later, was as follows: could Reagan, sans a constitutional amendment, give the vice president more duties and power, some of which were commensurate to those vested in the president? Even though Reagan eventually chose George H.W. Bush in lieu of Ford, and for any number of plausible reasons, he must have concluded the answer was no—the president could not confer on the vice president any permanent powers that were fairly proportionate to those held by the president.

That Dick Cheney was evidently unconcerned with the potential constitutional ramifications of what he and President Bush put into practice is not surprising. However, Gerald Ford had a different take on the nature of such an arrangement and, based on Alan Greenspan's retelling of events, "was skeptical that a 'super vice presidency' would actually work. For one thing, it raised constitutional questions ... For another thing, he doubted that any president could or should accept a dilution of power in carrying out his oath of office."[56] By this account, it would seem that Ford's concerns were founded on more than wariness about the creation of a super vice presidency, and instead lay equally with his inclination to put the presidency first. At the same time, Ford had used the expression "co-presidency" when describing the setup he might have with Reagan, emphasizing that if he were to accept Reagan's offer, it was imperative he have "a meaningful role across the board in the basic and the crucial and the important decisions."[57]

The ephemeral prospect of pairing Ronald Reagan with Gerald Ford in 1980 most likely collapsed because what they were trying to accomplish went well beyond the scope of the typical processes and negotiations involved in a presidential nominee settling on a running mate at a nominating convention.[58] Though the idea of restructuring the president-to-vice president arrangement resonated—as proposed by Reagan to Ford and established in practice by George W. Bush and Dick Cheney—it was equally frustrated by the persistent problem of where precisely the vice president belonged in the constitutional scheme. Cheney successfully assimilated the vice president's office into the president's office, profoundly refashioning the institution in the process. On account of his actions, he had also, perchance inadvertently, forced consideration of where the vice president belonged. In other words, was the vice president part of the executive branch or part of the legislative branch? Or did the vice president maybe inhabit a heretofore unrecognized fourth branch of government?

Historically there had been ambiguity about what to do with vice presidents. In many ways, the constitutional establishment of the vice presidency was delimited by the outwardly hybrid status of the office. Although Article 1 of the Constitution placed the vice president at the head of the Senate, the constitutional stipulation set forth in Article 2, for the powers of the president to devolve on the vice president in the event of succession, drew the vice president into the executive branch as well. For the broader public, if the vice president was thought of at all, it was in the context of a vice-presidential candidate seeking the office in the company of a presidential candidate, or when succession caused the occupant of the second office to move to the first. It made sense, then, to view the vice president in tandem with the president, and thus nearer the executive branch.

For Dick Cheney, when it was to his advantage, he was content giving divergent opinions on whether the vice president should be more closely aligned to the executive or to the legislature. Yet in adopting conflicting views on the office he held, Cheney further muddled interpretations of the proper place for the vice presidency. For instance, when the National Archives and Records Administration sought classified documents from the vice president's office, Cheney refused on the grounds that the vice president has only peripheral links to both the executive and the legislative branches, but is not considered an integral component of either, therefore there was no obligation for him to surrender any documents.[59] In effect, his argument was that by not being a definitive part of a specific, existent branch of the government, the vice presidency was its own branch.

Similarly, when the Office of Government Ethics—an agency within the executive branch empowered for oversight and resolution of possible conflicts of interest by government employees—tried to obtain records of travel expenses for personnel working in the vice president's office, they were denied. In this case, Cheney's legal counsel, David Addington, rebuffed the request on the basis of the rule on travel expense documentation being specific to executive agencies—and the Office of the Vice President was decidedly not an executive agency.[60]

Conversely, when assorted public interest and environmental groups pursued legal action against Cheney—in an attempt to compel him to release the names of all the participants of the task force on energy policy—the vice president's argument for refusal was calculated to emphasize the executive branch.[61] Even though the work of the energy task force was directed entirely by Cheney, and its final recommendations were known to reflect the preferences of the vice president, officially the task force functioned under the aegis of the president. And so the Bush administration argued: "Congress does not have the power to inhibit, confine or control the process through which the president formulates the legislative measures he proposes or the administration actions he orders."[62] In other words, if it matched Cheney's immediate interests—in this case maintaining the anonymity of unofficial participants in his task force's deliberations—the historic connection of the vice president to the president, and thus to the executive branch, was considered appropriate.

Because the Framers attached the vice president to two of the three branches of the American government, demarcation of a definitive place for that officer remains elusive. And if Dick Cheney offered shifting rationales for assigning the vice president to one or the other branch, he was not alone. Vice President Joe Biden, for example, when he was running for the second office, was unequivocal in disputing Cheney's conception of the vice president as a creature of the legislative branch. Late in the 2008 campaign, Biden declared that Cheney had "no authority relative to the Congress. The idea he's part of the legislative branch is a bizarre notion invented by Cheney to aggrandize the power of a unitary executive and look where it has gotten us. It has been very dangerous."[63] Parting from Biden's viewpoint, Dan Quayle sided with Cheney's suggestion of the vice president ultimately belonging with the national legislature. Obviously speaking from the vantage of one who has held the post, Quayle contended: "Cheney is right, the vice president is not part of the executive branch," and furthermore "your salary is paid by the Senate."[64]

Notwithstanding the assertions of the vice presidents just cited, or for that matter the opinions of any scholars or political pundits who periodically choose to weigh in, the vice presidency stands today, barring the constitutional restructuring of the office, a hybrid institution. With fixed ties to the executive branch and the president—principally founded on the precedent of succession and reinforced over the years by the munificence of assorted presidents towards their vice presidents—and by the delegation of duties for the vice president in the national legislature, specifically the Senate, the vice presidency is a surprisingly stable institution. And yet, despite the constancy of the institution, Dick Cheney managed to reshape the American vice presidency. More importantly, since the vice presidency has always mattered because of the presidency, the realignment of the president-to-vice president arrangement Cheney achieved is the most important outcome of his tenure.

It is difficult to determine how history will ultimately record the Cheney vice presidency. But since leaving office, Cheney has not faded entirely into political obscurity, as many earlier vice presidents did. Instead, in the first term of Barack Obama's presidency, Cheney began to develop an entirely new prototype for the role of a former vice president. From the outset, he has been a vociferous critic of President Obama, although thus far he appears unconcerned with his successor, Vice President Joe Biden.

Cheney's age and heath preclude his ever running for president, making his vigorous denunciations of the Obama administration unusual and unprecedented. Moreover, as it was when they held office, Cheney has been far more engaged than his former partner, George W. Bush, in the work of preserving a legacy for which they have a shared stake. At the end of the day, it just might be a case of the former vice president feeling that he has majority ownership of what is otherwise known as the Bush administration.

It is difficult to quantify the affect Dick Cheney had on the president-to-vice president dynamic. Still, in isolation, specific anecdotal evidence makes this much clear: never before in the history of the American vice presidency did an individual vice president so thoroughly dominate and define the vice president's relationship to the president as did Cheney. And in doing so, he changed popular perceptions about the American vice presidency while reshaping the vice-presidential institution, perhaps permanently.

8

THE VICE PRESIDENCY IN THE TWENTY-FIRST CENTURY

Certainly I had no desire or intention to seize an iota of presidential power. I was the Vice President and could be nothing more.

– Vice President Richard Nixon

The American vice presidency of the twenty-first century is a decidedly transformed political institution from the one created at the Federal Convention of 1787. As an officer of the national government, meant only to preside in one chamber of the Congress—with no vote except to break a tie among the members of that body, and intended to substitute for the president under specific circumstances, though for a time even that was a disputed notion—the vice president is now genuinely second only to the president. And yet, "the grotesqueness of the predicament" of the American vice presidency, as Franklin Roosevelt aptly characterized it in 1920, continues to escape the collective consciousness of the nation; it is, again turning to Roosevelt, as if the vice presidency has been accepted as it stands, taken purely "as a matter of course."[1]

Contrary to the attitude of indifference assumed by most Americans toward the vice presidency, the vice presidency is today a more substantial institution than it was when the Framers initially contemplated its creation at the Federal Convention. But how could such a transformation have happened? The vice presidency became a government institution by virtue of its establishment in the Constitution of the United States, yet the Constitution has not been amended for the purpose of granting additional functions and duties for the vice president beyond those already prescribed. And the two constitutional amendments with a direct bearing on the institution concerned ancillary matters, and were not duty related. The first of these, the Twelfth Amendment, was intended to sort out the election process for choosing the president and the vice president. And the second, the Twenty-fifth Amendment, reaffirmed the precedent of the vice president assuming the presidency upon the death, resignation, or impeachment of the president. In addition, the Twenty-fifth

Amendment provided a method for replacing the vice president on those occasions when the second office fell vacant, as well as for managing presidential inability and the procedures for installing the vice president as a temporary, acting president.

Other than making the vice president a permanent member of the National Security Council, the institutional framework of the office has stood as it was created, and maybe as it was intended. Hence, as an institution of the government essentially in name only, the vice presidency incrementally and subtly became much more. Twenty-one years into the twentieth century, the inclusion of the vice president in the president's cabinet fostered a more concrete attachment to the executive branch for the vice presidency; it was an attachment previously defined by the shared election of the only two officers of the government voted on by all the people of the nation. Subsequently, midway through the twentieth century, vice presidents were becoming indispensible deputies to the presidents they served, most notably Henry Wallace and Richard Nixon.

By the 1970s, the growth of the presidency, in tandem with the accumulation of institutional resources available to the president as well as to the vice president, conferred on the vice president an expanded reach and presence within the executive branch. In conjunction with increased resources came a corresponding level of vice-presidential influence. Even if the nature of such influence was colored by each specific president and vice president, a sizable measure of influence was exercised by every vice president, beginning in 1974 with Nelson Rockefeller. By that point, the growth of the institution was undeniable and in all likelihood irreversible. In addition, over time the formal Office of the Vice President began to match, though clearly not in density, the composition of the Executive Office of the President. In light of the preceding, and taken in the aggregate, the American vice presidency had finally arrived, in the process becoming a fully realized institution of the government.

WHAT TO DO ABOUT THE AMERICAN VICE PRESIDENCY?

In 1956, Clark Clifford, who served President Harry Truman in the capacity of special assistant, appeared before a Senate subcommittee considering a proposal for reorganizing the operations of the federal government. Specifically, Clifford was called to discuss what might be done about the vice presidency. During his testimony, Clifford juxtaposed the vice presidency with the presidency, describing the president as the foremost officer of the government, "with such tremendous responsibility and so wide a scope as oftentimes to be incredible; and we have the second job, exactly the opposite."[2] He went on to note how the Constitution was "the greatest instrument ever struck off by the hand of man."[3] But then, taking a swipe at the Framers, Clifford claimed that when it came to instituting the vice presidency, the Framers "didn't come up to the same high standard as they did in other phases of their constitutional effort."[4] Still, despite his reservations about the office of vice president, as it stood at that time, Clifford suggested it "could be built up into the important position that it should be."[5] And he was right.

At present, the American vice presidency is a substantial institution and differs from the office described in the Constitution; it is also an improved institution from the time Clark Clifford spoke of it at a Senate hearing in 1956. For these reasons the vice presidency merits the reevaluation it has received on the pages herein. And yet, if there has been one constant in regard to considerations of the vice presidency, it is this: apart from the surety of the position defined in the Constitution, it is an institution which has always evoked more questions than answers.

So, what should be done about the vice presidency? Surely the argument could be made to leave the institution as it now stands, the rationale being that the growth in the vice presidency, on the whole, has been an organic process. If the expanded reach of the vice presidency was not anticipated by the Framers, but changes to the institution have not been precipitously arrived at, then steady growth should be considered a progressive outcome for an institution conceived in a simpler era and with minimal expectations.

What necessitates a good look at the vice presidency is most likely underscored by the suspicion that, notwithstanding the enhanced utility of the office, it is now encroaching on the single institution for which it is intrinsically attached, and from where it derives its viability: the presidency. This premise is further underscored by the drift toward an institutional framework reflective of a collegial executive—an arrangement that was not the preference of the majority of the Framers—which is an outcome reflective of the symmetry of the Clinton-Gore pairing, and expressly manifest in the shared Bush-Cheney tenure.

Granting that the Framers pursued a course at the Federal Convention that precluded empowering a lone, monarchial-type executive atop the new government, broad sentiment in favor of a single officer to head the executive branch did emerge, though by no means was it a unanimous outlook. There were some at the Federal Convention, like Edmund Randolph, who opposed a unitary executive on the grounds that it was "the foetus of monarchy," and argued that it made no sense "why the great requisites for the Executive department, vigor, dispatch & responsibility could not be found in three men, as well as in one man. The Executive ought to be independent. It ought therefore in order to support its independence consist of more than one."[6]

Regardless of Edmund Randolph's predilection for the composition of the executive, the prevailing view in 1787 was to avoid the outlines of a collegial executive. Emblematic of such a view on the issue, and the one to carry the day, was that of John Rutledge, another delegate to the Federal Convention. According to James Madison, Rutledge suggested the best course "was for vesting the Executive power in a single person, tho' he was not for giving him the power of war and peace. A single man would feel the greatest responsibility and administer the public affairs best."[7]

If there was a general consensus on having a sole officer to head the executive branch, with executive power vested in the office of the president, then why have a vice president at all? Plainly it was not a simple matter of attaching a presiding officer to the Senate—that could be achieved easily enough with the appointment of an elected senator as the presiding officer, although pulling from the membership for such an officer was disquieting to many at the Federal Convention, for it was deemed undemocratic to deprive any state of one of its votes in the upper chamber. To this point, Alexander Hamilton advocated placing the vice president in the presiding officer's chair precisely because "to take the senator of any State from his seat as senator, to place him in that of President of the Senate, would be to exchange, in regard to the State from which he came, a constant for a contingent vote."[8]

Apart from predetermining an officer to manage the proceedings of the Senate, arranging to have the vice president for a suitable replacement for the president, if the need should arise, was the principal aim in establishing the position. Outlined earlier, the vice presidency was predominantly modeled on the position of the lieutenant governor found in many of the colonies and later replicated in ten of the states associated under the Articles of Confederation. One responsibility of the early lieutenant governors was to preside in the Senate; a second expectation for the lieutenant governor was to substitute for the governor. If the governor of a state required a designated substitute, then undoubtedly the president of the nation necessitated the same.

It stands to reason, then, that by including the vice president in the Constitution, two discrete purposes for the office were satisfied. The foremost use for the vice president was practical: to have an official of the government preside in the Senate. Another, subordinate use of the vice president was essentially precautionary, yet purposeful: to have an officer elected by all the people of the nation as a ready standby for the president. Hence, with the preceding being an accurate accounting of the origins of the vice presidency, and recognizing how greatly the office has changed over time, then it is appropriate to consider making more, or less depending on the view taken, of the American vice presidency.

By the time debate over the Twelfth Amendment commenced, suggestions for what to do about the vice presidency had already begun in earnest. One of the earliest and certainly simplest proposals for modifying how the president and the vice president were elected was to simply abolish the second office. Of this sentiment, it was recorded in the debates of the House of Representatives that one member "would have preferred the amendment ... went to abolish entirely the office of Vice President, to that which was then submitted to their consideration."[9] The suggestion went no further than to be put on paper, saving the vice presidency from abolishment. But the Twelfth Amendment was adopted and the vice presidency was never the same.

Another possible solution for what to do about the vice presidency is to alter the way the president and vice president are elected; specifically, to embrace a system whereby voters cast distinct ballots for the candidates for president and vice president. This method is presently in use in selected nations employing a presidential system—for example the Philippines—and it is the mode of selection in some parts of the United States when voting for governor and lieutenant governor. Under such a framework, political parties would continue to nominate a single ticket composed of a candidate for president and vice president. The critical difference would occur when it came time to vote and registered voters were allowed to cast distinct ballots for president and vice president—in effect, balloting in the same manner as the electors of the Electoral College have since the addition of the Twelfth Amendment.

Going to such an electoral arrangement would be problematic for a number of reasons, and there would likely be considerable resistance to the requisite amendment to the Constitution to put it in place. Resistance, however, would not necessarily be founded on constitutional or legal arguments; it would arise mainly from the volatility engendered by the partisanship inherent to the American political system. Realistically, the two major political parties functioning in the United States today—and in the Democratic Party's case, operating in name since the 1828 presidential election—would be loath to upsetting an electoral system which has continuously benefited both parties.

Elections for president and vice president are about outcomes, as all elections are, with the prime outcome being the determination of who won the election. But disrupting the process for electing the president and vice president could potentially impact another outcome of a presidential election, specifically governance. Even conceding that political parties are most about winning elections, the political parties continue to have an enduring stake in governance.

Besides the electoral consequences, the ramifications on governance if voters could cast distinct ballots for president and vice president would extend past the immediate concerns of the political parties and could cause the destabilization of any ideological mandate the winning presidential candidate earned. For instance, if the candidate for vice president of one political party was viewed more favorably than the opposition candidate, such a change to the electoral system would not preclude voting for individual candidates for president and vice president from opposing political parties. Presumably the outcome would be a mix of divergent ideological inclinations in the two national executive offices, the likes of which has not occurred since the uncomfortable union of Federalist President John Adams with Democratic-Republican Vice President Thomas Jefferson.

If opposition party candidates occupied the presidency and the vice presidency, and any provision of the Constitution pertaining to presidential succession or inability was subsequently evoked—with the powers of the president devolving to the vice president—the consequences would be profound. As with upsetting ideological mandates, in cases of the temporary incapacity of the president, if the elected president were replaced by a vice president who hailed from a different political party, then the preference of a plurality, or possibly a majority, of the electorate would be overturned.

The central outcome of a national executive team divided by partisan identification, however, would be the instantaneous futility of the vice president. This would be particularly acute for modern vice presidents since the predominant president-to-vice president association for the last three decades has been characterized by presidents who rely on their vice president for advice and support and by vice presidents who exercise influence and clout inside and out of the White House. With the election of an opposition party vice president, presidents would have no incentive to take the vice president into their confidence; likewise, there would be the persistent suspicion that the vice president was perpetually angling to replace the president.

Under the circumstances just outlined, the incumbent president could choose not to extend any of the substantive portfolios given to previous vice presidents, while restricting the vice president's access to critical information and participation in indispensible meetings of the president's inner circle. The president could even manage to restrict those prerogatives extended to the vice president via statute, circumspectly distinguishing what meetings mattered. Of course, in this scenario the president could not deprive the vice president entirely of responsibilities, as there is always the vice president's function as the president of the Senate.

The preceding points also reinforce the historic, and continuing, secondary status of vice-presidential candidates. In other words, when voting for president and vice president, the primary focus of the electorate continues to be the presidential candidates, and not the vice-presidential candidates. Moreover, irrespective of the frequency with which vice presidents have succeeded to the presidency, vice-presidential candidates continue to be dismissed as potential successors to the presidency, though there is a caveat to this with the notion of casting separate votes for president and vice president. A system giving voters the option, in a sense, to build their own electoral tickets would also provide them with the best opportunity to demonstrate they were actually paying attention to the candidates for vice president, and by extension acknowledging an established, essential vice-presidential institution.

Considering possible ways to alter the structure of the American vice presidency naturally raises the question of whether any change is necessary at all. At the same time, if the presidency became too much for one individual to handle, there is likewise a sound argument to be made for the vice president's job having become equally arduous, in a sense having outgrown its constitutional limitations. If this is the case, should additional powers be vested in the office of the vice president? Twelve years after failing in his bid for a second vice-presidential nomination, Henry Wallace emphatically answered no; he decried any proposals for adding to the constitutional or statutory authority of the vice president.[10] But Wallace was not necessarily concerned with restraining the growth of the office he once held; instead, he appeared to be most anxious about preserving the status of the office he sought unsuccessfully in 1948—the presidency. When Wallace stated, where "the law is concerned, one man should run the executive branch of government, not two," he obviously saw movement in that direction to be a threat to the efficacy of a unitary executive.[11]

If Wallace was right, was the solution to an overburdened presidency and vice presidency the retention of a single chief executive, with an increase in the number of vice presidents permitted under the system? Nations not nearly as complex or diverse as the United States, and therefore on many levels more governable, have constructed systems with more than one vice president. The constitutions of Peru and Costa Rica provide for a first and second vice president, and the Peruvian government also seats a prime minister, whereas the system in Cuba allows for a first vice president of the council of state and a first vice president of the council of ministers. And, putting aside the fundamental political and philosophical differences separating the United States and Iran, for comparative purposes it is worth noting that Iran has a system in place boasting a supreme leader and a president, both of whom are supported by twelve vice presidents and a council of ministers.

In the preceding sample of nations, in addition to other nations not included here, the vice president is an officer of the government who is either appointed by the president or elected by the national assembly. Conversely, there are places where the president and vice president are elected together, and in those nations with multiple vice presidents, for example Costa Rica, the president campaigns for office on an electoral ticket with two vice-presidential candidates for running mates. Finally, there is variation from nation-to-nation regarding whether the vice president, singular or plural, is added into the line of presidential succession. Indeed, in most nations where a presidential system is in place, the vice president is not integrated into the line of succession; instead, in the event of a vacancy in the presidency, a new election is held in lieu of the vice president ascending to the higher office.

If a president is unable to fulfill their term of office, the necessity of a ready successor to the presidency has long been among the strongest justifications for the inclusion of the vice president in a constitutionally stipulated line of succession. Not only is democratic legitimacy redoubled when the vice president replaces the president from a shared electoral ticket, but there is less uncertainty about continuity in governance of the type likely to arise in the time an election for a new president is organized, conducted, and certified. As such, validation for having the vice president in place for presidential succession may be found in the nine instances, thus far, when an American vice president has been obligated to move up to the presidency.

When the vice president is the constitutionally recognized successor to the president—a designation with no tangible ongoing tasks—and has defined, though far from demanding responsibilities in the legislative branch, as it is in the United States system of government, then making better use of the vice president has made sense. Still, the idea already introduced—that expectations for the vice presidency may now exceed the capacity of a single vice president—make the notion of having a second vice president appropriate to any reconfiguration of the American executive. And so, there is cause to reexamine the work of the Hoover Commission and its proposal for the addition of a second, administrative vice president.[12] Poignantly, the group was led by Herbert Hoover, a former president who shares with President Calvin Coolidge the distinction of using their vice president the least effectively of any of the vice presidents in the modern era.

In summary, the Hoover Commission recommended that the president appoint, with confirmation required by the Senate, a second vice president, sans constitutionally delegated responsibilities. The first vice president, having been elected with the president, would continue to function, per the direction of the Constitution, as the presiding officer of the Senate, possessing a vote only when the chamber is equally divided. In addition, the first vice president would be the set successor to the presidency. Presidential powers would transfer to the first vice president should the president die, resign, be impeached and convicted, or be deemed unable to discharge the powers and the duties of the presidential office, as clarified and expanded in the Twenty-fifth Amendment's inability provisions. In other words, the first vice president would continue to stand as the Framers of the Constitution intended.

By way of the Hoover Commission's recommendations, the second vice president would not be elected with the president and the first vice president, subsequently restricting the second vice president from succession. The advantage of this type of electoral setup is diminished political pressure, since the second vice president would not be viewed as the perpetual heir apparent, and would therefore be removed from much of the political jockeying that traditionally permeates the executive branch, especially in the first term of an administration.

The alternative, of course, to having the president appoint a second vice president is to have presidential nominees run for office on a ticket with two vice-presidential nominees, with each publicly designated for their respective position. Making the second vice president a third nationally elected officer of the government is a preferable configuration, as it would assuage the twin concerns of legitimacy and accountability in relation to the cabinet-rank status of the president's congressionally unconfirmed chief of staff.

A final point relevant to the place of the vice presidency in the American scheme of government, and one that has bearing irrespective of the number of individuals so designated, concerns the Twenty-second Amendment to the Constitution. Specifically, the Twenty-second Amendment was conceived in reaction to the unprecedented election of President Franklin Roosevelt to a fourth term in office. Proposed in 1947, just two years after Roosevelt's death moved Harry Truman from the vice presidency to the presidency, the amendment's intent was to ensure that future presidents would be barred from holding the office as long as Roosevelt.[13] It was an expedient measure guaranteed to inhibit the domination of the executive branch by any individual. Therefore, the Twenty-second Amendment stipulates the following: "No person shall be elected to the office of the President more than twice, and no person who has held the office of President, or acted as President, for more than two years of a term to which some other person was elected President shall be elected to the office of the President more than once."[14]

The impact of the Twenty-second Amendment on the development of the American vice presidency has been profound. Limiting the president to two terms fosters a scenario whereby the incumbent president, once reelected, steadily loses leverage in the final four years of their service, in essence becoming a weakened, though admittedly not completely powerless, political figure. But the principal outcome of the two-term limit is the increased prospect of the incumbent vice president seeking and receiving the nomination of their party for president.[15]

Pursuant to the Twenty-second Amendment, forcing the president to retire has helped to make the vice president the de facto head of their shared political party. Regardless of the current weakened state of political parties in the United States, for an incumbent vice president seeking a presidential nomination, becoming the figurehead of the party is sure to benefit their candidacy; it also explains why every incumbent vice president, with the exception of Dick Cheney, who has served with a lame duck president since the ratification of the Twenty-second Amendment in 1951, has received the ensuing presidential nomination.

Indeed, Richard Nixon, Hubert Humphrey, George H.W. Bush, and Al Gore all served with lame duck presidents. In Humphrey's case, President Lyndon Johnson could have run in the 1968 election for another term because he had served less than two years of President Kennedy's unfulfilled term—an exemption stipulated in the

Twenty-second Amendment. Nonetheless, once Johnson finally took himself out of the running, the machinery of the Democratic Party coalesced around Vice President Humphrey.

Besides the passage previously quoted from the Twenty-second Amendment, just two additional sentences comprise the amendment in its entirety. Oddly, in the three sentences that are the Twenty-second Amendment, the vice president is not referenced. It is a curious omission, with the amendment in no way limiting the tenure of the occupant of the vice presidency. In theory, the incumbent vice president could serve continuously or intermittently, depending on practical politics and the electorate's inclination for returning a specific individual to the vice presidency time and again.

In this way, a vice president elected to successive terms, and possibly with different presidents, as happened on occasion in the earliest years of the American government, would establish an invaluable institutional memory. In turn, this could lead to effective and sustained administration of the executive branch. Naturally, even if the Twenty-second Amendment puts a perpetual vice presidency into the realm of possibility, and taking into account the augmented state of the modern vice presidency, it is an untenable proposition that any political figure will settle for the vice presidency if the presidency is in reach.

IN BRIEF: VICE-PRESIDENTIAL CANDIDATES AND GENDER

That a woman has never been elected president or vice president of the United States, to date, speaks volumes about the role gender currently and historically plays in American politics. It is equally telling, in fielding candidates for the two nationally elected offices, that neither of the major political parties in the United States has ever nominated a woman candidate for president, and each party has accorded the vice-presidential nomination to a woman on just one occasion.

The paucity of women candidates gaining a spot on a presidential ticket is in part explained by the consistent dismissal of the seriousness of the presidential ambitions of women candidates by the media.[16] It is a phenomenon unusually endemic to female candidates for the presidency, as from the outset their candidacies are often taken for subterfuge, with their presumed actual goal being the vice-presidential nomination. To this point, one scholar writing prior to Senator Hillary Clinton's 2008 run for the presidency claimed that in those instances when women ran "for the presidential nomination of the major parties, the vice presidency was mentioned as a desired goal of each of their bids, and … were more likely to be mentioned for the vice presidency than were their male counterparts. The women were regularly framed as though the vice presidency (and not the presidency) was their true ambition."[17] In turn, this perpetuates the notion that a woman would be fine for vice president, but not necessarily for president.

Intrinsically, where the vice presidency is concerned, there is irony to be found. And in terms of gender and candidates for the vice presidency, it is no exception. Plainly the choice of the vice-presidential nominee always matters because of succession. In other words, from the moment an individual takes the vice-presidential oath of office, that individual is first in line to succeed to the presidency. For this reason, every nominee for vice president, female or male, should be measured for their potential as the next chief executive. The irony, then, is this: because women candidates theoretically have a better chance at being nominated and elected vice president—as opposed to earning the nomination for, and election to, the presidency—due to the continuing attitude of indifference displayed toward the second office, the candidacies of women running for vice president will likely be the route by which a woman will first, and finally, make it to the presidency.

As women advance in politics and government, working their way closer to the highest elected executive offices, there are numerous cultural and institutional barriers that continue to inhibit their progress. Much of this is founded on a persistent gender bias that hinders perceptions of women as elected executives capable of dealing with policies thought to be more masculine, such as economics and security.[18] With the persistent emphasis on the need for presidents and governors to be tough on economic and security issues, it was not surprising when the 2008 presidential election cycle featured a viable female candidate for president who was a senator, Hillary Clinton, as well as a female candidate for vice president, Sarah Palin, who was a governor at the time. Still, even with two prominent female candidates in the 2008 election season, one for president and one for vice president, each lost their respective races.

Of the two female candidacies briefly considered, of most concern here is the candidacy of Sarah Palin for vice president. Only time will tell what impact the Palin candidacy will have on future women candidates for vice president and president. Palin's missteps as governor, and when she was the Republican vice-presidential nominee, will continue to bring increased scrutiny of future female candidates for the two nationally elected executive offices. It should likewise be noted that the first and thus far only other time a woman, Congresswoman Geraldine Ferraro, was nominated for vice president occurred twenty-four years prior to the Palin nomination. Hence, it does not bode well for women seeking presidential and vice-presidential nominations that, of the two times women were selected as the vice-presidential nominees of the major political parties, they lost. By extension, perhaps the only obstacle remaining for a woman to reach the presidency may be the necessity of a woman vice-presidential candidate finally ending up on a winning presidential ticket.

THE VICE PRESIDENCY SERVED: AT PRESENT

On October 19, 2009, a photo of Vice President Joe Biden appeared on the cover of *Newsweek* magazine. It was just one day shy of nine months since Biden had taken the oath of office, becoming the forty-seventh vice president of the United States. The title of the cover story said it all: "Why Joe Is No Joke."[19] Indicative of the present, enhanced state of the institutional vice presidency, it would have been fitting to have substituted Biden's official title—the vice president—for his first name, for no longer is the American vice presidency just a political punch line.

By no means is the prominence of Biden's portrait on the cover of a newsmagazine meant to imply that a significant portion of the electorate no longer overlooks the vice presidency and vice-presidential candidates. Data generated throughout the 2008 presidential campaign indicates that the vice-presidential candidates were generally an ancillary concern for the majority of voters.[20] As such, the notion of an electorate continuing to discount the potential outcome of their vote if a less than stellar vice president were to succeed to the presidency is compounded.

Electoral disregard is also manifest when gauging incumbent candidates for vice president.[21] This is a puzzling expression of voter disinterest in vice-presidential candidates, especially in light of the transparent growth of the institution. What is more, modern vice presidents—dissimilar from the lot of their eighteenth and nineteenth century counterparts—are actively engaged by a comprehensive set of political and policy portfolios, and they likewise have an abundance of institutional resources at their disposal. Furthermore, under certain circumstances they are able to operate semi-autonomously, thus slightly disconnected from their president. Accordingly, incumbent modern vice presidents now have a record to run on, which stands somewhat apart from that of the president.

But if the proposition is true that vice presidents of the modern period have a measure of autonomy, they conversely remain inalterably linked to the president with whom they came to office. The continuity of connection with the presidency is a positive outcome of the growth of the modern vice-presidential institution because, other than the Constitution, the presidency is the only source of vice-presidential powers and responsibilities. And if the president is capable of extending and retracting vice-presidential prerogative, the president is equally in command of the scope of the president-to-vice president association, and whether or not it exemplifies a meaningful collaboration.

Based on the example set by his most recent predecessors, Al Gore and Dick Cheney, Joe Biden came to office with the expectation that he would be taking on an enhanced political institution. More importantly, he could be confident that Gore and Cheney, by their relations with their respective presidents, had further established the indispensability of the vice president to the president. During the 2008 campaign, Biden framed his then hypothetical vice presidency precisely along these lines when he stated:

> I would be the point person for the legislative initiatives in the United States Congress for our administration. I would also, when asked if I wanted a portfolio, my response was, no. But Barack Obama indicated to me he wanted me with him to help him govern. So every major decision he'll be making, I'll be sitting in the room to give him my best advice. He's president, not me, I'll give my best advice.[22]

Once inaugurated, Vice President Biden became an unceasing presence by the side of President Obama. And just as Gore and Cheney did before him, Biden was equally involved in the post-election and transition activities. This included the placement of key personnel, ensuring he continues to exercise influence on the president, even on those occasions when he is not nearby. Where Biden has transparently differed from Gore and Cheney, however, is in his aversion to the prime ministerial portfolios which helped define the tenures of his predecessors, although it would be a mischaracterization to claim that Biden has escaped entirely the tradition of the vice president leading any number of commissions established by the president, with the most prominent of these being his chairmanship of the Middle Class Task Force. Overall, Biden appears to be involved with President Obama in determining the priorities of the administration while forging a productive partnership with his president.[23]

To the benefit of both men, Obama has continued the practice of employing the vice president in the conduct of the administration's foreign policy, sending Biden on a diplomatic mission even before Secretary of State Hillary Clinton's inaugural trip abroad. By the end of his second year in office, Biden had traveled to twenty-five nations—including perpetually troubled areas such as Lebanon, Israel, Iraq, and Kosovo—engaging in substantive discussions in all. This made sense, not only because vice presidents routinely supplant the secretary of state in representing an administration on the world stage, but because Biden, again like Cheney and Gore, had more experience with foreign policy and national security issues than did the president. To be sure, when Biden was tapped for the vice-presidential nomination, foreign policy was perhaps the most robust feature of his thirty-five year legislative career; it was a sorely needed asset he brought to the Obama-Biden ticket.

The span of Biden's service in Congress, and the time he spent as a member of the Senate Foreign Relations Committee, gave him more than credibility in foreign policy. He had developed a network of alliances, Democratic and Republican, over the years that continues to be of immeasurable value to the Obama administration. And because he possesses a legislative background his president could not begin to approach, of necessity Biden has affected a reemphasis on the vice president in the national legislature. This is a return to form, of sorts, and characterized the modern era vice presidencies of John Nance Garner, Alben Barkley, Lyndon Johnson, and Hubert Humphrey, all of whom, like Biden, were creatures of the legislative branch. Indeed, Barkley and Humphrey were so at home there that both returned to the Senate after four years of service in the vice presidency.

Yet where Biden differs most from his recent predecessors is the consistency with which he is in the Capitol building. He regularly exercises in the Senate gymnasium, and when Congress is in session he frequently works in the ceremonial office of the vice president.[24] But he rarely presides, shirking, as it were, the principal constitutionally sanctioned function of the position he holds. For the most part, Biden is adhering to what is now a ritual of the vice presidency—tending to the deliberations of the Senate only when it is apparent that the vice president's tie-breaking vote will be required. Still, Biden's activism in and around the Congress extends past presiding and is grounded principally in his interactions with individual members and, of course, the Democratic caucuses of both chambers.

Since taking office, Vice President Biden's role on Capitol Hill has grown. The extent of Biden's involvement in the legislative branch has been driven in equal parts by fluctuations in the partisan makeup and tenor of the Congress, the cohesiveness of the Democratic Party, and the future political fortunes of both major political parties. It is the capacity of modern vice presidents to shift their focus from the executive to the legislative realm—and back again, when necessary—that makes the hybrid form of the institution so invaluable. And it is the flexibility of the institution that further compounds the usefulness of the vice president to the president.

After Obama's first chief of staff, Rahm Emanuel, left the scene, it was widely understood that Biden's access to Congress would be even more essential.[25] From the beginning, Biden had an equitable association with President Obama, yet he was not integrated into Obama's inner circle of advisers, many of whom had known the president well before the election. Emanuel could be counted among that group. Of greater import, Emanuel followed the model of an autocratic chief of staff, akin to H.R. Haldeman or Dick Cheney. It was an abrupt mode of operation which Emanuel applied equally to his dealings within the White House and when he pushed for the president's agenda before Congress. Emanuel's approach, which was the converse to Biden's approach, never helped ingratiate the chief of staff with those who came into contact with him in the Capitol.[26]

To Biden's advantage, when he took office the institutional vice presidency was better equipped to resist the machinations of a Haldeman or a Cheney in the chief of staff posting. In other words, from the moment his term of office began in 2009, as the vice president, Biden had a measure of clout that would have been unfamiliar to Spiro Agnew in 1969 or Nelson Rockefeller in the closing days of 1974. In the first two years of his vice presidency, Biden successfully strengthened his position with Obama by always supporting the president, even where they disagreed, and particularly in helping the untested president navigate the political waters of Washington. For these reasons, when Emanuel stepped down, it was the vice president who was poised and prepared to fill the vacuum caused by the exit of an abrasive, though influential, chief of staff.

Joe Biden's time in office, thus far, is not simply about his taking over a fully actualized government institution. There are features of his initial candidacy for vice president that highlight specific trends endemic to the modern vice presidency. To start, vice-presidential candidates tend to have more experience in the national government than do their presidential nominee counterparts. Predating the Obama-Biden team, these types of ticket-pairings may be found in the modern era as early as the 1928 election, when Herbert Hoover was put with the long serving Senator Charles Curtis, and next, in 1932, when President Hoover and Vice President Curtis were challenged, and defeated, by Franklin Roosevelt and then-Speaker of the House John Nance Garner. While there have been recent anomalies—notably, Senator John Kerry's choice of Senator John Edwards, and Senator John McCain's pick of Governor Sarah Palin—on the whole, experience in government typically resides with the vice-presidential nominees.

In concert with comparisons of nominee experience, a second feature of Biden's vice-presidential candidacy worthy of note was the construction of an electoral ticket wherein the vice-presidential nominee was considerably older than the presidential nominee. Biden holds a twenty year edge on President Obama, making him sixty-six to Obama's forty-six at the time of their nominations. But he is not alone among candidates for vice president. Among others, when Senator Alben Barkley ran for vice president in 1948 with President Harry Truman, Barkley had served in the Congress since 1913, and he was seventy-one at the time of his nomination, though he was merely seven years senior to Truman.

On occasion there is parity in the age of presidential and vice-presidential nominees, while other times the age, or youth, of one or the other of the two nominees is compensated for in the converse. Therefore, nominating vice-presidential candidates who are older than presidential nominees has not emerged as a pervasive pattern—but it could. Once elected, if the incumbent vice president is significantly older than the president, then their tenure comes to represent the model of the vice president as caretaker: prepared to move up to the presidency should the need arise, but never actively pursuing the top job while serving in the second job. Perhaps of more significance, under the preceding scenario, the sitting vice president will not necessarily be perceived as an inevitable presidential nominee.

During the latter part of the modern era, the vice president has come to be seen as a future presidential nominee and heir apparent to the presidency. This idea has persisted notwithstanding outcomes which have not supported such a conclusion. After the Twelfth Amendment to the Constitution, when election to the presidency and vice presidency became a team affair, only Martin Van Buren and George H.W. Bush ascended to the presidency from the vice presidency by winning their own term in office. Once there, both failed to win a second term as president. The other nine vice presidents who moved up to the presidency did so by succession, and of those, only Theodore Roosevelt, Calvin Coolidge, Harry Truman, and Lyndon Johnson won a term of their own. Of the preceding four, just Roosevelt and Coolidge left the presidency more popular than when they first took office. Though for Roosevelt, his popularity was of insufficient strength to sustain his attempt to regain the presidency four years hence.

Of modern incumbent vice presidents—specifically Richard Nixon, Hubert Humphrey, and Al Gore—all earned the presidential nomination of their party, but failed to win the ensuing election. Nixon did eventually win the presidency, but eight years had elapsed from the end of his vice presidency to the commencement of his presidency. Of the incumbent vice presidents to lose their bids for a second term— Walter Mondale and Dan Quayle—both failed to later win the presidency. In Mondale's case, he was successful in winning the Democratic nomination for president after being turned out of the vice presidency, but Quayle's stab at the Republican nomination for president never gelled beyond an exploratory committee and a condensed candidacy.

It is possible that Barack Obama selected Joe Biden to run with him, in part, because he knew that after potentially serving two terms as vice president, Biden was unlikely to run for president, his age being the salient factor. If this was a consideration for Obama, then Biden would not pose a threat to the president's legacy, nor would he be inclined to overshadow the president while they were in office. His place by Obama's side could be seen, then, as entirely supportive and by no means competitive.

If Obama's motivation for choosing Biden was founded in the surety of the latter man being in the twilight of his political career, it is a selection rationale dating back to Thomas Jefferson and the imprudent pick of George Clinton for Jefferson's second vice president. Without question, Jefferson favored Clinton because he was not a political threat to Jefferson, or to Jefferson's preferred heir apparent, James Madison. Using the same reasoning, Richard Nixon's choice of Spiro Agnew in 1968 finally makes sense. Whether it is acknowledged or not, modern presidential nominees, including George W. Bush and Barack Obama, may be selecting running mates because of their weightier résumés, as well as for the improbability of their someday outshining the president.

Another question to consider is if a younger, aspiring political figure is nominated for, and then gains, the vice presidency, what bearing will their future ambitions have over the course of their term of office? It would not be beyond the scope of a modern vice president to position themselves in opposition to the president on unusually prominent or controversial issues—much as John Calhoun and John Nance Garner did, in turn, to Andrew Jackson and Franklin Roosevelt. As a rule, however, politicians are risk averse, and publicly opposing their president would isolate the vice president inside the administration. If such a scenario were to occur, particularly in the first term, then the vice president would have the advantage of appearing independent and bold, consequently gaining an enviable position for the next presidential election. Conversely, depending on the president's response to the situation, and regardless of the issue, the vice president might be portrayed solely for the naked ambition underlying an abandonment of the president.

No matter the reasons for putting together electoral tickets, since the addition of the Twelfth Amendment to the Constitution, when voters cast their ballot for president, they vote for a single presidential ticket, with one candidate designated for the presidency and the other for the vice presidency. What appears to escape the notice of much of the electorate is that in voting for a presidential ticket, voters are actually choosing two potential presidents at once. In theory, this idea predates the Twelfth Amendment, since the Constitution directed, under the circumstances calling for succession, the powers of the presidency to devolve onto the vice president. In other words, from the outset, it was always in the realm of possibility that the individual who landed in the vice presidency could wind up president.

The notion that voters in the United States fail to appreciate the double value of their ballot for president was captured well at the 1988 debate of vice-presidential candidates. Addressing the American electorate broadly, the Democratic nominee, Senator Lloyd Bentsen, asserted:

> This debate tonight is not about the qualifications for the vice presidency. The debate is whether or not Dan Quayle and Lloyd Bentsen are qualified to be president of the United States ... And if that tragedy should occur, we have to step in there without any margin for error, without time for preparation, to take over the responsibility for the biggest job in the world, that of running this great country of ours; to take over the awesome responsibility for commanding the nuclear weaponry that this country has. No, the debate tonight

is about the presidency itself, and a presidential decision that has to be made by you. The stakes could not be higher.[27]

Senator Bentsen was stating the obvious. Heeding the institutional growth of the American vice presidency, the presidency is still why the vice presidency matters. Therefore, no candidate for vice president should be looked at as anything less than as another candidate for president. It is thus a potentially dangerous oversight on the part of voters to dismiss a thorough consideration of the nominees affixed to a presidential ticket, even if, ostensibly, the candidate is meant for the vice presidency.

If serving as vice president has effectively ended numerous political careers, the same may be said for losing vice-presidential nominees. As of this writing, only one vice-presidential nominee of either major political party in the United States—Franklin Roosevelt—who lost their bid for the second office has recovered sufficiently from that loss to later win the vice presidency or the presidency.[28]

And yet, because the public's perception of the vice presidency as an institution has improved so vastly, there seems to be a change in how defeated candidates for vice president are viewed. Put another way: due to the enhanced stature of the modern vice presidency, even being the nominee for vice president on an unsuccessful presidential ticket increases the viability of a future candidacy for president by the defeated vice-presidential nominee. Although, curiously, former nominees for vice president will disavow any interest in seeking the vice presidency again, even when it is obvious their presidential ambitions are futile. In recent years, such was the case with former vice-presidential nominees Edmund Muskie, Sargent Shriver, Robert Dole, and John Edwards—all of whom emphasized they had no interest in running for vice president again, only president.

This too was the scenario to unfold in 2008 with respect to the defeated vice-presidential nominee of the Republican Party. In the aftermath of the Obama-Biden ticket's convincing victory over John McCain and Sarah Palin, it was Palin, not McCain, who was immediately touted as a certain contender for the 2012 presidential nomination, and yet never mentioned for another vice-presidential nomination. That vice-presidential candidates are considered viable future candidates for president—win or lose—speaks volumes for how far the vice presidency has traveled.

Further illustrating this point, two presidential elections stand out where gaining a vice-presidential nomination, or not, likely affected the political fortunes of the figures involved. Both Abraham Lincoln and John Kennedy were considered for the vice-presidential nomination of their respective political parties four years prior to their winning the presidential nomination.[29] Whereas Lincoln seemed not to care whether he won what was the first vice-presidential nomination of the incipient Republican Party, Kennedy coveted the second spot, and with the help of his younger brother Robert, made an organized charge for the vice-presidential nomination. Neither Lincoln nor Kennedy was successful in making it onto the ticket of their party; instead, the vice-presidential nominees were a former senator from New Jersey, William Dayton, for the Republicans, and Senator Estes Kefauver of Tennessee, for the Democrats.

Had Lincoln in 1856, or Kennedy in 1956, been selected to run for vice president, it is uncertain, but doubtful, that either would have made the critical difference between victory and defeat for their respective tickets; consequently, both would have been candidates on losing presidential tickets. Coming off losing bids for the vice presidency, it is difficult to imagine Lincoln or Kennedy regaining the forward movement their political careers were undergoing at the time of the nominating conventions. As such, Lincoln might never have been a viable candidate for United States senator in 1858, as he was, and in 1958, Kennedy might have failed to achieve the resounding Senate reelection victory he did. In either case, running for vice president and losing almost surely would have dashed their future prospects for winning the presidency, as it did for Dayton and Kefauver.

Another characteristic more familiar to modern vice presidencies is that the vice president must meet the specific needs of their president. In the past, it was of no consequence if a vice president such as Elbridge Gerry, John Breckenridge, or Charles Fairbanks added to the executive government, since they were viewed as superfluous by the presidents they served. Conversely, a modern vice president, like Dan Quayle, offered what was needed of him to President George H.W. Bush. If Quayle endured consistent mocking for statements he had once made, he persisted as an effective, modern vice president, meeting the expectations of the president and fitting the precise niche tailored for him within the administration.

For a political institution beset by irony, perhaps the most telling one is this: of the two functions delegated to the vice president by the Constitution—presiding in the Senate and casting a vote in the chamber only if there is a tie—the vice president rarely does either. With regard to the vice president breaking ties in the Senate, the data indicates there is rarely cause for its use. During their terms as vice president, modern occupants of the office—such as Calvin Coolidge, Lyndon Johnson, Gerald Ford, Nelson Rockefeller, and Dan Quayle—were never called upon to break a tie vote in the Senate.[30] And whereas John Adams broke twenty-nine ties in his eight years as vice president, Dick Cheney was called on just eight times to do the same. Naturally, the political climate and the composition of the Senate play a part in the reduced need for the vice president's vote. Then again, it is conceivable that the vice presidency is simply an institution which has outgrown its constitutional place in the government.

In 1956, the political scientist and historian Clinton Rossiter published a book titled *The American Presidency*. Near the end of the text, Rossiter appealed to his readers to forgive his inclusion of "four or five" pages on the vice presidency; he then went on to describe the vice presidency as "a hollow shell of an office" occupied by "no one we should like to see" in the presidency.[31] Since Rossiter was writing in the era of the modern vice presidency, for the time, his words were an exaggeration of the plight of the office. By the mid-1950s the institutional capacity of the vice presidency had been on an upward trajectory for thirty-five years, but Rossiter, and many others like him, had not noticed.

The American vice presidency is insuperably linked to the presidency. This continues despite the transparent augmentation of the vice-presidential institution, and in the face of the, generally, improved caliber of individuals who are willing to run for the job. On the whole, it is an appropriate connection, for were it not for certain presidents, the vice presidency would surely still be identified for the hollow shell Clinton Rossiter described. And yet, while the presidency has made the vice presidency matter, the presidency continues to overwhelm the lesser institution. In this way, what sustains the vice presidency will always, equally, be the bane of the institution.

From the time of the two world wars, and particularly during and after the Second World War, the growth in the American presidency was astonishing. No institution in the political system could keep up with it, let alone be competitive with it—especially the vice presidency. But while institutions such as the Congress or the state governments have tried but failed to reclaim their prominence, the vice presidency moved forward, incrementally and subtly.

Still, and even in light of the power and the prestige of the presidency, to reread the words John Quincy Adams wrote about John Tyler when he became the first vice president to succeed to the presidency is a testament to how far the second office in the land has come. Adams, son of the first vice president, claimed Tyler had "all the interests and passions and vices of slavery rooted in his moral and political constitution—with talents not above mediocrity, and a spirit incapable of expansion to the dimensions of the station upon which he has been cast by the hand of Providence, unseen through the apparent agency of chance."[32] It is unfathomable that a modern vice president might be described by an objective writer with such contempt or be of such ill repute.

As it stands, there continues to be a single vice president in the American constitutional system. Either by their wisdom or by chance, when the Framers of the Constitution attached the vice president, in more or less equal parts, to the legislative and the executive branches, they had established a dormant institution. Under apparently suitable conditions, the vice presidency has developed beyond compare to the institution created in 1787. Yet in the end, so long as the president remains at the apex of the American system, the vice president will always be second best.

ENDNOTES

CHAPTER 1

INTRODUCTION: THE AMERICAN VICE PRESIDENCY RECONSIDERED

1   Kennedy, *Robert Kennedy in His Own Words*, p. 20.

2   In addition to the nine vice presidents to succeed to the presidency, John Adams, Thomas Jefferson, Martin Van Buren, Richard Nixon, and George H.W. Bush served as vice president before winning a term as president in their own right. After winning the presidency, only Jefferson and Nixon were elected to a second term, and with Nixon's resignation, only Jefferson completed his second term as president. And of the nine vice presidents to succeed to the presidency, only Theodore Roosevelt, Calvin Coolidge, Harry Truman, and Lyndon Johnson won an additional term as president on their own.

3   See Appendix C for the text of the Twenty-fifth Amendment to the Constitution of the United States of America.

4   Learned, "Casting Votes of the Vice-Presidents, 1789–1915."

5   Roosevelt, "The Three Vice-Presidential Candidates and What They Represent."

6   Ibid., p. 290.

7   Roosevelt, "Can the Vice President be Useful?"

8   Ibid., p. 8.

9   For congressional testimony on the Hoover Commission's findings, see U.S. Congress, Senate, 84th Cong., 2nd sess., January 16, 24, and 25, 1956. Subcommittee on Reorganization of the Committee on Government Operations: Proposal to Create Position of Administrative Vice President, passim.

10   Of the numerous journal articles devoted to improving the vice presidency, one of the better is Clinton L. Rossiter's "The Reform of the Vice Presidency," published in 1948 by the Academy of Political Science. Among the articles focused on vice-presidential candidates and their impact in elections, see Lee Sigelman and Paul T. Whalbeck's article, "'Veepstakes': Strategic Choice in Presidential Running Mate Selection." Finally,

one of the more prominent scholars to suggest abolishing the office of the vice president is Arthur M. Schlesinger Jr. Schlesinger Jr. makes his case in his article "On the Presidential Succession."

11   Waugh, *Second Consul.*

12   Among the better texts on the vice presidency published in the 1980s are Joel Goldstein's *The Modern American Vice Presidency: The Transformation of a Political Institution* and Paul Light's, *Vice-Presidential Power: Advice and Influence in the White House.*

13   The book referenced is *The Vice Presidency in Foreign Policy: From Mondale to Cheney.* It should be noted that only a minimal, cursory examination of the text was made by the author, and the conclusions therein are not significantly revisited.

14   Ibid., p. 13.

15   Wilson, *Constitutional Government*, p. 14.

16   The members of Barack Obama's vice-presidential selection committee were Caroline Kennedy, Eric Holder, and James Johnson. Johnson later resigned from the committee when questionable financial improprieties were linked to him.

17   There were innumerable print and broadcast reports of Senator Hillary Clinton grudgingly admitting that Senator Barack Obama was likely going to win the Democratic presidential nomination. Usually included in such analysis was attention to Clinton's initial, defiant concession, and then her lukewarm endorsement of Obama. For an international take on the inevitability of Obama's nomination, see the June 8, 2008, story in the UK's online edition of *The Sunday Times*, by Tom Baldwin, titled "Hillary Clinton Prepares to Admit Defeat with a Final Show of Strength."

18   Transcript, Candy Crowley interview with Senator Barack Obama, June 5, 2008, CNN transcripts archive.

19   According to a CBS News-*New York Times* random sample of delegates to the Democratic convention—conducted July 16–August 17, 2008—Senator Hillary Clinton was the choice for the vice-presidential nomination of 24 percent of the delegates polled, followed by 6 percent for Senator Joe Biden and 4 percent each for John Edwards, Bill Richardson, and Senator Evan Byah. Results of the poll were released August 18, 2008.

20   For a brief account of Senator John McCain's consideration of Joe Lieberman and the likely opposition to making the latter man the Republican vice-presidential nominee, see the *Washington Post* story of August 28, 2008, "McCain is Said to be Set to Unveil Running Mate Tomorrow," by Robert Barnes, Chris Cillizza, and Jon Cohen.

21   According to the ABC News Poll, "The Palin Pick," released September 5, 2008, 24 percent of registered Democrats held a favorable view of Sarah Palin at the time of her selection for the vice-presidential nomination, while 85 percent of registered Republicans and 53 percent of voters identified as independents held a favorable view of Palin. In the same poll, 19 percent of the Republicans surveyed suggested they were "less likely" to vote for McCain for president because of his choice of Palin.

22   In a *USA Today*-Gallup Poll, from August 23, 2008, 47 percent of respondents suggested Senator Joe Biden was an "excellent" or "pretty good" vice-presidential nominee choice; 57 percent suggested Biden was qualified to serve as president.

23   ABC News Poll, "The Palin Pick," September 5, 2008.

24   Ibid.

25   Gallup tracking poll conducted August 1–28, 2008; released August 29, 2008.

26   Governor Palin's comments on the vice president in the Senate were recounted by countless media outlets, including in Michael Kranish's "VP's Role a Matter of Debate: Even Candidates Seem Unsure," *The Boston Globe*, October 24, 2008.

27   Documented in Ryan Lizza's worthwhile article, "Biden's Brief," *The New Yorker*, October 20, 2008.

28   Transcript, Biden-Palin Vice-Presidential Debate, October 2, 2008, p. 34.

29   Jane Mayer notes the brief encounters Senator John McCain and Governor Sarah Palin had with one another prior to McCain tapping Palin for the vice-presidential nomination in "The Insiders," *The New Yorker*, October 27, 2008.

30   Transcript, Biden-Palin Vice-Presidential Debate, October 2, 2008, p. 33.

CHAPTER 2

IN THE BEGINNING: VICE-PRESIDENTIAL SELECTION, AARON BURR, AND THE TWELFTH AMENDMENT

1   Madison, *Notes of Debates*, p. 368.

2   Ibid., p. 596.

3   Schlesinger, "On the Presidential Succession," p. 489.

4   Guerrero, *John Adams' Vice Presidency*, p. 21.

5   Hamilton, *Writings*, pp. 149–150. Also, for a concise retelling of the origins of the vice presidency and of Hamilton's role, see Williams, *Rise of the Vice Presidency*, pp.14–20.

6   Hamilton, *Writings*, p. 149.

7   In Pennsylvania, "Vice-President" was the title given to the lieutenant governor; as noted in Williams, *Rise of the Vice Presidency*, p. 16.

8   Hamilton, *Federalist*, p. 445.

9   Ibid., pp. 444–445.

10   In "On the Presidential Succession," historian Arthur M. Schlesinger Jr. emphasizes that "the Constitutional Convention did not resort to the Vice Presidency in order to solve the problem of succession," and that the delegates to the Convention "already had a solution to that problem," p. 488.

11   Madison, *Notes of Debates*, p. 596.

12   For a brief delineation of Alexander Hamilton's "sketch of his frame of government which was patterned after the England of George II," see Feerick, *From Failing Hands*, p. 42–43.

13   Madison, *Notes of Debates*, p. 596.

14   Ibid.

15   In his *Notes of Debates*, James Madison recorded that Elbridge Gerry, Gouverneur Morris, Edmund Randolph, Hugh Williamson, and George Mason were opposed to the vice president's role as presiding officer of the Senate, p. 596.

16   Ibid.

17   Ibid.

18   U.S. Constitution, art. 2, sec. 1.

19   In *Second Consul*, Edgar Waugh makes the point that it became the "practice of our major political parties to get their Presidential and Vice Presidential nominees from different regions of the nation," p. 31.

20   Hamilton, *Federalist* (No. 68), p. 444.

21   On the merits of choosing two candidates for president at the same time, among others see Waugh, *Second Consul*, p. 26, and Schlesinger's "On the Presidential Succession," p. 490.

22   In *Second Consul*, Waugh makes the same point on achieving the ideal balance in the first administration of the United States government, p. 31.

23   Arthur Schlesinger Jr. once suggested that Aaron Burr was "a man of undoubted talents who, however, was trusted by no one in the long course of American history, except for his daughter Theodosia and Gore Vidal"; in "On the Presidential Succession," p. 491.

24   Hamilton, *Federalist*, (No. 10) p. 54.

25   Ibid., p. 57.

26   Washington, *Writings*, p. 225.

27   Although Thomas Jefferson and his adherents—including James Madison and James Monroe—often described themselves as Republicans, they and their associates were also described as Democratic-Republicans. Since the association of Democratic-Republicans later became the Democratic Party, and was never identified with what became the Republican Party, when describing the former group in this text, only the label of Democratic-Republican is used.

28   Although John Adams was the acknowledged leader of the Federalists, his domination of the party was not complete, as Alexander Hamilton was certainly recognized as a rival leader within the party.

29   John Quincy Adams, the sixth president of the United States, is often identified as a Democratic-Republican; however, on occasion he is identified as a National Republican.

30   In his essay, "Election of 1828," Robert V. Remini asserts that Martin Van Buren was "essential" in the creation of the "Democratic" party, p. 418. Curiously, on the same page, Remini notes that the coalition of Andrew Jackson, John Calhoun, and Martin Van Buren represented the beginning of the Democratic-Republicans, thus omitting Thomas Jefferson, James Madison, James Monroe, and many others who used that party label.

31   Thompson, *Essay*, p. 22. Both the Democratic-Republicans and the Federalists held a caucus of their congressional members in 1796, but there are no official records; it is therefore uncertain how formally organized either gathering was.

32   Among others, see Thompson's *Essay* with regard to the presumptive nominees for president and vice president of the two competing congressional caucuses of 1796, p. 22.

33   See Smith, "Election of 1796," p. 71, and Ferling, *Adams vs. Jefferson*, p. 85.

34   There are countless references to Aaron Burr's alleged designs in the elections of 1796 and 1800. One such example comes from historian John Ferling, who notes the "suspicions among some" that Aaron Burr was aiming more for the presidency than for the vice presidency; in *Adams vs. Jefferson*, p. 85.

35   Smith, "Election of 1796," p. 71.

36   Page Smith makes the point that Jefferson's followers "had hit upon the strategy of the future by working to create ... grass-roots sentiment for their party and their candidate"; in "Election of 1796," p. 71.

37   U.S. Constitution, art. 2, sec. 4.

38   See Smith, "Election of 1796," p. 71, and Ferling, *Adams vs. Jefferson*, pp. 87–89.

39   Ferling, *Adams vs. Jefferson*, pp. 87-88.

40   See Smith, "Election of 1796," pp. 70–71. In addition, Cohen, etc., note the choice of Burr for vice president in 1796 and 1800 specifically because of his connection to New York, which would serve as an effective counter to Thomas Jefferson hailing from Virginia, in *Party Decides*, p. 63.

41   Smith, "Election of 1796," p. 71, and Ferling, *Adams vs. Jefferson*, pp. 87–94.

42   Smith, "Election of 1796," pp. 71–72.

43   See Lomask's *Aaron Burr*, pp. 247–255, for a retelling of the machinations and obstructions preceding Burr's eventual selection. Also, in *Adams vs. Jefferson*, Ferling points out that the Democratic-Republican caucus, unlike the Federalists caucus, expressly "stipulated a choice for president. Their electors were told that Jefferson was the party's first choice," p. 132.

44   Lomask, *Aaron Burr*, pp. 254–255.

45   Ibid., p. 242.

46   For a comprehensive description of Burr's role in the New York election see Nathan Schachner's early, definitive text *Aaron Burr: A Biography*, pp. 167–187. For a similar delineation of Burr's activities in New York that year, see Lomask, *Aaron Burr*, pp.238–247.

47   Lomask comments on how critical it was to obtain New York's twelve electoral votes in *Aaron Burr*, p. 237. Also, in Ferling's *Adams vs. Jefferson*, the author notes John Adams was "stunned" when he discovered that the Democratic-Republicans had captured the state assembly; Adams knew that meant New York's electors were destined to go for the opposition, p. 127.

48   See Cunningham, "Election of 1800," pp. 108–109; Lomask, *Aaron Burr*, pp. 237–240; and Ferling, *Adams vs. Jefferson*, p. 130.

49   Lomask, *Aaron Burr*, p. 240.

50   Ibid., pp. 240, 244.

51   For a description of John Adams's ostensible campaign travels, see Cunningham, "Election of 1800," pp. 115–116. Interestingly, in *Adams vs. Jefferson*, Ferling delineates Adams's itinerary as well; however, he does not characterize Adams's trip as especially political or successful, p. 139.

52   Cunningham, "Election of 1800," p. 115, and Ferling, *Adams vs. Jefferson*, p. 140.

53   For reference to Burr's campaign activities after the New York contest, see Schachner, *Aaron Burr*, pp. 183–184.

54   The complete text of the letter is reprinted in Hamilton, *Writings*, "Letter from Alexander Hamilton, Concerning the Public Conduct and Character of John Adams, Esq. President of the United States," pp. 934–971.

55   For an assessment of Alexander Hamilton's derogatory letter about John Adams and the probable ramifications of it, see Ferling, *Adams vs. Jefferson*, pp. 140–143. In addition, a

review of Aaron Burr's success in obtaining and further circulating Hamilton's letter may be found in Lomask, *Aaron Burr*, pp. 257–259.

56   For a useful and interesting take on the Electoral College vote of 1800, see Ackerman and Fontana's "Thomas Jefferson Counts Himself into the Presidency," passim.

57   According to John Ferling in *Adams vs. Jefferson*, there were rumors "of a Federalist conspiracy to assassinate Jefferson," p. 180, as well as indications that "Virginia would secede if Jefferson was not elected," p. 188, and for a detailed exposition of the machinations the 1800 election when it went to the House of Representatives for resolution, review pp. 175–196.

58   Ferling examines the role played by James Bayard in *Adams vs. Jefferson*, pp. 189–195.

59   Ferling, *Adams vs. Jefferson*, p. 193. The idea that Thomas Jefferson struck a deal with Federalists is based on letters written by Aaron Burr and James Bayard, as well as on depositions made by Bayard and Samuel Smith.

60   Hofstadter, *American Political Tradition*, p. 44.

61   For a retelling of Aaron Burr's role in obtaining and distributing copies of Alexander Hamilton's damning letter about John Adams, see Lomask's *Aaron Burr*, pp. 257–258.

62   Hamilton, *Writings*, p. 514.

63   One alternative for amending the Constitution stipulates that two-thirds of the state legislatures must ask Congress to call a national convention to propose amendments; however, this method has never been utilized.

64   *Annals of the Congress*, 8th Cong., 1st sess., p. 673.

65   For a brief summation of the Twelfth Amendment, including the debate in Congress indicating some sentiment for abolishing the vice presidency, see Feerick, *From Failing Hands*, pp. 72–75.

66   Madison, *Notes of Debates*, p. 368.

67   *Annals of the Congress*, 8th Cong., 1st sess., p. 693. James Elliot was a member of the House of Representatives.

68   Quote from Representative Roger Griswold, recorded in *Annals of the Congress*, 8th Cong., 1st sess., p. 674.

69   Ibid.

70   Ibid.

71   The text of Alexander Hamilton's "Proposal for the New York Legislature for Amending the Constitution" is included in Hamilton's *Writings*, p. 982.

72   Ibid.

73   Ibid.

74   Appendix A is the text of the Twelfth Amendment to the United States Constitution.

75   The Twelfth Amendment's cementing of the pattern of political parties offering a team of candidates for president and vice president is fairly obvious, and has been noted elsewhere; for one early reference to this pattern, see Waugh, *Second Consul*, p. 50.

76   Ibid., p. 48.

77   Ibid., pp. 56–58.

CHAPTER 3

THE AMERICAN VICE PRESIDENCY: THE PRE-MODERN ERA

1   Maclay, *Journal*, p. 3.
2   For a thorough review of the debate on formal, procedural titles for the president and vice president, see Guerrero, *John Adams'*, pp. 112–120. Also, it is noted in Maclay's *Journal* that the "business of titles" occupied the two chambers of Congress, with the Senate adopting "pompous and lordly distinctions" for itself as a means for establishing its preeminence over the House, p. 13.
3   Maclay, *Journal*, p. 3.
4   See Guerrero, *John Adams'*, p. 117 on nobility and p. 120 on stature.
5   Ibid., p. 116 and McCullough, *John Adams*, p. 404–405.
6   Gail S. Cleere's text, *The House on Observatory Hill: Home of the Vice President of the United States*, offers an informative history of "Admirals House," located at the Naval Observatory in Washington, DC.
7   Feerick, *From Failing Hands*, p. 68.
8   Ibid., pp. 68–69.
9   *Annals of Congress*, 1st Congress, 1st sess., pp. 60, 78, 79.
10 Feerick, *From Failing Hands*, p. 69 and Guerrero, *John Adams'*, pp. 72–74.
11 Hatfield, *Vice Presidents*, p. 12, n.1. John Adams casting twenty-nine tie-breaking votes was verified by the Senate Historical Office. Hatfield also notes that Vice President George Dallas took "personal satisfaction" in holding the record for tie-breaking votes with thirty; however, only nineteen of Dallas's votes have ever been verified, pp. 158–159, and p.162, n. 35. In addition, Henry Learned, in "Casting Votes of the Vice-Presidents," notes twenty-nine tie-breaking votes to the first vice president, followed by John Calhoun with twenty-eight and George Dallas with nineteen, p. 571. However, Linda Guerrero, in her text *John Adams'*, places the number of tie-breaking votes by Adams at thirty-one, p. 128.
12 Guerrero, *John Adams'*, pp. 28, 145.
13 Ibid., p. 76.
14 See Learned, "Casting Votes of the Vice-Presidents," for the "power of removal" precedent, p. 574.
15 In *John Adams*, David McCullough points to George Washington's singularity in that Washington was "immensely popular, elected unanimously, and all but impervious to criticism," p. 484.
16 Guerrero, *John Adams'*, p. 187.
17 Ibid., p. 186.
18 Interview with Francis J. Attig, United States Senate Historical Office—Oral History Project, April 5, 1978, p. 73. Interview conducted by Donald A. Ritchie.
19 Article II, sec. 2.
20 The president's power to appoint the heads of the executive departments is granted in Article II, sec. 2 of the Constitution.

21   Guerrero notes: "Significantly for Adams' relationship with Washington, the New Englander viewed his office as strictly residing in the legislative branch," in *John Adams'*, p. 185.

22   Ibid.

23   John Adams in reply to a letter from James Lovell; from McCullough, *John Adams*, p. 414.

24   Guerrero notes that John Adams was so dissatisfied with the vice presidency that he considered resigning from office, in *John Adams'*, pp. 66–67.

25   Jefferson, *Best Letters*, p. 89. From a letter to James Madison dated January 1, 1797.

26   According to one biographer, Vice President Jefferson "presided discreetly over the Senate when that body was in session." Schachner, *Thomas Jefferson*, p. 590.

27   For an account of Jefferson privately recording "every bit of gossip he could" on Adams and the Federalists, see Schachner, *Thomas Jefferson*, p. 591. And regarding Jefferson distancing himself from Adams and his administration, David McCullough notes that Vice President Jefferson "had so effectively separated himself ... that he could be held accountable for nothing that had disappointed, displeased, or infuriated anyone," in *John Adams*, p. 544.

28   Jefferson, *Best Letters*, p. 89.

29   For a brief description of Thomas Jefferson presiding in the Senate and how it differed from when John Adams presided, see McCullough, *John Adams*, p. 535.

30   Jefferson, *Best Letters*, p. 91.

31   See Hatfield for the importance of Thomas Jefferson's manual, in *Vice Presidents*, p. 25, as well as McCullough's *John Adams* for the same, p. 535.

32   Jefferson, *Best Letters*, p. 90.

33   Lomask, *Aaron Burr*, p. 298.

34   Hatfield, *Vice Presidents*, p. 37.

35   Ibid., pp. 37–39.

36   Burr's return to the Senate, under indictment for murder, has been recounted innumerable times; for one concise retelling, see Young, *American Roulette*, pp. 17–18.

37   On February 11, 2006, Vice President Cheney was quail hunting with Harry Whittington, a contributor to the Bush-Cheney campaigns of 2000 and 2004, when he accidentally shot Whittington in the face and chest with bird pellet, seriously wounding the seventy-eight year old man and landing him in intensive care.

38   *Senate Journal.* 8th Cong., 2nd sess., March 2, 1805, p.71.

39   Schachner, *Thomas Jefferson*, p. 790.

40   Williams, *Rise of the Vice Presidency*, p. 33.

41   For specific reference to George Clinton's strategy for gaining the presidential and vice-presidential nominations at the same time, see Brant, "Election of 1808," p. 202; likewise, Brant offers a broad summary of Clinton's efforts to gain the presidency in 1808, pp. 195–212.

42   Ibid., p. 202.

43   Ibid., p. 201.

44   Although the procedures for filling vacancies in the presidency were modified in 1967 by the Twenty-fifth Amendment, the Constitution, in Article 2, sec. 1, originally directed that "the Congress may by Law provide for the Case of Removal, Death, Resignation or

Inability, both of the President and Vice President, declaring what Officer shall then act as President, and such Officer shall act accordingly, until the Disability be removed, or a President shall be elected."

45   Feerick, *From Failing Hands*, pp. 60–61.

46   Ibid., pp. 61–62.

47   For a broad treatment of the Succession Act of 1886, see Feerick, *From Failing Hands*, pp. 140–146.

48   In President Truman's June 19, 1945, message to Congress, Truman argued "the office of the President should be filled by an elective officer," and not by individuals nominated by the president.

49   Feerick, *From Failing Hands*, p. 205.

50   Appendix B contains the complete text of the Presidential Succession Act of 1947.

51   Madison, *Notes of Debates*, p. 596.

52   Williams, *Rise of the Vice Presidency*, p. 20.

53   Risjord, "Election of 1812," p. 252.

54   The impetus for the term arose when then-Governor Gerry and members of his party in the Massachusetts legislature redrew the state's electoral map in a shape similar to a salamander. At the time, political pundits combined Gerry's name with salamander, creating the term gerrymandering, and forever using it pejoratively.

55   According to Risjord, in "Election of 1812," Elbridge Gerry was nominated for vice president because "he was too old to threaten the Virginia succession in 1816," p. 252.

56   See Ray Irwin's *Daniel D. Tompkins*, pp. 209–210, for three possible explanations of how Tompkins became the vice-presidential nominee, instead of the presidential nominee.

57   In *Daniel D. Tompkins*, Irwin provides Jabez Hammond's concise summation of the complex but innocent financial situation that plagued Tompkins: "He was irregular and unmethodical in business; not systematical in keeping his accounts; employed too many agents; mingled his own private funds with those of the public; was naturally careless about money, and sometimes profuse in his expenses ... No candid man charged him with intentional dishonesty in his pecuniary transactions," p. 203.

58   In his *Autobiography*, Martin Van Buren describes Daniel Tompkins and the emotional and physical toll of his financial problems, as well as Van Buren's efforts to resolve some of Tompkins's affairs, pp. 94–98.

59   According to Irwin, it was nearly twenty-two years after Tompkins's death, before resolution of his finances was achieved and his heirs realized some restitution; in *Daniel D. Tompkins*, p. 307.

60   The absence of Tompkins at the inauguration is noted in Irwin's *Daniel D. Tompkins*, p. 264. Also, Tompkins attempted to regain the governorship of New York in the election of 1820; however, he failed in that effort, but he was reelected vice president.

61   Ibid., p. 264.

62   Adams, *Diary*, p. 314. The diary entry referenced was recorded January 25, 1824.

63   Jackson, *Correspondence*, Vol. 3, p. 148. The passage referenced is from a letter to Andrew Jackson from Dr. James C. Bronaugh, dated February 8, 1822.

64   For the Virginia presidents and Tompkins, see Irwin, *Daniel D. Tompkins*, pp. 307–308. And with regard to Tompkins working for the abolition of slavery in New York, Irwin

notes: "One of Tompkins' most highly-commended public acts before resigning the governorship had to do with slavery in New York. On January 28, 1817, the Governor sent a special message to the legislature, requesting that body to make further and more specific provision for the abolition of slavery throughout the state," p. 211.

65   Hopkins, "Election of 1824," p. 360.

66   For a summary of the candidate preference contests held in 1824, see Hopkins, "Election of 1824," pp. 360–363.

67   Van Buren, *Autobiography*, p. 514; and Hopkins, "Election of 1824," p. 367.

68   In terms of the secretary of state moving to the presidency: through the election of 1824, presidents Thomas Jefferson, James Madison, James Monroe and John Quincy Adams all served as secretary of state prior to gaining the presidency, with only Jefferson, of the previous group, and President John Adams moving directly from the vice presidency to the presidency.

69   On John Calhoun's move toward Andrew Jackson, see Remini, "Election of 1828," pp. 414–415.

70   For a discussion of Vice President Calhoun's congressionally approved role selecting Senate committee members, see Hatfield, *Vice Presidents*, pp. 87–88. And for a review of Senate measures to abolish the Electoral College, attempts to limit the president to two terms in office, and efforts at better defining the vice president's proper place in Senate proceedings, again reference the Hatfield text, pp. 89–92.

71   Learned, "Casting Votes of the Vice-Presidents," p. 572.

72   Ibid., p. 571, fn. 1.

73   See Van Buren, *Autobiography*, on the efforts of Vice President Calhoun and others in the Senate to defeat Van Buren's ministerial nomination, pp. 512–513 and pp. 532–534.

74   Ibid., p. 509. Passage is in a letter from Martin Van Buren to WM. L. Marcy Esq., dated March 14, 1832.

75   Richard Hofstadter offers a compelling summation of the political thought and career of John Calhoun in his seminal text, *The American Political Tradition: And the Men Who Made It*, pp. 87–118.

76   According to Hatfield, Jackson "prevailed" in getting the VP nomination for Van Buren; in *Vice Presidents*, p. 109.

77   With Andrew Jackson's choice of Martin Van Buren in 1832, it was not until the 1940 Democratic convention, when President Franklin Roosevelt insisted on making his agriculture secretary, Henry A. Wallace, his running mate, that a presidential candidate played such a decisive role when choosing a running mate.

78   Van Buren, *Autobiography*, p. 506.

79   Ibid.

80   Hatfield asserts that Martin Van Buren was the first vice president in over thirty years to have "assumed the office as the heir apparent" to the presidency; in *Vice Presidents*, p.105.

81   Van Buren, *Autobiography*, p. 673.

82   See Van Buren for an explanation of his reluctance to interfere in the Senate committee selection process; in *Autobiography*, p. 673. Also, Hatfield provides a succinct summa-

tion of the politics surrounding the Senate committee selection process in 1833; in *Vice Presidents*, pp. 111–112.

83 Van Buren devotes considerable attention to Andrew Jackson and the Bank of the United States in his *Autobiography*, passim. Also, for a summary pertaining to Jackson's fight with the Senate over the Bank of the United States, see Hatfield, *Vice Presidents*, pp. 112–114.

84 Hatfield, *Vice Presidents*, pp. 112–113.

85 Ibid., p. 113.

86 According to Hatfield, no vice president prior to Van Buren had "a greater measure of influence" on the president; in *Vice Presidents*, p. 105 and p. 111.

87 Ibid., p. 114.

88 In his *Autobiography*, Martin Van Buren rarely references Richard Johnson; moreover, not once in the entire text does Van Buren indicate that Johnson served as his running mate or as his vice president.

89 Hatfield, *Vice Presidents*, p. 128.

90 Ibid., p. 129.

91 On Richard Johnson's wives and mistresses, among others, see May, *John Tyler*, pp. 3–4, and Hatfield, *Vice Presidents*, p. 129.

92 Jackson, *Correspondence*, Vol. 6., p. 246.

93 Sirgiovanni, "Dumping the Vice President: An Historical Overview and Analysis," p. 768.

94 Ibid.

95 Jackson, *Correspondence*, Vol. 6., p. 246. From a letter to Martin Van Buren dated November 11, 1843.

96 Tyler was described as "His Accidency" by any number of his contemporaries, and later biographers, though the originator of the unfortunate moniker remains unknown. Among others, Peterson notes the preceding descriptor for Tyler in *Presidencies of William Henry Harrison & John Tyler*, p. 50.

97 Adams, *Diary*, pp. 520–521.

98 Schlesinger, Jr., "On the Presidential Succession," p. 488.

99 Madison, *Notes of Debates*, p. 594.

100 Ibid., p. 594.

101 U.S. Constitution, Article 2, sec. 1, paragraph 6.

102 Peterson, *Presidencies of William Henry Harrison & John Tyler*, p. 45. Peterson also offers a broad consideration of some of the questions to arise about the vice president and presidential succession on pp. 45–50.

103 Ibid., p. 48.

104 Monroe, *Republican Vision of John Tyler*, p. 81. In the same passage, Monroe claims Tyler's decision to retain the Harrison cabinet was one he would regret.

105 See Belohlavek's *George Mifflin Dallas* for the politics of the Tariff of 1846, pp. 110–118.

106 *Congressional Globe*, 29th Cong., 1st sess., 1846, p. 1156.

107 Ibid. Also, Belohlavek notes Dallas's idea of a vice-presidential veto in *George Mifflin Dallas*, p. 112.

108 Belohlavek, *George Mifflin Dallas*, p. 114.

109 *Congressional Globe*, 29th Cong., 1st sess., 1846, p. 1156.

110   See Hatfield, *Vice Presidents*, on the first meeting between Dallas and Polk, p. 155. Franklin Roosevelt also points to the strength of the Polk-Dallas association in "Can the Vice President be Useful?" p. 82.

111   Polk's *Diary* contains examples of President Polk's interactions with Vice President Dallas, including references to business before the Senate, pp. 52, 251, Vol. 2; foreign affairs, p. 181, Vol. 1; expansion of the United States, pp. 106, 456-457, Vol. 1; and social events, p. 292, Vol. 2.

112   Belohlavek, *George Mifflin Dallas*, pp. 110–111.

113   Ibid., pp. 134–136.

114   Elbert Smith, in *Presidencies of Zachary Taylor & Millard Fillmore*, makes the point that Fillmore had considerable legislative skills gained from many years in the House of Representatives; however, "Taylor and his cabinet made no effort whatsoever to use Fillmore's talents as a legislative manager," p. 165.

115   According to one account, James Buchanan was offered the vice-presidential spot on the ticket with Franklin Pierce, but he was unwilling to settle for the vice presidency; in Baker, *James Buchanan*, p. 57. However, William King's principal biographer, Daniel Fate Brooks, does not mention Buchanan's ever being offered or declining the vice-presidential nomination; instead, Brooks contends that Buchanan's supporters willingly backed Pierce for the presidential nomination, but only if King's name was attached to the ticket; in "The Faces of William Rufus King," pp. 21–22.

116   Baker covers James Buchanan's alleged homosexuality and Buchanan's friendship with William King in *James Buchanan*, pp. 25–26. Also, see Brooks for reference to the King-Buchanan relationship in "The Faces of William Rufus King," p. 18.

117   Baker, *James Buchanan*, p. 25.

118   Ibid., p. 25. Allegedly, the nieces of King and of Buchanan agreed to destroy the letters between the two men upon Buchanan's election to the presidency.

119   For a summation of the health of William King, and of his futile effort to recover in Cuba, refer to Brooks, "The Faces of William Rufus King," pp. 22–23.

120   According to the pamphlet, "The Vice President's Room," produced by the Office of Senate Curator: "Due to lack of space in the Capitol's old Senate wing, early vice presidents often shared their room with the president. Following the 1850s extension of the building, the Senate formally set aside a room for the vice president's exclusive use."

121   Binder, *James Buchanan*, p. 223.

122   There are countless retellings of the events of the 1860 presidential election; for a succinct review, see Morison's "Election of 1860," pp. 1097–1122. The appendix to Morison's essay also provides the platforms of the two factions of the Democratic Party, as well as the platforms of the Republican Party and the Constitutional Union Party, pp. 1123–1127.

123   Hamlin, *Life and Times*, p. 367.

124   Ibid., pp. 367–375. Also see Nickolay's *Abraham Lincoln* for reference to Lincoln and Hamlin's first meeting, as well as Lincoln seeking input on possible cabinet appointments from a number of different individuals, p. 347. And Feerick similarly notes Lincoln's overtures to Hamlin for advice on the cabinet and other matters in *From Failing Hands*, p. 107.

125 Hannibal Hamlin suggested Gideon Welles of Connecticut for secretary of the navy—a choice he later claimed to regret; in Hamlin, *Life and Times*, p.369, and pp. 415–417.

126 Ibid., p. 412.

127 Ibid.

128 Ibid., pp. 428–429.

129 Ibid., p. 429.

130 Ibid., pp. 429–433.

131 Hay, *Inside Lincoln's White House*, p. 18.

132 Feerick, *From Failing Hands*, pp. 107–108; and Hyman, "Election of 1864," p. 1168.

133 See Hamlin for a comprehensive assessment of Andrew Johnson's nomination for vice president and the conflicting views of Abraham Lincoln's role, or lack of, in securing Johnson's nomination; in *Life and Times*, pp. 461–489. Conversely, see Hyman's "Election of 1864" for his unequivocal assertion that "the President swung the convention to this view so successfully that the Johnson nomination did not require a second ballot and so adroitly that the party's factions accepted the choices," p. 1168.

134 For documentation of the effort by John G. Nicolay and others to correct the record on Abraham Lincoln's preference for Hannibal Hamlin's nomination for a second term in 1864, see "Supplement" in Hamlin, *Life and Times*, pp. 591–615.

135 For a first-hand account of Andrew Johnson's activities prior to, and during, his inaugural, see Hamlin, *Life and Times*, pp. 497–498.

136 Among others, see Hatfield's description of Andrew Johnson's behavior at his inauguration, including Johnson's inability to swear-in new senators; in *Vice Presidents*, p. 213.

137 As of this writing, Schuler Colfax and John Nance Garner are the only vice presidents to have served as Speaker of the House before winning the vice presidency. And James Polk is, thus far, the only former Speaker of the House to make it to the presidency.

138 Smith, *Schuyler Colfax*, p. 332. Colfax's words appeared in a public letter he had penned to Fredrick Douglas, Jr., on May 7, 1872, and which was subsequently published in an Indiana newspaper on May 10, 1872.

139 *Joint Resolution Proposing to Amend the Constitution*. S Res. 7, 42nd Cong., 2nd sess., (May 30, 1872), pp. 1–5.

140 Ibid., p. 5.

141 Smith, *Schuyler Colfax*, p. 330.

142 U.S. Congress. *Senate Journal*. 41st Cong., 1st sess., May 23, 1871, p. 178.

143 Schuyler Colfax had a substantial and successful career writing and lecturing. For a consideration of this aspect of his life, see Smith, *Schuyler Colfax*, passim.

144 Ibid., p. 327.

145 Ibid., pp. 331–332.

146 Ibid., pp. 338–345.

147 The machinations that resulted in Colfax not gaining the nomination in 1872 are covered in Smith's *Schuyler Colfax*, pp. 345–355.

148 For a brief review of the scandal that ended Schuyler Colfax's political career, see Hatfield, *Vice Presidents*, pp. 228–229, and for a detailed account of the affair, see Smith, *Schuyler Colfax*, pp. 369–416.

149 McFeely, *Grant*, p. 385.

150   Hatfield, *Vice Presidents*, pp. 246–247.

151   Howe, *Chester A. Arthur*, p. 152 and Feerick, *From Failing Hands*, pp. 123–128.

152   Feerick documents Vice President Arthur's behavior for the entirety of Garfield's ordeal, as well as the attention paid by the nation and the press to how Arthur responded in *From Failing Hands*, pp.121–123 and pp. 127–128.

153   According to Feerick, from the moment that President Garfield was shot until his death nearly three months later, Vice President Arthur "was never able to meet and speak with Garfield," in *From Failing Hands*, p. 123.

154   Feerick notes that such restrictions were imposed in spite of Garfield's explicit request to meet with his entire cabinet; in *From Failing Hands*, pp.125–127.

155   Howe, *Chester A. Arthur*, p. 152.

156   President Chester Arthur Message to Congress, December 6, 1881.

157   By one account, when Cleveland discovered that "many men in high office, including Vice President Hendricks, were lending their clout to undesirable applicants, the President began to wonder just who in his official family he could trust," in Brodsky, *Grover Cleveland*, p. 123.

158   Levi Morton served as minister to France in the Garfield and Arthur administrations.

159   Levi Morton owed his vice-presidential nomination to the New York political machine headed by Thomas Platt; his loyalty to Platt never wavered in the four years he was Benjamin Harrison's vice president.

160   Morgan, "Election of 1892," p. 1716.

161   Adlai Stevenson's nomination came about for balance, in part because Stevenson was for silver, while Cleveland was for gold, and also because Cleveland insisted on the selection of Stevenson; in Morgan, "Election of 1892," p. 1720. Also, Alyn Brodsky notes in his text, *Grover Cleveland*, that "Stevenson was a soft-money man; it was hoped he would help the party among the western silverites in general and in Illinois in particular," p. 274. And in terms of Stevenson's reputation for patronage politics: in the first Cleveland administration he was appointed first assistant postmaster general; once installed, he replaced approximately 40,000 Republican postmasters with Democratic postmasters; in Hatfield, *Vice Presidents*, p. 280.

162   Hatfield, *Vice Presidents*, pp.281–282.

163   Brodsky, *Grover Cleveland*, pp. 310–311.

164   Ibid., pp. 313–315.

165   Magie, *Life of Garret Augustus Hobart*, p. 167.

166   Ibid., p. 169; and Feerick, *From Failing Hands*, pp. 152–153.

167   Dawes, *Journal of the McKinley Years*, p. 207.

168   See Thayer's *Theodore Roosevelt*, pp. 143–150 and pp. 208–209. Also, Dunn's *From Harrison to Harding* includes an extended account of the factions and machinations behind Roosevelt's nomination for vice president, pp. 331–337.

169   Thayer, *Theodore Roosevelt*, pp. 143–144.

170   For a good portrait of Theodore Roosevelt's restless vigor, see *Theodore Rex* by Edmund Morris, and his retelling of Captain Archibald Butt's visit to Roosevelt's summer home, Sagamore Hill, pp. 529–533. Also, William Roscoe Thayer offers a first-hand description of

Roosevelt's energy, activities, and character in *Theodore Roosevelt*, Chapter 27, "Roosevelt at Home," pp. 255–280.

171 Roosevelt, *Works of Theodore Roosevelt*, p. 78.

172 Thayer, *Theodore Roosevelt*, p. 153.

173 Roosevelt, "The Three Vice-Presidential Candidates," p. 289.

174 Thayer, *Theodore Roosevelt*, p. 327. Also, in *Theodore Rex*, Edmund Morris describes Fairbanks this way: "At six foot four, Fairbanks moved and spoke as if he had no life of his own. His voice seemed to emanate from some inner Edison cylinder, and his gestures were correct but mechanical, as if jerked by hidden wires," p. 353.

175 On the occasion of Theodore Roosevelt leaving town for a hunting trip, Edmund Morris claims: "Rather than leave the White House in charge of Vice President Fairbanks, who had been relegated to near-total obscurity since the Inauguration, Roosevelt assigned crisis-management powers to William Howard Taft," in *Theodore Rex*, p. 380.

176 Thayer, *Theodore Roosevelt*, p. 314 and Gould, *Presidency of Theodore Roosevelt*, pp. 283–284.

177 Gould notes that first Charles Evans Hughes, and then Albert J. Beveridge, refused offers for the nomination; in *Presidency of Theodore Roosevelt*, p. 284. In addition, at the time of James Sherman's nomination, Hughes was approached on behalf of both Theodore Roosevelt and William Howard Taft and offered the nomination for vice president; Hughes was told that if he accepted, a bonus of $100,000 was his for the taking; in Morris, *Theodore Rex*, p. 527, n. 735.

178 Gould notes the assumed seamlessness of the transition from the Roosevelt to the Taft administration on account of the closeness of the two principals; in *Presidency of Theodore Roosevelt*, p. 290.

179 Gould, *Four Hats in the Ring*, p. 156.

180 Learned, "Casting Votes of the Vice-Presidents," p. 575. In total, Vice President James Sherman cast only four tie-breaking votes. The fourth tie-breaking vote was on an amendment to what eventually became the Seventeenth Amendment to the United States Constitution, initiating the direct election of senators and, at the time, raising questions about the legitimate role of the vice president and amendments to the Constitution.

181 Gould, *Four Hats in the Ring*, p. 74 and p. 156.

182 Wilson, *Congressional Government*, p. 162.

183 Marshall, *Recollections*, p. 234.

184 Ibid., p. 230.

185 Herbert Hoover offers a succinct account of President Wilson's stroke and the handling of the affair in *Ordeal of Woodrow Wilson*, pp. 271–278. Also, see Feerick's chapter dealing exclusively with Wilson's inability in *From Failing Hands*, pp. 162–180.

186 Hoover, *Ordeal of Woodrow Wilson*, p. 275, and Feerick, *From Failing Hands*, pp. 170–171.

187 Feerick, *From Failing Hands*, pp. 176–179.

188 Ibid., p. 164.

Chapter 4

The Modern Vice Presidency: From Coolidge to Johnson

1   For a useful review of Calvin Coolidge's time as a state legislator, lieutenant governor, and governor, see Fuess, *Calvin Coolidge*, pp. 94–233. Also, for a summary of Coolidge's time in the Massachusetts legislature, and when he was state senate president, see Gilbert, *Tormented President*, pp. 70–76.

2   Gilbert, *Tormented President*, p. 74.

3   Fuess, *Calvin Coolidge*, p. 160. Gilbert also includes the same passage from Coolidge in *Tormented President*, p. 79.

4   For Calvin Coolidge's early political career and his progressive policy views, see Gilbert's *Tormented President*, pp. 61–90. And for a contrasting view, based on Coolidge's later years as a national figure, Herbert Hoover asserted in his *Memoirs* that "Mr. Coolidge was a real conservative, probably the equal of Benjamin Harrison," p. 56.

5   In *Road to Normalcy*, Wesley Bagby includes Calvin Coolidge with those floated for the presidential nomination at the 1920 Republican convention, p. 83. Also, see McCoy, "Election of 1920," p. 2353 and p. 2358, for Coolidge as a potential presidential nominee, and pp. 2359–2360 for Coolidge's eventual vice-presidential nomination. And for Coolidge's nomination for vice president, see Gilbert's *Tormented President*, pp. 99–101.

6   Hatch, *History of the Vice-Presidency*, p. 378.

7   Harry Daugherty, President Harding's adviser and attorney general, wrote in his memoirs, *The Inside Story of the Harding Tragedy*, that it was his idea, not Harding's, to make the cabinet open to Coolidge, pp. 277–278.

8   Ibid., p. 106. Contrary to popular views of the role Vice President Calvin Coolidge played in the Harding administration, Claude Fuess asserts that "Harding had great confidence in Coolidge, consulted him frequently, and was influenced by him to a marked degree," in *Calvin Coolidge*, p. 288. Oddly, in the same text, Fuess suggests Coolidge "seldom participated in the cabinet discussions," p. 289.

9   Coolidge, *Autobiography*, pp. 163–164.

10   Ibid., p. 161.

11   Ibid., p. 162.

12   Ibid.

13   See Schachner, *Thomas Jefferson*, p. 591.

14   Coolidge, *Autobiography*, pp. 160–161

15   Ibid., pp. 159–160.

16   McCoy, *Calvin Coolidge*, p. 145.

17   For an illuminating retelling of the circumstances of Calvin Coolidge taking the oath of office in his father's home in Vermont, see the April 1924 article in *The Ladies Home Journal*, "The Midnight Oath," pp. 17, 236.

18   Ibid., 17.

19   Because Calvin Coolidge's father was a notary in Vermont, and thus was legally empow-
       ered to swear in officials solely of that state, Coolidge took the presidential oath a second
       time, upon his arrival in the capital, and this time administered by a federal judge.

20   Fuess, *Calvin Coolidge*, p. 345.

21   William Allen White offers an amusing play-by-play of Frank Lowden's nomination, and
       then the presentation of a letter of refusal from Lowden—all of which was broadcast across
       the nation by radio; in *Puritan in Babylon*, p. 304. Also, see Burner, "Election of 1924," p.
       2467.

22   Charles Dawes, in his *Notes as Vice President*, asserts that during the 1924 campaign
       he "traveled fifteen thousand miles in a special train and made one hundred and eight
       speeches," p. 19. Also, David Burner suggests that, for Dawes, the principal task in the
       campaign was to "carry on the partisan campaign for Coolidge"; in "Election of 1924," p.
       2467.

23   Gilbert, *Tormented President*, p. 175.

24   Robert Gilbert's text, *The Tormented President: Calvin Coolidge, Death, and Clinical
       Depression*, provides an exhaustive examination of Calvin Coolidge's life-long battle with
       depression. In brief, Gilbert's thesis is that Coolidge suffered from depression beginning
       in his boyhood and the death of his favorite son was the culminating tragedy in a series
       of such events, subsequently causing the president to suffer an emotional breakdown, and
       diminishing the remaining years of the Coolidge presidency.

25   Coolidge, *Autobiography*, p. 189.

26   Dawes, *Notes as Vice President*, p. 19.

27   Ibid., pp. 33–34.

28   Hatfield also notes the omission of Charles Dawes from Calvin Coolidge's autobiography
       in *Vice Presidents*, p. 364.

29   For the text of Charles Dawes's inaugural address, see his *Notes as Vice President*, pp.
       57–61.

30   Ibid., p. 61.

31   Ibid., pp. 183–184.

32   See Dawes, *Notes as Vice President*, pp. 5–8, and also Gilbert, *Tormented President*, p.
       203.

33   McCoy, *Calvin Coolidge*, p. 325.

34   Washington Correspondent, "Heap Big Chief," p. 405.

35   McCoy, *Calvin Coolidge*, pp. 268–269.

36   Hoover, *Memoirs*, Vol. 2, p. 194.

37   The childhood and adolescence of Charles Curtis is nicely summarized in Hatfield, *Vice
       Presidents*, pp. 373–375. Also, Curtis's sister, Dolly Gann, wrote a memoir, *Dolly Gann's
       Book*, which gives a decidedly biased view of her brother's life and career, particularly when
       he was the vice president and she served as his hostess, passim.

38   As to Charles Curtis and the presidential nomination: Fuchs notes that "Curtis was willing,
       but he was never really in the running," in "Election of 1928," p. 2603.

39   Washington Correspondent, "Heap Big Chief," p. 404.

40   Joseph Robinson, Alben Barkley, and Charles McNary are among the longest serving lead-
       ers in the Senate, having served fourteen, twelve, and eleven years, respectively. Charles

Curtis also served as Republican whip for nine years prior to becoming majority leader. Hubert Humphrey was Democratic whip in the Senate from 1961 until his nomination for vice president in 1964. Also, when Robert Dole was nominated for vice president, in 1976, he was on track for his party's leadership and later served as both minority and majority leader. And Dick Cheney was the Republican whip in the House of Representatives for a brief time, but he resigned from the position, and from the House, to join the cabinet of President George H.W. Bush in 1989.

41   In 1928, the Democratic nominee for vice president was Senate minority leader Joseph Robinson, and in 1932, Democrats nominated the Speaker of the House, John Nance Garner.

42   In a curious oversight, political scientist Joel Goldstein claims that John Nance Garner was the first vice president to regularly attend cabinet meetings; then, later in the same text, he identifies Calvin Coolidge as the first vice president to meet with the cabinet, only to follow that by incorrectly asserting, on the same page, that Herbert Hoover never invited Charles Curtis to attend cabinet meetings; in *Modern American*, p. 8 and p. 136.

43   See Hoover, *Memoirs of Herbert Hoover*, Vol. 1–3. Goldstein also notes Hoover "acknowledged no contribution Curtis made to his administration in his memoirs," in *Modern American*, p. 9.

44   Dawes, *Notes as Vice President*, p. 13. Also, Vice President Alben Barkley, who served in the Senate when Curtis was the vice president, commented on the efficacy with which Curtis presided; in "An Interview with Alben Barkley," University of Kentucky Oral History Program, August 5, 1953, BARK 17, Side #1; Reel #16, p. 7. Interview conducted by Sidney Shalett. Permission of use granted to the author by the University of Kentucky.

45   For reference to the haughtiness of Charles Curtis after his ascension to the vice presidency, see James, *Mr. Garner of Texas*, p. 141, as well as Hatfield, *Vice Presidents*, p. 380. In addition, Alben Barkley tells a story about Curtis and his insistence that senators never address him by his first name, only by his title; in "An Interview with Alben Barkley," University of Kentucky Oral History Program, August 5, 1953, BARK 17, Side #1, Reel #16, p. 7. Interview conducted by Sidney Shalett. Permission of use granted to the author by the University of Kentucky.

46   Washington Correspondent, "Heap Big Chief," p. 411.

47   Ibid., p. 405 and p. 406.

48   Ibid., p. 406.

49   In Freidel, "Election of 1932," p. 2716.

50   See Timmons, *Garner of Texas*, pp. 165–166 and p.168, and Freidel, "Election of 1932," pp. 2728–2729.

51   Key, Jr., *Politics*, p. 672.

52   See Barkley, "The Vice-Presidency," p. 13.

53   Timmons, *Garner of Texas*, p. 178.

54   Ibid., p. 184 and p. 193. Also, see James, *Mr. Garner of Texas*, p. 144.

55   Timmons, *Garner of Texas*, pp. 238–241. Also, for an explanation of Garner's personal conflict with Roosevelt's policies, see Schapsmeier, *Henry A. Wallace of Iowa*, p. 249.

56   In the 1936 election, Roosevelt and Garner received nearly twenty-eight million votes out of the over forty-five million popular votes cast, and in the Electoral College they received 523 of 531 electoral votes.

57   Timmons, *Garner of Texas*, pp. 215–217.

58   Ibid., p. 216.

59   For a colorful review of the circumstances that contributed to the defeat of Roosevelt's court-packing plan, see Timmons, *Garner of Texas*, pp. 217–225.

60   Ibid., pp. 230–237

61   See Garner, "Wisconsin Must Choose," p. 1.

62   Apparently John Nance Garner was not the only one who thought he should be president, though it came with a caveat. According to a Gallup poll conducted July 28–August 2, 1939 (Survey #165-A), 46 percent of Democratic voters suggested that they would like to see Garner get the 1940 presidential nomination of their party if Franklin Roosevelt did not seek a third term; in Gallup, *Gallup Poll, 1935–1971*. Vol. 1, p. 171.

63   Timmons, *Garner of Texas*, p. 240. Timmons notes that December 18, 1938, marks the last time that Garner and Roosevelt ever met alone—with an entire year still remaining in their term—and any meetings after that date were in the presence of other individuals.

64   Schapsmeier, *Henry A. Wallace of Iowa*, p. 265 and p. 267.

65   Roosevelt, "Can the Vice President Be Useful?", p. 82.

66   Schapsmeier, *Henry A. Wallace of Iowa*, p. 269.

67   "Reminiscences of Henry Agard Wallace," November 1950–May 1951, Columbia University Oral History Research Office Collection, p. 1308. Interview conducted by Dean Albertson. Permission of use granted to the author by Columbia University.

68   For a useful review of the Wallace-Jones conflict, see the chapter devoted exclusively to it in Schapsmeier, *Prophet in Politics*, pp. 50–71.

69   Ibid., pp. 50–51.

70   For the authoritative consideration of Henry Wallace's century of the common man, see his text of the same name: *The Century of the Common Man*, New York: Reynal and Hitchcock, 1943. In addition, in Schapsmeier's *Prophet in Politics*, pp. 35–36, the authors cover some of Wallace's ideas in this area, emphasizing that Roosevelt never entirely signed on to every one of Wallace's notions.

71   There is ample opinion on Henry Wallace's supposed mystical side. Alben Barkley, vice president to Harry Truman, claimed he was "troubled by some of the symptoms Wallace was displaying of the increasing mysticism which later made it possible for some left-wing groups to take advantage of him," in *That Reminds Me*, p. 186.

72   Schapsmeier, *Prophet in Politics*, pp. 14–17.

73   For a brief summary of Henry Wallace's trip to Mexico when he was the vice president-elect, see Schapsmeier, *Henry A. Wallace of Iowa*, pp. 279–280. In addition, see Culver, *American Dreamer*, pp. 246–249, for a recounting of the same trip.

74   James Buchanan also served as secretary of state before winning the presidency.

75   For Henry Wallace's description of his journey through Russia and China in 1944, see the text he authored, *Soviet Asia Mission*, New York: Reynal and Hitchcock, 1946. Also, for Wallace's day-by-day thoughts on the trip, see *Price of Vision*, pp. 334–360.

76 In Henry Wallace's published diary, *Price of Vision*, he notes that his "first speech in Russian … was well received," p. 343. For reference to Wallace's efforts toward learning Russian and then making "several speeches in Russian," see Schapsmeier, *Prophet in Politics*, p. 87, and see p. 88 for note of Wallace's "first major address given … to a Russian audience."

77 Henry Wallace embarked on his trip to the Soviet Union with the foreknowledge that the Soviets had the capability to produce an atomic bomb should they so choose; consequently, the display of technological advancements the Soviets offered Wallace when he visited Siberia no doubt hastened his concerns for what the host nation might be up to. For reference to Wallace's knowledge of Soviet atomic capabilities, see his *Price of Vision*, p. 42. And for Soviet scientists possibly being on par with American scientists, as well as the Soviet government making sure that Wallace saw an idyllic version of Siberia and the Russian people while he was there, see Schapsmeier, *Prophet in Politics*, p. 89 and pp. 91–92, respectively.

78 Among other references to the use of atomic energy for peaceful purposes, see Wallace, *Price of Vision*, p. 316 and pp. 522–523.

79 References to Henry Wallace's goals on his trip to China, specifically, as well as what the Chinese government hoped to gain from the trip are covered in Wallace's *Price of Vision*, pp. 347–359. And for a brief summary of Wallace's diplomatic efforts with China, see Schapsmeier, *Prophet in Politics*, p. 91–92.

80 For a good summary of Vice President Henry Wallace's tour of the Latin American nations, see Schapsmeier, *Prophet in Politics*, pp. 38–49.

81 Nelson Rockefeller was Coordinator of Inter-American Affairs for President Franklin Roosevelt and worked with Henry Wallace as a member of the Economic Defense Board.

82 Schapsmeier, *Prophet in Politics*, p. 46.

83 There is a great deal of anecdotal evidence of Henry Wallace's discomfort in the Senate. For one such account of Wallace in the Senate, see Schapsmeier, *Prophet in Politics*, pp. 7–8.

84 Miller, *Plain Speaking*, p. 187.

85 "An Interview with Alben Barkley," University of Kentucky Oral History Program, July 22, 1953, BARK 07, Tape #1, Side #2, Reel #5, p. 13. Interview conducted by Sidney Shalett. Permission of use granted to the author by the University of Kentucky.

86 Friedman, "Election of 1944," p. 3023.

87 Gallup, *Gallup Poll*, Vol. 1, p. 454.

88 On the first ballot for the vice-presidential nomination at the 1944 Democratic convention Henry Wallace received 429 ½ votes to 319 ½ for Harry Truman; the remainder of votes were split among assorted other candidates.

89 Friedman, "Election of 1944," p. 3024.

90 Wallace, *Price of Vision*, p. 367.

91 A thorough account of how Henry Wallace was kept off the Democratic Party ticket in 1944 may be found in "Defeat at the Democratic Convention and Victory in the Campaign of 1944," in Schapsmeier's *Prophet in Politics*, pp. 100–119. For Wallace's retelling of the people and circumstances depriving him of re-nomination, see *Price of Vision*, pp. 360–382.

92 Wallace, *Price of Vision*, p. 367.

93   For an account of the Senate confirmation process of Henry Wallace for secretary of commerce, see Schapsmeier, *Prophet in Politics*, pp. 121–124.

94   Miller, *Plain Speaking*, p. 209.

95   Ibid.

96   Marshall, *Recollections*, p. 201.

97   Alben Barkley discusses his weekly meetings with President Franklin Roosevelt, Vice President Henry Wallace, Speaker of the House Sam Rayburn, and House Majority Leader John McCormack in "An Interview with Alben Barkley," University of Kentucky Oral History Program, July 21, 1953; BARK 06, Tape #1, Side #2, p. 15–16. Interview conducted by Sidney Shalett. Permission of use granted to the author by the University of Kentucky.

98   Interview with Floyd M. Riddick, "Interview #3: The Office of Parliamentarian," United States Senate Historical Office—Oral History Project, July 12, 1978, p. 66 and p. 67. Interview conducted by Donald A. Ritchie.

99   Barkley, *That Reminds Me*, p. 207.

100   Executive Order No. 10016—Coat of Arms, Seal, and Flag of the Vice President of the United States, November 10, 1948, President Harry S. Truman. Truman's executive order revoked Executive Order No. 7285—Prescribing the Official Flag of the Vice President of the United States, February 7, 1936, President Franklin D. Roosevelt. Roosevelt's order initiated the creation of the first official flag for the vice president.

101   Alben Barkley discusses traveling across the nation to explain what the government does, and to advocate for the Truman administration, and how it was an unprecedented role for a vice president in "An Interview with Alben Barkley," University of Kentucky Oral History Program, July 22, 1953; BARK 07, Reel #6, Side #1, p. 20. Interview conducted by Sidney Shalett. Permission of use granted to the author by the University of Kentucky.

102   Costello, *Facts About Nixon*, p. 89.

103   According to Richard Nixon's friend and biographer, Earl Mazo: "Eisenhower informed his running mate that he viewed the Vice-Presidency as an important, meaningful office and believed the Vice-President should be an active participant with full knowledge of all that went on in an administration," in *Richard Nixon*, p. 90. Also, Ambrose notes that "Eisenhower wanted him [Nixon] present partly because he thought FDR had made a serious blunder in not keeping Harry Truman informed ... but, primarily because Nixon filled a real need—he could always be counted on to point out the political implications of any decision"; in *Nixon*, p. 309.

104   Ambrose discusses President Eisenhower's assignment of administrative tasks to Vice President Nixon; in *Nixon*, p. 30.

105   Data on Nixon's travels comes from Costello, *Facts About Nixon*, p. 247.

106   Mazo, *Richard Nixon*, p. 180.

107   Nixon's travels, in particular his first trip to Asia in 1953, is reviewed by Ambrose in *Nixon*, pp. 318–327.

108   Ibid., p. 319.

109   Mazo, *Richard Nixon*, p. 184.

110   Ibid., pp. 180–224. Mazo details alleged communist opposition to Nixon in the time he was traveling overseas, including claims that communist forces fomented riots and violence directed specifically toward him.

111   Kengor, "The Vice President, Secretary of State, and Foreign Policy," p. 183.

112   Nixon, *RN*, p. 205.

113   Ambrose, *Nixon*, p. 309.

114   Dwight Eisenhower is quoted by Richard Nixon in *RN*, pp. 87–88.

115   Nixon, *Six Crises*, "Section Three: The Heart Attack," pp. 131–181.

116   Ibid., p. 134.

117   Ibid., p. 143.

118   Feerick, *From Failing Hands*, pp. 227–228.

119   For the most important passages from President Eisenhower's directive see the White House Press Release of March 3, 1958, or Nixon, *Six Crises*, p. 179.

120   Nixon, *Six Crises*, p. 179.

121   Ibid.

122   Among others, see Ambrose's *Nixon*, pp. 384–408, for a detailed account of President Eisenhower vacillating about keeping Richard Nixon on the ticket in 1956. Also, Nixon weighs in on the speculation about his being retained for a second vice-presidential nomination in *Six Crises*, pp. 164–166.

123   See Nixon, *Six Crises*, pp. 158, 160, and 162.

124   Ibid., p. 162.

125   Interview with George A. Smathers, "Interview #6: Senate Democratic Leadership," United States Senate Historical Office—Oral History Project, September 19, 1989, p. 118. Interview conducted by Donald A. Ritchie.

126   O'Donnell, "*Johnny We Hardly Knew Ye*," p. 463. Quote is from President Lyndon Johnson on Senator Mike Mansfield's reluctance to join Vice President Hubert Humphrey in 1968 as Humphrey's vice-presidential running mate.

127   Sorensen, *Kennedy*, p. 162. From an unidentified interview with Senator John Kennedy.

128   O'Donnell, "*Johnny We Hardly Knew Ye*," pp. 221–222.

129   Transcript, James E. Webb Oral History Interview I, April 29, 1969, by T.H. Baker, Internet Copy, LBJ Library, p. 7.

130   Interview with George A. Smathers, "Interview #4: Kennedy and Johnson," United States Senate Historical Office—Oral History Project, September 5, 1989, pp. 88–89. Interview conducted by Donald A. Ritchie. In addition, for Lyndon Johnson's attempt to lead the Senate Democratic caucus as vice president, see Transcript, Hubert H. Humphrey Oral History Interview I, August 17, 1971, by Joe B. Frantz, Internet Copy, LBJ Library, p. 21.

131   Katherine Scott, United States Senate Historical Office, personal communication with the author, June 11, 2010. What was commonly referred to as the Old Executive Office Building (OEOB) was renamed the Eisenhower Executive Office Building. Every vice president since Lyndon Johnson has maintained a suite of offices in the building. Curiously, some scholars have incorrectly stated that Richard Nixon was the first vice president to have offices in the OEOB, including Richard Neustadt in his essay "Vice Presidents as National Leaders," p. 187. When Nixon was vice president he had offices in the building housing the Department of State, now named the Harry S. Truman Building.

132   President Kennedy's secretary of the interior, Stewart Udall, makes the point that Vice President Lyndon Johnson was used too sporadically by the administration in its dealings

with the Congress; in Transcript, Stewart L. Udall Oral History Interview I, April 18, 1969, by Joe B. Frantz, Internet Copy, LBJ Library, p. 11.

133 There are countless retellings of Vice President Lyndon Johnson's antics when traveling overseas, including a concise account in Doris Kearns's *Lyndon Johnson*, pp. 167–168. It should be noted that the Kearns text on Johnson's life devotes not quite nine pages of a 400 page manuscript to the Johnson vice presidency. Also, for how Johnson's travels abroad were perceived around the world as well as within the Kennedy administration, see Transcript, John Chancellor Oral History Interview I, April 25, 1969, by Dorothy Pierce McSweeny, Internet Copy, LBJ Library, pp. 8–9.

134 O'Donnell, *"Johnny We Hardly Knew Ye,"* p. 221.

135 Kearns, *Lyndon Johnson*, p. 164.

CHAPTER 5

THE MODERN VICE PRESIDENCY AND THE TWENTY-FIFTH AMENDMENT: FROM HUMPHREY TO QUAYLE

1 In *Hubert Humphrey*, Solberg notes that Humphrey was considered for the vice-presidential nomination in 1956, p. 174, and in 1960, p. 212.

2 Humphrey, "Changes in the Vice Presidency," p. 59.

3 Humphrey, *Education*, p. 415.

4 Ibid., p. 417.

5 There are assorted references to the incident related here. For a concise retelling of the events leading to Johnson's eventual ostracism of Humphrey from discussions on the United States policy on Vietnam—all of which stemmed from the incident—see Solberg, *Hubert Humphrey*, pp. 270–275.

6 Solberg, *Hubert Humphrey*, p. 274.

7 Valenti, *Very Human President*, p. 144.

8 On more than one occasion, President Johnson simply reclaimed any authority Vice President Humphrey held over a presidential task force, giving responsibility for formulation and implementation of the specific policy to an alternate individual or administration entity, instead.

9 Humphrey, "Changes in the Vice Presidency," p. 59.

10 Wattenberg, "The Clinton 2000 Effect in Perspective," pp. 166–167.

11 In his book, *One Heartbeat Away: Presidential Disability and Succession*, Senator Birch Bayh documents the arduous task of initiating, drafting, and passing the Twenty-fifth Amendment to the Constitution, passim.

12 For the entire text of the Twenty-fifth Amendment to the United States Constitution, see Appendix C.

13 For the text of the Presidential Succession Act of 1947, see Appendix B.

14 Schlesinger, "On the Presidential Succession," p. 500.

15   Ibid.

16   In addition to the pointed criticisms leveled by Arthur Schlesinger, Jr. in "On the Presidential Succession," Marie Natoli likewise offers brief, but specific criticism of the Twenty-fifth Amendment in her article "The Twenty-Fifth Amendment: Opening a Pandora's Box," passim.

17   Schlesinger, "On the Presidential Succession," p. 500.

18   Richard Nixon's deliberations on the choice of a running mate are reviewed at length in Theodore White's *Making of the President 1968*, pp. 249–253.

19   Humphrey, *Education*, p. 437.

20   Nixon, *RN*, p. 310.

21   White, *Making of the President 1968*, p. 143.

22   In 1968, Alabama Governor George Wallace ran as an independent candidate for president. Wallace, an avowed segregationist, tried to capitalize on the fear and anger many white Americans felt due to the prevalence of violence and riots in the late 1960s.

23   Interview with Floyd M. Riddick, "Interview #3: The Office of Parliamentarian," United States Senate Historical Office—Oral History Project, July 12, 1978, p. 68. Interview conducted by Donald A. Ritchie. Spiro Agnew's effort towards becoming a competent presiding officer is also noted in Hatfield's *Vice Presidents*, pp. 482–483.

24   Interview with Floyd M. Riddick, "Interview #3: The Office of Parliamentarian," United States Senate Historical Office—Oral History Project, July 12, 1978, pp. 67–68. Interview conducted by Donald A. Ritchie.

25   There are numerous retellings of Spiro Agnew's ostracism from the Senate; for one example see Hatfield, *Vice Presidents*, p. 483.

26   Elbridge Gerry quoted in Madison, *Notes of Debates*, p. 596.

27   For a brief review of Richard Nixon's proposal, see Lodge, *As it Was*, pp. 208–210.

28   Agnew, *Go Quietly*, p. 36.

29   Ibid.

30   "Reminiscences of Henry Agard Wallace," November 1950–May 1951, Columbia University Oral History Research Office Collection, p. 1308. Interview conducted by Dean Albertson. Permission of use granted to the author by Columbia University.

31   Agnew, *Go Quietly*, p. 35.

32   Ibid., p. 36.

33   Ibid., p. 34.

34   Ibid., p. 38 and p.128.

35   Ibid., p. 128.

36   Ibid., p. 130 and p. 202.

37   Ibid., p. 202. In *RN*, former president Richard Nixon noted that, with Agnew's resignation, "all it did was to open the way to put pressure on the President to resign as well," p. 1005.

38   Richard Nixon notes Agnew's suggestion to destroy the Watergate tapes twice in *RN*, first on p. 901, and then again on p. 1004.

39   Ibid., p. 814.

40   Haig, *Inner Circles*, p. 367.

41 Richard Nixon's preference for John Connally for vice president is frequently noted; including in his memoir *RN*, with Connally mentioned as an optional replacement candidate for Spiro Agnew in 1972, pp. 674–675, and later to fill the vacancy created by Spiro Agnew's resignation, pp. 925–926. Also, Agnew references Nixon's preference for Connally in *Go Quietly*, p. 130 and p. 201, as does Al Haig in *Inner Circles*, p. 363.

42 See Nixon, *RN*, p. 674 and p. 925, and Agnew, *Go Quietly*, p. 201.

43 Cannon, "Gerald R. Ford and Nelson A. Rockefeller," p. 135.

44 In a footnote in his memoirs, *Time to Heal*, Gerald Ford admits that John Connally, Nelson Rockefeller, and Ronald Reagan were Richard Nixon's preferred choices for the vice presidency, but Nixon knew Connally could not be confirmed, and choosing Rockefeller or Reagan "would split the party ideologically," therefore Ford was "the 'safest' choice," p. 107.

45 Ibid., p. 106.

46 Ibid., p. 105.

47 For the Senate hearings: see the transcript of the Hearings Before the Committee on Rules and Administration on the Nomination of Gerald R. Ford of Michigan to be Vice President of the United States, pp. 1–379. And for the House of Representatives: see the transcript of the Hearings Before the Committee on the Judiciary on Nomination of Gerald R. Ford to be the Vice President of the United States, pp. 1–798.

48 Ford, *Time to Heal*, p. 106.

49 In *Time to Heal*, Ford documents his conversation with his wife on the night Nixon asked him to be the nominee, p. 106; and he then notes that at his confirmation hearings he suggested he had only wanted to serve as Speaker of the House, p. 110.

50 Ford describes Nixon's ideas for a Ford vice presidency in *Time to Heal*, p. 105, and on p. 114.

51 Gerald Ford's brief speech made after he was sworn in as the fortieth vice president can be found reprinted in numerous publications; however, the simplest means for locating the text of Ford's remarks is by accessing "The Digital Ford Presidential Library: Vice Presidency," located at the website of the Gerald R. Ford Library and Museum.

52 According to Arthur Schlesinger, Jr., in "On the Presidential Succession": "Nixon, even in his feeble condition of 1974, was no more disposed to share power with Ford than he had shared power with Agnew," p. 478.

53 Cannon, "Gerald R. Ford and Nelson A. Rockefeller," p. 136.

54 Ibid. For a further evaluation of Ford's time as vice president, see James Cannon's review of that time period in *Time and Chance: Gerald R. Ford's Appointment With History*.

55 Ford, *Time to Heal*, p. 114.

56 Humphrey, *Education*, p. 426.

57 Ford notes his preparation for the presidency, while still vice president, in *Time to Heal*, p. 121, as does Cannon, in "Gerald R. Ford and Nelson A. Rockefeller," p. 136.

58 Ford, *Time to Heal*, p. 142.

59 Ibid.

60 According to Gerald Ford, in his memoir *Time to Heal*: other than Nelson Rockefeller, Richard Nixon "didn't identify anyone else by name," for a possible replacement vice president, p. 29.

61 Broder, "Election of 1968," p. 3729; and Solberg, *Hubert Humphrey*, p. 351.

62 Ford, *Time to Heal*, p. 143.

63 There are many references to Nelson Rockefeller's disavowal of any interest in the vice presidency; for one see Cannon, "Gerald R. Ford and Nelson A. Rockefeller," p. 137.

64 In "Finding a Policy Role for the Vice President," Michael Turner reviews the confirmation process Nelson Rockefeller endured, specifically with regard to the financial holdings of Rockefeller's extended family, pp. 73–81.

65 Transcripts from the House of Representatives, Hearings Before the Committee on the Judiciary on Nomination of Nelson A. Rockefeller to be Vice President of the United States, p. 2.

66 Ibid., pp. 1–1,455.

67 Rockefeller's lengthy confirmation hearings having an impact on his vice presidency has been noted over the years; for a sampling, see Ford, *Time to Heal*, pp. 223–224; Cannon, "Gerald R. Ford and Nelson A. Rockefeller," pp. 138–139; Turner, "Finding a Policy Role," passim; and Light, *Vice-Presidential Power*, pp. 180–183.

68 Cannon, "Gerald R. Ford and Nelson A. Rockefeller," pp. 137-138.

69 For various accounts of Nelson Rockefeller's expectations for his vice presidency, see Ford, *Time to Heal*, p. 145, Turner, "Finding a Policy Role," passim, and specifically pp. 262–271, as well as Light, *Vice-Presidential Power*, p. 179.

70 The practice of weekly private meetings between the president and vice president is often credited to President Jimmy Carter and Vice President Walter Mondale, when it was actually Gerald Ford and Nelson Rockefeller who began the ritual. Among others, Ford describes his meetings with the vice president in *Time to Heal*, p. 327.

71 One example of the obstructionism Nelson Rockefeller faced from within the White House comes from Henry Kissinger, who claimed that "the White House staff systematically undercut Rockefeller's role as vice chairman of the Domestic Council, to which Ford had appointed him"; in *Years of Renewal*, p. 188.

72 Ford, *Time to Heal*, p. 296.

73 For a brief review of staff rivalries, see Light, *Vice-Presidential Power*, pp. 129–131.

74 Ambrose, *Nixon*, p. 303.

75 Ford, *Time to Heal*, p. 145, and Light, *Vice-Presidential Power*, p. 179.

76 Kissinger, *Years of Renewal*, p. 188.

77 In Cannon, "Gerald R. Ford and Nelson A. Rockefeller," p. 139; and Light, *Vice-Presidential Power*, p. 179.

78 See Light for reference to Donald Rumsfeld coveting the vice-presidential nomination in 1974, as well as in 1976, in *Vice-Presidential Power*, pp. 189–190.

79 For a brief recounting of Nelson Rockefeller's arduous confirmation hearings, and how the length and complications of that process undermined his time in office, see Light, *Vice-Presidential Power*, pp. 180–183. Much of what Light suggests is covered more extensively, and earlier, in Michael Turner's "Finding a Policy Role," pp. 51–80, 261–270.

80 Light, *Vice-Presidential Power*, pp. 187–192.

81 Ford, *Time to Heal*, pp. 234–235.

82 Cheney is quoted by Warshaw in *Powersharing*, p. 87.

83 Ibid., pp. 90–91.

84   Ford, *Time to Heal*, p. 327.

85   Ibid., pp. 327–328.

86   Ibid., p. 328; and Kissinger, *Years of Renewal*, p. 837.

87   Kissinger, *Years of Renewal*, p. 188.

88   Cannon, "Gerald R. Ford and Nelson A. Rockefeller," p. 142.

89   Ford, *Time to Heal*, p. 280, and Cannon, "Gerald R. Ford and Nelson A. Rockefeller," p. 142.

90   For a concise, though skeptical review of the various investigations into the Central Intelligence Agency during the 1970s, see Kissinger, *Years of Renewal*, pp. 310–343.

91   The papers of Rayburn D. Hanzlik, Coordinator of Public Forums and Associate Director of Intergovernmental Affairs, offer a comprehensive record of Vice President Rockefeller's public policy forums. Hanzlik's papers are held by the Gerald R. Ford Presidential Library and Museum.

92   Light, *Vice-Presidential Power*, p. 73.

93   Beginning with Vice President Spiro Agnew, the office of the vice president, and the vice president's top aides, were listed in the *United States Government Organization Manual 1972/73*, p. 89. It has been suggested that including the vice president's office in the government publication, though a "simple" act, has furthered the institutionalization of the office; in Light, *Vice-Presidential Power*, p. 70.

94   Lewis, *Mondale*, pp. 14, 185.

95   Mondale, "Sideman," p. 4. The manuscript provided by Walter Mondale of his lecture is capitalized in its entirety; therefore, for all direct quotations from the lecture, capitalization choices have been made at the author's discretion.

96   Ibid., pp. 6–7. A scanned PDF file of the memorandum Walter Mondale submitted to Jimmy Carter is available from the Minnesota Historical Society, dated December 9, 1976, and titled: "The Role of the Vice President in the Carter Administration."

97   Mondale, "Sideman," p. 7. Also see Carter, *Keeping Faith*, p. 39.

98   Mondale, "Sideman," p. 7.

99   Carter, *Keeping Faith*, p. 39.

100   Ibid.

101   Mondale, "Sideman," p. 7.

102   Ibid., p. 8.

103   Ibid.

104   Ibid., pp. 10–12.

105   Ibid., p. 9.

106   There are numerous newspaper accounts of Mondale's early mission to South Africa; however, for a concise retelling of the trip, see Lewis, *Mondale*, pp. 221–224.

107   Mondale was sent abroad for the first time as vice president just three days after taking office. On that occasion he traveled to Japan, a nation to which he would return sixteen years later as the United States ambassador, having been appointed to the post by President Bill Clinton.

108   In his biography of Walter Mondale, Finlay Lewis claims that South Africa was a "sovereign nation whose politicians were notoriously sensitive about outside meddling," in *Mondale*, p. 223.

109   Ibid., p. 222.

110   Ibid., pp. 222–223. Vice President Mondale's advocacy for universal suffrage in South Africa came at a press conference on the closing day of the Vienna summit.

111   Mondale summarizes his involvement in the Camp David accords in "Sideman," pp. 16–17.

112   Ibid., pp. 13–15. Mondale briefly describes the Indochinese refuge problem, and his personal satisfaction with the speech he delivered to the special conference of the United Nations held in Geneva, Switzerland, July 20–21, 1979.

113   According to *The 1980 World Book Yearbook*, $190 million was pledged in relief for the Indochinese refugees, p. 514.

114   Carter, *Keeping Faith*, p. 39.

115   The work of the Hoover Commission resulted in voluminous recommendations. For a summation of the proposal for an administrative vice president, see the following document: U.S. Congress, Senate, 84th Cong., 2nd sess., January 16, 24, and 25, 1956. Subcommittee on Reorganization of the Committee on Government Operations: Proposal to Create Position of Administrative Vice President, passim.

116   Mondale, "Sideman," p. 8; and Carter, *Keeping Faith*, pp. 39–40.

117   Carter, *Keeping Faith*, p. 40.

118   Mondale is quoted without attribution in Lewis, *Mondale*, p. 231.

119   Mondale, "Sideman," p. 19.

120   Untermeyer, "Looking Forward," p. 158.

121   The possible electoral pairing of Ronald Reagan and Gerald Ford in 1980 is addressed extensively in Chapter 7.

122   The estimated mileage George H.W. Bush traveled in the eight years he was vice president was provided by the George Bush Presidential Library and Museum, located in College Station, Texas.

123   Bush, *Looking Forward*, pp. 224–225.

124   There are countless retellings of the appropriateness of Vice President Bush's deportment in the wake of the assassination attempt on President Reagan, including brief, insider accounts in Helene Von Damm's, *At Reagan's Side*, p. 195; as well as in Chase Untermeyer's essay, "Looking Forward," pp. 161–162.

125   On January 21, 1981, President Reagan appointed Vice President Bush to head the Task Force on Regulatory Relief.

126   Transcript, press conference of Secretary of State Alexander Haig, the White House, March 30, 1981.

127   For a useful review of the Iran-contra affair, see the 1997 book by Lawrence E. Walsh, *Firewall: The Iran-Contra Conspiracy and Cover-Up*.

128   For a compelling overview of the Reagan presidency and Ronald Reagan's disengagement specifically, see *Landslide: The Unmaking of the President, 1984–1988*, by Jane Mayer and Doyle McManus.

129   Thomas Jefferson and Martin Van Buren both served for two years as secretary of state before winning a term as vice president. John Calhoun also served as secretary of state in the Tyler administration, but he did so after having resigned from the vice presidency.

130   From an interview for *Business Week*, August 1986.

131   For the official assessment of Vice President George Bush's involvement in the Iran-Contra scandal, see the *Final Report of the Independent Counsel for Iran/Contra Matters*, Vol. 1, Chapter 28 "George Bush," pp. 473–484.

132   Quotation is from Proclamation 6518—Grant of Executive Clemency, President George H.W. Bush, December 24, 1992. Although presidential documents are accessible from any number of sources, including presidential libraries, executive orders are easily located in print or online from the vast data maintained by the National Archives and Records Administration.

133   Von Damm, *At Reagan's Side*, p. 165.

134   There are countless references to the broad apprehension many conservative Republicans held for the more moderate George H.W. Bush. For one such account, see Von Damm's *At Reagan's Side*, and the concerns adherents of Ronald Reagan maintained about Bush and his trusted adviser James Baker, pp. 165–166.

135   For a review of Dan Quayle's efforts to attract the attention of then-Vice President George Bush, see Broder, *Man Who Would Be President*, pp. 20–26.

136   For a concise summation of Dan Quayle's career in Congress, including his work with Senator Edward Kennedy, see Hatfield, *Vice Presidents*, pp. 545–547.

137   There were countless negative references by the media about Dan Quayle in the hours and days after he received the 1988 Republican nomination for vice president. For a consideration of Quayle's woes on this front, see Broder, *Man Who Would Be President*, p. 57 and p. 59.

138   Quayle, phone interview with the author, March 4, 2009.

139   Ibid.

140   Ibid.

141   Broder, *Man Who Would Be President*, p. 130.

142   For a concise take on Vice President Quayle and his efforts with the National Space Council, see *The New York Times* article of February 15, 1992, "Quayle's Influence Seen in NASA Shake-Up," by Warren E. Leary.

143   Quayle, phone interview with the author, March 4, 2009.

144   For a brief review of the reaction of conservative Republicans to President Bush's proposed tax hike, see Quayle, "Standing Firm: Personal Reflections," p. 177.

145   Vice President Quayle offered the number of nations he visited and a brief retelling of the importance of his meetings with foreign leaders to the author in a phone interview conducted on March 4, 2009.

146   Ibid. Vice President Quayle described specifics of the vetting process used at the time of his nomination for vice president; it was an account that ran contrary to the popular perception of how he was chosen.

147   See Broder, *Man Who Would Be President*, pp. 95–97. Broder claims that there were a number of instances in the time surrounding the Gulf War, in which Quayle was not included at the center of decision making, and on at least one occasion, a media event was staged in order to demonstrate the supposed involvement of the vice president.

148   There are a number of accounts of the tensions and resentments existent between Vice President Quayle and James Baker during the 1988 campaign, as well as in the time they served together in the Bush administration. For just one consideration, see Paul Kengor's

critique of the Quayle-Baker relationship, and its impact on Quayle's role in foreign policy, in "The Vice President, Secretary of State, and Foreign Policy," pp. 77–86.

149 Quayle, "Standing Firm: Personal Reflections," p. 173.

150 Ibid.

151 Dan Quayle formed an exploratory committee for the presidential elections of 1996 and 2000. In 2000, Quayle declared his candidacy for president, but withdrew from the race not long afterwards.

CHAPTER 6

THE VICE PRESIDENCY AUGMENTED: THE CASE OF GORE

1 When Albert Gore Sr. was asked if he thought he would see his son elected president, he reportedly stated: "I've been negotiating with the Lord to let me live to see that something like that happens. But I haven't been able to get a commitment yet." The elder Gore is quoted in Richard L. Berke's article "The Good Son," *The New York Times*, February 20, 1994.

2 Dawes, *Notes as Vice President*, p. 3.

3 Bill Clinton and Al Gore had met only briefly, on a few occasions, before Clinton formally interviewed Gore, and then offered him a spot on the ticket. For two takes on Clinton's selection of Gore for a running mate, see Clinton, *My Life*, pp. 413–414, and Woodward, *Agenda*, pp. 52–53.

4 More impressive than the 10 percent boost Bill Clinton's candidacy gained from adding Al Gore to the Democratic ticket was a July 9, 1992, CNN/Time poll that indicated 33 percent of registered voters were more likely to vote for Clinton because of Gore's presence on the Democratic ticket.

5 Transcript of the Gore-Quayle-Stockdale Vice-Presidential Debate, October 13, 1992, pp. 4–5.

6 Ibid., p. 6.

7 Ibid.

8 Ibid., p. 5.

9 Bush, *Looking Forward*, p. 227.

10 Clinton, *My Life*, 516.

11 Woodward, *Agenda*, pp. 280–281. This encounter appears in a variety of sources, but Woodward's version appears to be the initial account of Gore's response to Clinton.

12 Mark Gearan quoted in Ann Devroy and Stephen Barr's "Gore Bucks Tradition in Vice President's Role," *The Washington Post*, February 18, 1995. In addition, George Stephanopoulos is quoted as saying nearly the same as does Gearan, in Elaine Sciolino and Todd S. Purdum's article "Al Gore, One Vice President Who is Eluding the Shadows," *The New York Times*, February 19, 1995.

13 Clinton, *My Life*, p. 414.

14   Elaine Sciolino and Todd S. Purdum, "Al Gore, One Vice President Who is Eluding the Shadows," *The New York Times*, February 19, 1995.

15   Christopher, *Chances of a Lifetime*, pp. 155–156.

16   For simplicity, when referring to the Executive Office of the President (EOP), the White House Office, or WHO, is included as a part of the EOP.

17   It should be noted that the individuals designated chief of staff, at least prior to James Baker in the Reagan administration, were not always formally designated the chief of staff; instead, even if the individual was accepted as the chief of staff, like Hamilton Jordan in the Carter administration, they were given the title of Assistant to the President.

18   New York Senator Kenneth Keating introduced S.J. Res. 35, calling for a second vice president to be elected with the president and to be placed in the line of succession directly after the first vice president, but before the Speaker of the House.

19   Bayh, *One Heartbeat Away*, p. 55.

20   Nessen, *It Sure Looks Different*, p. 249.

21   According to journalist Bob Woodward, Al Gore was "relentless" during the transition; in *Agenda*, p. 59.

22   For Warren Christopher's insights on the value of the chief of staff position, see *Chances of a Lifetime*, pp. 161–163.

23   Ibid., p. 163.

24   Among others, James D. King and James W. Riddlesperger Jr. note in their article "Presidential Management and Staffing: An Early Assessment of the Clinton Presidency," that Al Gore was effective in placing intimates and his own Senate staffers "into top-level positions in the new administration," p. 501.

25   There are numerous evaluations of the National Performance Review. For two of the best assessments, see J.R. Thompson's article "Reinvention as Reform: Assessing the National Performance Review," *Public Administration Review*, Vol. 60, no. 6, (November-December, 2000), pp. 508–520, and L. Lenkowky and J.L. Perry's article "Reinventing Government: the Case for National Service," *Public Administration Review*, Vol. 60, no. 4, (July–August, 2000), pp. 298–307. And for Al Gore's assessment of specific outcomes of the National Performance Review, as applied to the executive in the federal bureaucracy, see his article "The New Job of the Federal Executive," *Public Administration Review*, Vol. 54, no. 4, (July–August, 1994), pp. 317–321.

26   Clinton, *My Life*, p. 647.

27   Ibid., p. 648.

28   With regard to the four respective foreign policy groups, Gore was partnered with a leader from Russia, South Africa, Egypt, and the Ukraine.

29   In his article "The Vice President, Secretary of State, and Foreign Policy," Paul Kengor described the Gore-Chernomyrdin relationship as "the main channel between the administration and Moscow," p. 196.

30   Converting Russian nuclear plants to civilian purposes was the result of an agreement Vice President Gore and Prime Minister Chernomyrdin signed in June of 1994.

31   With regard to the first secretary of state in the Clinton administration, Warren Christopher, Paul Kengor claims in "The Vice President, Secretary of State, and Foreign Policy," that the

number "of foreign policy [assignments] Christopher granted to Gore is quite astonishing," p. 196.

32   Albright, *Madam Secretary*, p. 180.

33   Ibid.

34   Ibid., p. 221.

35   Richard L. Berke, "The Good Son," *The New York Times*, February 20, 1994.

36   Cohen, "'The Polls': Popular Views of the Vice President and Vice Presidential Favorability," p. 354. See Cohen for a very brief, but useful consideration of vice-presidential favorability polls, juxtaposed with presidential favorability polls, and the effect of the latter on the former.

37   Whether or not serving in the vice presidency helps or hurts the chances of the incumbent vice president to land in the presidency is given a cursory consideration by Marie Natoli in her article: "The Vice Presidency: Stepping Stone or Stumbling Block?"

38   Clinton, *My Life*, p. 414.

39   Of the 303 votes of the Electoral College held for the presidential election of 1860, Lincoln and Hamlin received 180 votes; Breckinridge and Lane, 72 votes; John Bell and Edward Everett, 39 votes; and Douglas and his running mate, Herschel Johnson, 12 votes.

40   Richard L. Berke, "The Good Son," *The New York Times*, February 20, 1994.

41   Ibid.

42   In "'The Polls': Popular Views of the Vice President and Vice Presidential Favorability," Jeffrey Cohen asserts, "the president casts a long shadow on the vice president," p. 356.

43   See Marie Natoli's article "The Humphrey Vice Presidency in Retrospect" for an effective deconstruction of a speech given by Hubert Humphrey during the 1968 presidential campaign, pp. 607–609. In the speech, Humphrey explained his previous support for the Vietnam War, while offering a plan to end the war if elected president.

44   In David Halberstam's seminal text on the Kennedy-Johnson years, *The Best and the Brightest*, Halberstam framed Richard Nixon's challenge of Hubert Humphrey in the 1968 election in this way: "It was like running against Johnson without Johnson. Humphrey bore the burdens of the Johnson years without the strengths," p. 803.

45   Aggregate approval ratings were derived from Gallup online polling archives.

46   Cohen, "'The Polls': Popular Views of the Vice President and Vice Presidential Favorability," p. 356.

47   Ibid.

48   For a brief review of approval and favorability polling for Al Gore shifting after his announced candidacy for the presidency, and as the 2000 election drew nearer, see Jeffrey Cohen's articles, "'The Polls': Popular Views of the Vice President and Vice Presidential Approval," pp. 145–146; and "'The Polls': Popular Views of the Vice President and Vice Presidential Favorability," pp. 355–356.

49   A comprehensive review of the online archives of the Gallup polling organization, as well as other competing polling organizations, indicated that when Al Gore was vice president he had wider name recognition than any of his predecessors.

50   There were a number of accusations made against Vice President Gore with respect to suspect fundraising activities. Prior to the 1996 presidential election, among the most prominent of these was Gore's visit to a Buddhist temple in Los Angeles, California for

an event that was not billed as a fundraiser, but indeed benefited the Democratic National Committee. Gore was also accused of improperly using the vice president's personal office in the White House to make phone calls soliciting campaign funds.

51 According to Cohen, there has been an increase in the sheer number of polls wherein the vice president is the topic of the poll since the tenure of Walter Mondale, which then correlates with the increasing prominence of the vice president; in "'The Polls': Popular Views of the Vice President and Vice Presidential Approval," p. 143.

52 Gallup Survey No. 151-A, March 10–15, 1939, p. 147.

53 Gallup Poll No. 196, May 23, 1940.

54 Gallup Poll No. 230, February 14, 1941. In the same poll respondents were also asked if the runner-up in the presidential election should be made a U.S. senator for life.

55 For one instance when this question was asked, see Gallup Poll No. 417, April 21, 1948. Slight variations of the same question are asked in an assortment of Gallup surveys over the years.

56 Gallup Poll No. 520, September 12–17, 1953.

57 See Jeffery Cohen's "'The Polls': Popular Views of the Vice President and Vice Presidential Approval," and "'The Polls': Popular Views of the Vice President and Vice Presidential Favorability," both of which trace fluctuations in approval and favorability polling on Al Gore when he was vice president.

58 Cohen, "'The Polls': Popular Views of the Vice President and Vice Presidential Approval," pp. 145–146; and Cohen, "'The Polls': Popular Views of the Vice President and Vice Presidential Favorability," pp. 355–356.

59 Cohen, "'The Polls': Popular Views of the Vice President and Vice Presidential Approval," p. 144.

60 For just one example, see the CBS News Poll Database for a December 1999 survey in which a hypothetical presidential contest between Vice President Al Gore and Governor George W. Bush stood at 51 percent of respondents for Bush, versus 39 percent for Gore.

61 Quote is from Richard Nixon's 1964 testimony before the Senate Judiciary Committee, reprinted and cited in "Selected Materials on the Twenty-fifth Amendment," Senate Document 93-42, p. 95.

62 Wattenberg, "The Clinton 2000 Effect in Perspective: The Impact of Retiring Presidents on Their Parties' Chances of Retaining the White House," pp. 164–165.

63 John M. Murphy and Mary E. Stuckey assess the four presidents and vice presidents considered here—specifically the "rhetorical strategies" used by the outgoing presidents when campaigning for their vice president—in their article "Never Cared to Say Goodbye: Presidential Legacies and Vice Presidential Campaigns," pp. 46–66.

64 President Lyndon Johnson did not actively campaign in New Hampshire in 1968, yet he managed to win 50 percent of the vote, to Senator Eugene McCarthy's 41 percent.

65 As referenced in Chapter 5, from the outset Vice President Humphrey had been treading a fine line with President Johnson with respect to the Vietnam War. When, at a meeting with the president, Humphrey voiced reservations about the conduct of the war, Johnson isolated the vice president for a time for what he perceived as disloyalty by Humphrey.

66 Murphy, "Never Cared to Say Goodbye: Presidential Legacies and Vice Presidential Campaigns," p. 62.

67   For one take on why Al Gore chose not to emphasize his ties to President Clinton and the Clinton administration, see Martin P. Wattenberg's brief but useful article, "The Clinton 2000 Effect in Perspective: The Impact of Retiring Presidents on Their Parties' Chances of Retaining the White House."

68   For further consideration of vice-presidential nominee selection, broadly, and Al Gore's selection of Senator Joseph Lieberman, specifically, see Hite, "A Paradigm for Vice-Presidential Nominee Selection," passim.

69   For a cogent collection of essays on the 2000 election, see the 2002 text *Bush v. Gore*, edited by Bruce Ackerman.

70   Transcript of the Lieberman-Cheney Vice-Presidential Debate, October 5, 2000, p. 17.

71   Identical language is used in Article II, sec. 1 of the United States Constitution and the Twelfth Amendment.

72   Hatfield references this series of procedures in *Vice Presidents*, p. 198.

73   Henry Wallace was the presidential nominee of the Progressive Party in 1948. Wallace's vice-presidential running mate was Senator Glen Taylor of Idaho.

74   President Clinton is quoted in Richard L. Berke's "The Good Son," *The New York Times*, February 20, 1994.

75   President Johnson's remarks are recounted in Humphrey, *Education of a Public Man*, p. 301.

CHAPTER 7

THE VICE PRESIDENCY UNBOUNDED: THE CASE OF CHENEY

1   As noted previously in Chapter 3, the thirteenth vice president, William Rufus Devane King, took the vice-presidential oath of office on the island of Cuba, in 1853.

2   *Senate Journal*. 63rd Cong., Special Senate Session, March 4, 1913, p. 306. Over the years, Thomas Marshall's remarks with regard to the four years of silence he faced have been incorrectly recounted and embellished. In addition, it has consistently and erroneously been implied that Marshall's remarks came at the opening of his speech before the Senate, instead of at the conclusion, as was actually the case.

3   In 1937, John Nance Garner became the first vice president to take the oath of office outdoors with the president.

4   For a good summation of Dick Cheney and the vice-presidential selection and nomination in 2000, see the August 7, 2000 article in *Time*, "Republican Convention: How Bush Decided," by James Carney and John F. Dickerson.

5   It should be noted that not all of the interviews with potential vice-presidential candidates were held in Texas; on occasion interviews were held in other states.

6   Quote is from "Bush Officially Introduces Cheney as His Running Mate," July 25, 2000, press conference, CNN transcripts archive.

7   Ibid.

8   Researching the daily archives of any of the major news services, such as CNN or CBS, is the best means for assessing Dick Cheney's travel itinerary during the 2000 campaign; it is then simple to extrapolate from the data why Cheney went where he did.

9   The 1924 campaign of Calvin Coolidge and Charles Dawes, and the aggressive electioneering of vice-presidential candidates, broadly, is succinctly reviewed in Chapter 4.

10 There are innumerable sources for information on the 2000 transition initiated by Dick Cheney. For a useful chronology of the transition, see "The New Administration Takes Shape" at www.gwu.edu/~action/chrntran.html.

11 "Transcript of Former Secretary Richard Cheney's News Conference," *Washington Post*, November 27, 2000.

12 Ibid.

13 Ibid.

14 Ibid.

15 Although it is uncertain if the original suggestion that George W. Bush and Dick Cheney shared a "co-presidency" originated with Shirley Warshaw, for a book length treatment of the idea, see her text *The Co-Presidency of Bush and Cheney*.

16 For a useful review of collegial executive designs, see Shugart, *Presidents and Assemblies*, pp. 20–21, 93–105, 219, 285.

17 In a presidential system the veto is broadly recognized for being "the primary check of the president on congressional power," in Shugart, *Presidents and Assemblies*, p. 134.

18 Wilson, *Constitutional Government*, p. 14.

19 Ibid.

20 As in Chapter 6, when referring to the Executive Office of the President (EOP), the White House Office (WHO) is treated as a part of the EOP.

21 As noted in Chapter 5, Michael Turner exhaustively documents Vice President Rockefeller's efforts to have a substantial role in policymaking in the Ford administration; he likewise reviews Donald Rumsfeld's counter efforts to restrict that role for Rockefeller; in "Finding a Policy Role for the Vice President."

22 Ibid.

23 For note of Lewis Libby and his access to the White House, see Warshaw, *Co-Presidency*, pp. 64–65.

24 For Dick Cheney's brief musings on the efforts of the Congress to reestablish equilibrium with the presidency, see Cheney, "The Significance of Campaign '84," passim. Also, for a concise take on the American presidency after Watergate, see Howard J. Silver's article "Presidential Power and the Post-Watergate Presidency."

25 See Arthur Schlesinger Jr.'s text *The Imperial Presidency*, New York: Houghton Mifflin, 1973.

26 Cheney, "The Significance of Campaign '84," p. 336.

27 Ibid., p. 335.

28 Transcript, Lieberman-Cheney Vice-Presidential Debate, October 5, 2000, p. 17.

29 The most revealing and useful exposition of Dick Cheney's preference for a disproportionately strong executive is his article, "The Significance of Campaign '84."

30   Quote is from the text of an article written by Walter Mondale and sent by fax from his office to the author. The article was published in *The Washington Post* on July 29, 2007, and was titled "Answering to No One."

31   For a detailed consideration of the dynamics involved in vice-presidential nominee selection, see Hite, "A Paradigm for Vice-Presidential Nominee Selection," passim.

32   Dukakis, personal communication with the author, February 3, 2009.

33   Transcript, Edwards-Cheney Vice-Presidential Debate, October 5, 2004, p. 25.

34   Martin Gold comments on Dick Cheney's frequent absence from presiding in the Senate, but notes that "as long as his presence can be felt … as it very much is in the case of Dick Cheney, then I think that that probably is all that can be expected of a modern vice president"; in Martin Gold, Counsel to the Senate Republican Leader, 1979–1982, 2003–2004, Oral History Interviews, Senate Historical Office, Washington, DC, Interview 5, p. 121 (Donald A. Ritchie, interviewer).

35   Bruck, "Odd Man Out," p. 54.

36   Ibid., pp. 54, 56.

37   In "Power Grab," journalist Elizabeth Drew describes President Bush's signing statement frenzy as a "power grab" and notes "the Constitution distinguishes between the power of the Congress and that of the president by stating that Congress shall 'make all laws' and the president shall 'take care that the laws be faithfully executed.' Bush claims the power to execute the laws as he interprets them, ignoring congressional intent," p. 1.

38   See Halstead, "Presidential Signing Statements," for an overview of the historical use of executive signing statements. What was particularly uncharacteristic of any prior presidents who employed executive signing statements was the arrogance President Bush displayed toward the Congress when using the statements, as well as the passiveness of the Congress in responding to the transparent incursions by the executive into the legislative sphere. According to Halstead, with Andrew Jackson and John Tyler, the Congress strenuously objected to such actions by the executive; likewise, "Presidents Polk and Pierce apologized for the issuance of signing statements," in part because they were disinclined to incur the scorn of Congress. And President Grant went so far as to proclaim that a signing statement "was an 'unusual method of conveying the notice of approval,'" p. 2.

39   There are several accounts of Vice President Cheney reviewing legislation and then finding cause to use executive signing statements; for just two reviews of this practice, see Warshaw, *Co-Presidency*, p. 254, fn. 43, and Savage, *Takeover*, p. 236.

40   The specific role of David Addington and executive signing statements is succinctly addressed in Savage, *Takeover*, p. 236.

41   According to the Senate Historical Office: as of 2011 there have been 2,564 presidential vetoes since George Washington was inaugurated in 1789.

42   See Shugart, *Presidents and Assemblies* for a comprehensive review of the differences in presidential and parliamentary systems, including executive arrangements, passim.

43   Bagehot, *English Constitution*, passim.

44   In *Presidents and Assemblies*, Shugart defines "premier-presidentialism" systems on pp. 23–24, and then defines "president-parliamentary" systems on pp. 24–25.

45   Transcript, Lieberman-Cheney Vice-Presidential Debate, October 5, 2000, p. 11.

46   Presidential memorandum, President George W. Bush, January 29, 2001.

47 For the composition of the National Energy Policy Development Group, see the hierarchical representation of the group in the United States General Accounting Office report, "Energy Task Force," GAO-03-894, p. 7.

48 Among the better accounts of the consistent disengagement of President George W. Bush during his first years in office is Ron Suskind's entertaining book, *The Price of Loyalty: George W. Bush, the White House, and the Education of Paul O'Neill*.

49 For an unusual take on a possible Reagan-Ford ticket, based on an interview by Walter Cronkite with former President Gerald Ford, see Rebecca Cline's article, "The Cronkite-Ford Interview at the 1980 Republican National Convention: A Therapeutic Analogue."

50 Academic assessments of Ronald Reagan's offer of the vice-presidential nomination to Gerald Ford in 1980 are nearly nonexistent. One of the only scholarly considerations, aside from the attention given to the topic in this book, is Michael Turner's article "Reagan and the Vice Presidency," which appeared in the journal *Politics* in 1981.

51 Cline, "The Cronkite-Ford Interview at the 1980 Republican National Convention: A Therapeutic Analogue," p. 94.

52 Greenspan, *Age of Turbulence*, p. 90.

53 According to Alan Greenspan: "a ticket of Ronald Reagan and Jerry Ford would pick up 2 or 3 percentage points, enough to win," *Age of Turbulence*, p. 89.

54 Cline, "The Cronkite-Ford Interview at the 1980 Republican National Convention: A Therapeutic Analogue," p. 95.

55 After Ronald Reagan and Gerald Ford met privately and decided their deal was off, Reagan "quickly selected George H.W. Bush as his vice presidential candidate and made the announcement that very night," in Greenspan, *Age of Turbulence* p. 91.

56 Ibid., p. 90.

57 Transcript, Walter Cronkite interview with former President Gerald Ford, "Campaign '80: The Republican National Convention," July 16, 1980, CBS News.

58 Greenspan, *Age of Turbulence*, p. 91.

59 Referencing the incident with the National Archives in "The Darksider," Hendrik Hertzberg stated: "Cheney provoked widespread hilarity by pleading executive privilege (in order to deny one set of documents to the Senate Judiciary Committee) while simultaneously maintaining that his office is not part of the executive branch (in order to deny another set to the Information Security Oversight Office of the National Archives). On Cheney's version of the government organization chart, it seems, the location of the Office of the Vice-President is undisclosed. So are the powers that, in a kind of rolling, slow-motion coup d'état, he has gathered unto himself," p. 36.

60 The best resource for information on Dick Cheney's claims that the OVP is exempt from the travel disclosure rules that are applicable to the rest of executive branch is the nonpartisan Center for Public Integrity.

61 Among the various accounts of litigants seeking the names of all the participants in the Cheney energy force meetings, *The New York Times* article of April 25, 2004, "Administration Says a 'Zone of Autonomy' Justifies Its Secrecy on Energy Task Force," by Linda Greenhouse, is one of the more concise. Also, for a more scholarly treatment of the same topic, see Halstead's "The Law: Walker v. Cheney: Legal Insulation of the Vice President from GAO Investigations," pp. 635–648.

62   Quote is from Cheney v. United States District Court, No. 03-475.

63   Transcript, Biden-Palin Vice-Presidential Debate, October 2, 2008, p. 35.

64   Quayle, phone interview with the author, March 4, 2009.

Chapter 8

The Vice Presidency in the Twenty-First Century

1   Roosevelt, "Can the Vice President be Useful?" p. 8.

2   Testimony of Clark Clifford, U.S. Congress, Senate, 84th Cong., 2nd sess., January 16, 24, and 25, 1956. Subcommittee on Reorganization of the Committee on Government Operations: Proposal to Create Position of Administrative Vice President, p. 56.

3   Ibid.

4   Ibid.

5   Ibid., p. 57

6   Madison, *Notes of Debates*, p. 46.

7   Ibid., p. 46.

8   Hamilton, *The Federalist*, p. 445.

9   *Annals of the Congress*, 8th Cong., 1st sess., p. 693. The sentiment for abolishment of the vice presidency, cited here, was expressed by John Randolph, a member of the House of Representatives from Virginia.

10   Wallace, "How a Vice President is Picked—Inside Look at U.S. Politics," p. 86.

11   Ibid.

12   For congressional testimony on the Hoover Commission's findings, specific to the vice presidency, see: U.S. Congress, Senate, 84th Cong., 2nd sess., January 16, 24, and 25, 1956. Subcommittee on Reorganization of the Committee on Government Operations: Proposal to Create Position of Administrative Vice President, passim.

13   The Twenty-second Amendment to the United States Constitution was proposed by resolution of Congress on March 24, 1947. Ratification of the Twenty-second Amendment was completed on February 27, 1951.

14   U.S. Constitution, Twenty-second Amendment, sec. 1.

15   Richard Nixon was the first incumbent vice president to benefit from the Twenty-second Amendment. After Nixon, and apart from Nelson Rockefeller, Dan Quayle, and Dick Cheney, every individual to serve as vice president went on to gain the presidential nomination of their party. With respect to Rockefeller and Cheney: neither ever tried to win the presidency after serving in the vice presidency, but Quayle did.

16   Falk, *Women for President*, passim.

17   Ibid., p. 64.

18   In "Women as Executive Branch Leaders," Karen Hult addresses the idea that gendered bias influences perceptions of women elected executives and their ability to handle policies assumed to be more masculine, like economics and security.

19   Vice President Biden appears on the cover of the October 19, 2009, edition of *Newsweek*, with Holly Bailey and Evan Thomas's accompanying article about Biden, "An Inconvenient Truth Teller."

20   Apart from initial interest in the vice-presidential candidacy of Sarah Palin, a comprehensive survey by the author of polling data from the 2008 campaign confirmed that voters were most concerned with the candidates for president.

21   A broad review by the author of polling data from the 1992, 1996, and 2004 presidential campaigns indicated a consistent disregard on the part of the electorate toward the incumbent candidates for vice president.

22   Transcript, Biden-Palin Vice-Presidential Debate, October 2, 2008, p. 34.

23   Thomas, "An Inconvenient Truth Teller," passim.

24   See Helene Cooper's article, "As the Ground Shifts, Biden Plays a Bigger Role," *The New York Times*, December 11, 2010.

25   Ibid.

26   In juxtaposing the contrasting styles of Vice President Biden and Rahm Emanuel, New York Congressman Anthony Weiner said: "Biden brings everything that Rahm Emanuel brings, but the major difference is everyone likes Joe Biden." Wiener is quoted in Helene Cooper's article, "As the Ground Shifts, Biden Plays a Bigger Role," *The New York Times*, December 11, 2010.

27   Transcript, Bentsen-Quayle Vice-Presidential Debate, October 5, 1988, p. 2.

28   Franklin Roosevelt was a candidate for vice president in 1920, on the ticket with Governor James Cox. Roosevelt later captured the 1932 Democratic nomination for president, and won. Senator Robert Dole was the vice-presidential nominee of the Republican Party in 1976, running on the ticket with President Gerald Ford. Twenty years later, Dole won the Republican nomination for president, but he and his running mate, Jack Kemp, were defeated by President Bill Clinton and Vice President Al Gore.

29   Among others, see Lorant, *Life of Abraham Lincoln*, p. 72 for a cursory reference to Abraham Lincoln and the vice-presidential nomination in 1856. And for John Kennedy and the vice-presidential nomination in 1956, see O'Donnell *"Johnny We Hardly Knew Ye,"* pp. 134–142.

30   Based on data verified by the Senate Historical Office; included in the document: "Occasions When Vice Presidents Have Voted to Break Tie Votes in the Senate," March 13, 2008.

31   Rossiter, *American Presidency*, p. 100

32   Adams, *Diary*, p. 520. Adams's entry is dated April 4, 1841.

APPENDIX A

THE TWELFTH AMENDMENT TO THE CONSTITUTION OF THE UNITED STATES OF AMERICA

P roposed by resolution of the Congress on December 9, 1803; declared ratified by three fourths of the States on September 25, 1804.

ARTICLE (XII)

The Electors shall meet in their respective states, and vote by ballot for President and Vice-President, one of whom, at least, shall not be an inhabitant of the same state with themselves; they shall name in their ballots the person voted for as President, and in distinct ballots the person voted for as Vice-President, and they shall make distinct lists of all persons voted for as President, and of all persons voted for as Vice-President, and of the number of votes for each, which lists they shall sign and certify, and transmit sealed to the seat of the government of the United States, directed to the President of the Senate;-- The President of the Senate shall, in the presence of Senate and House of Representatives, open all the certificates and the votes shall then be counted;--The person having the greatest number of votes for President, shall be the President, if such number be a majority of the whole number of Electors appointed; and if no person have such majority, then from the persons having the highest numbers not exceeding three on the list of those voted for as President, the House of Representatives shall choose immediately, by ballot, the President. But in choosing the President, the votes shall be taken by states, the representation from each state having one vote; a quorum for this purpose shall consist of a member or members from two-thirds of the states, and a majority of all the states shall be necessary to a choice. [And if the House of Representatives shall not choose a President whenever the right of choice shall devolve upon them, before the fourth day of March next following, then the Vice-President shall act as President, as in the case of the death or other constitutional disability of the President.] The person having the greatest number of votes as Vice-President, shall be the Vice-President, if such a number be a majority of the whole number of Electors appointed, and if no person have a majority, then from the two highest numbers on the list, the Senate shall choose the Vice-President; a quorum for the purpose shall consist of two-thirds of the whole number of Senators, and a majority of the whole number shall be necessary to a choice. But no person constitutionally ineligible to the office of President shall be eligible to that of Vice-President of the United States.

APPENDIX B

THE PRESIDENTIAL SUCCESSION ACT OF 1947

An act to provide for the performance of the duties of the office of President in case of the removal, resignation, death, or inability both of the President and Vice President.

July 18, 1947
61 U.S. Stat. 380

"Be it enacted, etc., That (a) (1) if, by reason of death, resignation, removal from office, inability, or failure to qualify, there is neither a President nor Vice President to discharge the powers and duties of the office of President, then the Speaker of the House of Representatives shall, upon his resignation as Speaker and as Representative in Congress, act as President.

"(2) The same rule shall apply in case of the death, resignation, removal from office, or inability of an individual acting as President under this subsection.

"(b) If, at the time when under subsection (a) a Speaker is to begin the discharge of the powers and duties of the office of President, there is no Speaker, or the Speaker fails to qualify as Acting President, then the President pro tempore of the Senate shall, upon his resignation as President pro tempore and as Senator, act as President.

"(c) An individual acting as President under subsection (a) or subsection (b) shall continue to act until the expiration of the then current Presidential term, except that—

(1) if his discharge of the powers and duties of the office is founded in whole or in part on the failure of both the President-elect and the Vice President-elect to qualify, then he shall act only until a President or Vice President qualifies; and

(2) if his discharge of the powers and duties of the office is founded in whole or in part on the inability of the President or Vice President, then he shall act only until the removal of the disability of one such individuals.

"(d) (1) If, by reason of death, resignation, removal from office, inability, or failure to qualify, there is no President pro tempore to act as President under subsection (b), then the officer of the United States who is highest on the following list, and who is not under disability to discharge the powers and duties of the office of President shall act as President: Secretary of State, Secretary of the Treasury, Secretary of War, Attorney General, Postmaster General, Secretary of the Navy, Secretary of the Interior, Secretary of Agriculture, Secretary of Commerce, Secretary of Labor.

"(2) An individual acting as President under this subsection shall continue so to do until the expiration of the then current Presidential term, but not after a qualified and prior-entitled individual is able to act, except that the removal of the disability of an individual higher on the list contained in paragraph (1) or the ability to qualify on the part of an individual higher on such list shall not terminate his service.

"(3) The taking of the oath of office by an individual specified in the list in paragraph (1) shall be held to constitute his resignation from the office by virtue of the holding of which he qualifies to act as President.

"(e) Subsections (a), (b), and (d) shall apply only to such officers as are eligible to the office of President under the Constitution. Subsection (d) shall apply only to officers appointed, by and with the advice and consent of the Senate, prior to the time of the death, resignation, removal from office, inability, or failure to qualify, of the President pro tempore, and only to officers not under impeachment by the House of Representatives at the time the powers and duties of the office of President devolve upon them.

"(f) During the period that any individual acts as President under this Act, his compensation shall be at the rate then provided by law in the case of the President.

"(g) Sections 1 and 2 of the Act entitled 'An Act to provide for the performance of the duties of the office of President in case of the removal, death, resignation, or inability both of the President and Vice President', approved January 19, 1886 (24 Stat. 1; U.S.C., 1940 edition, title 3, secs. 21 and 22), are repealed."

Appendix C

The Twenty-Fifth Amendment to the Constitution of the United States of America

P roposed by resolution of the Congress on July 6, 1965; declared ratified by the legislatures of thirty-nine of the fifty States on February 23, 1967.

Article (XXV)

Section 1. In case of the removal of the President from office or of his death or resignation, the Vice President shall become President.

Sec. 2. Whenever there is a vacancy in the office of the Vice President, the President shall nominate a Vice President who shall take office upon confirmation by a majority of vote of both Houses of Congress.

Sec. 3. Whenever the President transmits to the President pro tempore of the Senate and the Speaker of the House of Representatives his written declaration that he is unable to discharge the powers and duties of his office, and until he transmits to them a written declaration to the contrary, such powers and duties shall be discharged by the Vice President as Acting President.

Sec. 4. Whenever the Vice President and a majority of either the principal officers of the executive departments or of such other body as Congress may by law provide, transmit to the President pro tempore of the Senate and the Speaker of the House of Representatives their written declaration that the President is unable to discharge the powers and duties of his office, the Vice President shall immediately assume the powers and duties of the office as Acting President.

Thereafter, when the President transmits to the President pro tempore of the Senate and the Speaker of the House of Representatives his written declaration that no inability exists, he shall resume the powers and duties of his office unless the Vice President and a majority of either the principal officers of the executive department or of such other body as Congress may by law provide, transmit within four days to the President pro tempore of the Senate and the Speaker of the House of Representatives their written declaration that the President is unable to discharge the powers and duties of his office. Thereupon Congress shall decide the issue, assembling within forty-eight hours for that purpose if not in session. If the Congress, within twenty-one days after receipt of the latter written declaration, or, if Congress is not in session, within twenty-one days after Congress is required to assemble, determines by a two-thirds vote of both Houses that the President is unable to discharge the powers and duties of his office, the Vice President shall continue to discharge the same as Acting President; otherwise, the President shall resume the powers and duties of his office.

Appendix D

Statements on the Vice Presidency and Vice Presidents

"I am Vice President. In this I am nothing, but I may be everything."
  —Vice President John Adams, speaking before the Senate for the first
    time, 1789

"It was necessary to make Mr. Adams Vice-President to keep him quiet."
  —Gouverneur Morris, letter to William Maclay, 1789

 "Any man is foolish to want to be vice-president, unless he cares nothing for active life, and is willing to be a nonentity in the great debates which go on in his presence, without being able to express an opinion."
  —Vice President William Almon Wheeler, 1877

"I can't help feeling more and more that the Vice-Presidency is not an office in which I could do anything and not an office in which a man who is still vigorous and not past middle life has much chance of doing anything ... Now, as Governor, I can achieve something, but as Vice-President I should achieve nothing."
  —Governor Theodore Roosevelt, 1900

"The Vice President is like a man in a cataleptic state; he cannot speak; he cannot move; he suffers no pain; and yet he is perfectly conscious of everything that is going on about him."
  —Vice President Thomas Marshall, date unknown

"I can do only two things here [in the Senate]. One of them is to sit up here on this rostrum and listen to you birds talk without the ability to reply. The other is to look at the newspapers every morning to see how the President's health is."
  —Vice President Charles Dawes, comment to Senator Alben Barkley,
    date unknown

"Being Vice President sort of ruined Charlie Curtis"
    —Vice President John Nance Garner, date unknown

"I don't want those constables guarding me. There is not anybody crazy enough to shoot a vice president."
    —Vice President John Nance Garner, date unknown

"I felt that [the vice presidency] offered opportunities that I had really never had before. I … never felt the vice presidency was a comedown from anything except the presidency."
    —President Lyndon Johnson, date unknown

"Whatever the miseries and inadequacies of the vice presidency, I had considered it an honored position, and to have been succeeded by Spiro Agnew did not please me."
    —Vice President Hubert Humphrey, 1976

"I could have no such man-to-man talk with President Nixon … I was never allowed to come close enough to participate with him directly in any decision."
    —Vice President Spiro Agnew, 1980

"I know something about power—at least I did before I became vice president"
    —Vice President Gerald Ford, 1974

"I never wanted to be vice president of anything."
    —Vice President Nelson Rockefeller, 1974

"Under Carter, for the first time, the other elected national figure became an engaged participant in all the important issues confronting the president."
    —Vice President Walter Mondale, 2002

"The modern vice presidency is the most misunderstood elective office in our political system. People either make too little or too much of it."
    —Vice President George H.W. Bush, 1987

"Based on my personal experience, the vice presidency can be a rather awkward office."
    —Vice President Dan Quayle, 1997

"I've got a job I think matters now, as chairman of the Foreign Relations Committee … And so it wasn't self-evident to me that being Vice-President would be a better job …"
    —Senator Joe Biden, 2008

"When presidents die—that's why they have the vice president mostly."
    —Calvin J. Hite, 2010

BIBLIOGRAPHY

Ackerman, Bruce and David Fontana. "Thomas Jefferson Counts Himself into the Presidency." *Virginia Law Review*, Vol. 90, no. 2, (April 2004), pp. 551–643.

Adams, John Q. *The Diary of John Quincy Adams, 1794–1845*, edited by Allan Nevins. New York: Fredrick Ungar Publishing Co., 1969. First published in 1951 by Fredrick Ungar Publishing Co. Page references are to the 1969 edition.

Agnew, Spiro T. *Go Quietly ... or Else*. New York: William Morrow and Company, Inc., 1980.

Albright, Madeleine and Bill Woodward. *Madam Secretary*. New York: Miramax Books, 2003.

Ambrose, Stephen E. *Nixon: The Education of a Politician, 1913–1962*. New York: Simon and Schuster, 1987.

Atkeson, Lonna Rae. "From the Primaries to the General Election: Does a Divisive Nomination Race Affect a Candidate's Fortunes in the Fall?" in *Pursuit of the White House 2000: How We Choose Our Presidential Nominees*, edited by William Mayer, pp. 285–312. New York: Chatham House Publishers, 2000.

Bagby, Wesley M. *The Road to Normalcy: The Presidential Campaign and Election of 1920*. Baltimore, MD: The Johns Hopkins Press, 1962.

Bagehot, Walter. *The English Constitution*. New York: Cornell University Press, 1966.

Bailey, Holly and Evan Thomas. "An Inconvenient Truth Teller." *Newsweek*, October 19, 2009, pp. 30–35.

Baker, Jean H. *James Buchanan*. New York: Time Books, Henry Holt and Company, 2004.

Barkley, Alben W. "The Vice-Presidency." May 1952, unpublished. Box 164, Alben W. Barkley Collection, University of Kentucky, Special Collections Library.

That Reminds Me. New York: Doubleday & Company, Inc., 1954. A facsimile of the first edition. Ann Arbor, MI: University Microfilms, 1970.

Bayh, Birch. *One Heartbeat Away: Presidential Disability and Succession.* New York: The Bobbs-Merrill Company, Inc., 1968.

Belohlavek, John M. *George Mifflin Dallas: Jacksonian Patrician.* University Park: The Pennsylvania State University Press, 1977.

Beschloss, Michael R. *Taking Charge: The Johnson White House Tapes, 1963–1964.* New York: Simon & Schuster, 1997.

Binder, Fredrick Moore. *James Buchanan and the American Empire.* Cranbury, NJ: Associated University Presses, 1994.

Brands, H. W. *Andrew Jackson: His Life and Times.* New York: Doubleday, 2005.

Brant, Irving. "Election of 1808." In *History of American Presidential Elections, 1789–1968,* edited by Arthur M. Schlesinger, Jr., Fred L. Israel, and William P. Hansen, Vol. 1, pp. 185–221. New York: Chelsea House Publishers, 1971.

Broder, David S. "Election of 1968." In *History of American Presidential Elections, 1789–1968,* edited by Arthur M. Schlesinger, Jr., Fred L. Israel, and William P. Hansen, Vol. 4, pp. 3705–3752. New York: Chelsea House Publishers, 1971.

Broder, David S. and Bob Woodward. *The Man Who Would Be President: Dan Quayle.* New York: Simon & Schuster, 1992.

Brodsky, Alyn. *Grover Cleveland: A Study in Character.* New York: St. Martin's Press, 2000.

Brooks, Daniel Fate. "The Faces of William Rufus King." *Alabama Heritage,* Issue 69, (Summer 2003), pp. 14–23.

Bruck, Connie. "Odd Man Out: Chuck Hagel's Republican Exile." *The New Yorker,* November 3, 2008, pp. 54, 56, 63.

Burner, David. "Election of 1924." In *History of American Presidential Elections, 1789–1968,* edited by Arthur M. Schlesinger, Jr., Fred L. Israel, and William P. Hansen, Vol. 3, pp. 2459–2490. New York: Chelsea House Publishers, 1971.

Bush, George and Victor Gold. *Looking Forward.* New York: Doubleday, 1987.

Cannon, James. "Gerald R. Ford and Nelson A. Rockefeller: A Vice-Presidential Memoir." In *At the President's Side: The Vice Presidency in the Twentieth Century,* edited by Timothy Walch, pp. 135–143. Columbia: University of Missouri Press, 1997.

Carney, James and John F. Dickerson. "Republican Convention: How Bush Decided." *Time,* August 7, 2000, pp. 86–89.

Carter, Jimmy. *Keeping Faith: Memoirs of a President.* New York: Bantam Books, 1982.

Cheney, Richard B. "The Significance of Campaign '84." *Presidential Studies Quarterly*, Vol. 14, no. 3, Campaign '84: The Contest for National Leadership (Part Three) (Summer 1984), pp. 335–340.

Christopher, Warren. *Chances of a Lifetime*. New York: Scribner, 2001.

Cleere, Gail S. *The House on Observatory Hill: Home of the Vice President of the United States*. Washington, DC: U.S. Government Printing Office, 1989.

Cline, Rebecca. "The Cronkite-Ford Interview at the 1980 Republican National Convention: A Therapeutic Analogue." *Central States Speech Journal*, Vol. 36, no. 1–2, (Spring/Summer 1985), pp. 92–104.

Clinton, Bill. *My Life*. New York: Alfred A. Knopf, 2004.

Cohen, Jeffrey E. "'The Polls': Popular Views of the Vice President and Vice Presidential Approval." *Presidential Studies Quarterly*, Vol. 31, no. 1, (March 2001), pp. 142–149.

"'The Polls': Popular Views of the Vice President and Vice Presidential Favorability." *Presidential Studies Quarterly*, Vol. 31, no. 2, (June 2001), pp. 349–357.

Cohen, Marty, David Karol, Hans Noel, and John Zaller. *The Party Decides: Presidential Nominations Before and After Reform*. Chicago: The University of Chicago Press, 2008.

Coolidge, Calvin J. *The Autobiography of Calvin Coolidge*. New York: Cosmopolitan Book Corporation, 1929.

Costello, William. *The Facts About Nixon: An Unauthorized Biography*. New York: The Viking Press, 1960.

Culver, John C. and John Hyde. *American Dreamer: The Life and Times of Henry A. Wallace*. New York: W.W. Norton and Company, Inc., 2000.

Cunningham, Noble E., Jr. "Election of 1800." In *History of American Presidential Elections, 1789–1968*, edited by Arthur M. Schlesinger, Jr., Fred L. Israel, and William P. Hansen, Vol. 1, pp. 101–134. New York: Chelsea House Publishers, 1971.

Daugherty, Harry M. *The Inside Story of the Harding Tragedy*. New York: The Churchill Company, 1932.

David, Paul T. "The Vice Presidency: Its Institutional Evolution and Contemporary Status." *The Journal of Politics*, Vol. 29, no. 4, (November 1967), pp. 721–748.

Dawes, Charles G. *Notes as Vice President 1922–1929*. Boston: Little, Brown, and Company, 1935.

A Journal of the McKinley Years, edited by Bascom N. Timmons. Chicago: The Lakeside Press, R.R. Donnelley & Sons Company, 1950.

Drew, Elizabeth. "Power Grab." *The New York Review of Books*, Vol. 53, no. 11, (June 22, 2006), pp. 1–2.

Dukakis, Michael. Personal communication with the author, February 3, 2009.

Dunn, Arthur Wallace. *From Harrison to Harding: A Personal Narrative, Covering a Third of a Century, 1888–1921*. Vol. 1. New York: G. P. Putnam's Sons; The Knickerbocker Press, 1922.

Falk, Erika. *Women for President: Media Bias in Eight Campaigns*. Chicago: University of Illinois Press, 2008.

Feerick, John D. *From Failing Hands: The Story of Presidential Succession*. New York: Fordham University Press, 1965.

Ferling, John. *Adams vs. Jefferson: The Tumultuous Election of 1800*. New York: Oxford University Press, 2004.

Ferraro, Geraldine A. *Ferraro: My Story*. New York: Bantam Books, 1985.

Ford, Gerald R. *A Time to Heal: The Autobiography of Gerald R. Ford*. New York: Harper & Row Publishers, 1979.

Freidel, Frank. "Election of 1932." In *History of American Presidential Elections, 1789–1968*, edited by Arthur M. Schlesinger, Jr., Fred L. Israel, and William P. Hansen, Vol. 3, pp. 2707–2739. New York: Chelsea House Publishers, 1971.

Friedman, Leon. "Election of 1944." In *History of American Presidential Elections, 1789–1968*, edited by Arthur M. Schlesinger, Jr., Fred L. Israel, and William P. Hansen, Vol. 4, pp. 3009–3038. New York: Chelsea House Publishers, 1971.

Fuchs, Lawrence H. "Election of 1928." In *History of American Presidential Elections, 1789–1968*, edited by Arthur M. Schlesinger, Jr., Fred L. Israel, and William P. Hansen, Vol. 3, pp. 2585–2609. New York: Chelsea House Publishers, 1971.

Fuess, Claude M. *Calvin Coolidge: The Man From Vermont*. Hamden, CT: Archon Books, 1965.

Gallup, George H. *The Gallup Poll: Public Opinion, 1935–1971*. Vol. 1, *1935–1948*. New York: Random House, 1972.

Garner, John N. "Wisconsin Must Choose: A Third Term for Mr. Roosevelt or a First Term for John Nance Garner," 1940. Milwaukie, WI: Wisconsin Garner for President Club.

Gilbert, Robert E. *The Tormented President: Calvin Coolidge, Death, and Clinical Depression*. Westport, CT: Praeger Publishers, 2003.

Goldberg, Robert A. *Barry Goldwater*. New Haven, CT: Yale University Press, 1995.

Goldstein, Joel K. *The Modern American Vice Presidency: The Transformation of a Political Institution*. New Jersey: Princeton University Press, 1982.

Gould, Lewis L. *The Presidency of Theodore Roosevelt*. Lawrence: University Press of Kansas, 1991.

Four Hats in the Ring: The 1912 Election and the Birth of Modern American Politics. Lawrence: University Press of Kansas, 2008.

Greene, John Robert. "I'll Continue to Speak Out": Spiro T. Agnew as Vice President." In *At the President's Side: The Vice Presidency in the Twentieth Century*, edited by Timothy Walch, pp. 124–132. Columbia: University of Missouri Press, 1997.

Greenspan, Alan. *The Age of Turbulence: Adventures in a New World*. New York: The Penguin Press, 2007.

Guerrero, Linda Dudik. *John Adams' Vice Presidency, 1789–1797: The Neglected Man in the Forgotten Office*. New York: Arno Press, 1982.

Haig, Alexander M. Jr. *Inner Circles: How America Changed the World, A Memoir*. New York: Warner Books, Inc., 1992.

Halberstam, David. *The Unfinished Odyssey of Robert Kennedy*. New York: Random House, 1968.

The Best and the Brightest. New York: Fawcett Crest, 1973. First published in 1969 by Random House. Page references are to the 1973 edition.

War in a Time of Peace: Bush, Clinton, and the Generals. New York: Simon & Schuster, 2002. First published in 2001 by Simon & Schuster. Page references are to the 2002 edition.

Halstead, T.J. "The Law: Walker v. Cheney": Legal Insulation of the Vice President from GAO Investigations." *Presidential Studies Quarterly*, Vol. 33, no. 3, The Permanent War (Sep., 2003), pp. 635–648.

"Presidential Signing Statements: Constitutional and Institutional Implications." *CRS Report for Congress*. Washington DC: Congressional Research Service, 2007.

Hamilton, Alexander. *Writings*. New York: The Library of America, 2001.

Hamilton, Alexander, John Jay, and James Madison. *The Federalist: A Commentary on the Constitution of the United States*. New York: The Modern Library, 1941.

Hamlin, Charles Eugene. *The Life and Times of Hannibal Hamlin*. Vol. 2. New York: Kennikat Press, 1971. First published 1899 by Kennikat Press.

Hatch, Louis Clinton. *A History of the Vice-Presidency of the United States*, revised and edited by Earl L. Shoup. New York: The American Historical Society, Inc., 1934. A facsimile of the first edition. Ann Arbor, MI: University Microfilms, 1969.

Hatfield, Mark O. *Vice Presidents of the United States: 1789–1993*, edited by Wendy Wolff. Washington, DC: U.S. Government Printing Office, 1997.

Hay, John. *Inside Lincoln's White House: The Complete Civil War Diary of John Hay*, edited by Michael Bulingame and John R. Turner Ettlinger. Carbondale: Southern Illinois University Press, 1997.

Hertzberg, Hendrik. "The Darksider." *The New Yorker*, July 9 & 16, 2007, pp. 35–36.

Hite, James E. "A Paradigm for Vice-Presidential Nominee Selection." (Forthcoming.)

Hofstadter, Richard. *The American Political Tradition: And the Men Who Made It*. New York: Vintage Books, 1989. First published in 1948 by Alfred Knopf, Inc. Page references are to the 1989 edition.

Hoover, Herbert. *The Memoirs of Herbert Hoover*. Vol. 2, *The Cabinet and the Presidency, 1920–1933*. New York: The Macmillan Company, 1952.

The Ordeal of Woodrow Wilson. New York: McGraw-Hill Book Company, Inc., 1958.

Hopkins, James F. "Election of 1824." In *History of American Presidential Elections, 1789–1968*, edited by Arthur M. Schlesinger, Jr., Fred L. Israel, and William P. Hansen, Vol. 1, pp. 349–381. New York: Chelsea House Publishers, 1971.

Howe, George F. *Chester A. Arthur: A Quarter-Century of Machine Politics*. New York: Frederick Ungar Publishing Co., 1957. First published in 1935 by Dodd, Mead and Company, Inc. Page references are to the 1957 edition.

Hult, Karen M. "Women as Executive Branch Leaders." In *Rethinking Madam President: Are We Ready for a Woman in the White House?*, edited by Lori Cox Han and Caroline Heldman. Boulder, CO: Lynne Rienner Publishers, 2007.

Humphrey, Hubert H. "Changes in the Vice Presidency." *Current History*, 67 (August 1974), pp. 58–59, 89–90.

The Education of a Public Man: My Life and Politics, edited by Norman Sherman. New York: Doubleday & Company, Inc., 1976.

Hyman, Harold M. "Election of 1864." In *History of American Presidential Elections, 1789–1968*, edited by Arthur M. Schlesinger, Jr., Fred L. Israel, and William P. Hansen, Vol. 2, pp. 1155–1178. New York: Chelsea House Publishers, 1971.

Irwin, Ray W. *Daniel D. Tompkins: Governor of New York and Vice President of the United States*. New York: The New-York Historical Society, 1968.

Jackson, Andrew. *Correspondence of Andrew Jackson*, edited by John Spencer Bassett. Vol. 3, *1820–1828*. New York: Kraus Reprint CO., 1969. First published in 1928 by Carnegie Institution of Washington. Page references are to the 1969 edition.

James, Marquis. *Mr. Garner of Texas*. New York: The Bobbs-Merrill Company, 1939.

Jefferson, Thomas. *The Best Letters of Thomas Jefferson*, edited by J.G. De Roulhac. Massachusetts: Houghton Mifflin Company, 1926.

Kearns, Doris. *Lyndon Johnson and the American Dream*. New York: Harper & Row Publishers, 1976.

Kengor, Paul. "The Foreign Policy Role of Vice President Al Gore." *Presidential Studies Quarterly*, Vol. 27, no. 1, Bill Clinton and Al Gore: Retrospect and Prospect (Winter 1997), pp. 14–38.

"The Vice President, Secretary of State, and Foreign Policy." *Political Science Quarterly*, Vol. 115, no. 2, (Summer 2000), pp. 175–199.

Kennedy, Robert F. *Robert Kennedy in His Own Words: The Unpublished Recollections of the Kennedy Years*, edited by Edwin O. Guthman and Jeffrey Shulman. Toronto: Bantam Books, 1988.

Key, V.O. Jr. *Politics, Parties, and Pressure Groups*. 2nd ed. New York: Thomas Y. Crowell Company, 1948.

King, James D. and James W. Riddlesperger Jr. "Presidential Management and Staffing: An Early Assessment of the Clinton Presidency." *Presidential Studies Quarterly*, Vol. 26, no. 2, Presidential Elections: Past and Present (Spring,1996), pp. 496–510.

Kissinger, Henry. *Years of Renewal*. New York: Simon & Schuster, 1999.

Learned, Henry Barrett. "Casting Votes of the Vice-Presidents, 1789–1915." *The American Historical Review*, 20, no. 3. (April 1915), pp. 571–576.

Leonard, Thomas M. *James K. Polk: A Clear and Unquestionable Destiny*. Wilmington, DE: Scholarly Resources Inc., 2001.

Lewis, Finlay. *Mondale: Portrait of an American Politician*. New York: Perennial Library, 1984. First published in 1980 by Harper & Row Publishers, Inc., hardcover edition. Page references are to the 1984 edition.

Light, Paul C. *Vice-Presidential Power: Advice and Influence in the White House*. Baltimore, MD: The Johns Hopkins University Press, 1984.

Lizza, Ryan. "Biden's Brief." *The New Yorker*, October 20, 2008, pp. 48–53.

Lodge, Henry Cabot. *As it Was: An Inside View of Politics and Power in the '50s and '60s*. New York: W.W. Norton & Company, Inc., 1976.

Lomask, Milton. *Aaron Burr: The Years From Princeton to Vice President, 1756–1805*. New York: Farrar, Straus, Giroux, 1979.

Lorant, Stefan. *The Life of Abraham Lincoln*. New York: Bantam Books, 1976.

Maclay, William and Edgar Stanton Maclay. *Journal of William Maclay: United States Senator from Pennsylvania, 1789–1791*. New York: D.A. Appleton and Co., 1890.

Madison, James. *Notes of Debates in the Federal Convention of 1787*. New York: W.W. Norton & Company, Inc., 1966.

Magie, David. *Life of Garret Augustus Hobart: Twenty-fourth Vice-President of the United States.* New York: G.P. Putnam's Sons; The Knickerbocker Press, 1910.

Marshall, Thomas R. *Recollections of Thomas R. Marshall: A Hoosier Salad.* Indianapolis: The Bobbs-Merrill Company, 1925.

May, Gary. *John Tyler.* New York: Henry Holt and Company, 2008.

Mayer, Jane. "Contract Sport." *The New Yorker*, February 16 & 23, 2004, pp. 40–44.

"The Insiders." *The New Yorker*, October 27, 2008, pp. 38–42.

Mayer, Jane and Doyle McManus. *Landslide: The Unmaking of the President, 1984–1988.* Boston, MA: Houghton Mifflin, 1988.

Mayer, William G. "A Brief History of Vice Presidential Selection." In *Pursuit of the White House 2000: How We Choose Our Presidential Nominees*, edited by William G. Mayer, pp. 313–374. New York: Chatham House Publishers, 2000.

Mazo, Earl. *Richard Nixon: A Personal and Political Portrait.* New York: Avon Books, 1960. First published in 1959 by Harper & Brothers. Page references are to the 1960 edition.

McCoy, Donald R. *Calvin Coolidge: The Quiet President.* New York: The Macmillan Company, 1967.

"Election of 1920." In *History of American Presidential Elections, 1789–1968*, edited by Arthur M. Schlesinger, Jr., Fred L. Israel, and William P. Hansen, Vol. 3, pp. 2349–2385. New York: Chelsea House Publishers, 1971.

McCullough, David. *John Adams.* New York: Simon & Schuster, 2001.

McFeely, William S. *Grant: A Biography.* New York: W.W. Norton & Company, 1981.

McGovern, George. *Grassroots: The Autobiography of George McGovern.* New York: Random House, 1977.

"The Midnight Oath." *The Ladies Home Journal*, Vol. 41, April 1924, pp. 17, 236.

Miller, Merle. *Plain Speaking: An Oral Biography of Harry S. Truman.* New York: Berkley Medallion Books, 1974. First published in 1973 by Berkley Publishing Corporation. Page references are to the 1974 edition.

Mondale, Walter F. "Sideman: Reflections on the Vice Presidency." Lecture at Macalester College, St. Paul, Minnesota, May 6, 2002. Page references are to the manuscript copy provided to the author by Walter F. Mondale.

Monroe, Dan. *The Republican Vision of John Tyler.* College Station: Texas A & M University Press, 2003.

Morgan, H. Wayne. "Election of 1892." In *History of American Presidential Elections, 1789–1968*, edited by Arthur M. Schlesinger, Jr., Fred L. Israel, and William P. Hansen, Vol. 2, pp. 1703–1732. New York: Chelsea House Publishers, 1971.

Morison, Elting. "Election of 1860." In *History of American Presidential Elections, 1789–1968,* edited by Arthur M. Schlesinger, Jr., Fred L. Israel, and William P. Hansen, Vol. 2, pp. 1097–1122. New York: Chelsea House Publishers, 1971.

Morris, Edmund. *Theodore Rex.* New York: Modern Library, 2002. First published in 2001 by Random House. All page references are to the 2002 edition.

Murphy, John M. and Mary E. Stuckey. "Never Cared to Say Goodbye: Presidential Legacies and Vice Presidential Campaigns." *Presidential Studies Quarterly,* Vol. 32, no. 1, (March 2002), pp. 46–66.

Natoli, Marie D. "The Twenty-Fifth Amendment: Opening a Pandora's Box." *Presidential Studies Quarterly,* Vol. 6, no. 4, (Fall 1976), pp. 48–50.

"The Vice Presidency: Gerald Ford as Healer." *Presidential Studies Quarterly,* Vol. 10, no. 4, (Fall 1980), pp. 662–664.

"The Humphrey Vice Presidency in Retrospect." *Presidential Studies Quarterly,* Vol. 12, no. 4, Perceptions on the Presidency, Leadership, and Statesmanship (Fall 1982), pp. 603–609.

"The Vice Presidency: Stepping Stone or Stumbling Block?" *Presidential Studies Quarterly,* Vol. 18, no. 1, The Presidency in a Bicentennial and Quadrennial Election Year (Winter 1988), pp. 77–79.

"Harry S. Truman and the Contemporary Vice Presidency." *Presidential Studies Quarterly,* Vol. 18, no. 1, The Presidency in a Bicentennial and Quadrennial Election Year (Winter 1988), pp. 81–84.

Nessen, Ron. *It Sure Looks Different From the Inside.* Chicago: Playboy Press, 1978.

Neustadt, Richard E. "Vice Presidents as National Leaders." In *At the President's Side: The Vice Presidency in the Twentieth Century,* edited by Timothy Walch, pp. 183–196. Columbia: University of Missouri Press, 1997.

Nickolay, John G. and John Hay. *Abraham Lincoln: A History.* Vol. 3. New York: The Century Company, 1917. First published in 1886 by The Century Company. Page references are to the 1917 edition.

Nixon, Richard M. *Six Crises.* New York: Doubleday & Company, Inc., 1962.

RN: The Memoirs of Richard Nixon. New York: Grosset & Dunlap, 1978.

O'Donnell, Kenneth P., Dave F. Powers, and Joe McCarthy. *"Johnny We Hardly Knew Ye": Memories of John Fitzgerald Kennedy.* New York: Pocket Books, 1973. First published in 1972 by Little, Brown and Company. Page references are to the 1973 edition.

Orren, Karen and Stephen Skowronek. *The Search for American Political Development.* Cambridge, UK: Cambridge University Press, 2004.

Peterson, Norma Lois. *The Presidencies of William Henry Harrison & John Tyler*. Lawrence: University Press of Kansas, 1989.

Polk, James K. *The Diary of James K. Polk: During His Presidency, 1845–1849*. Edited by Milo Milton Quaife. 4 vols. New York: Kraus Reprint Co. 1970. First published in 1910 by A.C. McClurg & Co. Page references are to the 1970 edition.

Quayle, Dan. Phone interview with the author, March 4, 2009.

"Standing Firm: Personal Reflections on Being Vice President." In *At the President's Side: The Vice Presidency in the Twentieth Century*, edited by Timothy Walch, pp. 169–179. Columbia: University of Missouri Press, 1997.

Remini, Robert V. "Election of 1828." In *History of American Presidential Elections, 1789–1968*, edited by Arthur M. Schlesinger, Jr., Fred L. Israel, and William P. Hansen, Vol. 1, pp. 413–436. New York: Chelsea House Publishers, 1971.

Risjord, Norman K. "Election of 1812." In *History of American Presidential Elections, 1789–1968*, edited by Arthur M. Schlesinger, Jr., Fred L. Israel, and William P. Hansen, Vol. 1, pp. 249–272. New York: Chelsea House Publishers, 1971.

Roosevelt, Franklin D. "Can the Vice President be Useful?" *The Saturday Evening Post*, October 16, 1920, pp. 8, 81–82.

Roosevelt, Theodore. "The Three Vice-Presidential Candidates and What They Represent." *Review of Reviews*, (September 1896), pp. 289–297.

The Works of Theodore Roosevelt: National Edition. Vol. 15, *State Papers as Governor and President, 1899–1909*. New York: Charles Scribner's Sons, 1926.

Rossiter, Clinton L. "The Reform of the Vice Presidency," *Political Science Quarterly*, Vol. 63, no. 3, (September 1948), pp. 383–404.

The American Presidency. New York: The New American Library, 1956.

Savage, Charlie. *Takeover: The Return of the Imperial Presidency and the Subversion of American Democracy*. New York: Back Bay Books, 2008. First published in 2007 by Little, Brown and Company, hardcover edition. Page references are to the 2008 edition.

Schachner, Nathan. *Aaron Burr: A Biography*. New York: Frederick A. Stokes Company, 1937.

Thomas Jefferson: A Biography. New York: Thomas Yoseloff Ltd., 1957. First published in 1951 by Thomas Yoseloff Ltd. in two volumes. All page references are to the 1957 printing of a single volume.

Schapsmeier, Edward L. and Fredrick H. Schapsmeier. *Henry A. Wallace of Iowa: The Agrarian Years, 1910–1940*. Ames: The Iowa State University Press, 1968.

Prophet in Politics: Henry A. Wallace and the War Years, 1940–1965. Ames: The Iowa State University Press, 1970.

Schlesinger, Arthur M. Jr. *The Imperial Presidency*, New York: Houghton Mifflin, 1973.

"On the Presidential Succession." *Political Science Quarterly*, 89, no. 3, (Autumn 1974), pp. 475–505.

Robert Kennedy and His Times. New York: Ballantine Books, 1978.

Shriver, R. Sargent. "Acceptance Speech." Address delivered before the Democratic Party National Committee, August 9, 1972. Baltimore, Maryland: Archives of the Sargent Shriver Peace Institute.

Shugart, Matthew Soberg and John M. Carey. *Presidents and Assemblies: Constitutional Design and Electoral Dynamics*. UK: Cambridge University Press, 1992.

Sigelman, Lee and Paul T. Whalbeck. "Veepstakes": Strategic Choice in Presidential Running Mate Selection." *The American Political Review*, Vol. 91, no. 4, (December 1997), pp. 855–864.

Silver, Howard J. "Presidential Power and the Post-Watergate Presidency." *Presidential Studies Quarterly*, Vol. 8, no. 2, Presidential Power and Democratic Constraints (Spring 1998), pp. 199–214.

Sirgiovanni, George, S. "Dumping the Vice President: An Historical Overview and Analysis." *Presidential Studies Quarterly*, Vol. 24, no. 4, Forming a Government (Fall 1994), pp. 765–782.

Smith, Elbert B. *The Presidencies of Zachary Taylor & Millard Fillmore*. Lawrence: University Press of Kansas, 1988.

Smith, Page. "Election of 1796." In *History of American Presidential Elections, 1789–1968*, edited by Arthur M. Schlesinger, Jr., Fred L. Israel, and William P. Hansen, Vol. 1, pp. 59–80. New York: Chelsea House Publishers, 1971.

Smith, Willard H. *Schuyler Colfax: The Changing Fortunes of a Political Idol*. Indianapolis: Indiana Historical Bureau, 1952.

Solberg, Carl. *Hubert Humphrey*. New York: W.W. Norton & Company, Inc., 1984.

Sorensen, Theodore C. *Kennedy*. New York: Harper & Row Publishers, 1965. Reprinted with introduction by Theodore C. Sorensen. New York: Perennial Library, 1988. Page references are to the 1988 edition.

"Election of 1960." In *History of American Presidential Elections, 1789–1968*, edited by Arthur M. Schlesinger, Jr., Fred L. Israel, and William P. Hansen, Vol. 4, pp. 3449–3469. New York: Chelsea House Publishers, 1971.

Suskind, Ron. *The Price of Loyalty: George W. Bush, the White House, and the Education of Paul O'Neill*. New York: Simon & Schuster, 2004.

Thayer, William Roscoe. *Theodore Roosevelt: An Intimate Biography*. New York: Grosset & Dunlap, 1919.

Thompson, Charles S. *An Essay On: The Rise and Fall of the Congressional Caucus as a Machine for Nominating.* New Haven, CT: Yale University, 1902. A facsimile of the first publication of the essay. Ann Arbor, MI: University Microfilms, 1971.

Timmons, Bascom N. *Garner of Texas: A Personal History.* New York: Harper & Brothers Publishers, 1948.

Turner, Michael. "Finding a Policy Role for the Vice President: The Case of Nelson A. Rockefeller." PhD diss., State University of New York, 1978.

"Reagan and the Vice Presidency." *Politics,* Vol. 1, no. 1, (April 1981), pp. 29–35.

Untermeyer, Chase. "Looking Forward: George Bush as Vice President." In *At the President's Side: The Vice Presidency in the Twentieth Century,* edited by Timothy Walch, pp. 157–168. Columbia: University of Missouri Press, 1997.

U.S. Congress. *Annals of the Congress of the United States, 1789–1824.* 42 vols. Washington, DC, 1834–56.

U.S. Congress. *Congressional Globe.* 46 vols. Washington, DC, 1834–73.

U.S. Congress. *Senate Journal.* 41st Cong., 1st sess., May 23, 1871.

U.S. Congress. Senate. *Joint Resolution Proposing to Amend the Constitution.* S Res. 7, 42nd Cong., 2nd sess., (May 30, 1872), pp. 1–5.

U.S. Congress. *Senate Journal.* 63rd Cong., Special Senate Session, March 4, 1913.

U.S. Congress, Senate, 84th Cong., 2nd sess., January 16, 24, and 25, 1956. Subcommittee on Reorganization of the Committee on Government Operations: Proposal to Create Position of Administrative Vice President, pp. 1–108.

U.S. Congress, Senate, 93rd Cong., 1st sess., (1973). Senate Judiciary Committee, Selected Materials on the Twenty-fifth Amendment, Senate Document 93-42.

U.S. Congress. Senate, 93rd Cong., 1st sess., November 1, 5, 7, and 14, 1973. Hearings Before the Committee on Rules and Administration on the Nomination of Gerald R. Ford of Michigan to be Vice President of the United States, pp. 1–379.

U.S. Congress. House, 93rd Cong., 1st sess., November 15, 16, 19, 20, 21, and 26, 1973. Hearings Before the Committee on the Judiciary on Nomination of Gerald R. Ford to be the Vice President of the United States, pp. 1–798.

U.S. Congress. House, 93rd Cong., 2nd sess., November 21, 22, 25, 26, 27; December 2, 3, 4, and 5, 1974. Hearings Before the Committee on the Judiciary on Nomination of Nelson A. Rockefeller to be Vice President of the United States, pp. 1–1,455.

Valenti, Jack. *A Very Human President.* New York: Pocket Book, 1977. First published in 1976 by W.W. Norton, hardcover edition. Page references are to the 1977 edition.

Van Buren, Martin. *The Autobiography of Martin Van Buren,* edited by John C. Fitzpatrick. Washington, DC: Government Printing Office, 1920.

Von Damm, Helene. *At Reagan's Side*. New York: Doubleday, 1989.

Wallace, Henry A. "How a Vice President is Picked—Inside Look at U.S. Politics." *U.S. News & World Report*, April 6, 1956, pp. 86–89. Full text of an address delivered to the Harvard Law School Forum, March 30, 1956.

The Price of Vision: The Diary of Henry A. Wallace, 1942–1946, edited by John Morton Blum. Boston, MA: Houghton Mifflin Company, 1973.

Walsh, Lawrence E. *Firewall: The Iran-Contra Conspiracy and Cover-Up*. New York: Norton, 1997.

Warshaw, Shirley A. *Powersharing: White House-Cabinet Relations in the Modern Presidency*. New York: State University of New York Press, 1996.

The Co-Presidency of Bush and Cheney. Stanford, CA: Stanford University Press, 2009.

Washington Correspondent, A. "Heap Big Chief." *The American Mercury*, Vol. 17, no. 68, (August 1929), pp. 401–411.

Washington, George. *The Writings of George Washington: From the Original Manuscript Sources, 1745–1799*, edited by John C. Fitzpatrick. Vol. 35, *March 30, 1796–July 31, 1797*. Westport, CT: Greenwood Press, Publishers, 1970. First published in 1940 by the United States Government Printing Office. Page references are to the 1970 edition.

Wattenberg, Martin P. "The Clinton 2000 Effect in Perspective: The Impact of Retiring Presidents on Their Parties' Chances of Retaining the White House." *Presidential Studies Quarterly*, Vol. 33, no 1, 2000 Presidential Election, (March 2003), pp. 164–171.

Waugh, Edgar W. *Second Consul: The Vice Presidency: Our Greatest Political Problem*. New York: The Bobbs-Merrill Company, Inc., 1956.

White, Theodore H. *The Making of the President 1968*. New York: Atheneum Publishers, 1969.

The Making of the President 1972. New York: Atheneum Publishers, 1973.

White, William A. *A Puritan in Babylon: The Story of Calvin Coolidge*. New York: The Macmillan Company, 1938.

Williams, Irving G. *The Rise of the Vice Presidency*. Washington, DC: Public Affairs Press, 1956.

Wilson, Woodrow. *Congressional Government: A Study in American Politics*. New York: Riverside Press, Houghton Mifflin Company, 1885. Reprinted with introduction by Walter Lippmann. New York: Meridian Books, 1956. Reprinted 2006 by Dover Publications, paperback edition. Page references are to the 2006 edition.

Constitutional Government in the United States. New York: The Columbia University Press, 1908.

Woodward, Bob. *The Agenda: Inside the Clinton Administration.* New York: Simon & Schuster, 1994.

The 1980 World Book Yearbook. Chicago, IL: World Book—Childcraft, 1980.

Young, Donald. *American Roulette: The History and Dilemma of the Vice Presidency.* 2nd ed. New York: Holt, Rinehart and Winston, 1972.

INDEX

CREDITS

"Amendment XII," from the U.S. Constitution. Copyright in the Public Domain.

"The Presidential Succession Act of 1947," 61 U.S. Stat. 380. Copyright in the Public Domain.

"Amendment XXV," from the U.S. Constitution. Copyright in the Public Domain.

Permission of use granted to the author by the Columbia University Oral History Research Office Collection for specific cited material from the transcripts of the "Reminiscences of Henry Agard Wallace."

Permission of use granted to the author by the University of Kentucky Oral History Program for specific cited material from the transcripts of "An Interview with Alben Barkley."

CPSIA information can be obtained at www.ICGtesting.com
Printed in the USA
BVOW09s2243290315

393773BV00019B/394/P